Praise for *Database Design for Mere Mortals™, Second Edition*

"This book takes the somewhat daunting process of database design and breaks it into completely manageable and understandable components. Mike's approach whilst simple is completely professional, and I can recommend this book to any novice database designer."

—Sandra Barker, Lecturer, University of South Australia, Australia

"Databases are a critical infrastructure technology for information systems and today's business. Mike Hernandez has written a literate explanation of database technology—a topic that is intricate and often obscure. If you design databases yourself, this book will educate you about pitfalls and show you what to do. If you purchase products that use a database, the book explains the technology so that you can understand what the vendor is doing and assess their products better."

—Michael Blaha, consultant and trainer, author of *A Manager's Guide to Database Technology*

"If you told me that Mike Hernandez could improve on the first edition of *Database Design for Mere Mortals* I wouldn't have believed you, but he did! The second edition is packed with more real-world examples, detailed explanations, and even includes database-design tools on the CD-ROM! This is a must-read for anyone who is even remotely interested in relational database design, from the individual who is called upon occasionally to create a useful tool at work, to the seasoned professional who wants to brush up on the fundamentals. Simply put, if you want to do it right, read this book!"

—Matt Greer, Process Control Development, The Dow Chemical Company

"Mike's approach to database design is totally common-sense based, yet he's adhered to all the rules of good relational database design. I use Mike's books in my starter database-design class, and I recommend his books to anyone who's interested in learning how to design databases or how to write SQL queries."

—Michelle Poolet, President, MVDS, Inc.

"Slapping together sophisticated applications with poorly designed data will hurt you just as much now as when Mike wrote his first edition, perhaps even more. Whether you're just getting started developing with data or are a seasoned pro; whether you've read Mike's previous book or this is your first; whether you're happier letting someone else design your data or you love doing it yourself—this is the book for you. Mike's ability to explain these concepts in a way that's not only clear, but fun, continues to amaze me."

—From the Foreword by Ken Getz, MCW Technologies, coauthor *ASP.NET Developer's JumpStart*

"The first edition of Mike Hernandez's book *Database Design for Mere Mortals* was one of the few books that survived the cut when I moved my office to smaller quarters. The second edition expands and improves on the original in so many ways. It is not only a good, clear read, but contains a remarkable quantity of clear, concise thinking on a very complex subject. It's a must for anyone interested in the subject of database design."

—Malcolm C. Rubel, Performance Dynamics Associates

"Mike's excellent guide to relational database design deserves a second edition. His book is an essential tool for fledgling Microsoft Access and other desktop database developers, as well as for client/server pros. I recommend it highly to all my readers."

—Roger Jennings, author of *Special Edition Using Access 2002*

"There are no silver bullets! Database technology has advanced dramatically, the newest crop of database servers perform operations faster than anyone could have imagined six years ago, but none of these technological advances will help fix a bad database design, or capture data that you forgot to include! *Database Design for Mere Mortals*™, *Second Edition*, helps you design your database right in the first place!"

—Matt Nunn, Product Manager, SQL Server, Microsoft Corporation

"When my brother started his professional career as a developer, I gave him Mike's book to help him understand database concepts and make real-world application of database technology. When I need a refresher on the finer points of database design, this is the book I pick up. I do not think that there is a better testimony to the value of a book than that it gets used. For this reason I have wholeheartedly recommended to my peers and students that they utilize this book in their day-to-day development tasks."

—Chris Kunicki, Senior Consultant, OfficeZealot.com

"Mike has always had an incredible knack for taking the most complex topics, breaking them down, and explaining them so that anyone can 'get it.' He has honed and polished his first very, very good edition and made it even better. If you're just starting out building database applications, this book is a must-read cover to cover. Expert designers will find Mike's approach fresh and enlightening and a source of great material for training others."

—John Viescas, President, Viescas Consulting, Inc., author of *Running Microsoft Access 2000* and coauthor of *SQL Queries for Mere Mortals*

"Whether you need to learn about relational database design in general, design a relational database, understand relational database terminology, or learn best practices for implementing a relational database, *Database Design for Mere Mortals*™, *Second Edition*, is an indispensable book that you'll refer to often. With his many years of real-world experience designing relational databases, Michael shows you how to analyze and improve existing databases, implement keys, define table relationships and business rules, and create data views, resulting in data integrity, uniform access to data, and reduced data-entry errors."

—Paul Cornell, Site Editor, MSDN Office Developer Center

Praise for the First Edition

"[A]n astoundingly fresh approach to the 'nasty' task of database design . . . Anyone who has anything to do with creating applications using a database product should buy this book and read it cover to cover."

—John Viescas, President, Viescas Consulting, Inc., author of *Running Microsoft Access 2000* and coauthor of *SQL Queries for Mere Mortals*

"[A] must-have for anyone new to relational database design . . . [Mike's] attention to detail is marvelous, and the explanations of the interview process are a must-read for anyone, including experienced relational database designers."

—Jim Booth, Principal Consultant, James Booth Consulting

"Mike has done us a favor by taking an academic topic and making it logical, approachable, and comprehensible for us mortals. Anyone interested in making their database design better should read this book. It contains good information for every level of database developer."

—Malcolm C. Rubel, Contributing Editor, *Databased Advisor* and *FoxPro Advisor*

"*Database Design for Mere Mortals* is sure to help both aspiring and practicing database designers alike! Michael delivers the major points of logical database design with a clear, common-sense approach that makes this book an excellent resource and a pleasure to read."

—Nick Evans, Contributing Editor, *PowerBuilder Advisor Magazine*

"No matter what specific database package you're using (or, perhaps, no package at all), the concepts in this book will make sense, and will apply to your database design projects."

—From the Foreword by Ken Getz, MCW Technologies, coauthor, *ASP.NET Developer's JumpStart*

Database Design
for Mere
Mortals™
Second Edition

Addison-Wesley presents the
For Mere Mortals® *Series*

Series Editor: Michael J. Hernandez

The goal of the *For Mere Mortals*® *Series* is to present you with information on important technology topics in an easily accessible, common-sense manner. The primary audience for *Mere Mortals* books is that of readers who have little or no background or formal training in the subject matter. Books in the Series avoid dwelling on the theoretical and instead take you right into the heart of the topic with a matter-of-fact, hands-on approach. The books are not designed to address all the intricacies of a given technology, but they do not avoid or gloss over complex, essential issues either. Instead, they focus on providing core, foundational knowledge in a way that is easy to understand and that will properly ground you in the topic. This practical approach provides you with a smooth learning curve and helps you to begin to solve your real-world problems immediately. It also prepares you for more advanced treatments of the subject matter, should you decide to pursue them, and even enables the books to serve as solid reference material for those of you with more experience. The software-independent approach taken in most books within the Series also teaches the concepts in such a way that they can be applied to whatever particular application or system you may need to use.

Titles in the Series:

Project Management for Mere Mortals®
Claudia M. Baca. ISBN: 0321423453

User Interface Design for Mere Mortals™
Eric Butow. ISBN: 0321447735

Database Design for Mere Mortals®, *Second Edition:*
A Hands-On Guide to Relational Database Design
Michael J. Hernandez. ISBN: 0201752840

Microsoft Office Project for Mere Mortals®:
Solving the Mysteries of Microsoft Office Project
Patti Jansen. ISBN: 0321423429

UML for Mere Mortals®
Robert A. Maksimchuk and Eric J. Naiburg. ISBN: 0321246241

VSTO for Mere Mortals™
Kathleen McGrath and Paul Stubbs. ISBN: 0321426711

SQL Queries for Mere Mortals®:
A Hands-On Guide to Data Manipulation in SQL, Second Edition
John L. Viescas and Michael J. Hernandez. ISBN: 0321444434

For more information, check out the series web site at
www.awprofessional.com/ForMereMortalsSeries.

Database Design
▶ for Mere
▶ Mortals™
Second Edition

*A Hands-On Guide
to Relational
Database Design*

Michael J. Hernandez

✦Addison-Wesley

Boston ▪ San Francisco ▪ New York ▪ Toronto ▪ Montreal
London ▪ Munich ▪ Paris ▪ Madrid
Capetown ▪ Sydney ▪ Tokyo ▪ Singapore ▪ Mexico City

Many of the designations used by manufacturers and sellers to distinguish their products are claimed as trademarks. Where those designations appear in this book, and Addison-Wesley was aware of a trademark claim, the designations have been printed with initial capital letters or in all capitals.

The author and publisher have taken care in the preparation of this book, but make no expressed or implied warranty of any kind and assume no responsibility for errors or omissions. No liability is assumed for incidental or consequential damages in connection with or arising out of the use of the information or programs contained herein.

The publisher offers discounts on this book when ordered in quantity for bulk purchases and special sales. For more information, please contact:

U.S. Corporate and Government Sales
(800) 382-3419
corpsales@pearsontechgroup.com

For sales outside of the U.S., please contact:

International Sales
(317) 581-3793
international@pearsontechgroup.com

Visit Addison-Wesley on the Web: www.awprofessional.com

Library of Congress Cataloging-in-Publication Data

Hernandez, Michael J. (Michael James), 1955–
    Database design for mere mortals : a hands-on guide to relational database
design / Michael J. Hernandez—2nd ed.
        p.   cm.
    Includes bibliographic references and index.
    ISBN 0-201-75284-0 (alk. paper)
    1. Database design.   2. Relational databases.   I. Title.
    QA76.9.D26 H477 2003
    005.75'6—dc21   2002034545

ISBN 0-201-75284-0

Text printed in the United States on recycled paper at Courier Stoughton in Stoughton, Massachusetts.

13th Printing   February 2008

For my wife, Kendra, who has always believed in me.

In loving memory of our cats, Chico and Bugs. Writing just isn't the same without them.

Dedicated to anyone who has unsuccessfully attempted to design a relational database.

About the Author

Michael J. Hernandez currently works at Microsoft as a program manager for the Developer Tools team of the Visual Studio .NET group. Previously, he was an independent relational database consultant specializing in relational database design. Mike is a veteran database developer with more than 14 years of experience developing applications for a wide variety of clients in diverse industries. He has worked with several relational database management systems throughout his career and has been working exclusively with Access since Version 1.0 and with SQL Server since version 7.0. Mike is coauthor of the best-selling *SQL Queries for Mere Mortals* and has been a contributing author to, columnist for, and technical editor of various database books and periodicals.

Aside from his work on various database development projects and writing projects, Mike has also been a veteran instructor for nationally recognized training organizations such as AppDev, Deep Training, and Focal Point, Inc., and traveled across the nation teaching Microsoft Access, SQL Server, SQL/92 query construction, and relational database design. For more than 13 years, Mike trained thousands of students from Fortune 500 companies, the military, the government, and the private sector. He consistently received top ratings from his students and became one of the premiere instructors in the country. He's spoken at various national and international conferences, such as the 2001 Microsoft Office Deployment and Development Conference in Orlando, Florida, and the 2002 Microsoft Office Solutions Conference in Palm Springs, California. Mike became deeply involved in Microsoft's .NET initiative and was one of the first 200 Microsoft-authorized .NET instructors. He participated in Microsoft's nationwide .NET Developers Training Tour and in Deep Training's .NET Training Tour in San Jose, Costa Rica. Now he travels across the country on behalf of Microsoft.

Mike has been studying the guitar since 1967 and was actually a professional guitarist for 15 years, playing a wide variety of styles. His ability to enthuse his audiences comes from years of entertaining, and Mike has a reputation among his colleagues for being quite uninhibited. He's played the guitar for his students, subjected anyone within earshot to a collection of the world's worst puns, played the game Charades to illustrate a point, and caused minor uproars with his imitations of George Bush, Sr., and Ross Perot.

Some of Mike's musician friends have talked him into coming out of retirement, and he is playing once again in front of gracious and appreciative audiences. He's taken to playing a lot of Bossa Nova and finger-style jazz and is even composing his own music. With any kind of luck, he'll eventually have enough material to produce his own music CD.

On those rare occasions when he has free time, Mike usually spends it at one of three places: drinking a "Tall Americano with room" at any immediately available Starbucks, hanging out in the database section at any Barnes & Noble bookstore, or hitting golf balls at the local driving range and pretending he is Lee Trevino.

If you'd like to contact Mike, you can e-mail him at mjhernandez@msn.com.

Contents

PART II: THE DESIGN PROCESS   75

Chapter 4: Conceptual Overview   77

Foreword

I don't see Mike Hernandez as much as I used to. Both our professional lives have changed a great deal since I first wrote the foreword to his original edition. If nothing else, we travel less, and our paths cross less often than they did. If you'll indulge me, I might try to add that the entire world has changed since that first edition. On the most mundane level, my whole development life has changed, since I've bought into this Microsoft .NET thing whole-heartedly and full-time. One thing that hasn't changed, however, is the constant need for data, and well-designed data. Slapping together sophisticated applications with poorly designed data will hurt you just as much now as when Mike wrote his first edition—perhaps even more. Whether you're just getting started developing with data, or are a seasoned pro; whether you've read Mike's previous book, or this is your first time; whether you're happier letting someone else design your data, or you love doing it yourself—this is the book for you. Mike's ability to explain these concepts in a way that's not only clear, but fun, continues to amaze me.

—Ken Getz
October 10, 2002

From the First Edition . . .

Perhaps you're wondering why the world needs another book on database design. When Mike Hernandez first discussed this book with me, *I* wondered. But the fact is—as you may have discovered from leafing through pages before landing here in the foreword—the world *does* need a book like this one. You can certainly find many books detailing the theories and concepts behind the science of database design, but you won't find many (if any) written from Mike's particular perspective. He has made it his goal to provide a book that is clearly based on the sturdy principles of mathematical study, but has geared it toward practical use instead of theoretical possibilities. No matter what specific database package you're using, the concepts in this book will make sense and will apply to your database-design projects.

I knew this was the book for me when I turned to the beginning of Chapter 6 and saw this suggestion:

> Do not adopt the current database structure as the basis for the new database structure.

If I'd had someone tell me this when I was starting out on this database developer path years ago I could have saved a *ton* of time! And that's my point here: Mike has spent many years designing databases for clients; he has spent lots of time thinking, reading, and studying about the *right* way to create database applications; and he has put it all here, on paper, for the rest of us.

This book is full of the right stuff, illustrated with easy-to-understand examples. That's not to say that it doesn't contain the hardcore information you need to do databases right—it does, of course. But it's geared toward real developers, not theoreticians.

I've spent some time talking with Mike about database design. Over coffee, in meetings, writing courseware, it's always the same: Mike is passionate about this material. Just as the operating system designer seeks the perfect, elegant algorithm, Mike spends his time looking for just the right way to solve a design puzzle and—as you will read in this book—how best to explain it to others. I've learned much of what I know

about database design from Mike over the years and feel sure that I
have a lot more to learn from this book. After reading through this concise, detailed presentation of the information you need to know in order
to create professional databases, I'm sure you'll feel the same way.

—Ken Getz
MCW Technologies
KenG@mcwtech.com

Preface
(Second Edition)

Life, as the most ancient
of all metaphors insists, is a journey . . .
—Jonathan Raban
For Love and Money

I believe that learning about database design
is an ongoing process. I'm always learning
more and more about the intricacies
and nuances of design—and so will you.
—Michael J. Hernandez
Database Design for Mere Mortals

In the six years since the first edition of this book was published, I've continued my journey along the database path. I've dug deeper into the intracacies of design and probed further into the philosophy of good design. I've learned much from numerous conversations with my database students and industry colleagues and from the correspondence I've had with those who have read my book. As a result, I've been able to hone my design methodology and revise some of its processes, making it clearer and more thorough than ever before.

Although I'll take a brief break (writing can be quite a mental exercise), I know that my journey will soon continue. There is still so much more to explore, discover, and learn. I find that designing and working with databases is much like mountain climbing—there's always a new and exciting challenge ahead of you! Perhaps six years from now, I'll have a chance to share my experiences with you once again.

Acknowledgments

Despite what anyone tells you, writing is truly a cooperative effort. I am so thankful that there are editors, colleagues, friends, and family who continue to be ready and willing to lend their help. It is these people who provide encouragement and keep you focused on the task at hand, and it is to them that I extend my most heartfelt appreciation.

First, I wish to thank my editor, Mary O'Brien, for the opportunity to write this new edition. Her patience, kindness, leadership, and steady hand guided this project and helped me bring it to successful completion. I'd also like to thank Mary's assistants, Alicia Carey, Stacie Parillo, and Brenda Mulligan. Alicia and Stacey displayed great patience and provided unwavering support throughout the many months I was working on this edition, and Brenda was an invaluable partner throughout the production process. And a special thanks to John Fuller and his production staff—great job, as always! A hearty thanks to Tyrrell Albaugh for guiding the production process so smoothly, and to Jennifer Kelland for her meticulous and thorough editing work. With such a wonderful team as this, I just can't imagine why I'd ever want to write for anyone else.

Next, I'd like to acknowledge my distinguished technical review team: Sandy Barker, Michael Blaha, Matt Greer, and Michelle Poolet. These folks graciously and generously gave their time, effort, and expertise to provide me with a wealth of valuable feedback and suggestions. This book definitely benefitted from their contributions. Thanks once again to all of you for your time and input and for helping to make this edition even better than I first envisioned.

I want to extend a very special thanks to Ken Getz for once again providing the foreword for my book. Ken is a well-respected database/VB/.NET expert, a colleague, and a good friend. I'm so pleased to have his thoughts and comments at the beginning of the book.

A special thanks also goes to all of those readers who took the time to send me their thoughts and comments. I am humbled by their praise and support and particularly appreciative of the good, constructive criticism that eventually helped me to improve that material in this edition. I also wish to thank all the academic institutions, government agencies, and commercial organizations that have adopted my book and made it "standard reading" for those just beginning their database careers. I am honored by their support of my work.

Finally, I want to thank my wife, Kendra, for her unending patience while I was enmeshed in my writing. Her help and support have been invaluable, and yet again, I owe her a great debt. I would tell you exactly how I feel about her, but she abhors any sort of PDA (public display of affection). Instead of a big verbal hug, I'll just say this:

Well, Ked, now we can take a nice, long, well-deserved break. . . .

Preface
(First Edition)

If the Lord Almighty had consulted me before embarking upon Creation, I should have recommended something simpler.
—Alfonso X, King of Castile and Leon

Creating a database can be like creating a universe, only more complicated. At least when the universe was created, there was no one around to complain.
—Michael J. Hernandez

It all started with a simple question: How do I properly design a database?

It was a question that propelled me onto an interesting journey—a journey to find someone or some book that could provide the answer. This journey has taken me to a number of bookstores and put me in the path of many interesting and fascinating people. I've read a variety of books on the subject, from the totally incomprehensible to the sorely lacking in content, and had conversations with people ranging from those who were in my position to those who really knew their craft. I was fortunate to have a few people in the latter category become my mentors, and I learned a great deal from them.

Books were a different story. There came a moment when I realized that current books on database design were just not written for people like me. If you had a background in mathematics, a computer science degree, and had been working in the computer industry for some time, *then* you were the audience the authors of these books were trying to reach. Otherwise, there was very little available. The few attempts at "simplified" texts simply failed to teach effectively, often because the authors seemed to assume that the reader was simpleminded.

I believed that there should be a book for people who did not have high levels of specialized education; a book that was straightforward and easy to read, thorough but not tedious; a book that used examples that were relatively easy to understand. So I wrote a special report on the fundamentals of database design for a local publisher, and it met with some success. Encouraged by this, I decided that someday I would write a book on the complete process of relational database design.

Early in my journey, I became a successful database developer and instructor. I've developed databases for a number of diverse organizations and businesses and have taken pleasure in instructing people on how to use a variety of database software programs. Throughout all this I've kept my sights on my goal.

It was at the 1995 Database Summit in Seattle, Washington, that I met Kathleen Tibbetts, a Developers Press editor for Addison-Wesley. At that moment my journey took quite a positive turn. She was looking for people with something to say, and I was definitely that type of person. Kathleen listened very patiently to the story of the journey upon which I had embarked. She determined that this would be a good time for me to work on realizing my goal—to finally commit to paper all that I had learned about database design.

The book you now hold in your hands is a result of the culmination of this particular journey. I've shaped and molded the knowledge I accumulated into what I believe is a clear and straightforward database-design method. I've tried very hard to make it accessible to everyone, regardless of previous experience. I have sought a presentation that would be easier to learn and understand than traditional design methods, yet would yield the same results.

I believe that learning about database design is an ongoing process. I'm always learning more and more about the intricacies and nuances of design—and so will you. Database design is more of an art than an exact science, involving as much intuition as pure theoretical and technical knowledge. It also involves communication skills and the ability to see things in the long term, as well as the short term. Database design can be a fascinating subject once you really get into it.

Acknowledgments

I've discovered that writing a book is something of a cooperative effort. I am thankful that there are always editors, colleagues, friends, and family who are ready and willing to lend their help. It is these people who provide encouragement and keep you focused on the task at hand. Without them, you could easily "put it off until tomorrow."

First and foremost, I would like to thank Kathleen Tibbetts at Addison-Wesley for her unwavering support and for providing me with the opportunity to write this book. She has been just as enthusiastic about this project as I have been. I look forward to working with her on further projects.

Next, my deepest thanks to my good friend, colleague, and technical editor, Jim Booth. I have a great deal of respect for Jim's knowledge on the subject of database design, and his comments have been invaluable. He and I have a thick porterhouse steak and a bottle of fine red wine waiting for us once this book is out on the market.

I also owe a debt of gratitude to my good friend and colleague Christopher R. Weber. In spite of a busy consulting and lecture schedule, Chris reviewed a number of chapters and provided valuable feedback. Now, if we could both find the time to sit down and discuss music . . . (we're both musicians.)

I'd like to acknowledge some of the many people who have shared their experience and knowledge with me and have had a positive influence on my career in the field of database management: Karen Watterson, Mike Johnson, Karl Fischer, Paul Litwin, John Viescas, Ken Getz, and Gregory Piercy. My thanks to you all.

My sincerest and deepest appreciation goes to my very dear friend and mentor, Alastair Black. Not only was he gracious enough to review every word in the entire book; he and his wife, Julia, opened their home to me and treated me as one of their own. His immeasurable and invaluable help in the writing of this book cannot be overstated. I've learned more about the *craft* of writing in these past months than at any other time in my professional or personal life.

Last, but certainly not least, a special thanks to my wife, Kendra. Every married author realizes, by the end of the work, how much he owes to the patience of the spouse and is moved to recognize the priceless contribution of interest and forbearance. But I am enjoined not to make as much of this as it deserves, because Kendra strongly opposes public displays of affection (PDAs as she calls them), whether in person or in print. So the only thing I'll say is this: Thanks, Ked. Now we can resume a normal life.

Introduction

Plain cooking cannot be entrusted to plain cooks.
—COUNTESS MORPHY

In the past, the process of designing a database has been a task performed by information technology (IT) personnel and professional database developers. These people usually had mathematical, computer science, or systems design backgrounds and typically worked with large mainframe databases. Many of them were experienced programmers and had coded a number of database application programs consisting of thousands of lines of code. (And these people were usually very overworked due to the nature and importance of their work!)

People designing database systems at that time needed to have a solid educational background because most of the systems they created were meant to be used companywide. Even when creating databases for single departments within a company or for small businesses, database designers still required extensive formal training because of the complexity of the programming languages and database application programs that they were using. As technology advanced, however, those educational requirements evolved.

Since the mid-1980s, many software vendors have developed database software programs that run on desktop computers and can be more easily programmed to collect, store, and manage data than their mainframe counterparts. They have also produced software that allows groups of people to access and share centralized data within a variety of environments, such as client/server architectures on computers connected within local-area networks (LANs) and wide-area networks (WANs), and even via the Internet. People within a company or organization are no longer strictly dependent on mainframe databases or on having their information needs met by centralized IT departments. Over the years, vendors have added new features and enhanced the tool sets in their database software, enabling database developers to create more powerful and flexible database applications. They've also improved the ease with which the software can be used, inspiring many people to create their own database applications. Today's database software greatly simplifies the process of creating efficient database structures and intuitive user interfaces.

Most programs provide sample database structures that you can copy and alter to suit your specific needs. Although you might initially think that it would be quite advantageous for you to use these sample structures as the basis for a new database, you should stop and reconsider that move for a moment. Why? Because you could easily and unwittingly create an improper, inefficient, and incomplete design. Then you would eventually encounter problems in what you believed to be a dependable database design. This, of course, raises the question, "What types of problems would I encounter?"

Most problems that surface in a database fall into two categories: *application* problems and *data* problems. Application problems include such things as problematic data entry/edit forms, confusing menus, confusing dialog boxes, and tedious task sequences. These problems typically arise when the database developer is inexperienced, is unfamiliar with a good application-design methodology, or knows too little about the software he's using to implement the database. Problems of this nature are common and important to address, but they are beyond the scope of this work.

> ❖ **Note** One good way to solve many of your application problems is to purchase and study third-party "developer" books that cover the software you're using. Such books discuss application-design issues, advanced programming techniques, and various tips and tricks that you can use to improve and enhance an application. Armed with these new skills, you can revamp and fine-tune the database application so that it works correctly, smoothly, and efficiently.

Data problems, on the other hand, include such things as missing data, incorrect data, mismatched data, and inaccurate information. Poor database design is typically the root cause of these types of problems. A database will not fulfill an organization's information requirements if it is not structured properly. Although poor design is typically generated by a database developer who lacks knowledge of good database-design principles, it shouldn't necessarily reflect negatively on the developer. Many people, including experienced programmers and database developers, have had little or no instruction in any form of database-design methodology. Many are unaware that design methodologies even exist. Data problems and poor design are the issues that this work will address.

What's New in the Second Edition

I revised this edition to improve readability, update or extend existing topics, add new content, and enhance its educational value. Here is a list of the changes you'll find in this edition:

- Much of the text has been rewritten to improve clarity and reader comprehension.

- Many of the figures and illustrations have been revised to improve clarity.

- New figures and illustrations have been added as warranted by revisions of or additons to existing text.

- Discussions of *relational database management systems* and the *relational model* in Chapter 1 have both been expanded to include brief content on recent technological advances and general industry direction.

- The premise behind the design methodology presented in this book is explained in Chapter 2.

- Discussion of *nulls* and the *many-to-many relationship* in Chapter 3 have both been expanded to provide greater detail on these subjects.

- Web-page-based examples are now included as appropriate in Chapter 6.

- Discussions of *multivalued fields* and the *subset tables* in Chapter 7 have both been expanded to provide greater detail on these subjects.

- The discussion of *primary keys* in Chapter 8 has been expanded to provide greater detail on this subject.

- The Field Specifications sheet has been updated and redesigned for improved flow and readability.

- The discussion of the *Data Type* field specification element in Chapter 9 has been expanded to include an introduction to Structured Query Language (SQL) data types.

- Discussions of *self-referencing relationships* and the *Deny, Nullify,* and *Set Default* deletion rules have been added to Chapter 10.

- Review questions have been added at the end of Chapters 1 through 12, and the answers to the questions appear in Appendix A.

- A flowchart of the design process has been provided as a quick reference tool and is included in Appendix B.

- All of the various design guidelines have been compiled in Appendix C.

- A glossary has been added to provide a quick reference for various terms used throughout the book.

- The accompanying CD includes files in Adobe Acrobat PDF format. These files contain the material in Appendixes B through F.

Who Should Read This Book

No previous background in database design is necessary to read this book. The reason you have this book in your hands is to learn how to design a database properly. If you're just getting into database management and you're thinking about developing your own databases, this book will be very valuable to you. It's better that you learn how to create a database properly from the beginning than that you learn by trial and error. The latter method takes much longer, believe me.

If you fall into the category of those people who have been working with database programs for a while and are ready to begin developing new databases for your company or business, you should read this book. You probably have a good feel for what a good database structure should look like, but aren't quite sure how database developers arrive at an effective design. Maybe you're a programmer who has created a number of databases following a few basic guidelines, but you have always ended up writing a lot of code to get the database to work properly. If this is the case, this book is also for you.

It would be a good idea for you to read this book even if you already have some background in database design. Perhaps you learned a design methodology back in college or attended a database class that discussed design, but your memory is vague about some details, or there were parts of the design process that you just did not completely understand.

Those points with which you had difficulty will finally become clear once you learn and understand the design process presented in this book.

This book is also appropriate for those of you who are experienced database developers and programmers. Although you may already know many of the aspects of the design process that are presented here, you'll probably find that there are some elements that you've never before encountered or considered. You may even come up with fresh ideas about how to design your databases by reviewing the material in this book because many of the design processes familiar to you are presented here from a different viewpoint. At the very least, this book can serve as a great refresher course in database design.

> ❖ **Note**   Those of you who have a burning desire to immerse yourselves in the depths of the database field (i.e., to learn the intricacies of database theory and design, analysis, implementation, administration, application development, and so on) should make a point of reading most of the books on my recommended reading list. Although I do not cover any of the aforementioned topics, my book does serve as the beginning of your journey into the realm of the database professional.

The Purpose of This Book

In general terms, there are three phases to the overall database-development process.

1. *Logical design:* The first phase involves determining and defining tables and their fields, establishing primary and foreign keys, establishing table relationships, and determining and establishing the various levels of data integrity.

2. *Physical implementation:* The second phase entails creating the tables, establishing key fields and table relationships, and using the proper tools to implement the various levels of data integrity.

3. *Application development:* The third phase involves creating an application that allows a single user or group of users to interact with the data stored in the database. The application-development phase itself can be divided into separate processes, such as determining end-user tasks and their appropriate sequences, determining information requirements for report output, and creating a menu system for navigating the application.

You should always go through the logical design first and execute it as completely as possible. After you've created a sound structure, you can then implement it within any database software you choose. As you begin the implementation phase, you may find that you need to modify the database structure based on the pros and cons or strengths and weaknesses of the database software you've chosen. You may even decide to make structural modifications to enhance data-processing performance. Performing the logical design first ensures that you make conscious, methodical, clear, and informed decisions concerning the structure of your database. As a result, you help minimize the potential number of further structural modifications you might need to make during the physical-implementation and application-development phases.

This book deals with only the logical-design phase of the overall development process, and the book's main purpose is to explain the process of relational database design without using the advanced, orthodox methodologies found in an overwhelming majority of database-design books. I've taken care to avoid the complexities of these methodologies by presenting a relatively straightforward, commonsense approach to the design process. I also use a simple and straightforward data-modeling method as a supplement to this approach, and present the entire process as clearly as possible and with a minimum of technical jargon.

There are many database-design books out on the market that include chapters on implementing the database within a specific database product, and some books even seem to meld the design and implementation phases together. (I've never particularly agreed with the idea of combining these phases, and I've always maintained that a database developer should perform the logical-design and implementation phases separately to ensure maximum focus, effectiveness, and efficiency.) The main drawback that I've encountered with these types of books is that it can be difficult for a reader to obtain any useful or relevant information from the implementation chapters if he or she doesn't work with the particular database software or programming language that the book incorporates. It is for this reason that I decided to write a book that focuses strictly on the logical design of the database.

> ❖ **Note** I *do not* cover implementation issues, SQL, or application-programming issues in this work, but there are various books that I do recommend on these topics. You can review my recommendations by accessing my Web site at **http://www.ForMereMortals.com**.

This book should be easier to read than other books you may have encountered on the subject. Many of the database-design books on the market are highly technical and can be difficult to assimilate. I think most of these books can be confusing and overwhelming if you are not a computer science major, database theorist, or experienced database developer. The design principles you'll learn within these pages are easy to understand and remember, and the examples are common and generic enough to be relevant to a wide variety of situations.

Most people I've met in my travels around the country have told me that they just want to learn how to create a sound database structure without having to learn about normal forms or advanced mathematical theories. Many people are not as worried about implementing a structure within a specific database software as they are about learning how to optimize their data structures and how to impose data integrity. In this book, you'll learn how to create efficient database structures, how to impose *several* levels of data integrity, as well as how to relate tables together to obtain information in an almost infinite number of ways. Don't worry; this isn't as difficult a task as you might think. You'll be able to accomplish all of this by understanding a few key terms and by learning and using a specific set of commonsense techniques and concepts.

You'll also learn how to analyze and leverage an existing database, determine information requirements, and determine and implement business rules. These are important topics because many of you will probably inherit old databases that you'll need to revamp using what you'll learn by reading this book. They'll also be just as important when you create a new database from scratch.

When you finish reading this book, you'll have the knowledge and tools necessary to create a good relational database structure. I'm confident that this entire approach will work for a majority of developers and the databases they need to create.

How to Read This Book

I strongly recommend that you read this book in sequence from beginning to end, regardless of whether you are a novice or a professional. You'll keep everything in context this way and avoid the confusion that generally comes from being unable to see the "big picture" first. It's also a good idea to learn the process as a whole before you begin to focus on any one part.

If you are reading this book to refresh your design skills, you could read just those sections that are of interest to you. As much as possible, I've tried to write each chapter so that it could stand on its own; nonetheless, I would still recommend that you glance through each of the chapters to make sure that you're not missing any new ideas or points on design that you may not have considered up to now.

How This Book Is Organized

Here's a brief overview of what you'll find in each part and each chapter.

Part I: Relational Database Design

This section provides an introduction to databases, the idea of database design, and some of the terminology you'll need to be familiar with in order to learn and understand the design process presented in this book.

Chapter 1, *The Relational Database*, provides a brief discussion of the types of databases you'll encounter, common database models, and a brief history of the relational database.

Chapter 2, *Design Objectives*, explores why you should be concerned with design, points out the objectives and advantages of good design, and provides a brief introduction to normalization and normal forms.

Chapter 3, *Terminology*, covers the terms you need to know in order to learn and understand the design methodology presented in this book.

Part II: The Design Process

Each aspect of the database-design process is discussed in detail in Part II, including establishing table structures, assigning primary keys, setting field specifications, establishing table relationships, setting up views, and establishing various levels of data integrity.

Chapter 4, *Conceptual Overview*, provides an overview of the design process, showing you how the different components of the process fit together.

Chapter 5, *Starting the Process*, covers how to define a mission statement and mission objectives for the database, both of which provide you with an initial focus for creating your database.

Chapter 6, *Analyzing the Current Database*, covers issues concerning the existing database. We look at reasons for analyzing the current database, how to look at current methods of collecting and presenting data, why and how to conduct interviews with users and management, and how to compile initial field lists.

Chapter 7, *Establishing Table Structures*, covers topics such as determining and defining what subjects the database should track, associating fields with tables, and refining table structures.

Chapter 8, *Keys*, covers the concept of keys and their importance to the design process, as well as how to define candidate and primary keys for each table.

Chapter 9, *Field Specifications*, covers a topic that a number of database developers tend to minimize. Besides indicating how each field is created, field specifications determine the very nature of the values a field contains. Topics in this chapter include the importance of field specifications, types of specification characteristics, and how to define specifications for each field in the database.

Chapter 10, *Table Relationships*, explains the importance of table relationships, types of relationships, setting up relationships, and establishing relationship characteristics.

Chapter 11, *Business Rules*, covers types of business rules, determining and establishing business rules, and using validation tables. Business rules are very important in any database because they provide a distinct level of data integrity.

Chapter 12, *Views*, looks into the concept of views and why they are important, types of views, and how to determine and set up views.

Chapter 13, *Reviewing Data Integrity*, reviews each of the levels of integrity that have been defined and discussed in previous chapters. Here you learn that it's a good idea to review the final design of the database structure to ensure that you've imposed data integrity as completely as you can.

Part III: Other Database-Design Issues

This section deals with topics such as avoiding bad design and bending the rules set forth in the design process.

Chapter 14, *Bad Design—What Not to Do*, covers the types of designs you should avoid, such as a flat-file design and a spreadsheet design.

Chapter 15, *Bending or Breaking the Rules*, discusses those rare instances in which it may be necessary to stray from the techniques and concepts of the design process. This chapter tells you when you should consider bending the rules, as well as how it should be done.

Part IV: Appendixes

Appendix A, *Answers to Review Questions*, contains the answers to all of the review questions in Chapters 1 through 12.

Appendix B, *Diagram of the Database Design Process*, provides a diagram that maps the entire database design process.

Appendix C, *Design Guidelines*, provides an easy reference to the various sets of design guidelines that appear throughout the book.

Appendix D, *Documentation Forms*, provides blank copies of the Field Specifications, Business Rule Specifications, and View Specifications sheets, which you can copy and use on your database projects.

Appendix E, *Database Design Diagram Symbols*, contains a quick and easy reference to the diagram symbols used throughout the book.

Appendix F, *Sample Designs*, contains sample database designs that can serve as the basis for ideas for databases you may want or need to create.

Appendix G, *Recommended Reading*, provides a list of books that you should read if you are interested in pursuing an in-depth study of database technology.

Glossary contains concise definitions of various words and phrases used throughout the book.

IMPORTANT: READ THIS SECTION!

A Word About the Examples and Techniques in This Book

You'll notice that there are a wide variety of examples in this book. I've made sure that they are as generic and relevant as possible. However, you may notice that several of the examples are rather simplified, incomplete, or even on occasion incorrect. Believe it or not, I created them that way on purpose.

I've created some examples with errors so that I could illustrate specific concepts and techniques. Without these examples, you wouldn't see how the concepts or techniques are put to use, as well as the results you should expect from using them. Other examples are simple because, once again, the focus is on the technique or concept and not on the example itself. For instance, there are many ways that you can design an order-tracking database. However, the structure of the sample order-tracking database I use in this book is simple because the focus is specifically on the *design process,* not on creating an elaborate order-tracking database system.

So what I'm really trying to emphasize here is this:

> Focus on the concept or technique and its intended results, *not on the example used to illustrate it.*

A New Approach to Learning

Here's an approach to learning the design process (or pretty much anything else, for that matter) that I've found very useful in my database-design classes.

Think of all the techniques used in the design process as a set of tools; each tool (or technique) is used for a specific purpose. The idea here is that once you learn generically how a tool is used, you can then use that tool in any number of situations. The reason you can do this is *because you use the tool the same way in each situation.*

Take a Crescent wrench, for example. Generically speaking, you use a Crescent wrench to fasten and unfasten a nut to a bolt. You open or close the jaw of the wrench to fit a given bolt by using the adjusting screw located on the head of the wrench. Now that you have that clear, try it out on a few bolts. Try it on the legs of an outdoor chair, or the valve cover on an engine, or the side panel of an outdoor cooling unit, or the hinge plates of an iron gate. Do you notice that regardless of where you encounter a nut and bolt, you can always fasten and unfasten the nut by using the Crescent wrench in the same manner?

The tools used to design a database work in *exactly* the same way. Once you understand how a tool is used generically, it will work the same way regardless of the circumstances under which it is used. For instance, consider the tool (or technique) for decomposing a field value. Say you have a single Address field in a CUSTOMERS table that contains the street address, city, state, and zip code for a given customer. You'll find it difficult to use this field in your database because it contains more than one item of data; you'll certainly have a hard time retrieving information for a particular city or sorting the information by a specific zip code.

The solution to this apparent dilemma is to decompose the Address field into smaller fields. You do this by identifying the distinct items that make up the value of the field, and then treating each item as its own separate field. That's all there is to it! This process constitutes a "tool" that you can now use on *any* field containing a value composed of two or more distinct data items, such as these sample fields. Figure I.1 shows the results of the decomposition process.

Current Field Name	Sample Value	New Field Names
Address	7402 Kingman Dr., Seattle, WA 98012	Street Address, City, State, Zip Code
Phone	(206) 555-5555	Area Code, Phone Number
Name	Michael J. Hernandez	First Name, Middle Initial, Last Name
EmployeeCode	ITDEV0516	Department, Category, ID Number

Figure I.1. *Decomposing fields containing multiple data items.*

❖ **Note** You'll learn more about decomposing field values in Chapter 7, "Establishing Table Structures."

You can use all of the techniques ("tools") that are part of the design process presented in this book in the same manner. You'll be able to design a sound database structure using these techniques regardless of the type of database you need to create. Just be sure to remember this:

Focus on the concept or technique being presented and its intended results, *not on the example used to illustrate it.*

■■ Part I
Relational Database Design

The Relational Database

A fish must swim three times—
in water, in butter, and in wine.
—POLISH PROVERB

Topics Covered in This Chapter

Types of Databases

Early Database Models

The Relational Database Model

Relational Database Management System

Beyond the Relational Model

What the Future Holds

Summary

Review Questions

The relational database has been in existence for over 25 years. It has spawned a multi-billion dollar industry, is the most widely used type of database in the world today, and is an essential part of our everyday lives. It is very likely that you are using a relational database every time you purchase goods at a store, make travel plans with your travel agent, check out a book at the library, or make a purchase on the Internet.

Before we delve into the design process, let's take a look at a brief history of the relational database—where it has come from, where it is now, and where it's going in the future.

Types of Databases

What is a database? As you probably know, a database is an organized collection of data used for the purpose of modeling some type of organization or organizational process. It really doesn't matter whether you're using paper or a computer software program to collect and store the data. As long as you're gathering data in some organized manner for a specific purpose, you've got a database. Throughout the remainder of this discussion, we'll assume that you're using a computer software program to collect and maintain your data.

There are two types of databases found in database management, *operational databases* and *analytical databases*.

Operational databases are the backbone of many companies, organizations, and institutions throughout the world today. This type of database is primarily used in *on-line transaction processing* (OLTP) scenarios, that is, in situations where there is a need to collect, modify, and maintain data on a daily basis. The type of data stored in an operational database is *dynamic*, meaning that it changes constantly and always reflects up-to-the-minute information. Organizations, such as retail stores, manufacturing companies, hospitals and clinics, and publishing houses, use operational databases because their data is in a constant state of flux.

In contrast, analytical databases are primarily used in *on-line analytical processing* (OLAP) scenarios, where there is a need to store and track historical and time-dependent data. An analytical database is a valuable asset when there is a need to track trends, view statistical data over a long period of time, and make tactical or strategic business projections. This type of database stores *static* data, meaning that the data is never (or very rarely) modified. The information gleaned from an analytical database reflects a point-in-time snapshot of the data. Chemical labs, geological companies, and marketing-analysis firms are examples of organizations that use analytical databases.

Analytical databases often use data from operational databases as their main data source, so there can be some amount of association between them; nevertheless, operational and analytical databases fulfill very specific types of data-processing needs, and creating their structures requires radically different design methodologies. This book focuses on designing an operational database because it is still the most widely used type of database in the world today.

Early Database Models

In the days before the relational database model, two data models were commonly used to maintain and manipulate data—the *hierarchical database model* and the *network database model*.

❖ **Note** Although use of these models is rapidly waning, I've provided a brief overview of each for historical purposes. In an overall sense, I believe it is useful for you to know what preceded the relational model so that you have a basic understanding of what led to its creation and evolution.

In the following overview I briefly describe how the data in each model is structured and accessed, how the relationship between a pair of tables is represented, and one or two of the advantages or disadvantages of each model.

Some of the terms you'll encounter in this section are explained in more detail in Chapter 3, "Terminology."

The Hierarchical Database Model

Data in this type of database is structured hierarchically and is typically diagrammed as an inverted tree. A single table in the database acts as the "root" of the inverted tree and other tables act as the

branches flowing from the root. Figure 1.1 shows a diagram of a typical hierarchical database structure.

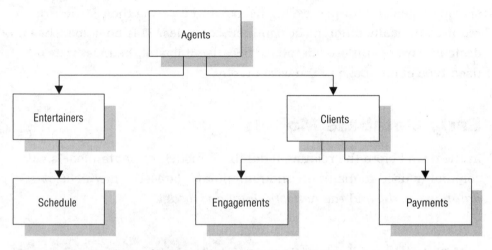

Figure 1.1. *Diagram of a typical hierarchical database.*

Agents Database In the example shown in Figure 1.1, an agent
books several entertainers, and each entertainer has his own
schedule. An agent also maintains a number of clients whose
entertainment needs are met by the agent. A client books engagements through the agent and makes payments to the agent for
his services.

A relationship in a hierarchical database is represented by the term
parent/child. In this type of relationship, a parent table can be associated with one or more child tables, but a single child table can be associated with only one parent table. These tables are explicitly linked via a
pointer or by the physical arrangement of the records within the tables. A
user accesses data within this model by starting at the *root* table and
working down through the tree to the target data. This access method
requires the user to be very familiar with the structure of the database.

One advantage to using a hierarchical database is that a user can retrieve data very quickly because there are explicit links between the table structures. Another advantage is that *referential integrity* is built in and automatically enforced. This ensures that a record in a child table must be linked to an existing record in a parent table, and that a record deleted in the parent table will cause all associated records in the child table to be deleted as well.

A problem occurs in a hierarchical database when a user needs to store a record in a child table that is currently unrelated to any record in a parent table. Consider an example using the *Agents* database shown in Figure 1.1. A user cannot enter a new entertainer in the ENTERTAIN-ERS table until the entertainer is assigned to an agent in the AGENTS table. Recall that a record in a child table (in this case, ENTERTAIN-ERS) *must* be related to a record in the parent table (AGENTS). Yet in real life, entertainers commonly sign up with the agency well before they are assigned to specific agents. This scenario is difficult to model in a hierarchical database. The rules can be bent without breaking them if a dummy agent record is inserted in the AGENTS table; how-ever, this option is not really optimal.

This type of database cannot support complex relationships, and there is often a problem with redundant data. For example, there is a many-to-many relationship between clients and entertainers; an entertainer will perform for many clients, and a client will hire many entertainers. You can't directly model this type of relationship in a hierarchical data-base, so you'll have to introduce redundant data into both the SCHEDULE and ENGAGEMENTS tables.

- The SCHEDULE table will now have client data (such as client name, address, and phone number) to show for whom and where each entertainer is performing. This particular data is redun-dant because it is currently stored in the CLIENTS table.

- The ENGAGEMENTS table will now contain data on entertainers (such as entertainer name, phone number, and type of entertainer) to indicate which entertainers are performing for a given client. This data is redundant as well because it is currently stored in the ENTERTAINERS table.

The problem with this redundancy is that it opens up the possibility of allowing a user to enter a single piece of data inconsistently. This, in turn, can result in producing inaccurate information.

A user can solve this problem in a roundabout manner by creating one hierarchical database specifically for entertainers and another specifically for agents. The new *Entertainers* database will contain only the ENTERTAINERS table, and the revised *Agents* database will contain the AGENTS, CLIENTS, PAYMENTS, and ENGAGEMENTS tables. The SCHEDULE table is no longer needed in the *Entertainers* database because you can define a *logical child relationship* between the ENGAGEMENTS table in the *Agents* database and the ENTERTAINERS table in the *Entertainers* database. With this relationship in place, you can retrieve a variety of information, such as a list of booked entertainers for a given client or a performance schedule for a given entertainer. Figure 1.2 shows a diagram of the new model.

As you see, a person designing a hierarchical database must be able to recognize the need to use this technique for a many-to-many relationship. Here the need is relatively obvious, but many relationships are more obscure and may not be discovered until very late in the design process or, more disturbingly, well after the database has been put into operation.

The hierarchical database lent itself well to the tape storage systems used by mainframes in the 1970s and was very popular in companies that used those systems. But, despite the fact that the hierarchical database provided fast and direct access to data and was useful in a number of circumstances, it was clear that a new database model was

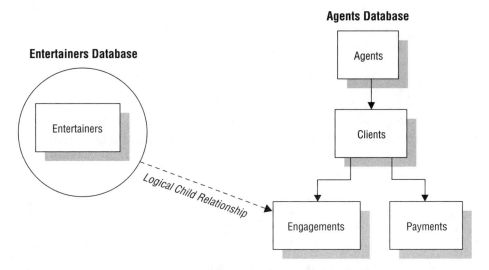

Figure 1.2. *Using two hierarchical databases to resolve a many-to-many relationship.*

needed to address the growing problems of data redundancy and complex relationships among data.

The Network Database Model

The network database was, for the most part, developed as an attempt to address some of the problems of the hierarchical database. The structure of a network database is represented in terms of *nodes* and *set structures*. Figure 1.3 shows a diagram of a typical network database.

Agents Database In the example shown in Figure 1.3, an agent represents a number of clients and manages a number of entertainers. Each client schedules any number of engagements and makes payments to the agent for his or her services. Each entertainer performs a number of engagements and may play a variety of musical styles.

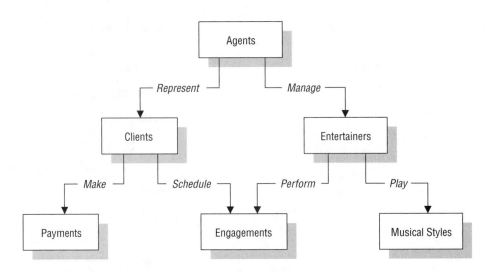

Figure 1.3. *Diagram of a typical network database.*

A *node* represents a collection of records, and a *set structure* establishes and represents a relationship in a network database. It is a
transparent construction that relates a pair of nodes together by using
one node as an *owner* and the other node as a *member*. (This is a valuable improvement on the parent/child relationship.) A set structure
supports a one-to-many relationship, which means that a record in the
owner node can be related to one or more records in the member node,
but a single record in the member node is related to *only one record* in
the owner node. Additionally, a record in the member node cannot exist
without being related to an existing record in the owner node. For
example, a client *must* be assigned to an agent, but an agent with no
clients can still be listed in the database. Figure 1.4 shows a diagram
of a basic set structure.

One or more sets (connections) can be defined between a specific pair
of nodes, and a single node can also be involved in other sets with
other nodes in the database. In Figure 1.3, for instance, the CLIENTS
node is related to the PAYMENTS node via the *Make* set structure. It is

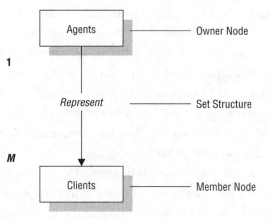

Figure 1.4. *A basic set structure.*

also related to the ENGAGEMENTS node via the *Schedule* set structure. Along with being related to the CLIENTS node, the ENGAGE-
MENTS node is related to the ENTERTAINERS node via the *Perform* set
structure.

A user can access data within a network database by working through
the appropriate set structures. Unlike the hierarchical database, where
access must begin from a root table, a user can access data from within
the network database, starting from any node and working backward
or forward through related sets. Consider the *Agents* database in
Figure 1.3 once again. Say a user wants to find the agent who booked
a specific engagement. She begins by locating the appropriate engagement record in the ENGAGEMENTS node, and then determines which
client "owns" that engagement record via the *Schedule* set structure. Finally, she identifies the agent that "owns" the client record via the *Represent* set structure. The user can answer a wide variety of questions *as
long as she navigates properly through the appropriate set structures.*

One advantage the network database provides is fast data access. It
also allows users to create queries that are more complex than those

they created using a hierarchical database. A network database's main disadvantage is that a user has to be very familiar with the structure of the database in order to work through the set structures. Consider the *Agents* database in Figure 1.3 once again. It is incumbent on the user to be familiar with the appropriate set structures if she is to determine whether a particular engagement has been paid. Another disadvantage is that it is not easy to change the database structure without affecting the application programs that interact with it. Recall that a relationship is explicitly defined as a set structure in a network database. You cannot change a set structure without affecting the application programs that use this structure to navigate through the data. If you change a set structure, you must also modify all references made from within the application program to that structure.

Although the network database was clearly a step up from the hierarchical database, a few people in the database community believed that there must be a better way to manage and maintain large amounts of data. As each data model emerged, users found that they could ask more complex questions, thereby increasing the demands made upon the database. And so, we come to the relational database model.

The Relational Database Model

The relational database was first conceived in 1969 and has arguably become the most widely used database model in database management today. The father of the relational model, Dr. Edgar F. Codd, was an IBM research scientist in the late 1960s and was at that time looking into new ways to handle large amounts of data. His dissatisfaction with the database models and database products of the time led him to begin thinking of ways to apply the disciplines and structures of mathematics to solve the myriad of problems he had been encountering. Being a mathematician by profession, he strongly believed that he could apply specific branches of mathematics to solve problems, such as data redundancy, weak data integrity, and a database structure's overdependence on its physical implementation.

Dr. Codd formally presented his new relational model in a landmark work entitled "A Relational Model of Data for Large Shared Databanks"[1] in June of 1970. He based his new model on two branches of mathematics—set theory and first-order predicate logic. Indeed, the name of the model itself is derived from the term *relation*, which is part of set theory. (A widely held misconception is that the relational model derives its name from the fact that tables within a relational database can be related to one another.)

A relational database stores data in *relations*, which the user perceives as tables. Each relation is composed of *tuples*, or records, and *attributes*, or fields. (I'll use the terms *tables, records,* and *fields* throughout the remainder of the book.) The physical order of the records or fields in a table is completely immaterial, and each record in the table is identified by a field that contains a unique value. These are the two characteristics of a relational database that allow the data to exist independently of the way it is physically stored in the computer. As such, a user isn't required to know the physical location of a record in order to retrieve its data. This is unlike the hierarchical and network database models, in which knowing the layout of the structures is crucial to retrieving data.

The relational model categorizes relationships as *one-to-one, one-to-many,* and *many-to-many*. (These relationships are covered in detail in Chapter 10.) A relationship between a pair of tables is established implicitly through matching values of a shared field. In Figure 1.5, for example, the CLIENTS and AGENTS tables are related via an AGENT ID field; a specific client is associated with an agent through a matching AGENT ID. Likewise, the ENTERTAINERS and ENGAGEMENTS tables are related via an ENTERTAINER ID; a record in the ENTERTAINERS table

---

1. Edgar F. Codd, "A Relational Model of Data for Large Shared Databanks," *Communications of the ACM*, June 1970, 377–87.

Agents

Agent ID	Agent First Name	Agent Last Name	Date of Hire	Agent Home Phone
100	Mike	Hernandez	05/16/95	553-3992
101	Greg	Piercy	10/15/95	790-3992
102	Katherine	Ehrlich	03/01/96	551-4993

Clients

Client ID	Agent ID	Client First Name	Client Last Name	Client Home Phone	......
9001	100	Stewart	Jameson	553-3992	......
9002	101	Shannon	McLain	790-3992	......
9003	102	Estela	Pundt	551-4993	......

Entertainers

Entertainer ID	Agent ID	Entertainer First Name	Entertainer Last Name	......
3000	100	John	Slade	......
3001	101	Mark	Jebavy	......
3002	102	Teresa	Weiss	......

Engagements

Client ID	Entertainer ID	Engagement Date	Start Time	Stop Time
9003	3001	04/01/96	1:00 PM	3:30 PM
9009	3000	04/13/96	9:00 PM	1:30 AM
9001	3002	05/02/96	3:00 PM	6:00 PM

Figure 1.5. *Examples of related tables in a relational database.*

can be associated with a record in the ENGAGEMENTS through matching ENTERTAINER IDs.

As long as a user is familiar with the relationships among the tables in the database, he can access data in an almost unlimited number of ways. He can access data from tables that are directly related and from tables that are indirectly related. Consider the *Agents* database in Figure 1.5. Although the CLIENTS table is indirectly related to the ENTERTAINERS table, the user can produce a list of clients and the entertainers who have performed for them. (Of course, it really depends on how the tables are actually structured, but I digress. This example serves our purpose for now.) He can do this easily because CLIENTS is directly related to ENGAGEMENTS and ENGAGEMENTS is directly related to ENTERTAINERS.

Retrieving Data

You retrieve data in a relational database by using *Structured Query Language* (SQL). SQL is the standard language used to create, modify, maintain, and query relational databases. Figure 1.6 shows a sample SQL query statement you can use to produce a list of all clients in the city of El Paso.

```
SELECT ClientLastName, ClientFirstName, ClientPhoneNumber
FROM Clients
WHERE City = "El Paso"
ORDER BY ClientLastName, ClientFirstName;
```

Figure 1.6. *A sample SQL query statement.*

The three components of a basic SQL query are the SELECT...FROM statement, the WHERE clause, and the ORDER BY clause. You use the

SELECT clause to indicate the fields you want to use in the query and the FROM clause to indicate the table(s) to which the fields belong. You can filter the records the query returns by imposing criteria against one or more fields with the WHERE clause, and then sort the results in ascending or descending order with the ORDER BY clause.

Most of today's major relational database software programs incorporate various forms of SQL implementations, ranging from windows in which users can manually enter "raw" SQL statements to graphical tools that allow users to build queries using various graphic elements. For example, a user working with R:BASE Technologies's R:BASE can opt to build and execute SQL query statements directly from a command prompt, while someone using Microsoft Access may find it easier to build queries using Access's graphical query builder. Regardless of how the queries are built, the user can save them for future use.

It's not always necessary for you to know SQL in order to work with a database. If your database software provides a graphical query builder or you're using a custom-built application to work with the data in your database, you'll never need to write a single SQL statement. It's a good idea, however, for you to gain a basic understanding of SQL. It will help those of you using query-building tools to understand and troubleshoot the queries you create with these tools, and it will definitely be to your advantage should you need to work high-end database software programs, such as Oracle and Microsoft SQL Server.

> ❖ **Note** Although a detailed discussion of SQL is beyond the scope of this book, you should understand that SQL is a language directly related to the relational database model. If you have a desire or need to study SQL, you could start by reading my second book, *SQL Queries for Mere Mortals*, and then move on to any of the other SQL books that are on my recommended reading list in Appendix G.

Advantages of a Relational Database

The relational database provides a number of advantages over previous models, such as the following:

- *Built-in multilevel integrity:* Data integrity is built into the model at the field level to ensure the accuracy of the data; at the table level to ensure that records are not duplicated and to detect missing primary key values; at the relationship level to ensure that the relationship between a pair of tables is valid; and at the business level to ensure that the data is accurate in terms of the business itself. (Integrity is discussed in detail as the design process unfolds.)

- *Logical and physical data independence from database applications:* Neither changes a user makes to the logical design of the database, nor changes a database software vendor makes to the physical implementation of the database, will adversely affect the applications built upon it.

- *Guaranteed data consistency and accuracy:* Data is consistent and accurate due to the various levels of integrity you can impose within the database. (This will become quite clear as you work through the design process.)

- *Easy data retrieval:* At the user's command, data can be retrieved either from a particular table or from any number of related tables within the database. This enables a user to view information in an almost unlimited number of ways.

These and other advantages have proved beneficial to the business community and to all those who need to collect and manage data. Indeed, the relational database has become the database of choice in many circumstances.

Until recently, one perceived disadvantage of the relational database was that software programs based on it ran very slowly. This was not a fault of the relational model itself, but of the ancillary technology available at the time of the model's introduction. Processing speed, memory, and storage were simply insufficient to provide database software vendors with a platform on which to build a full implementation of the relational database, so the initial relational database software programs fell woefully short of their full potential. Since the early 1990s, however, advances in both hardware technology and software engineering have made processing speed an insignificant issue and have allowed vendors to make significant gains in their efforts to support the model more fully.

You'll learn more about the relational database model as you work through the design process presented in this book. Some of the topics you'll encounter include creating tables, establishing data integrity, working with relationships, and establishing business rules.

Relational Database Management Systems

A *relational database management system* (RDBMS) is a software program you use to create, maintain, modify, and manipulate a relational database. Many RDBMS programs also provide the tools you need to create end-user applications that interact with the data stored in the database. Of course, the quality of an RDBMS is a direct function of the extent to which it supports the relational database model. Even among "true" RDBMSs, support for the relational database varies among vendors, and there is yet to be a *full* implementation of the relational model's potential. Despite this, all RDBMS programs continue to evolve and become more full-featured and powerful than ever before.

Since the early 1970s, a number of RDBMS programs have been produced by a variety of software vendors, encompassing various types of computer hardware, operating systems, and programming environments. As we continue our voyage into the beginning of the twenty-first century, it's safe to say that RDBMS programs are as ubiquitous and integrated into our daily lives as cellular phones.

In the earliest days of the relational database, RDBMSs were written for use on mainframe computers. (Didn't everything start on a mainframe?) Two RDBMS programs prevalent in the early 1970s were System R, developed by IBM at its San Jose Research Laboratory in California, and Interactive Graphics Retrieval System (INGRES), developed at the University of California at Berkeley. These two programs contributed greatly to the general appreciation of the relational model.

As the benefits of the relational database became more widely known, many companies decided to make a slow move from hierarchical and network database models to the relational database model, thus creating a need for more and better mainframe RDBMS programs. The 1980s saw the development of various commercial RDBMSs for mainframe computers, such as Oracle, developed by Oracle Corporation, and IBM's DB2.

The early to mid-1980s saw the rise of the personal computer, and with it the development of PC-based RDBMS programs. Some of the early entries in this category, such as dBase by Ashton-Tate and FoxPro from Fox Software, were nothing more than elementary file-based database-management systems. True PC-based RDBMS programs began to emerge with the introduction of R:BASE, originally developed by Microrim, and Paradox, originally developed by Ansa Software. Each of these products helped to spread the idea and potential of database management from the mainframe-dominated domain of information systems departments to the desktop of the common end user.

The need to share data became apparent as more and more users worked with databases throughout the late 1980s and early 1990s. The concept of a centrally located database that could be made available to multiple users seemed a very promising idea. This would certainly make data management and database security much easier to implement. Database vendors responded to this need by developing *client/server* RDBMS programs.

As Figure 1.7 illustrates, the data in this type of system resides on a computer acting as a *database server*, and users interact with the data through applications residing on their own computer, or *database client*. The database developer uses the client/server RDBMS program to create and maintain the database and attendant end-user application programs. She implements data integrity and data security on the database server, giving her the ability to base a variety of user applications on the same set of data without affecting the data's integrity or security.

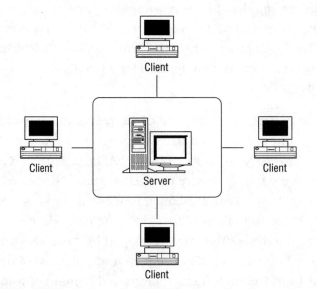

Figure 1.7. *A typical client/server architecture.*

Client/server RDBMS programs have been widely used for quite some time to manage large volumes of shared data. Some of the more recent entries in the client/server RDBMS category are Microsoft SQL Server

2000 from Microsoft Corporation and Oracle9i Application Server, from Oracle Corporation.

Beyond the Relational Model

Although RDBMSs have been widely accepted for use in typical business applications, such as inventory control, patient management, banking, order processing, and event scheduling, they have proven to be (currently, at least) lacking for such applications as computer-aided design (CAD), geographic information systems (GIS), and multimedia storage systems. Two new database models eventually emerged in response to this problem: the *object-oriented* database and the *object-relational* database.

The object-oriented model incorporates all of the characteristics of an object-oriented programming language and essentially relegates the relational database to the status of a data store. The fundamental idea here is that the database developer handles every aspect of the database, including the sets of operations that manipulate the data in the database from within the object-oriented database programming software. No longer is there a clear separation between the database software and the application programming software. (As with any other model, there are pros and cons to this approach.) Versant ODBMS by Versant Corporation and UniData by IBM are two of the most recent examples of object-oriented database software.

Unlike the relational model, which has a solid theoretical basis in two distinct branches of mathematics, the object-oriented database model has no specific theoretical foundation. As such, there is no singular, cohesive consensus as to its definition. There is, however, a version of the model proposed by the Object Management Group (OMG) that has become somewhat of a de facto standard for object-oriented database-management systems.

> ❖ **Note** The OMG is a nonprofit international group that addresses the issues of object standards. It was founded in 1989 and comprises more than 800 member organizations. It is important to note that the OMG is not a standards body, such as the American National Standards Institute (ANSI), but merely an advisory and certification group.

The object-relational model (formerly known as the *extended relational data model*), on the other hand, extended the relational database model by incorporating various object-oriented elements and characteristics, such as classes, encapsulation, and inheritance. The idea was that these extensions would allow a relational database to manage and manipulate more complex types of data, such as audio streams, video clips, and architectural drawings. Though many in the database industry believed this to be a move in the right direction, they still maintained that it did not go far enough to deal with advanced database applications. The model is still being refined and used, however, as evidenced most recently by the entry of IBM's IBM Informix Dynamic Server 9.30.

Object-oriented supporters and relational database proponents are still debating various issues to this day. Both sides agree that the relational database will not work for certain types of applications, but disagree as to the appropriate solution to the problem. The issues are quite complex and well beyond the scope of this work, but suffice it to say that these debates are likely to go on until one side gives up or technology renders them irrelevant.

What the Future Holds

The manner in which databases are used has evolved immensely in the past several years. There came a time when many organizations began to realize that there was a lot of useful information that could be gathered from data they stored in various relational and nonrelational databases. This prompted them to question whether there was a way to mine the data for useful analytical information that they could then use to make critical business decisions. Furthermore, they wondered if they could consolidate and integrate their data into a viable knowledgebase for their organizations. Indeed, these would be difficult questions to answer.

IBM proposed the idea of a *data warehouse*, which, as originally conceived, would allow organizations to access data stored in any number of nonrelational databases. They were unsuccessful in their first attempts at implementing data warehouses, primarily because of the complexities and performance problems associated with such a task. It has been only recently that the possibility of implementing a data warehouse has become more viable and practical. Bill Inmon, widely regarded as the father of the data warehouse, is a strong and vocal advocate of the technology and has been instrumental in its evolution. Data warehouses are now becoming more commonplace as companies move to leverage the vast amounts of data they've stored in their databases over the years.

The Internet has had a great influence on the way organizations use databases. Many companies and businesses are using the Web to expand their consumer base, and much of the data they share with and gather from these consumers is stored in a database. The Internet has even spawned a potentially viable solution to the problem of consolidating data from various relational and nonrelational systems. eXtensible Markup Language (XML) is quickly becoming a de facto data transfer standard for sharing data across heterogeneous systems. It is platform- and system-agnostic, so a database system that can write to and read from an XML document can share data with other systems that can do the same. As the Internet continues to become a dominant force in the world of business and commerce, more and more database vendors are rushing to incorporate XML capabilities into their products.

> ❖ **Note** I've really only pricked the surface of XML; it does far more than I've suggested in this brief introduction.

A Final Note

RDBMSs now have a long history, and they continue to play a huge role in the way people, businesses, and organizations interact with their data. Their role is constantly expanding and evolving as data becomes more accessible via the Internet and businesses move at an ever-increasing pace to gain a presence on the Web. Numerous organizations are heavily invested in their relational database systems, and they are not likely to disappear anytime soon.

Summary

We opened this chapter by defining the two types of databases currently used in database management: operational databases and analytical databases.

We then briefly discussed the hierarchical database model and the network database model. Our discussion covered the data structures, relationships, and data-access methods used in both models, as well as their chief disadvantages. You learned that these models were widely used in the early days of database management and led to the eventual development and introduction of the relational database model.

Next, we provided a detailed discussion of the relational database model, its history, and its features. We noted that it is based on specific branches of mathematics and that this mathematical foundation is what makes the model so structurally sound. Then we explored the model's data structures and relationships, and the role SQL plays in accessing data within the model. You'll remember, no doubt, that SQL is the standard language used to work with relational databases. We ended this section by reviewing the advantages of the relational database model.

We then took a look at a brief history of relational database management systems, beginning with the mainframe systems of the early 1970s and progressing through the PC-based systems of the 1980s to the client/server systems of the 1990s. At this point you should have a sense of the progression of circumstances that have led to the development of the database systems we use today.

The chapter continued with a brief discussion of the object-relational and object-oriented database models. Here you learned that these models emerged ostensibly as a means to deal with advanced database applications, and that they each incorporate various object-oriented elements and characteristics. You also learned that object-oriented databases are still in a state of flux and that debates still continue between object-oriented supporters and relational database proponents over the viability of object-oriented solutions.

Finally, we closed the chapter with a brief discussion of data warehouses and XML. You learned that data warehouses are used to consolidate and integrate data from heterogeneous sources and that the possibility of truly using them has only recently become more viable and practical. Next, you learned that XML is quickly becoming a de facto data transfer standard for sharing data across relational and nonrelational data sources. You also understand that relational databases are likely to be used for quite some time, despite the great impact the Internet has had on the way organizations use databases.

In the next chapter, we'll discuss why you should be concerned with database design and why theory is important. We'll also cover the objectives and advantages of good design.

Review Questions

1. Name the two main types of databases in use today.

2. What type of data does an analytical database store?

3. True or False: An operational database is used primarily in on-line transaction processing (OLTP) scenarios.

4. What two data models were commonly used in the days before the relational database model?

5. Describe a parent/child relationship.

6. What is a set structure?

7. Name one of the branches of mathematics on which the relational model is based.

8. How does a relational database store data?

9. Name the three types of relationships in a relational database.

10. How do you retrieve data in a relational database?

11. State two advantages of a relational database.

12. What is a relational database management system?

13. What is the premise behind the object-relational model?

14. What is the purpose of a data warehouse?

15. What is XML and why is it significant?

2

Design Objectives

Everything factual is, in a sense, theory.
The blue of the sky exhibits the basic laws of chromatics.
There is no sense in looking for something behind
phenomena; they are theory.
—GOETHE

Topics Covered in This Chapter

Why Should You Be Concerned with Database Design?

Some of you who work with RDBMS software programs may wonder why you should be concerned with database design. After all, most RDBMS programs come with sample databases that you can copy and modify to suit your own needs, and you can even borrow tables from the sample databases and use them in other databases that you've created. Some programs also provide tools that will guide you through the process of defining and creating tables. However, these tools don't actually help you *design* a database—they merely help you create the physical tables that you will include in the database.

What you must understand is that it's better for you to use these tools *after you've created the logical database structure*. RDBMS programs provide the design tools and the sample databases to help minimize the time it takes you to *implement* the database structure physically. Theoretically, reducing implementation time gives you more time to focus on creating and building end-user applications.

Yet the primary reason you should be concerned with database design is that it's crucial to the consistency, integrity, and accuracy of the data in a database. If you design a database improperly, it will be difficult for you to retrieve certain types of information, and you'll run the risk that your searches will produce inaccurate information. *Inaccurate information is probably the most detrimental result of improper database design—it can adversely affect your organization's bottom line.* In fact, if your database affects the manner in which your business performs its daily operations, or if it's going to influence the future direction of your business, you *must* be concerned with database design.

Let's look at this from a different perspective for a moment: Think about how you would go about having a custom home built for you. What's the first thing you're going to do? Certainly you're not going to hire a contractor immediately and let him build your home however he wishes. *Surely* you will first engage an architect to design your new home *and then* hire a contractor to build it. The architect will explore your needs and express them as a set of blueprints, recording decisions about size and shape and requirements for various systems (structural, mechanical, electrical). Next, the contractor will procure the labor and materials, including the listed systems, and then assemble them according to the drawings and specifications.

Now let's return to our database perspective and think of the logical database design as the architectural blueprints and the physical database implementation as the completed home. The logical database design describes the size, shape, and necessary systems for a database; it addresses the informational and operational needs of your business. You then build the physical implementation of the logical database design, using your RDBMS software program. Once you've created your tables, set up table relationships, and established the appropriate levels of data integrity, your database is complete. Now you're ready to create applications that allow you to interact easily with the data stored in the database, and you can be confident that these applications will provide you with timely and, above all, accurate information.

Although you can implement a poor design in an RDBMS, implementing a good design is far more to your advantage because it will yield accurate information, store data more efficiently and effectively, and will be easier for you to manage and maintain.

The Importance of Theory

❖ **Note** In this chapter, I use the term *theory* to represent "general propositions used as principles" and not "conjectures or proposals."

A number of major disciplines (and their associated design methodologies) have some type of theoretical basis. Structural engineers design an unlimited variety of structures using the theories of physics. Composers create beautiful symphonies and orchestral pieces using the concepts found in music theory. The automobile industry uses aerodynamics theories to design more fuel-efficient automobiles. The airplane industry uses the same theories to design airplane wings that reduce wind drag.

These examples demonstrate that theory is relevant and very important. The chief advantage of theory is that it helps you predict outcomes; it allows you to predict what will happen if you perform a certain action or series of actions. You know if you drop a stone, it will fall to the ground. If you are agile, you can get your toes out of the way of Newton's theory of gravity. The point is that it works *every time*. If you chisel a stone flat and place it on another flat stone, you can predict that it will stay where you put it. This theory allows you to design pyramids and cathedrals and brick outhouses. Now consider a database example. Let's assume you have a pair of tables that are related to each other. You know that you can draw data from both tables simultaneously simply because of the way relational database theory works. The data you draw from both tables is based on matching values of a shared field between the tables themselves. Again, your actions have a predictable result.

The relational database is based on two branches of mathematics known as *set theory* and *first-order predicate logic*. This very fact is what allows the relational database to guarantee accurate information. These branches of mathematics also provide the basis for formulating good design methodologies and the building blocks necessary to create good relational database structures.

You might harbor an understandable reluctance to study complicated mathematical concepts simply to carry out what seems to be a rather limited task. You're sure to hear claims that the mathematical theories on which the relational database and its associated design methodologies are based don't have any relevance to the real world, or that they are somehow impractical. This is not true: Math is central to the relational model and is what guarantees the model's viability. But cheer up—it isn't really necessary for you to know anything about set theory or *first-order* predicate logic in order to use a relational database! You certainly don't have to know all the details of aerodynamics just to drive an automobile. Aerodynamic theories may help you understand and appreciate how an automobile can get better gas mileage, but they won't help you learn how to parallel park.

Mathematical theory provides the foundation for the relational database model, and thus makes the model predictable, reliable, and sound. Theory describes the basic building blocks used to create a relational database and provides guidelines for how it should be arranged. Arranging building blocks to achieve a desired result is defined as "design."

The Advantage of Learning a Good Design Methodology

You could learn how to design a database properly by trial and error, but it would take you a very long time, and you would probably have to repair many mistakes along the way. The best approach is to learn a good database-design methodology, such as the one in this book, and then embark on designing your database.

You'll gain several advantages from learning and using a good design methodology.

- *It gives you the skills you need to design a sound database structure.* A large number of data-processing problems can be attributed to the presence of redundant data, duplicate data, and invalid data, or the absence of required data. All of these problems produce erroneous information and make certain queries and reports difficult to run. You can avoid almost all of these problems by employing a good design methodology.

- *It provides you with an organized set of techniques that will guide you step-by-step through the design process.* The organization of the techniques enables you to make informed decisions on every aspect of your design.

- *It helps you keep your missteps and design reiterations to a minimum.* Of course, you will naturally make *some* mistakes when you're designing a database, but a good methodology helps you recognize errors in your design and gives you the tools to correct them. Additionally, the organization of the techniques within the methodology keeps you from unnecessarily repeating a given design process.

- *It makes the design process easier and reduces the amount of time you spend designing the database.* You will inevitably waste valuable time taking an arbitrary trial-and-error approach to design because it lacks the logic and organization that a good methodology provides.

- *It will help you understand and use your RDBMS software more fully and effectively.* As your knowledge of proper design expands and grows, you'll actually begin to understand *why* a given RDBMS provides certain tools and *how* you can use them to implement the structure within the RDBMS program.

Regardless of whether you use the design methodology presented in this book or some other established methodology, you should choose a design methodology, learn it as well as you can, and use it faithfully to design your databases.

Objectives of Good Design

There are distinct objectives you must achieve in order to design a good, sound database structure. You can avoid many of the problems mentioned in the previous section if you keep these objectives in mind and constantly focus on them while you're designing your database.

- *The database supports both required and ad hoc information retrieval.* The database must store the data necessary to support information requirements defined during the design process and any possible ad hoc queries that may be posed by a user.

- *The tables are constructed properly and efficiently.* Each table in the database represents a single subject, is composed of relatively distinct fields, keeps redundant data to an absolute minimum, and is identified throughout the database by a field with unique values.

- *Data integrity is imposed at the field, table, and relationship levels.* These levels of integrity help guarantee that the data structures and their values will be valid and accurate at all times.

- *The database supports business rules relevant to the organization.* The data must provide valid and accurate information that is always meaningful to the business.

- *The database lends itself to future growth.* The database structure should be easy to modify or expand as the information requirements of the business change and grow.

You might find it difficult at times to fulfill these objectives, but you'll certainly be pleased with your final database structure once you've met them.

Benefits of Good Design

The time you invest in designing a sound database structure is time well spent. Good design *saves* you time in the long run because you do not have to constantly revamp a quickly and poorly designed structure. You gain the following benefits when you apply good design techniques:

- *The database structure is easy to modify and maintain.* Modifications you make to a field or table will not adversely affect other fields or tables in the database.

- *The data is easy to modify.* Changes you make to the value of a given field in a table will not adversely affect the values of other fields within the table. Furthermore, a well-designed database keeps duplicate fields to an absolute minimum, so you typically modify a particular data value in one field only.

- *Information is easy to retrieve.* You'll be able to create queries easily because the tables are well constructed and the relationships between them are properly established.

- *End-user applications are easy to develop and build.* You can spend more time on programming and addressing the data manipulation tasks at hand, instead of working around the inevitable problems that arise when you work with a poorly designed database.

Database-Design Methods

Traditional Design Methods

In general, traditional methods of database design incorporate three phases: *requirements analysis*, *data modeling*, and *normalization*.

The requirements-analysis phase involves an examination of the business being modeled, interviews with users and management to assess the current system and to analyze future needs, and an assessment of information requirements for the business as a whole. This process is relatively straightforward, and, indeed, the design process presented in this book follows the same line of thinking.

The data-modeling phase involves modeling the database structure using a data-modeling method, such as entity-relationship (ER) diagramming, semantic-object modeling, or object-role modeling. Each of these modeling methods provides a means of visually representing various aspects of the database structure, such as the tables, table relationships, and relationship characteristics. In fact, the modeling method used in this book is a basic version of ER diagramming. Figure 2.1 shows an example of a basic ER diagram.

Figure 2.1. *An example of a basic ER diagram.*

❖ **Note** I've incorporated the data-modeling method I use in this book into the design process itself rather than treating it separately. I'll introduce and explain each modeling technique as appropriate throughout the process.

Each data-modeling method incorporates a set of diagramming symbols used to represent a database's structure and characteristics. For example, the diagram in Figure 2.1 provides information on several aspects of the database.

- The rectangles represent two tables called AGENTS and CLIENTS.

- The diamond represents a relationship between these two tables, and the "1:N" within the diamond indicates that it is a one-to-many relationship.

- The vertical line next to the AGENTS table indicates that a client must be associated with an agent, and the circle next to the CLIENTS table indicates that an agent doesn't necessarily have to be associated with a client.

Fields are also defined and associated with the appropriate tables during the data-modeling phase. Each table is assigned a *primary key*, various levels of data integrity are identified and implemented, and relationships are established via *foreign keys*. Once the initial table structures are complete and the relationships have been established according to the data model, the database is ready to go through the normalization phase.

Normalization is the process of decomposing large tables into smaller ones in order to eliminate redundant data and duplicate data and to avoid problems with inserting, updating, or deleting data. During the normalization process, table structures are tested against *normal forms* and then modified if any of the aforementioned problems are found. A normal form is a specific set of rules that can be used to test a table structure to ensure that it is sound and free of problems. There are a number of normal forms, and each one is used to test for a particular set of problems. The normal forms currently in use are First Normal Form, Second Normal Form, Third Normal Form, Fourth Normal Form, Fifth Normal Form, Boyce-Codd Normal Form, and Domain/Key Normal Form.

The Design Method Presented in This Book

The design method that I use in this book is one that I've developed over the years. It incorporates a requirements analysis and a simple ER-diagramming method to diagram the database structure. However, it *does not* incorporate the traditional normalization process or involve the use of normal forms. The reason is simple: Normal forms can be confusing to anyone who has not taken the time to study formal relational database theory. For example, examine the following definition of Third Normal Form:

> A *relvar* is in *3NF* if and only if it is in *2NF* and every *non-key*
> *attribute* is *nontransitively dependent* on the *primary key.*[1]

This description is relatively meaningless to a reader who is unfamiliar with the terms *relvar, 3NF, 2NF, non-key attribute, transitively dependent,* and *primary key.*

The process of designing a database is not and should not be hard to understand. As long as the process is presented in a straightforward manner and each concept or technique is clearly explained, anyone should be able to design a database properly. For example, the following definition is derived from the *results* of using Third Normal Form against a table structure, and I believe most people will find it clear and easy to understand:

> A table should have a field that uniquely identifies each of its
> records, and each field in the table should describe the subject
> that the table represents.

The process I used to formulate this definition is the same one I used to develop my entire design methodology.

Back in the late 1980s, it occurred to me that the relational model had been in existence for almost 20 years and that people had been designing databases using the same basic methodology for about 12 years. I was using the traditional design methodology at that time, but I occasionally found it difficult to employ. The two things that bothered me the most about it were the normalization process (as a whole) and the seemingly endless iterations it took to arrive at a proper design. Of course, these seemed to be sore points with most of the other database developers that

---

1. C. J. Date, *An Introduction to Database Systems,* 7th ed. (Boston, MA: Addison-Wesley, 2000), 362; emphasis added.

I knew, so I certainly wasn't alone in my frustrations. I thought about these problems for quite some time, and then I came up with a solution.

I already knew that the purpose of normalization is to take an improperly or poorly designed table and transform it into a table with a sound structure. I also understood the process: Take a given table and test it against the normal forms to determine whether it is properly designed. If it isn't designed properly, make the appropriate modifications, retest it, and repeat the entire process until the table structure is sound. Figure 2.2 shows how I visualized the process at this point.

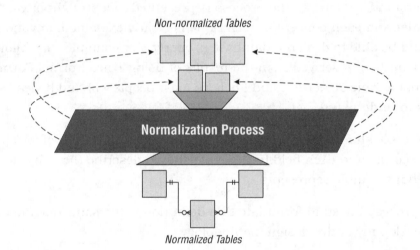

Figure 2.2. *A graphic representation of the general normalization process.*

I kept these facts in mind and then posed the following questions:

1. If we assume that a thoroughly normalized table is properly and efficiently designed, couldn't we identify the specific characteristics of such a table and state these to be the attributes of an ideal table structure?

2. Couldn't we then use that ideal table as a model for all tables we create for the database throughout the design process?

The answer to both questions, of course, is yes, so I began in earnest to develop the basis for my "new" design methodology. I first compiled distinct sets of guidelines for creating sound structures by identifying the final characteristics of a well-defined database that *successfully* passed the tests of *each* normal form. I then conducted a few tests, using the new guidelines to create table structures for a new database and to correct flaws in the table structures of an existing database. These tests went very well, so I decided to apply this technique to the entire traditional design methodology. I formulated guidelines to address other issues associated with the traditional design method, such as domains, subtypes, relationships, and referential integrity. After I completed the new guidelines, I performed more tests and found that my methodology worked quite well.

The main advantage of my design methodology is that it removes many aspects of the traditional design methodology that new database developers find intimidating. For example, normalization, in the traditional sense, is now transparent to the developer because it has been incorporated (via the new guidelines) throughout the design process. Another major advantage is that the methodology is clear and easy to implement. I believe much of this is due to the fact that I've written all the guidelines in plain English, making them easy for most anyone to understand.

It's important for you to understand that this design methodology will yield a fully normalized database structure *only if you follow it as faithfully as you would any other design methodology.* You cannot shortcut, circumvent, de-emphasize, or omit any part of this methodology (or any design methodology, for that matter) and expect to develop a sound structure. You must go through the process diligently, methodically, and completely in order reap the expected rewards.

There are a few basic terms you'll have to learn before you delve into the design process, and we'll cover them in the next chapter.

Summary

At the beginning of this chapter we looked at the importance of being concerned with database design. You now understand that database design is crucial to the integrity and consistency of the data contained in a database. We have seen that the chief problem resulting from improper or poor design is *inaccurate information*. Proper design is of paramount concern because bad design can adversely affect the information used by an organization.

Next, we entered into a discussion of the importance of theory, as well as its relevance to the relational database model, and you learned that the model's foundation in mathematical theory makes it a very sound and reliable structure.

Following this discussion, we looked at the advantages gained by learning a design methodology. Among other things, using a good methodology yields an efficient and reliable database structure, reduces the time it takes to design a database, and allows you to avoid the typical problems caused by poor design.

Next, we listed the objectives of good design. Meeting these objectives is crucial to the success of the database-design process because they help you ensure that the database structure is sound. We then enumerated the advantages of good design, and you learned that the time you invest in designing a sound database structure is time well spent.

We closed this chapter with a short discussion of traditional database-design methods and an explanation of the premise behind the design method presented in this book. By now, you understand that traditional design methods are complex and can take some time to learn and comprehend. On the other hand, the design method used in this book is presented in a clear and straightforward manner, is easy to implement, and will yield the same results as the traditional design methodology.

Review Questions

1. When is the best time to use an RDBMS program's design tools?

2. True or False: Design is crucial to the consistency, integrity, and accuracy of data.

3. What is the most detrimental result of improper database design?

4. What fact makes the relational database structurally sound and able to guarantee accurate information?

5. State two advantages of learning a design methodology.

6. True or False: You will use your RDBMS program more effectively if you understand database design.

7. State two objectives of good design.

8. What helps to guarantee that data structures and their values are valid and accurate at all times?

9. State two benefits of applying good design techniques.

10. True or False: You can take shortcuts through some of the design processes and still arrive at a good, sound design.

Terminology

"When I use a word," Humpty Dumpty said in rather a scornful tone, "it means just what I choose it to mean—neither more nor less."
—LEWIS CARROLL
THROUGH THE LOOKING GLASS

Topics Covered in This Chapter

Why This Terminology Is Important

Value-Related Terms

Structure-Related Terms

Relationship-Related Terms

Integrity-Related Terms

Summary

Review Questions

The terms in this chapter are important for you to understand before you embark upon learning the design process. Indeed, there are other terms that you'll need to learn, and I'll cover them as you work through the process. There's also a glossary in the back of the book that you can use to refresh your memory on any term you learn here or in the following chapters.

Why This Terminology Is Important

Relational database design has its own unique set of terms, just as any other profession, trade, or discipline. Here are three good reasons why it's important for you to learn these terms.

1. *They are used to express and define the special ideas and concepts of the relational database model.* Much of the terminology is derived from the mathematical branches of set theory and first-order predicate logic, which, as you already know, form the basis of the relational database model.

2. *They are used to express and define the database-design process itself.* The design process becomes clearer and much easier to understand once you know these terms.

3. *They are used anywhere a relational database or RDBMS is discussed.* You'll see these terms in publications such as trade magazines, RDBMS software manuals, educational course materials, and commercial RDBMS software books. You'll also hear these terms in conversations between various types of database practitioners.

This chapter covers a majority of the terms used to define the ideas and concepts of the design process, and each term is defined and discussed in some detail. (I provide pertinent details or necessary further discussion for a given term at the point where the term is expressly used within a specific technique in the design process.) There are several other terms that I introduce and discuss later in the book because they are more easily understood within the context of the specific idea or concept to which they relate.

> ❖ **Note** The glossary contains concise definitions for all of the terms presented here and throughout the book.

There are four categories of terms defined in this chapter: *value-related, structure-related, relationship-related,* and *integrity-related.*

Value-Related Terms

Data

The values you store in the database are *data.* Data is static in the sense that it remains in the same state until you modify it by some manual or automated process. Figure 3.1 shows some sample data.

```
George Edleman     92883     05/16/96     95.00
```

Figure 3.1. *An example of basic data.*

On the surface, this data is meaningless. For example, there is no easy way for you to determine what "92883" represents. Is it a zip code? Is it a part number? Even if you know it represents a customer identification number, is it one that is associated with George Edleman? There's just no way of knowing until you process the data.

Information

Information is data that you process in a manner that makes it meaningful and useful to you when you work with it or view it. It is dynamic in the sense that it constantly changes relative to the data stored in the database, and also in the sense that it can be processed and presented in an unlimited number of ways. You can show information as the result of a SELECT statement, display it in a form on your computer screen, or print it on paper as a report. The point to remember is that *you must process your data in some manner so that you can turn it into meaningful information.*

Figure 3.2 demonstrates how the data from the previous example can be processed and transformed into information. It has been manipulated in such a way—in this case as part of a patient invoice report—that it is now meaningful to anyone who views it.

Eastside Medical Clinic 7743 Kingman Dr. Seattle, WA 98032 (206) 555-9982	Patient Name: George Edelman Patient ID: 10884 Visit Date: 05/16/96 Physician: Daniel Chavez

Doctors Services	Service Code	Fee		Nursing Services	Service Code	Fee
[X] Consultation	92883	119.00	[ ]	R.N. Exam	89327	
[X] EKG	92773	95.00	[ ]	Supplies	82372	
[ ] Physical	98377		[ ]	Nurse Instruction	88332	
[ ] Ultrasound	97399		[ ]	Insurance Report	81368	

Figure 3.2. *An example of data transformed into information.*

It is very important for you to understand the difference between *data* and *information*. A database is designed to provide meaningful information to someone within a business or organization. This information can be provided only if the appropriate *data* exists in the database and the database is structured in such a way as to support that *information*. If you ever forget the difference between data and information, just remember this little axiom:

> *Data* is what you *store*; *information* is what you *retrieve*.

When you fully understand this single, simple concept, the logic behind the database-design process will become crystal clear.

> ❖ **Note** Unfortunately, *data* and *information* are two terms that are *still* frequently used interchangeably (and, therefore, errone-ously) throughout the database industry. You'll encounter this error in numerous trade magazines and commercial database books, and you'll even see the terms misused by authors who should know better.

Null

A *null* represents a missing or unknown value. You must understand from the outset that a null *does not* represent a zero or a text string of one or more blank spaces. The reasons are quite simple.

- A zero can have a very wide variety of meanings. It can represent the state of an account balance, the current number of available first-class ticket upgrades, or the current stock level of a particu-lar product.

- Although a text string of one or more blank spaces is guaranteed to be meaningless to most of us, it is definitely meaningful to a query language like SQL. A blank space is a valid character as far as SQL is concerned, and a character string composed of three blank spaces ('   ') is just as legitimate as a character string composed of three letters ('abc'). In Figure 3.3, a blank repre-sents the fact that Washington, D.C., is not located in any county whatsoever.

- A *zero-length* string—two consecutive single quotes with no space in between ('')—is also an acceptable value to languages such as SQL, and can be meaningful under certain circumstances. In an EMPLOYEES table, for example, a zero-length string value in a field called MiddleInitial may represent the fact that a particular employee does not have a middle initial in his name.

Clients

Client ID	Client First Name	Client Last Name	Client City	Client County	State	<< other fields >>
9001	Stewart	Jameson	Seattle	King	WA	......
9002	Shannon	McLain	Poulsbo		WA	......
9003	Estela	Pundt	Fremont	Alameda	CA	......
9004	Timothy	Ennis	Bellevue	King	WA	......
9005	Marvin	Russo	Washington		DC	......
9006	Kendra	Bonnicksen	Portland		OR	......

Figure 3.3. *An example of a table containing null values.*

❖ Note Due to space restrictions, I cannot always show all of the fields for a given sample table. I will, however, show the fields that are most relevant to the discussion at hand and use *<<other fields>>* to represent fields that are unessential to the example. You'll see this convention in many examples throughout the remainder of the book.

The Value of Nulls

A null is quite useful when you use it for its stated purpose, and the CLIENTS table in Figure 3.3 clearly illustrates this. Each null in the CLIENT COUNTY field represents a missing or unknown county name for the record in which it appears. In order for you to use nulls correctly, you must first understand why they occur at all.

Missing values are commonly the result of human error. For example, consider the record for Shannon McLain. If you're entering the data for Ms. McLain and you fail to ask her for the name of the county she lives in, that data is considered missing and is represented in the record as a null. Once you recognize the error, however, you can correct it by calling Ms. McLain and asking her for the county name.

Unknown values appear in a table for a variety of reasons. One reason may be that a specific value you need for a field is as yet undefined. For instance, you could have a CATEGORIES table in a *School Scheduling* database that doesn't currently contain a category for a new set of classes that you want to offer beginning in the fall session. Another reason a table might contain unknown values is that they are truly unknown. Refer to the CLIENTS table in Figure 3.3 once again and consider the record for Marvin Russo. Say that you're entering the data for Mr. Russo and you ask him for the name of the county he lives in. If he doesn't know the county name and you don't happen to know the county that includes the city in which he lives, then the value for the county field in his record is truly unknown and is represented within the record as a null. Obviously, you can correct the problem once either of you determines the correct county name.

A field value may also be null if none of its values applies to a particular record. Assume for a moment that you're working with an EMPLOYEES table that contains a SALARY field and a HOURLYRATE field. The value for one of these two columns is always going to be null because an employee cannot be paid both a fixed salary and an hourly rate.

It's important to note that there is a very slim difference between "does not apply" and "is not applicable." In the previous example, the value of one of the two fields literally does not apply. Now assume you're working with a PATIENTS table that contains a field called HAIRCOLOR and you're currently updating a record for an existing male patient. If that patient recently became bald, then the value for that field is definitely "not applicable." Although you could just use a null to represent a value that is not applicable, I always recommend that you use a true value such as "N/A" or "Not Applicable." This will make the information clearer in the long run.

As you can see, whether you allow nulls in a table depends on the manner in which you're using the data. Now that we've shown you the positive side of using nulls, let's take a look at the negative implication of using them.

The Problem with Nulls

The major disadvantage of nulls is that they have an adverse effect on mathematical operations. An operation involving a null evaluates to null. This is logically reasonable—if a number is unknown then the result of the operation is necessarily unknown. Note how a null alters the outcome of the operation in the following example:

$(25 \times 3) + 4 = 79$

$(\text{Null} \times 3) + 4 = \text{Null}$

$(25 \times \text{Null}) + 4 = \text{Null}$

$(25 \times 3) + \text{Null} = \text{Null}$

The PRODUCTS table in Figure 3.4 helps to illustrate the effects nulls have on mathematical expressions that incorporate fields from a table. In this case, the value for the TOTAL VALUE field is derived from the mathematical expression "[SRP] × [QTY ON HAND]." As you inspect the records in this table, note that the value for the TOTAL VALUE field is missing where the QTY ON HAND value is null, resulting in a null value for the TOTAL VALUE field as well. This leads to a serious *undetected* error that occurs when all the values in the TOTAL VALUE field are added together: an inaccurate total. This error is "undetected" because an RDBMS program will not inherently alert you of the error. The only way to avoid this problem is to ensure that the values for the QTY ON HAND field cannot be null.

Figure 3.5 helps to illustrate the effect nulls have on aggregate functions that incorporate the values of a given field in a table. The result of

Products

Product ID	Product Description	Category	SRP	Qty On Hand	Total Value
70001	Shur-Lok U-Lock	Accessories	75.00		
70002	SpeedRite Cyclecomputer		65.00	20	1,300.00
70003	SteelHead Microshell Helmet	Accessories	36.00	33	1,118.00
70004	SureStop 133-MB Brakes	Components	23.50	16	376.00
70005	Diablo ATM Mountain Bike	Bikes	1,200.00		
70006	UltraVision Helmet Mount Mirrors		7.45	10	74.50

Figure 3.4. *The nulls in this table will have an effect on mathematical operations involving the table's fields.*

an aggregate function, such as Count(<*fieldname*>), will be null if it is based on a field that contains null values. The table in Figure 3.5 shows the results of a summary query that counts the total number of occurrences of each category in the PRODUCTS table shown in Figure 3.4. The value of the TOTAL OCCURRENCES field is the result of the function expression Count([CATEGORY]). Notice that the summary query shows "0" occurrences of an unspecified category, implying that each product has been assigned a category. This information is clearly inaccurate because there are two products in the PRODUCTS table that have not been assigned a category.

Category Summary

Category	Total Occurrences
	0
Accessories	2
Bikes	1
Components	1

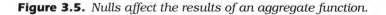

Figure 3.5. *Nulls affect the results of an aggregate function.*

The issues of missing values, unknown values, and whether a value will be used in a mathematical expression or aggregate function are all taken into consideration in the database-design process, and we will revisit and discuss these issues further in later chapters.

Structure-Related Terms

Table

According to the relational model, data in a relational database is stored in *relations*, which are perceived by the user as *tables*. Each relation is composed of *tuples* (records) and *attributes* (fields). Figure 3.6 shows a typical table structure.

Clients

Client ID	Client First Name	Client Last Name	Client City	<< other fields >>
9001	Stewart	Jameson	Seattle	....
9002	Shannon	McLain	Poulsbo	....
9003	Estela	Pundt	Tacoma	....
9004	Timothy	Ennis	Seattle	....
9005	Marvin	Russo	Bellingham	....
9006	Kendra	Bonnicksen	Tacoma	....

Records

Fields

Figure 3.6. *A typical table structure.*

Tables are the chief structures in the database and each table always represents a single, specific subject. The logical order of records and fields within a table is of absolutely no importance, and every table contains at least one field—known as a *primary key*—that uniquely identifies each of its records. (In Figure 3.6, for example, CLIENT ID is the primary key of the CLIENTS table.) In fact, data in a relational database can exist independently of the way it is physically stored in the computer because of these last two table characteristics. This is great news for the user because he or she isn't required to know the physical location of a record in order to retrieve its data.

The subject that a given table represents can either be an *object* or *event*. When the subject is an object, it means that the table represents something that is tangible, such as a person, place, or thing. Regardless of its type, every object has characteristics that can be stored as data. This data can then be processed in an almost infinite number of ways. Pilots, products, machines, students, buildings, and equipment are all examples of objects that can be represented by a table, and Figure 3.6 illustrates one of the most common examples of this type of table.

When the subject of a table is an event, it means that the table represents something that occurs at a given point in time having characteristics you wish to record. These characteristics can be stored as data and then processed as information in exactly the same manner as a table that represents some specific object. Examples of events you may need to record include judicial hearings, distributions of funds, lab test results, and geological surveys. Figure 3.7 shows an example of a table representing an event that we all have experienced at one time or another—a doctor's appointment.

A table that stores data used to supply information is called a *data table*, and it is the most common type of table in a relational database. Data in this type of table is dynamic because you can manipulate it (modify, delete, and so forth) and process it into information in some form or fashion. You'll constantly interact with these types of tables as you work with your database.

Patient Visit

Patient ID	Visit Date	Visit Time	Physician	Blood Pressure	<< other fields >>
92001	05/01/96	10:30	Hernandez	120/80	....
97002	05/01/96	13:00	Piercy	112/74	....
99014	05/02/96	09:30	Rolson	120/80	....
96105	05/02/96	11:00	Hernandez	160/90	....
96203	05/02/96	14:00	Hernandez	110/75	....
98003	05/03/96	09:30	Rolson	120/80	....

Figure 3.7. *A table representing an event.*

A *validation table* (also known as a *lookup table*), on the other hand, stores data that you specifically use to implement data integrity. A validation table usually represents subjects, such as city names, skill categories, product codes, and project identification numbers. Data in this type of table is static because it will very rarely change at all. Although you have very little *direct* interaction with these tables, you'll frequently use them *indirectly* to validate values that you enter into a data table. Figure 3.8 shows an example of a validation table.

Categories

Category ID	Category Name
10000	Accessories
20000	Bikes
30000	Clothing
40000	Components

Figure 3.8. *An example of a validation table.*

I'll discuss validation tables in more detail in Chapter 11.

Field

A *field* (known as an *attribute* in relational database theory) is the smallest structure in the database and it represents a characteristic of the subject of the table to which it belongs. Fields are the structures that actually store data. The data in these fields can then be retrieved and presented as information in almost any configuration that you can imagine. The quality of the information you get from your data is in direct proportion to the amount of time you've dedicated to ensuring the structural integrity and data integrity of the fields themselves. There is just no way to underestimate the importance of fields.

Every field in a *properly designed* database contains one and only one value, and its name will identify the type of value it holds. This makes entering data into a field very intuitive. If you see fields with names such as FIRSTNAME, LASTNAME, CITY, STATE, and ZIPCODE, you know exactly what type of values go into each field. You'll also find it very easy to sort the data by state or look for everyone whose last name is "Hernandez."

You'll typically encounter three other types of fields in an improperly or poorly designed database.

1. A *multipart* field (also known as a *composite* field), which contains two or more *distinct* items within its value.

2. A *multivalued* field, which contains multiple instances of the *same* type of value.

3. A *calculated* field, which contains a concatenated text value or the result of a mathematical expression.

Figure 3.9 shows a table with an example of each of these types of fields.

| | | | Calculated Field | | Multipart Field | Multivalued Field |

Clients

Client ID	Client First Name	Client Last Name	Client Full Name	Address	Client City, State, Zip	Account Rep
9001	Stewart	Jameson	Stewart Jameson	......	Seattle, WA 98125	John, Sandi
9002	Shannon	McLain	Shannon McLain	......	Poulsbo, WA 98370	Frits
9003	Estela	Pundt	Estela Pundt	......	Bellevue, WA 98005	John
9004	Timothy	Ennis	Timothy Ennis	......	Seattle, WA 98115	Frits, Sandi
9005	Marvin	Russo	Marvin Russo	......	Bellingham, WA 98225	Frits, John
9006	Kendra	Bonnicksen	Kendra Bonnicksen	......	Olympia, WA 98504	Sandi

Figure 3.9. *A table containing regular, calculated, multipart, and multivalued fields.*

I'll cover calculated, multipart, and multivalued fields in greater detail in Chapter 7.

Record

A *record* (known as a *tuple* in relational database theory) represents a unique instance of the subject of a table. It is composed of the entire set of fields in a table, regardless of whether or not the fields contain values. Because of the manner in which a table is defined, each record is identified throughout the database by a unique value in the primary key field of that record.

In Figure 3.9, each record represents a unique client within the table, and the CLIENT ID field is used to identify a given client throughout the database. In turn, each record includes all of the fields within the table, and each field describes some aspect of the client represented by the record. Consider the record for Timothy Ennis, for example. His record represents a unique instance of the table's subject ("Clients") and includes the total collection of fields in the table, treated as a unit. The values of those fields represent relevant facts about Mr. Ennis that are important to someone in the organization.

Records are a key factor in understanding table relationships because you'll need to know how a record in one table relates to other records in another table.

View

A *view* is a "virtual" table composed of fields from one or more tables in the database; the tables that comprise the view are known as *base tables*. The relational model refers to a view as "virtual" because it draws data from base tables rather than storing data on its own. In fact, the only information about a view that is stored in the database is its structure. Many major RDBMS programs support views, but some (such as Microsoft Access) refer to them as *saved queries*. Your specific RDBMS program will determine whether you refer to this object as a query or a view.

Views enable you to see the information in your database from many different aspects, providing you with a great amount of flexibility when you work with your data. You can create views in a variety of ways and they are especially useful when you base them on multiple related tables. In a school scheduling database, for example, you could create a view that consolidates data from the STUDENTS, CLASSES, and CLASS SCHEDULES tables.

Figure 3.10 shows a view called INSTRUMENT ASSIGNMENTS that is composed of fields taken from the STUDENTS, INSTRUMENTS, and STUDENT INSTRUMENTS tables. The view displays data that it draws from all of these tables simultaneously, based on matching values between the STUDENT ID fields in the STUDENTS and STUDENT INSTRUMENTS tables, and the INSTRUMENT ID fields in the INSTRU-MENTS and STUDENT INSTRUMENTS tables.

Students

Student ID	Student First Name	Student Last Name	Student Phone	<< other fields >>
60001	Zachary	Erlich	553-3992	....
60002	Susan	McLain	790-3992	....
60003	Joe	Rosales	551-4993	....

Student Instruments

Student ID	Instrument ID	Checkout Date
60002	1003	09/26/01
60001	1002	09/28/01
60003	1000	09/28/01

Instruments

Instrument ID	Instrument Description	Category	<< other fields >>
1000	Stratocaster	Guitar	....
1001	Player 2100 Multieffects	Multieffect Unit	....
1002	JCM 2000 Tube Super Lead	Amplifier	....
1003	Twin Reverb Reissue	Amplifier	....

Instrument Assignments (*View*)

Student First Name	Student Last Name	Instrument Description	Checkout Date
Zachary	Erlich	JCM 2000 Tube Super Lead	09/26/01
Susan	McLain	Twin Reverb Reissue	09/28/01
Joe	Rosales	Stratocaster	09/28/01

Figure 3.10. *An example of a typical view.*

There are three major reasons that views are important.

1. They allow you to work with data from multiple tables simultaneously. (In order for a view to do this, the tables must have connections, or *relationships*, to each other.)

2. They enable you to prevent certain users from viewing or manipulating specific fields within a table or group of tables. This capability can be very advantageous in terms of security.

3. You can use them to implement data integrity. A view you use for this purpose is known as a *validation view*.

You'll learn more about designing and using views in Chapter 12.

❖ **Note** Although every major database vendor supports the type of view I've described in this section, several vendors are now supporting what is known as an *indexed* (or *materialized*) view. An indexed view is different from a "regular" view in that it does store data, and its fields can be indexed to improve the speed at which the RDBMS processes the view's data. A full discussion of indexed views is beyond the scope of this book because it is a vendor-specific implementation issue. However, you should research this topic further if you are working with a client/server or mainframe RDBMS program.

Keys

Keys are special fields that play very specific roles within a table, and the type of key determines its purpose within the table. There are several types of keys a table may contain, but the two most significant ones are the *primary key* and the *foreign key*.

A primary key is a field or group of fields that uniquely identifies each record within a table; if a primary key is composed of two or more fields, it is known as a *composite* primary key. The primary key is absolutely the most important key in the entire table.

- A primary key **value** identifies *a specific record* throughout the entire database,

- The primary key **field** identifies *a given table* throughout the entire database.

- The primary key enforces table-level integrity and helps establish relationships with other tables in the database. (You'll learn more about relationships in the next section.)

Every table in your database should have a primary key!

The AGENT ID field in Figure 3.11 is a good example of a primary key. It uniquely identifies each agent within the AGENTS table and helps to guarantee table-level integrity by ensuring nonduplicate records. It can also be used to establish relationships between the AGENTS table and other tables in the database, such as the ENTERTAINERS table shown in the example.

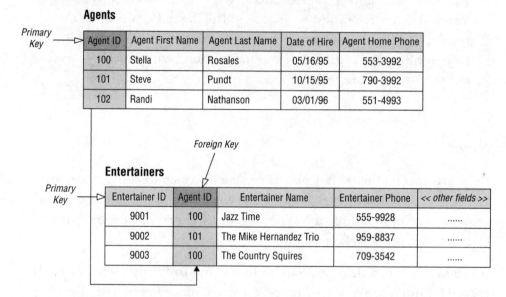

Figure 3.11. *An example of primary and foreign key fields.*

When you determine that two tables bear a relationship to each other, you typically establish the relationship by taking a copy of the primary key from the first table and incorporating it into the structure of the second table, where it becomes a foreign key. The name "foreign key" is derived from the fact that the second table already has a primary key of its own, and the primary key you are introducing from the first table is "foreign" to the second table.

Figure 3.11 also shows a good example of a foreign key. Note that AGENT ID is the primary key of the AGENTS table and a foreign key in the

ENTERTAINERS table. AGENT ID assumes this role because the ENTER-
TAINERS table already has a primary key—ENTERTAINER ID. As such,
AGENT ID establishes the relationship between both of the tables.

Besides helping to establish relationships between pairs of tables, foreign keys also help implement and ensure relationship-level integrity.
This means that the records in both tables will always be properly
related because the values of a foreign key *must match* existing values
of the primary key to which it refers. Relationship-level integrity also
helps you avoid the dreaded "orphaned" record, a classic example of
which is an order record without an associated customer. If you don't
know who made the order, you can't process it, and you obviously can't
invoice it. That'll throw your quarterly sales off!

Key fields play an important part in a relational database, and you
must learn how to create and use them. You'll learn more about primary keys in Chapters 8 and 10.

Index

An *index* is a structure an RDBMS provides to improve data processing. Your particular RDBMS program will determine how the index
works and how you use it. However, *an index has absolutely nothing
to do with the logical database structure!* The only reason I include the
term *index* in this chapter is that people often confuse it with the
term *key*.

Index and *key* are just two more terms that are widely and frequently
misused throughout the database industry and in numerous database-
related publications. (Remember my comments on *data* and *information*?) You'll always know the difference between the two if you
remember that keys are *logical structures* you use to identify records
within a table, and indexes are *physical structures* you use to optimize
data processing.

Relationship-Related Terms

Relationships

A relationship exists between two tables when you can in some way associate the records of the first table with those of the second. You can establish the relationship via a set of primary and foreign keys (as you learned in the previous section) or through a third table known as a *linking table* (also known as an *associative table*). The manner in which you establish the relationship really depends on the type of relationship that exists between the tables. (You'll learn more about that in a moment.) Figure 3.11 illustrates a relationship established via primary/foreign keys, and Figure 3.12 illustrates a relationship established with a linking table.

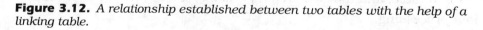

Students

Student ID	Student First Name	Student Last Name	Student Phone	<< *other fields* >>
60001	Zachary	Erlich	553-3992	......
60002	Susan	McLain	790-3992	......
60003	Joe	Rosales	551-4993	......

Student Schedule (*Linking Table*)

Student ID	Class ID
60003	900001
60001	900003
60003	900003
60002	900002
60001	900001

Classes

Class ID	Class Name	Instructor ID	<< *other fields* >>
900001	Intro. to Political Science	220087	......
900002	Adv. Music Theory	220039	......
900003	American History	220148	......

Figure 3.12. *A relationship established between two tables with the help of a linking table.*

A relationship is an important component of a relational database.

- It enables you to create multitable views.

- It is crucial to data integrity because it helps reduce redundant data and eliminate duplicate data.

You can characterize every relationship in three ways: by the type of relationship that exists between the tables, the manner in which each table participates, and the degree to which each table participates.

Types of Relationships

There are three specific types of relationship (traditionally known as a *cardinality*) that can exist between a pair of tables: *one-to-one*, *one-to-many*, and *many-to-many*.

One-to-One Relationships

A pair of tables bears a *one-to-one* relationship when a single record in the first table is related to only one record in the second table, and a single record in the second table is related to only one record in the first table. In this type of relationship, one table serves as a "parent" table and the other serves as a "child" table. You establish the relationship by taking a copy of the parent table's primary key and incorporating it within the structure of the child table, where it becomes a foreign key. This is a special type of relationship because it is the only one in which both tables may actually share the same primary key.

Figure 3.13 shows an example of a typical one-to-one relationship. In this case, EMPLOYEES is the parent table and COMPENSATION is the child table. The relationship between these tables is such that a single record in the EMPLOYEES table can be related to only one record in the COMPENSATION table, and a single record in the COMPENSATION

Employees

Employee ID	Employee First Name	Employee Last Name	Home Phone	<< other fields >>
100	Zachary	Erlich	553-3992	......
101	Susan	McLain	790-3992	......
102	Joe	Rosales	551-4993	......

Compensation

Employee ID	Hourly Rate	Commission Rate	<< other fields >>
100	25.00	5.0%	......
101	19.75	3.5%	......
102	22.50	5.0%	......

Figure 3.13. *An example of a one-to-one relationship.*

table can be related to only one record in the EMPLOYEES table. Note that EMPLOYEE ID is indeed the primary key in both tables. However, it will also serve the role of a foreign key in the child table.

One-to-Many Relationships

A *one-to-many* relationship exists between a pair of tables when a single record in the first table can be related to many records in the second table, but a single record in the second table can be related to *only one* record in the first table. (The parent/child model I used to describe a one-to-one relationship works here as well. In this case, the table on the "one" side of the relationship is the parent table, and the table on the "many" side is the child table.) You establish a one-to-many relationship by taking a copy of the parent table's primary key and incorporating it within the structure of the child table, where it becomes a foreign key.

The example in Figure 3.14 illustrates a typical one-to-many relationship. A single record in the AGENTS table can be related to one or more records in the ENTERTAINERS table, but a single record in the ENTERTAINERS table is related to only one record in the AGENTS table. As you probably have already guessed, AGENT ID is a foreign key in the ENTERTAINERS table.

Agents

Agent ID	Agent First Name	Agent Last Name	Date of Hire	Agent Home Phone
100	Stella	Rosales	05/16/95	553-3992
101	Steve	Pundt	10/15/95	790-3992
102	Randi	Nathanson	03/01/96	551-4993

Entertainers

Entertainer ID	Agent ID	Entertainer Name	Entertainer Phone	<< other fields >>
9001	101	Jazz Time	555-9928	......
9002	100	The Mike Hernandez Trio	959-8837	......
9003	100	The Country Squires	709-3542	......

Figure 3.14. *An example of a one-to-many relationship.*

This is by far the most common relationship that exists between a pair of tables in a database. It is crucial from a data-integrity standpoint because it helps to eliminate duplicate data and to keep redundant data to an absolute minimum.

Many-to-Many Relationships

A pair of tables bears a *many-to-many* relationship when a single record in the first table can be related to *many* records in the second table and a single record in the second table can be related to *many* records in the first table. You establish this relationship with a *linking table*. (You learned a little bit about this type of table at the beginning of this section.) A linking table makes it easy for you to associate records from one table with those of the other and will help to ensure that you have no problems adding, deleting, or modifying related data. You define a linking table by taking copies of the primary key of each table in the relationship and using them to form the structure of the new table. These fields actually serve two distinct roles: Together, they form the *composite primary key* of the linking table; separately, they each serve as a foreign key.

A many-to-many relationship that is not properly established is "unresolved." Figure 3.15 shows a classic and clear example of an unresolved many-to-many relationship. In this instance, a single record in the STUDENTS table can be related to *many* records in the CLASSES table and a single record in the CLASSES table can be related to *many* records in the STUDENTS table.

Students

Student ID	Student First Name	Student Last Name	Student Phone	<< other fields >>
60001	Zachary	Erlich	553-3992	......
60002	Susan	McLain	790-3992	......
60003	Joe	Rosales	551-4993	......

Classes

Class ID	Class Name	Instructor ID	<< other fields >>
900001	Intro. to Political Science	220087	......
900002	Adv. Music Theory	220039	......
900003	American History	220148	......

Figure 3.15. *An example of an unresolved many-to-many relationship.*

This relationship is unresolved due to the inherent peculiarity of the many-to-many relationship. The main issue is this: How do you *easily* associate records from the first table with records in the second table? To reframe the question in terms of the tables shown in Figure 3.15, how do you associate a single student with several classes or a specific class with several students? Do you insert a few STUDENT fields into the CLASSES table? Or do you add several CLASS fields to the STUDENTS table? Either of these approaches will make it difficult for you to work with the data and will affect data integrity adversely. The best approach for you to take is to create and use a linking table, which will resolve the many-to-many relationship in the most appropriate and effective manner. Figure 3.16 shows this solution in practice.

Students

Student ID	Student First Name	Student Last Name	Student Phone	<< other fields >>
60001	Zachary	Erlich	553-3992	......
60002	Susan	McLain	790-3992	......
60003	Joe	Rosales	551-4993	......

Student Schedule (*Linking Table*)

Student ID	Class ID
60003	900001
60001	900003
60003	900003
60002	900002
60001	900001

Classes

Class ID	Class Name	Instructor ID	<< other fields >>
900001	Intro. to Political Science	220087	......
900002	Adv. Music Theory	220039	......
900003	American History	220148	......

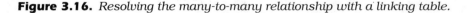

Figure 3.16. *Resolving the many-to-many relationship with a linking table.*

It's important for you to know the type of relationship that exists between a pair of tables because it determines how the tables are related, whether or not records between the tables are interdependent, and the minimum and maximum number of related records that can exist within the relationship. You'll learn much more about relationships in Chapter 10.

Types of Participation

A table's participation within a relationship can be either *mandatory* or *optional*. Say there is a relationship between two tables called TABLE_A and TABLE_B.

- TABLE_A's participation is *mandatory* if you must enter *at least one* record into TABLE_A before you can enter records into TABLE_B.

- TABLE_A's participation is *optional* if you are not required to enter *any* records into TABLE_A before you can enter records into TABLE_B.

Let's take a look at an example using the AGENTS and CLIENTS tables in Figure 3.17. The AGENTS table has a *mandatory* participation within the relationship *if an agent must exist* before a new client can be entered into the CLIENTS table. However, the AGENTS table's participation is *optional if there is no requirement for an agent to exist* in the table before a new client can be entered into the CLIENTS table. You can identify the appropriate type of participation for the AGENTS table by determining the way its data is being used in relation to the data in the CLIENTS table. For example, when you want to ensure that each client is assigned to an available agent, you make the AGENTS table's participation within the relationship mandatory.

Agents

Agent ID	Agent First Name	Agent Last Name	Date of Hire	Agent Home Phone
100	Stella	Rosales	05/16/95	553-3992
101	Steve	Pundt	10/15/95	790-3992
102	Randi	Nathanson	03/01/96	551-4993

Clients

Client ID	Agent ID	Client First Name	Client Last Name	Client Home Phone
9001	100	Stewart	Jameson	553-3992
9002	101	Shannon	McLain	790-3992
9003	102	Scott	Barker	551-4993

Figure 3.17. *The AGENTS and CLIENTS tables.*

Degree of Participation

The *degree of participation* determines the minimum number of records that a given table must have associated with a single record in the related table and the maximum number of records that a given table is allowed to have associated with a single record in the related table.

Consider, once again, a relationship between two tables called TABLE_A and TABLE_B. You establish the degree of participation for TABLE_B by indicating a minimum and maximum number of records in TABLE_B that can be related to a *single* record in TABLE_A. If a single record in TABLE_A can be related to no fewer than 1 but no more than 10 records in TABLE_B, then the degree of participation for TABLE_B is **1,10**. (The degree of participation is notated with the minimum number on the left and the maximum number on the right, separated by a comma.) You can establish the degree of participation for TABLE_A in the same manner. You can identify the degree of participation for each table in a relationship by determining the way the data in each table is related and how the data is being used.

Let's consider the AGENTS and CLIENTS tables in Figure 3.17 once more. If you require an agent to handle *at least one* client, but certainly no more than eight, then the degree of participation for the CLIENTS table is **1,8**. When you want to ensure that a client can only be assigned to one agent, then you indicate the degree of participation for the AGENTS table as **1,1**.

Integrity-Related Terms

Field Specification

A *field specification* (traditionally known as a *domain*) represents all the elements of a field. Each field specification incorporates three types of elements: *general*, *physical*, and *logical*.

- *General* elements constitute the most fundamental information about the field and include items such as Field Name, Description, and Parent Table.

- *Physical* elements determine how a field is built and how it is represented to the person using it. This category includes items such as Data Type, Length, and Display Format.

- *Logical* elements describe the values stored in a field and include items such as Required Value, Range of Values, and Default Value.

You'll learn all of the elements associated with a field specification, including those mentioned here, in Chapter 9.

Data Integrity

Data integrity refers to the validity, consistency, and accuracy of the data in a database. I cannot overstate the fact that the level of accuracy of the information you retrieve from the database is in direct proportion to the level of data integrity you impose upon the database. Data integrity is one of the most important aspects of the database-design process, and you cannot underestimate, overlook, or even partially neglect it. To do so would put you at risk of being plagued by errors that are very hard to detect or identify. As a result, you would be making important decisions on information that is inaccurate at best, or totally invalid at worst.

There are four types of data integrity that you'll implement during the database-design process. Three types of data integrity are based on various aspects of the database structure and are labeled according to the area (level) in which they operate. The fourth type of data integrity is based on the way an organization perceives and uses its data. The following is a brief description of each:

1. *Table-level integrity* (traditionally known as *entity integrity*) ensures that there are no duplicate records within the table and that the field that identifies each record within the table is unique and never null.

2. *Field-level integrity* (traditionally known as *domain integrity*) ensures that the structure of every field is sound; that the values in each field are valid, consistent, and accurate; and that fields of the same type (such as Cɪᴛʏ fields) are consistently defined throughout the database.

3. *Relationship-level integrity* (traditionally known as *referential integrity*) ensures that the relationship between a pair of tables is sound and that the records in the tables are synchronized whenever data is entered into, updated in, or deleted from either table.

4. *Business rules* impose restrictions or limitations on certain aspects of a database based on the ways an organization perceives and uses its data. These restrictions can affect aspects of database design, such as the range and types of values stored in a field, the type of participation and the degree of participation of each table within a relationship, and the type of synchronization used for relationship-level integrity in certain relationships. All of these restrictions are discussed in more detail in Chapter 11. Because business rules affect integrity, they must be considered along with the other three types of data integrity during the design process.

Summary

This chapter began with an explanation of why terminology is important for defining, discussing, or reading about the relational database model and the database-design process.

The section on *value-related terms* showed you that there is a distinct difference between data and information, and that understanding this difference is crucial to understanding the database-design process. You now know quite a bit about *nulls* and how they affect information you retrieve from the database.

Structure-related terms were covered next, and you learned that the core structures of every relational database are *fields*, *records*, and *tables*. You now know that *views* are virtual tables that are used, in part, to work with data from two or more tables simultaneously. We then looked at *key fields*, which are used to identify records uniquely within a table and to establish a relationship between a pair of tables. Finally, you learned the difference between a *key field* and an *index*. Now you know that an index is strictly a software device used to optimize data processing.

In the section on *relationship-related* terms, you learned that a connection between a pair of tables is known as a *relationship*. A relationship is used to help ensure various aspects of data integrity, and it is the mechanism used by a view to draw data from multiple tables. You then learned about the three characteristics of table relationships: the *type of relationship* (one-to-one, one-to-many, many-to-many), the *type of participation* (optional or mandatory), and the *degree of participation* (minimum/maximum number of related records).

The chapter ended with a discussion of *integrity-related terms*. Here you learned that a *field specification* establishes the general, physical, and logical characteristics of a field—characteristics that are an integral part of every field in the database. You then learned that *data integrity* is one of the most important aspects of the database-design process because of its positive effect on the data in the database. Also, you now know that there are four types of data integrity—three based on database structure and one based on the way the organization interprets and uses its data. These levels of integrity ensure the quality of your database's design and the accuracy of the information you retrieve from it.

Review Questions

1. Why is terminology important?

2. Name the four categories of terms.

3. What is the difference between *data* and *information*?

4. What does a *null* represent?

5. What is a null's major disadvantage?

6. What are the chief structures in the database?

7. Name the three types of tables.

8. What is a *view*?

9. State the difference between a *key* and an *index*.

10. What are the three types of *relationships* that can exist between a pair of tables?

11. What are the three ways in which you can characterize a relationship?

12. What is a *field specification*?

13. What three types of elements does a field specification incorporate?

14. What is *data integrity*?

15. Name the four types of data integrity.

■■■■■■■■■■ Part II
The Design Process

Conceptual Overview

I don't pretend to understand the
Universe—it's a great deal bigger than I am.
—THOMAS CARLYLE

Topics Covered in This Chapter

The Importance of Completing the Design Process

Defining a Mission Statement and Mission Objectives

Analyzing the Current Database

Creating the Data Structures

Determining and Establishing Table Relationships

Determining and Defining Business Rules

Determining and Defining Views

Reviewing Data Integrity

Summary

Review Questions

Understanding how to design a relational database isn't quite as hard as understanding the universe; in fact, it's much easier. It is important for you, however, to have an overall idea of the way the database-design process works and a general idea of the steps involved within the process. The purpose of this chapter is to provide an overview of the database-design process.

For the purpose of this overview, I've consolidated all of the techniques in the design process into seven phases, and I discuss each phase in general terms. This discussion provides a good overall picture of the database-design process, and I hope it will give you a much clearer understanding of each of the design techniques covered in Chapters 5 through 13.

You can use the design methodology in this book to design a new database completely from scratch, refine an existing database, or help you analyze an existing database so that you can design a new database based on the results of your analysis.

> ❖ **Note** A database can be designed by a single individual or a design team composed of two or more individuals. Throughout the remainder of the book, I use the phrase "database developer" and the word "developer" to refer to the person designing the database.

The Importance of Completing the Design Process

One thing I want to make perfectly clear from the very beginning is the importance of completing the design process. I'm often asked if it's truly necessary to go through the entire design process. My answer is always a resounding yes! I'm then asked whether it's still necessary if someone is only going to create a "simple" database. ("Simple" is one of the most dangerous words known to database developers. *Nothing* is ever "simple.") Again, my answer is yes, it's *still* necessary. The type, size, or purpose of the database is totally irrelevant to the value of undertaking a fully developed design. You should implement and follow the database-design process from beginning to end.

It is a well-known and proven fact that it is a bad idea to attempt to design a database without undertaking a complete database-design process. Many database problems are caused by poor database design, and *partially* following the design process is just about as bad as not using it at all. An incomplete design is a poor design. Only following through with a whole, unabbreviated design process assures a sound structure and data integrity

An important point to keep in mind is that the level of structural integrity and data integrity in your database is directly proportional to how thoroughly you follow the design process. The less time you spend on the design process, the greater the risk you run of encountering problems with the database. Although thoroughly following the database-design process may not eliminate all of the problems you may encounter when designing a database, it will greatly help to minimize them. As you work with your RDBMS software, you'll find that a well-designed database is easier to implement than a poorly designed one.

Databases are not hard to design; it just takes a little time to design them properly. When it seems as if the design process is taking too long, don't allow yourself to take shortcuts—just be patient and remember what a wise old sage once said:

> There's *never* time to do it right, but there's *always* time to do it over!

Defining a Mission Statement and Mission Objectives

The first phase in the database-design process involves defining a *mission statement* and *mission objectives* for the database. The mission statement establishes the purpose of the database and provides you with a distinct focus for your design work.

Every database is created for a specific purpose, whether it's to solve a specific business problem, to manage the daily transactions of a business or organization, or to be used as part of an information system. You identify the purpose of your database and define it within a *mission statement*. This will help ensure that you develop an appropriate database structure and that you collect the data necessary to support the intended purpose of the database.

Along with the mission statement, you'll define *mission objectives* in this phase. Mission objectives are statements that represent the general tasks your users can perform against the data in the database. You use these objectives to support your mission statement and to help you determine various aspects of the database structure.

There are two separate groups of people who will be involved in defining the mission statement and the mission objectives. The first group, which includes the database developer (you), the owner or head of the organization, and management personnel, is responsible for defining the mission statement. The second group, which includes the database developer (you again), management personnel, and end users, will be responsible for defining the mission objectives.

Analyzing the Current Database

The second phase in the database-design process involves analyzing the current database, if one exists. Depending on your organization, the database will typically be a *legacy database* or a *paper-based database*. A legacy database (also known as an *inherited* database) is one that has been in existence and in use for several years or more. A paper-based database, as you may already know, is a loose collection of forms, index cards, manila folders, and the like. Whatever the database type or condition, analyzing it will yield valuable information about the way your organization is currently using and managing its data. In addition, the analysis involves reviewing the way your organization is currently collecting and presenting the data. As the database developer, you look at how your organization uses paper to collect data (via forms) and present data (via reports). If your organization uses some software application program to manage and manipulate the data in the database, you study the way it collects and presents the data on-screen. Finally, you take into account how (if at all) your organization is using its data on the Web, and you review any browser-based applications that work with the database.

Another part of the analysis involves conducting interviews with users and management to identify how they interact with the database on a daily basis. As the database developer, you ask users how they work with the database and what their information requirements are at the current time. You then interview management personnel and ask them about the information they currently receive and about their perception of the overall information requirements for the organization. These interviews are an important component of your analysis because the questions you ask (or don't ask) will have a great impact on your final database structure. You must conduct full and complete interviews if you are to design a database that truly meets your organization's information needs.

Next, you use the information you've gathered from the analysis and the interviews to compile an initial list of fields. You then refine this list by removing all calculated fields and placing them on their own list; you'll use these calculated fields later in the design process. The refined list constitutes your organization's fundamental data requirements and provides a starting point for the design of a new database. (As you know, nothing is ever truly final. Rest assured that you'll extend and refine this field list further as you develop your design.)

Once your initial field list is complete, you send it to your users and management for a brief review and possible refinement. You encourage feedback and take their suggestions for modifications into consideration. If you think the suggestions are reasonable and well supported, you make the appropriate modifications, record the list in its current state, and move on to the next phase.

Creating the Data Structures

Creating the data structures for the database is the third phase in the database-design process. You define tables and fields, establish keys, and define field specifications for every field.

Tables are the first structures you define in the database. You determine the various subjects that the tables will represent from the mission objectives you wrote during the first phase of the design process and the data requirements you gathered during the second phase. Then you establish these subjects as tables and associate them with fields from the field list you compiled during the second phase of the design process. After you've completed this task, you review each table to ensure that it represents only one subject and that it does not contain duplicate fields.

Now you go on to review the fields within each table. You refine all multipart or multivalued fields in the table so that they each store only a single value, and you move or delete fields that do not represent distinct characteristics of the subject the table represents. When you complete this review, you then review and refine the table structures. This involves checking the work you performed on the fields to ensure that you didn't accidentally miss anything, and ensuring that each table structure is properly defined. Next, you establish the appropriate keys for each table. Your main task is to ensure that each table has a properly defined primary key; this particular key uniquely identifies each record within a table.

The final step in this phase is to establish field specifications for each field in the database. Here you conduct interviews with users and management to help you identify the specific field characteristics that are important to them and review and discuss any characteristics with which they may be unfamiliar. After you've completed these interviews, you define and document field specifications for each field. You then review the table structures and field specifications with users and management once more for possible refinements. The table structures are ready for the next phase once you complete the refinements (if any) that you identified during the review.

Determining and Establishing Table Relationships

The fourth phase of the database-design process involves establishing table relationships. You conduct interviews with users and management once again, identify relationships, identify relationship characteristics, and establish relationship-level integrity.

Working with users and management is a prudent exercise because they can assist you in identifying relationships among the data. You cannot possibly be familiar with every aspect of the data your organization uses, so leveraging whatever knowledge they have about the data they use will be very beneficial to you.

After you've identified the relationships, you establish a logical connection between the tables in each relationship with a primary key or with a linking table. What you actually use depends upon the type of relationship you're establishing between the tables. Next, you determine the type of participation and degree of participation for the tables in each relationship. In some cases, these participation characteristics will be obvious to you due to the nature of the data stored in the tables.

In other cases, you'll base the participation characteristics on specific business rules.

Determining and Defining Business Rules

Determining and defining business rules is the fifth phase of the database-design process. During this phase, you'll hold interviews, identify limitations on various aspects of the database, establish business rules, and define and implement validation tables.

The manner in which your organization views and uses its data will determine a set of limitations and requirements that you must build into the database. Your interviews with users and management will help you identify the specific constraints you will impose on the data, data structures, or relationships. You then establish and document these specifications as business rules.

The interviews you conduct with users will reveal *specific* limitations on various aspects of the database. For example, a user working with an order processing database is very aware of specific details, such as the fact that a ship date must occur later than an order date; that there must always be a daytime phone number; and that a shipping method should always be indicated. On the other hand, your interviews with management reveal *general* limitations on various aspects of the database. The office manager for an entertainment agency, for example, is familiar with general issues, such as the fact that an agent can represent no more than 20 entertainers and that promotional information for each entertainer must be updated every year.

Next, you define and implement validation tables as necessary to support certain business rules. For example, if you find that certain fields have a finite range of values because of the manner in which your organization uses them, you can use validation tables to ensure the consistency and validity of the values stored in those fields.

The level of integrity that business rules establish at this point is significant because it relates directly to the way your organization views and uses its data. As the organization grows, its perspective on the data will change, which means that the business rules must change as well. Determining and establishing business rules is an ongoing, iterative process, and you must be constantly diligent if you are going to maintain this level of integrity properly.

Determining and Defining Views

The sixth phase of the design process involves determining and defining views. Here you'll conduct interviews (once again), identify various ways of working with the data, and establish the views.

You identify the types of views you need to build in the database by interviewing users and management and determining how they work with their respective data. You may find, for example, that many users require detailed information to perform their work, while others need only summary information to help them make strategic decisions for the organization. Each group of users must access information in very specific ways, and you can use views to accommodate these situations.

Next, you define the views you've identified during the interview process using the appropriate tables and fields, and establish criteria for those views that are required to retrieve specific information. For instance, you would establish criteria for a view that must list all customers located in Texas or a view that must display the total number of authorized vendors (by city) in Washington State.

Reviewing Data Integrity

The seventh and final phase in the database-design process involves reviewing the final database structure for data integrity.

First, you review each table to ensure that it meets the criteria of a properly designed table, and you check the fields within each table for proper structure. You then resolve any inconsistencies or problems you encounter and review the structures once more. After you've made the appropriate refinements, you check table-level integrity.

Second, you review and check the field specifications for each field. You make necessary refinements to the fields and then check field-level integrity. This review reaffirms the field-level integrity you identified and established earlier in the database-design process.

Third, you review the validity of each relationship, confirm the relationship type, and confirm the participation characteristics for each table within the relationship. You then study relationship integrity to ensure that there are matching values between shared fields and that there are no problems inserting, updating, or deleting data in either of the tables within the relationship.

Finally, you review the business rules that you identified earlier in the database-design process and confirm the constraints you've placed on various aspects of the database. If there are any other limitations that have come to your attention since the last set of personnel interviews, you establish them as new business rules and add them to the existing set of business rules.

You're ready to implement your logical database structure in an RDBMS program once you've completed the entire database-design process. However, the process is never *really* complete because the database structure will always need refinement as your organization evolves.

Summary

We began this chapter with a discussion of the importance of completing the design process, and you learned that designing a database without the benefit of a good design method leads to poor and improper design. We also discussed the fact that the level of structural and data integrity is in direct proportion to how thoroughly you follow the design process. You then learned that inconsistent data and inaccurate information are two problems typically associated with poorly designed databases.

Next we looked at an overview of the entire database-design process. The process was consolidated into the following phases in order to provide you with a clear picture of the general steps involved in designing a database:

1. *Define a mission statement and mission objectives for the database.* The mission statement defines the purpose of the database, and the mission objectives define the tasks that are to be performed by users against the data in the database.

2. *Analyze the current database.* You identify your organization's data requirements by reviewing the way your organization currently collects and presents its data and by conducting interviews with users and management to determine how they use the database on a daily basis.

3. *Create the data structures.* You establish tables by identifying the subjects that the database will track. Next, you associate each table with fields that represent distinct characteristics of the table's subject, and you designate a particular field (or group of fields) as the primary key. You then establish field specifications for every field in the table.

4. *Determine and establish table relationships.* You identify relationships that exist between the tables in the database and establish the logical connection for each relationship using primary keys and foreign keys or by using linking tables. Then you set the appropriate characteristics for each relationship.

5. *Determine and define business rules.* You conduct interviews with users and management to identify constraints that must be imposed upon the data in the database. The manner in which your organization views and uses its data typically determines the types of constraints you must impose on the database. You then declare these constraints as business rules, and they will serve to establish various levels of data integrity.

6. *Determine and establish views.* You interview users and management to identify the various ways they work with the data in the database. When your interviews are complete, you establish views as appropriate. You define each view using the appropriate tables and fields, and you establish criteria for those views that must display a limited or finite set of records.

7. *Review data integrity.* This phase involves four steps. First, you review each table to ensure that it meets proper design criteria. Second, you review and check all field specifications. Third, you test the validity of each relationship. Fourth, you review and confirm the business rules.

Review Questions

1. Why is it important to complete the design process thoroughly?

2. True or False: The level of structural integrity is in direct proportion to how thoroughly you follow the design process.

3. What is the purpose of a *mission statement*?

4. What are *mission objectives*?

5. What constitutes your organization's fundamental data requirements?

6. How do you determine the various subjects that the tables will represent?

7. True or False: You establish field specifications for each field in the database during the second phase of the database-design process.

8. How do you establish a logical connection between the tables in a relationship?

9. What determines a set of limitations and requirements that you must build into the database?

10. What is it that you can design and implement to support certain business rules?

11. How do you determine the types of views you need to build in the database?

12. When can you implement your logical structure in an RDBMS program?

Starting the Process

"Where shall I begin, please your Majesty?" he asked.
"Begin at the beginning," the King said gravely,
"and go on till you come to the end: then stop."
—LEWIS CARROLL
ALICE'S ADVENTURES IN WONDERLAND

Topics Covered in This Chapter

Conducting Interviews

The Case Study: Mike's Bikes

Defining the Mission Statement

Defining the Mission Objectives

Summary

Review Questions

Everything has a beginning, and the database-design process is no different. Interestingly enough, you start the process by defining the end result. It is in the very first step of the database-design process that you identify and declare the purpose of the database. You also define and declare a list of the tasks that your users can perform against the data in the database. Both of these items provide you with a focus and direction for developing a database, and they help ensure that your final database structure supports the stated purpose and tasks.

Conducting Interviews

Interviews are an integral part of database design, and they play a key role during certain phases of the design process. Assuming that you work within some organization and need to design a database to support the work that you and your fellow employees perform, you should make certain that you conduct your interviews in the manner described in this book. This means that throughout the design process, you'll interact with some of your fellow employees, management personnel, and (depending on the size of the organization) the owner. If you work for a small organization that employs only a handful of people, or if you are only creating a database for yourself, you'll conduct "self-interviews"; you'll still conduct the interviews described in this book, but you will act as the interviewer *and* the interviewee. *You* will be the one who provides the answers to the questions.

> ❖ **Note** Interviewing is a skill that you can learn with some amount of patience, diligence, and practice. There are a variety of approaches and techniques you can use to conduct an interview, and there are numerous academic papers, articles, and books that have been written on the subject. Although an in-depth discussion of this topic is beyond the scope of this book, I've included several techniques and guidelines in this chapter that will help you conduct your interviews efficiently and effectively.

Interviews are important because they provide a valuable communication link between you (the developer) and the people for whom you're designing the database, help ensure the success of your design efforts, and provide critical information that can affect the design of the database structure. As you're working with table relationships, for example, you might find it difficult to determine the type of participation and degree of participation for a specific relationship. The only way for you to determine the proper values for these relationship characteristics is to conduct an interview with the appropriate people in your organization. You can then use the information you gathered during the interview to set the relationship characteristics. Using an interview as an information-gathering tool, you can gain new insights from participants regarding part of the database or clarify facts that you don't understand. Note that you must always conduct each of the interviews incorporated within this design process, regardless of the type of database you're designing or the number of people involved. You will inevitably miss some piece of important information when you neglect or omit any of the interviews, and this could adversely affect the final structure of your database.

> ❖ **Note** Throughout the remaining chapters, I use open-ended questions for all interviews that are part of the concept or technique under discussion. You can use these questions as a guide for formulating your own questions for a given interview.

Always establish guidelines for your interviews before you conduct them. This will help ensure that you conduct your interviews in a consistent manner and that they are always (or usually) successful. Here are some guidelines you can establish for the participants and for yourself.

Participant Guidelines

- *Make the participants aware of your intentions.* Many people are wary of interviews. They don't like to be "put on the spot" and they don't want to be asked "trick" questions. Let each person know the subject you wish to discuss, the names of the other participants, the time you want to start the session, and whether this interview is part of an ongoing series of interviews. If everyone participating in a given interview session knows how you're going to conduct it and what you expect of them, they're more likely to engage in the conversation at hand and be quite responsive to your questions. Above all, reassure them that the interview is not a disguised assessment of their performance; you want to make certain they feel comfortable talking to you openly and without reservation. This will go a long way toward building a foundation of trust between you and the participants.

- *Let the participants know that you appreciate their taking part in the interview and that their responses to the interview questions are valuable to the overall design project.* Earlier experiences are likely to make some people believe that whatever input they provide goes unnoticed and unappreciated at work. Even when in the past their input made a significant impact on a specific project, rarely did they get so much as a thank-you. In light of this, there's no real motivation for them to participate in your interview. Many, if not all, of your participants will start out with this attitude. But you can really increase their motivation by letting them know that you truly and honestly appreciate their participation and are very interested in their responses. Assure them that their feedback is truly valuable to the design process and that in many cases their responses can substantiate and validate decisions made throughout the design process. If you make yourself credible by being genuinely sincere, participants will help you in any way they can. Your job will be much easier and everyone will participate voluntarily and enthusiastically. It's very effective to show, on a second interview, how you have already used participants' earlier contributions.

- *Make sure everyone understands that you are the official arbitrator if and when a dispute arises.* It's inevitable that minor disputes will arise during an interview and that there will be some amount of tension until such disputes are resolved. You can avoid this situation by arbitrating these disputes yourself. As the database developer, you're in the best position to do this because you have an objective viewpoint and can see both sides of an issue. Additionally, the decision you make will always be in the best interests of the database structure. Always remember that disputes dealing with something other than the database structure can be referred to a more appropriate authority, if one exists.

Interviewer Guidelines (These Are for You)

- *Conduct the interview in a well-lit room, separated from distracting noise, with a large table and comfortable chairs, and have coffee and munchies on hand.* You'll greatly enhance your chances of carrying out a successful interview when you pay attention to atmosphere. Use a well-lit room because it allows the participants to read your interview materials very easily. A large table ensures that everyone has space to work, and comfortable chairs keeps them relaxed enough to concentrate on the conversation at hand. Always have plenty of coffee available, as this seems to be the preferred beverage of businesspeople everywhere. Finally, provide a good supply of munchies to help keep everyone in a good mood. People actually seem to think better when they have something to munch on—it keeps their mouths occupied while they're thinking. (The business climate has changed considerably since I first wrote this book. Many people are now conducting interviews and meetings in restaurants or at the local Starbucks. You might consider this as an option if you can't devise an appropriate setting for your interviews.)

- *Set a limit of 10 people for each interview.* Limiting the number of participants promotes a more relaxed atmosphere and makes it easier for you to encourage everyone to participate. One problem you'll find in conducting an interview with a large number of people is that the intimidation level of some of the participants will rise in direct proportion to the number of participants taking part in the interview as a whole. Some people are just afraid of looking ignorant or incompetent in front of their colleagues, whether or not there's truly any justification for such feelings. So, you do have a very good reason to restrict the number of participants in an interview.

- *Conduct separate interviews for users and management.* Separating the two groups is a good idea for a variety of reasons, including the "fear factor" noted above. Primarily, you want to separate them because each group has a different perspective on the organization as a whole and how the organization uses its data on a daily basis. Conducting separate interviews for each group allows you to leverage their unique perspectives to your advantage as you work through the database-design process. Another reason for keeping the interviews separate is to eliminate the conflicts that can arise when these groups disagree over certain aspects of the organization. It's quite common for there to be a lack of communication between them, and the odds are 50/50 that the interview will bring this problem to the surface. This may impel them to establish better lines of communication, or it may exacerbate the problem further. In any case, this communication problem can complicate and extend your interview and diffuse its results. Use your knowledge of the organization to help you judge whether to keep the interviews separate. If you need to conduct an interview with both groups at the same time, do so *intentionally*, with a specific purpose in mind, and be prepared for distractions.

- *When you have to interview several groups of people, designate a group leader for each group.* The group leader will help you ensure that the interview runs smoothly. She will be responsible for preparing each member of her group for the interview and for providing you with any new information she obtained from the group outside of the interview. During the interview, the group leader can direct your questions to the member best equipped to answer them.

You'll occasionally encounter a group leader who may want to dominate the interview and answer every one of your questions. When this happens, diplomatically and politely inform him that it is your job (and duty) to obtain feedback from all of the participants, so that you can make a complete assessment of the organization's overall information requirements. If this doesn't rectify the problem, you have the option of designating someone else as the group leader or refraining from including him in future interviews.

• *Prepare your questions prior to the interview.* You can conduct an interview rather easily if you have a set of prepared questions. (Coming up with questions off the top of your head is rarely a good idea, even if you're an experienced interviewer and are highly skilled at producing ad hoc questions.) Having a prepared list of questions allows you to provide a focus and direction for the interview, and it provides the participant with a continuity of thought. Your interview will flow more smoothly and will be more productive when your questions move easily from topic to topic.

As you prepare your list of interview questions, make sure you use *open-ended* questions. For example, "Did you feel our service was (a) poor, (b) average, or (c) good" is a *closed* question. A closed question isn't particularly useful because it supplies its own set of responses and does not allow an interviewee to provide an objective opinion or elaborate answer. On the other hand, an open-ended question, such as "How do you feel about our service?" is far more useful because it allows the interviewee to answer the question in a variety of ways. There are times when you may need to use closed questions, but it's better to use them intentionally, sparingly, and with a specific purpose in mind.

• *If you're not very good at taking notes, either assign that task to a dependable transcriber for each interview or get the group's permission to use a tape recorder to record the interview.* You conduct interviews to gather specific information about the organization, so it's important that you establish a detailed record of each interview. If you find it difficult to conduct an interview and take notes at the same time, you should enlist one of the participants as your assistant and have him take notes for you. (This is one good way to encourage participation from people who are normally quiet or reserved.) Choose your assistant carefully because the notes may suffer if he is at all distracted by the proceedings. Another option you have available is to use a tape recorder to record the interview. This might prove to be a better way to handle your notes because the tape recorder will capture the interview more accurately, and you'll be able to determine exactly who provided you with a given piece of information. (If you do decide to record the interview, be sure you first obtain permission from each of the participants. There may be privacy or confidentiality issues at stake, and you don't want to get yourself into any kind of trouble.)

- *Give everyone your equal and undivided attention.* This is a crucial point for you to remember: You must pay complete attention to the person who is speaking, and do so sincerely. If you give a participant the impression that you're bored, uninterested, or preoccupied, he will immediately reduce his level of participation within the interview. On the other hand, he will probably participate quite enthusiastically if he sees that you are interested in what he's saying and has your undivided attention.

There will be times when a participant responds to your questions with vague or incomplete answers. He may respond this way for several reasons. It may be that he doesn't quite know how to express the ideas he wants to convey or that he's not at liberty to divulge certain information. It could also be that he's just not comfortable talking about himself and what he does or that he is suspicious of you for some reason. In any case, you'll have to be patient and make him feel at ease so that he will provide you with the information you need. For example, you could try to state your best approximation of what he's said thus far and ask if it is what he meant to say.

- *Keep the pace of the interview moving.* You've probably attended meetings during which a particular point was belabored or much time was spent trying to extract information from a reluctant participant. You can prevent this from happening during your interviews by setting personal limits on the time you'll allow for a question to be answered and the time you'll spend on a specific topic. Don't inform the participants about this limit; instead, try to promote a sense of urgency.

- *Always maintain control of the interview.* This is the single most important guideline for every interview you conduct. Inevitably, something goes wrong the moment you lose control of the interview. For instance, say you have a situation where one of the participants begins to change the focus of the interview by discussing issues that have little or no relevance to the topics on your agenda. You'll certainly lose control of the interview unless you do something to redirect the discussion. Regaining control of the interview will be easy for you to do in some cases, but in others you'll just have to declare your portion of the interview "complete" and let the participants carry on with their discussion. You can avoid situations like this so long as you maintain control of the interview.

Interviews are an integral part of the design process, and I provide examples of them throughout the next several chapters. You'll find sample dialog that illustrates typical interview scenarios and examples of questions you might use during a given interview. (The sample questions always relate to the type of interview you're currently conducting.)

❖ **Note** The purpose of an interview example is to illustrate the *techniques* you use to conduct a specific type of interview, and I've kept the dialog relatively simple for this reason. However, the dialog will still provide you with good ideas for the types of conversations you conduct in the interview.

One final point: Keep in mind that the guidelines I've presented in this section are merely *recommendations*. I suspect that you won't be able to apply all of these guidelines to every interview you conduct. However, I would expect you to apply them in an ideal situation. Yes, I know—you don't come across ideal situations all the time. Neither do I. But you can still make it your goal to meet as many of these guidelines as possible. In the end, the person who stands to gain the most is you.

The Case Study: Mike's Bikes

There are numerous examples throughout the book that illustrate the concepts and techniques used in the database-design process. I've drawn these examples from a variety of databases and used them in an arbitrary fashion. Using them in this manner allows me to demonstrate that once you learn how to apply a particular concept or technique *generically*, you can then apply it to any other database you're designing. Therefore, your focus should always be on the concept or technique being presented, not on the example itself.

Nevertheless, I use a single database example as a case study to illustrate the steps involved in the design process. This enables me to present the process with some degree of continuity. As the database-design process unfolds, I apply each technique to designing the database for the fictitious company in the case study. I provide only a few details about the company in this chapter, but I'll supply more as I present each new concept or technique.

Mike's Bikes, our case-study business, is a new bike shop located in a small suburb called Greenlake, not far from downtown Seattle. It has been open for only two months, and business is growing steadily. Mike, the shop's owner, has been conducting his daily business on paper. He records sales on preprinted forms, maintains employee and vendor information on sheets of paper (storing them in manila folders), and writes information about his regular customers on index cards. As a result, Mike spends a lot of time maintaining all of this data. He owns a computer but uses it mainly to play games, write letters, and visit various golf sites. The only business-related task he performs on the computer is keeping track of the bike shop's inventory using a spreadsheet program.

Recently, Mike learned that using a database would be a good way to store and work with data related to his business. Using a database would greatly diminish the amount of time he currently spends maintaining his data, and he could always ensure that the data is up-to-date and that the information is accurate. Although he thinks a database is a good idea, he's aware of the fact that he doesn't know the first thing about properly designing a database. Undaunted, Mike has decided to hire a database consultant to design the database for him.

You are, in this fable, the consultant he has hired for the project. As the database-design process unfolds throughout the next several chapters, you'll apply each technique to design the database for Mike's Bikes. As you learn new concepts or techniques, Mike will supply you with the information you need to complete the design of his database.

Defining the Mission Statement

In the previous chapter, you learned that the *mission statement* declares the specific purpose of the database in general terms and that you define it at the beginning of the database-design process. Furthermore, it provides you with a focus for your design efforts and keeps you from getting diverted and making the database structure unnecessarily large or complex.

The Well-Written Mission Statement

A good mission statement is succinct and to the point. Verbose statements have a tendency to be confusing, ambiguous, or vague; they do more to obscure the purpose of the database than to clarify it. Here is an example of a typical mission statement:

> The purpose of the New Starz Talent Agency database is to maintain the data we generate, and to supply information that supports the engagement services we provide to our clients and the management services we provide to our entertainers.

This mission statement is well-defined and uncluttered by unnecessary statements or details. It is a very general statement, just as it should be. Think of a mission statement as the flame of a candle located at the end of a dark tunnel. The light produced by the flame guides you to the end of the tunnel, so long as you focus on it. In the same manner, the mission statement guides you to the end of the database-design process. Guided by your mission statement, you can focus on designing a database structure that will support the declared purpose of the database.

A well-written mission statement is free of phrases or sentences that explicitly describe *specific tasks*. If your mission statement contains these types of phrases or sentences, remove them and rewrite the statement. Be sure to keep the discarded phrases handy, though, because you may be able to use them to formulate mission objectives. (You'll learn about mission objectives in the next section.) Here's an example of a poorly worded mission statement:

> The purpose of the Whatcom County Hearing Examiner's database is to keep track of applications for land use, maintain data on applicants, keep a record of all hearings, keep a record of all decisions, keep a record of all appeals, maintain data on department employees, and maintain data for general office use.

It should be immediately apparent that there are a few things wrong with this mission statement.

- *It's slightly verbose.* Remember that the ideal mission statement should be succinct and to the point.

- *The specific purpose of the database is unclear.* This mission statement is written in such a way that it is difficult for you to ascertain the specific purpose of the database.

- *It describes several specific tasks.* Two issues arise when a mission statement is written in this manner. First, the description of the tasks does nothing to define the specific purpose of the database. Second, the statement somehow appears to be incomplete. It raises the question "Are there any tasks we've forgotten to include in the mission statement?"

You can fix this mission statement by removing the references to specific tasks (be sure to save them for the next step) and rewriting the statement. Here is an example of one of the possible ways you could rewrite this mission statement:

> The purpose of the Whatcom County Hearing Examiner's database is to maintain the data the examiner's office uses to make decisions on land-use requests submitted by citizens of Whatcom County.

Notice how the purpose of the database has become much clearer in this version. Also note that the statement is more succinct and doesn't give the impression of being incomplete. You'll always have a clear focus during the database-design process when you formulate your mission statements in this manner.

Composing a Mission Statement

The process of creating a mission statement involves conducting an interview with the owner or manager of the organization, learning about the organization, and determining the purpose of the new database.

You conduct the interview for this step with the owner of the organization or, if he directs, the appropriate staff. Either will be able to help you define the statement because each has an overall understanding of the organization and a general comprehension of why the database is necessary in the first place. Besides helping you to define the mission statement, this interview will also provide a great deal of information about the organization itself. This information is valuable because you can use it later in the design process.

As you conduct the interview, encourage the interview participant to discuss as many facets of the organization as she can, even if the discussion relates to issues that aren't directly relevant to the database. The idea here is for you to understand what the organization does and how it functions; the more you understand an organization, the better prepared you will be to design a database that will fulfill its needs. The organization's general need for a database will become clear to you once you have a better understanding of the organization itself. You can then translate this need into a mission statement.

Be sure to ask open-ended questions during the interview. In some cases, a good question can prompt the participant to state the purpose of the database without much effort. For example, say you posed the following question:

"How would you describe the purpose of your organization to a new client?"

This is a good open-ended question because it focuses on the issue yet gives the participant the freedom to respond with what she feels is a complete answer. Furthermore, this type of question will typically generate a response that you can translate directly into a mission statement.

Now assume you received the following reply:

"We supply entertainment services to our clientele for any and all occasions. We take care of all the details for the engagement so that it is as worry-free for the client as possible."

You can easily rewrite this type of response and turn it into a mission statement. In fact, when a response such as this one consists of two or more sentences or phrases, one of the sentences or phrases typically indicates the purpose of the database. For example, you can use the first sentence from the reply above to construct the mission statement. Here is one of several ways you could rewrite the reply:

The purpose of the All-Star Talent database is to maintain the data we use in support of the entertainment services we provide to our clientele.

The most important point to remember is that the mission statement should make sense to you (the database developer) and to those for whom you are designing the database. Different groups of people have different ways of phrasing statements, and the specific wording of the statement can depend greatly on industry-specific terminology. Your mission statement is complete when you have a sentence that describes the specific purpose of the database and that is understood and agreed upon by everyone concerned.

Here are a few sample questions that you can use to arrive at your mission statement:

How would you describe the purpose of your organization to a new client?

What would you say is the purpose of your organization?

What is the major function of your organization?

How would you describe what your organization does?

How would you define the single most important reason for the existence of your organization?

What is the main focus of your organization?

You may have noticed that some of these questions seem to be the same question rewritten in a different manner. Keep in mind that the observation regarding the phrasing of mission statements also applies to the interview questions you'll use throughout the database-design process. You can pose the *same question* to several people and receive different responses because each person may interpret the meaning of the question a little differently. In some cases, you may just get a long, "I haven't had my first espresso yet" type of stare. Experiment with different types of phrasing and determine which type works best for you. Your method of constructing and posing questions may be different from someone else's, but it doesn't matter as long as you have a method that suits you.

CASE STUDY

Now you need to define a mission statement for Mike's Bikes. Before you can define the mission statement, you must conduct an interview with the owner to gather information about his business. Assume you have an assistant named Zachary who is conducting the interview for you. The interview may go something like this:

ZACHARY: "Can you tell me why you believe you need a database?"

MIKE: "I think we need a database just to keep track of all our inventory. I'd also like to keep track of all our sales as well."

ZACHARY: "I'm sure the database will address those issues. Now, what would you say is the single most important function of your business?"

MIKE: "To provide a wide array of bicycle products and bicycle-related services to our customers. We have a lot of great customers. And regular ones, too! They're our biggest asset."

(The interview continues until Zachary has finished asking all the questions on his list.)

After the interview, review the information you've gathered and define the mission statement. You can ascertain a few points from the previous dialog with Mike, such as the fact that he'll need to be able to track products, customers, and customer sales. But the most valuable point is provided by his reply to the second question. You can use the first sentence in that reply to formulate the mission statement. Taking into account some of the other points you've identified in the interview, you can rewrite Mike's reply to create the following mission statement:

The purpose of the Mike's Bikes database is to maintain the data we need to support our retail sales business and our customer-service operations.

When you feel you have a good mission statement, review it with Mike and make sure that he understands and agrees with the declared purpose of the database. When you and Mike are satisfied with the mission statement, you can go on to the next step, which is defining the mission objectives.

Defining the Mission Objectives

To expand upon the overview in the previous chapter, *mission objectives* are statements that represent the *general* tasks supported by the data maintained in the database. Each mission objective represents a *single* task. These mission objectives provide information that you'll use throughout the database-design process. For example, mission objectives help you define table structures, field specifications, relationship characteristics, and views. They also help you establish data integrity and define business rules. Finally, mission objectives guide your development efforts and ensure that your final database structure supports the mission statement.

Well-Written Mission Objectives

A well-written mission objective is a declarative sentence that clearly defines a general task and is free from unnecessary details. It is expressed in general terms, succinct and to the point, and unambiguous. Here are some examples of typical mission objectives:

We need to maintain complete patient address information.

We need to keep track of all customer sales.

We need to make sure an account representative is responsible for no more than 20 accounts at any given time.

We need to keep track of vehicle maintenance.

We need to produce employee phone directories.

These mission objectives are well defined and easy to understand. Each mission objective represents a single general task and defines the task clearly without unnecessary details. For example, the last mission objective in the list states that employee directories need to be produced, but it doesn't indicate *how* they are to be produced. It is not necessary to indicate how the employee lists will be produced because that issue is part of the application-development process. Remember that the purpose of a mission objective is to help define various structures within the database and to help guide the overall direction of the database's development.

If a mission objective represents more than one general task, you should decompose it into two or more mission objectives. Here is an example of a poorly written mission objective:

> We need to keep track of the entertainers we represent and the type of entertainment they provide, as well as the engagements that we book for them.

There are two problems with this mission objective:

1. *It defines more than a single general task.* It is clear that there are two tasks represented in this statement: keeping track of entertainers and keeping track of engagements.

2. *It contains unnecessary detail.* It's unnecessary to refer to the entertainer's "type of entertainment" in this mission objective. The phrase "type of entertainment" either refers to a distinct characteristic of an entertainer, or it represents a new task that should be declared as a mission objective. If it refers to a distinct characteristic of an entertainer, it should be removed from the statement; otherwise, it should be used as the basis for a new mission objective.

You can fix this mission objective by removing the unnecessary detail and rewriting it as two mission objectives. (Keep the details you discard on a separate piece of paper; they may be useful later in the design process.) Here is an example of one possible revision:

> We need to maintain complete entertainer information.

> We need to keep track of all the engagements we book.

Notice that each mission objective now clearly defines a single general task and is easy to understand as well. Mission objectives such as these are easy to use as you design the database.

Composing Mission Objectives

Defining mission objectives is a process that involves conducting interviews with users and management and then writing appropriate mission objectives based on the information gathered from the interviews.

The purpose of the interview is to determine what types of general tasks need to be supported by the data in the database. You accomplish this by asking the participants open-ended questions and allowing them to elaborate on their replies as necessary. The mission statement and mission objectives interviews are the easiest ones you'll conduct during the design process because everyone is usually enthusiastic about participating. It's fairly easy to get people to discuss what they do on a daily basis and to give their perspective on the function of the organization. This is also one of the few interviews you'll conduct with both users and management; there should be a lot of common ground between the two groups due to the general nature of the interview.

One very important point to remember is that *the interviews you conduct here involve very general discussions*. The discussions are more conceptual than analytical; your intent here is not to analyze the current database or database application, but to get an overall idea of the general tasks the database should support. Keep in mind that one of the purposes of the mission objectives is to help guide the development of the database structure.

As you conduct the interview, be sure, once again, to ask open-ended questions. Remember that open-ended questions are apt to elicit better responses from your participants. Ask the participants questions regarding their daily work, how the organization functions, and what type of issues they believe need to be addressed by the database. Encourage them to discuss as many facets of their work and the organization as they possibly can. As they reply, try to record each response as a declarative sentence. You'll find it is much easier to transform a sentence into a mission objective if you can do this. Here are just a few examples of the types of questions you could pose during the interview:

What kind of work do you perform on a daily basis?

How would you define your job description?

What kind of data do you work with?

What types of reports do you generate?

What types of things do you keep track of?

What types of services does your organization provide?

How would you describe the type of work you do?

All of these questions are likely to evoke a good, lengthy response from the participant. One of the advantages of questions like these is that they provide the opportunity for you to ask follow-up questions. For example, say you received the following response to the last question in the list:

> "First, I try to determine the general problem with the vehicle. Then I fill out a work order and note my assessment of the problem. Finally, I send the vehicle to the next available service team."

You'll immediately notice that it's a lengthy response, which is fine. You should also note that you could easily ask a follow-up question, such as the following:

> "Is there any type of customer information incorporated within the procedure you just described?"

Even if the reply is no, the question is still open-ended enough for the participant to elaborate further on his original response. This type of follow-up question could also jar his memory and cause him to relay other information, which may be related to the subject of the original response.

Here is a set of mission objectives that you could derive from the participant's original response:

> We need to maintain information on customer vehicles.
>
> We need to keep track of work orders.
>
> We need to maintain information on our service teams.
>
> We need to maintain information on our mechanics.
>
> We need to maintain information on our customers.

Three of these objectives are derived directly from the response. They're easy for you to determine because their subjects are explicitly stated in the response itself. The last two mission objectives are derived from *assumptions* based on the response. This is a technique (which you can think of as "reading between the lines") that experienced database designers use quite often, and it is one that you should use when you're defining mission objectives. The technique relies on your ability to determine what information a response conveys *implicitly*, as well as what it conveys *explicitly*. So pay attention. Listen for implications. Without good assumptions, your overall set of mission objectives could be incomplete.

Review the following response and determine whether there is implicit information hidden within the response itself:

> "I book entertainment for our clientele, which consists of commercial and noncommercial clients. Our noncommercial clients are typically individuals or small groups who book weddings, birthdays, anniversaries, and the like. Our commercial clients, on the other hand, consist of businesses, such as nightclubs and corporations. The nightclubs book entertainment in six-week slots; the corporations book things, such as corporate parties, product rollouts, and various types of promotional functions."

Aside from the explicit information that this response conveys, there are at least two pieces of implicit information that you can uncover in this response. The first piece of implicit information concerns the need to maintain information on the entertainers booked for the engagements. An agent needs to know things such as the entertainer's name, phone number, mailing address, availability, and whether he will travel to out-of-town locations. The second piece of implicit information concerns the need to maintain information on the engagements themselves. An agent must know all the details concerning the engagement in order to ensure that the engagement runs smoothly.

Now that you know how important it is to look for implicit information, keep it in mind when you're defining mission objectives.

Here are the "final words" regarding mission objectives: Make sure that your mission objectives are both properly defined and well defined, that each objective makes sense to you and to those for whom you are designing the database, and that you look for any implicit information hidden within every participant's response.

CASE STUDY

It's time now to interview Mike and his staff so that they can help you define the mission objectives for the Mike's Bikes database. Here's a partial transcript of the interview with Mike. Once again, your assistant, Zachary, is conducting the interview.

ZACHARY: "Can you give me an idea of the things you'd like to track in the database?"

MIKE: "Oh sure, that's pretty easy. I want to keep track of our inventory, our customers, and our sales."

ZACHARY: "Is there anything else that you can think of that is related to these subjects?"

MIKE "Well, I guess if we're going to keep track of our inventory, we should know who our suppliers are."

ZACHARY: "What about the sales reps involved in each sale?"

MIKE: "Oh yeah, we should definitely keep information about our employees. If nothing else, it's a good idea to do this from a human-resources point of view. At least, that's what my wife tells me!"

(The interview continues until Zachary has finished asking all the questions on his list.)

When the interviews are complete, review all the information you've gathered and define the appropriate mission objectives. Be sure to keep the "final words" in mind as you define them. Here are a few possible mission objectives for the Mike's Bikes database.

We need to maintain complete inventory information.

We need to maintain complete customer information.

We need to track all customer sales.

We need to maintain complete supplier information.

We need to maintain complete employee information.

Once you've compiled a list of mission objectives, review them with Mike and his staff. When they are satisfied that they understand the mission objectives and that the list is relatively complete, commit the list to a document in your favorite word processor and save it for later use.

Summary

This chapter opened with a discussion of the *interview process*. You learned why interviews are an important part of the database-design process and why it's important to learn how to conduct an interview properly. You now know the difference between an *open-ended* question and a *closed* question, as well as when to use each kind of question. We ended this discussion by reviewing a set of interview guidelines, and you learned that you should use them to help you ensure that the interviews are productive and successful.

The *mission statement* was our next topic of discussion. We expanded upon the Chapter 4 overview by looking at how the mission statement states the specific purpose of the database. You now know that the process involves conducting interviews and learning about the organization, then formulating the mission statement from the information you gathered during these steps. We defined the characteristics of a good mission statement, and you learned that a well-defined mission statement establishes a clear focus for your design efforts.

Next, we discussed *mission objectives*, and we expanded upon the Chapter 4 overview once again. As you now know, mission objectives represent the tasks performed against the data in the database, and you define them after the mission statement. We then explored how to define a mission objective. Here, you learned that you conduct interviews with users and management and that the information you gather from these interviews provides the basis for each mission objective. We also discussed the characteristics of a well-written mission objective, and you learned that a clearly defined mission objective will help you define various structures within the database.

Review Questions

1. Why are interviews important?

2. What problem can arise when you conduct an interview with a large number of people?

3. What is the primary reason for conducting separate interviews with users and management?

4. True or False: You'll commonly use closed questions in your interviews.

5. What kind of responses should you try to evoke from the interview participants?

6. What is the single most important guideline for every interview you conduct?

7. What is a *mission statement*?

8. State two characteristics of a well-written mission statement.

9. True or False: You need not learn about the organization in order to compose a mission statement.

10. When is your mission statement complete?

11. What is a mission objective?

12. State two characteristics of a well-written mission objective.

13. True or False: You should interview users and management to help you define mission objectives.

14. How does the staff's daily work relate to the mission objectives?

15. True or False: A mission objective can describe more than one task.

16. State two ways that a mission objective can be derived from a response.

17. When is a mission objective complete?

Analyzing the Current Database

*To see what is in front of one's nose
needs a constant struggle.*
—GEORGE ORWELL
IN FRONT OF YOUR NOSE

Topics Covered in This Chapter

Getting to Know the Current Database

Conducting the Analysis

Looking at How Data Is Collected

Looking at How Information Is Presented

Conducting Interviews

Interviewing Users

Interviewing Management

Compiling a Complete List of Fields

Case Study

Summary

Review Questions

Getting to Know the Current Database

To determine where you should go, you must first understand where you are.

This maxim defines the entire philosophy behind this phase of the database-design process. You must devote some time to gaining a clear understanding of your organization's database for these reasons:

- To determine whether the database supports the organization's *current* information requirements

- To uncover existing structural deficiencies

- To determine how the database needs to evolve so that it will support the organization's *future* information requirements

You can use the existing database as a resource for developing a new database. However, you must carefully judge which aspects of the current database remain useful and which aspects should be discarded. You can make these judgments by answering the following questions:

What types of data does the organization use?

How does the organization use that data?

How does the organization manage and maintain that data?

The answers to these questions provide you with vital information that you can use to design a database that best suits your organization's needs.

You can best answer these questions by analyzing your organization's existing database. It's very likely that the organization is using some type of database, and it can probably be associated with one of the following categories:

- *Paper-based databases*—also known as *file systems*—typically consist of various forms and handwritten documents stored in file folders or bound in notebooks. The folders and notebooks are identified by some coding scheme (e.g., unique numbers or colored tabs) and stored in file cabinets. These cabinets are likely to be identified by some coding scheme as well, depending on the size of the database.

- *Legacy databases* have been in existence and in use for several years or more and consist of various types of data structures and character-based user interface screens that all reside on a mainframe computer or personal computer. The capability, functionality, and effectiveness of the structures and screens are quite dependent upon the programming language and database-management software used to create them. In general, the structures and screens are crude by today's standards because they were created at a time when programming languages and database software were not as sophisticated as those we've come to know since the mid-1990s.

- *Human-knowledge bases* (loosely defined) are based on the memory of one or more employees within an organization. These individuals have a specific amount of knowledge regarding a given aspect of the organization (e.g., customer information or product details), and they are crucial to conducting the organization's business.

The goal of your analysis is to determine the types of data the organization uses, how the organization manages and maintains that data, and how the organization views and uses the data. You can reduce the time it takes to define the preliminary field and table structures for the new database if you conduct this investigation properly.

During the analysis, you review the various ways the organization collects and presents its data, and you conduct a set of interviews with users and management. You then use the information you've gathered to define a preliminary field list and to help you determine the tables that should be included in the initial database structure. If your analysis reveals that the current database is poorly designed, you can take precautions to ensure that you don't make the same mistakes in the new database. Despite whatever shortcomings the current database may have, it can still help you identify a number of the fields and tables that you should include in the new database.

There's one rule you should keep first and foremost in your mind as you're analyzing the current database:

> **Do not adopt the current database structure as the basis for the new database structure.**

Following this rule will help you avert unnecessary errors and aid in maximizing your design efforts.

Every so often, there's a point during the analysis when a novice database developer (and sometimes an experienced one, as well) will stop and think, "This database doesn't look too bad. Let's just end the analysis here and use this database as the basis for the new one." This is a particularly bad idea because every hidden problem within the current database structure will be transferred into the new database. These types of problems include awkward table structures, poorly defined relationships, and inconsistent field specifications; they will invariably surface later and at the least opportune times. Therefore, you should do your best to avoid this perilous situation by following the rule above. Just remember that it's always better to define a new database structure explicitly than to copy an existing structure. After all, if the old database didn't have problems, you wouldn't be building a new one.

You'll typically analyze two types of databases during this part of the design process: paper-based databases and legacy databases. Many organizations use both types of databases to some degree, and you perform the same basic analysis process on each of them. There are minor differences in the way you analyze a paper-based database and a legacy database, to be sure, but the differences have more to do with the databases themselves than with the overall analysis process. You needn't be concerned with these differences, however, because I've seamlessly incorporated them into the analysis process presented in this book.

Paper-Based Databases

A *paper-based database* incorporates data that is literally collected, stored, and maintained on paper. The paper used in this type of database appears in a variety of shapes, sizes, and configurations. Some of the more common formats include index cards, hand-written reports, and various types of preprinted forms. Anyone who has ever worked in an office for a business or organization is very familiar with this type of database.

You'll find that analyzing this type of database can be a daunting task. One of your most immediate problems is finding someone who completely understands how the database works so you can learn its use and purpose. There are several problems with the paper-based database itself, especially in terms of the way data is collected and managed. This type of database typically contains inconsistent data, erroneous data, duplicate data, redundant data, incomplete entries, and old data that should have been purged from the database long ago. Clearly, the only reason you'd analyze this type of database is to identify items that you could incorporate into the new database. For example, you can extract individual pieces of data from various sections of a form in the paper-based database and transform them into fields in the new database.

Legacy Databases

A *legacy database* is a database that has been in existence and in use for five years or more. Mainframe databases typically fall into this category, as do older PC-based databases. There are several reasons that "legacy" is used as part of the name for this type of database. First, it suggests that the database has been around for a long time, possibly longer than anyone can clearly remember. Second, the word "legacy" may mean that the individual who originally created the database has either shifted responsibilities within the organization or is working for someone else, and, thus, the database has become his or her legacy to the organization. Third, the term implies the disturbing possibility that no single individual completely understands the database structure or how it is implemented in the DBMS software program.

Mainframe legacy databases present some special problems in the analysis process. One problem stems from the fact that a number of older mainframe databases are based on hierarchical or network database models. If neither you nor anyone in the organization has a firm understanding of these models, it will take you some time to decipher the structure of the database. In this case, you'll find it very helpful to make printouts of the data in each of the database structures.

Even if a legacy database is based on the relational model, there's no particular guarantee that the structure is sound. Unfortunately, there are many instances where the people who created these databases didn't completely understand the concept of a relational database. (After you have read this book, you won't fall into that group.) As a result, many older databases have improper or inefficient structures.

Numerous PC-based legacy databases are improperly or inefficiently designed as well. Many of them were originally designed and implemented in dBase II and dBase III, which were nonrelational database-management systems. As a result, the databases implemented within these systems could not take advantage of the benefits provided by the relational model. Two characteristics commonly associated with these types of databases are duplicate fields and redundant data, which (as you'll learn later) can cause serious problems with data integrity.

Analyzing a legacy database is somewhat easier than analyzing a paper-based database because a legacy database is typically more organized and structured than a paper-based database, the structures within the database are explicitly defined, and there is usually a software application program that people use to interact with the data in the database. (The application program is valuable to you during the analysis process because it can reveal a lot of information about the data structures and the tasks performed against the data in the legacy database.) The time it will take you to perform a proper analysis will depend to some degree on the platform (mainframe or PC), the DBMS used to implement the legacy database, and the software application program.

The key point to remember when you're analyzing either a paper-based or a legacy database is that you should proceed through the process patiently and methodically so that you can ensure a thorough and accurate analysis.

Conducting the Analysis

There are three steps in the analysis process: reviewing the way data is collected, reviewing the manner in which information is presented, and conducting interviews with users and management.

It will be necessary for you to speak to various people in the organization as you conduct the first two steps in this process. *Be sure your conversations relate purely to the reviews at hand.* You'll have the opportunity to ask them other in-depth questions later. Keep in mind that these reviews are an integral part of your preparation for the interviews that will follow. Indeed, these reviews help you determine the types of questions you'll need to ask in subsequent interviews.

Looking at How Data Is Collected

The first step in the analysis process involves reviewing the ways in which data is collected. This includes everything from index cards and hand-written lists to preprinted forms and data-entry screens (such as those used in a database software program or Web browser).

Begin this step by reviewing all paper-based items. Find out what types of paper documents the organization is using to record data, and then gather a single sample of each. Assemble these samples into a stack, and then store them in a folder for use later in the design process. For example, assume that the organization is collecting supplier data on index cards. Go through each of the index cards until you find one with an entry that is as complete as possible. When you've found an appropriate sample, make a copy of it and place the copy in your stack of samples. Proceed through this process for each type of paper record being used. Figure 6.1 shows two examples of how the organization might use a paper record to collect data.

A1 Office Supplies	
Suite 133	
7739 Alpine Way SE	
Seattle, WA 98115	
Susan McLain	519-5883
FAX	519-9948

Employee Fact Sheet				
Name: George Chavez		Date Hired: June 30, 1995		
Address: 7527 Taxco Drive		City: Seattle	State: WA	Zip: 98115
Phone: 553-0399	Date of Birth: 09/22/55		SSN: 456-92-0049	
Education: *Name of Academic Organization*		*Location*		*Year Graduated*
University of Texas at El Paso		El Paso, TX		1977

Figure 6.1. *Examples of paper-based items used to collect data.*

Next, review all of the computer software programs that the organization uses to collect data. The objective here is to gather a set of sample screen shots that represent how the organization uses these programs to work with data. A word of caution: Many people have discovered unique and ingenious ways to use common programs, such as word processors and spreadsheets, as a way to collect and manage data. Make sure you speak with someone who is familiar with the way the computers are being used within the organization and determine which programs the organization is using to manage its data.

As you review each program, find a screen that best represents how the program collects data. You're looking for screens similar to those in Figure 6.2.

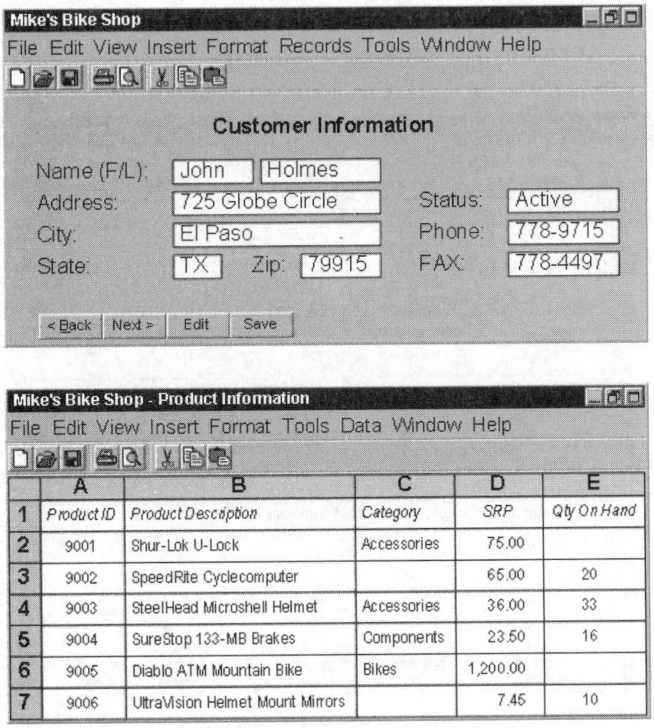

Figure 6.2. *A typical database screen and a typical spreadsheet screen.*

The first screen is typical of those you would find in a database program, and the second screen is typical of those you would find in a spreadsheet program. When you've found an appropriate sample, create a screen shot (use [ALT]-[PRTSC] or a screen-capture program), paste it into a document in your word-processing program, indicate the name of the source program and the date you created the screen shot, and then print the document. Continue reviewing the program and repeat this procedure as appropriate. Then repeat the entire process for each program. Once you've printed copies of all the appropriate screen shots, assemble them together and store them in a folder for use later in the design process.

Now examine the Web pages that the organization uses to collect data via the Internet. The pages you're interested in will look very similar to the data-entry forms you would find in a database application program. Figure 6.3 shows an example of such a page.

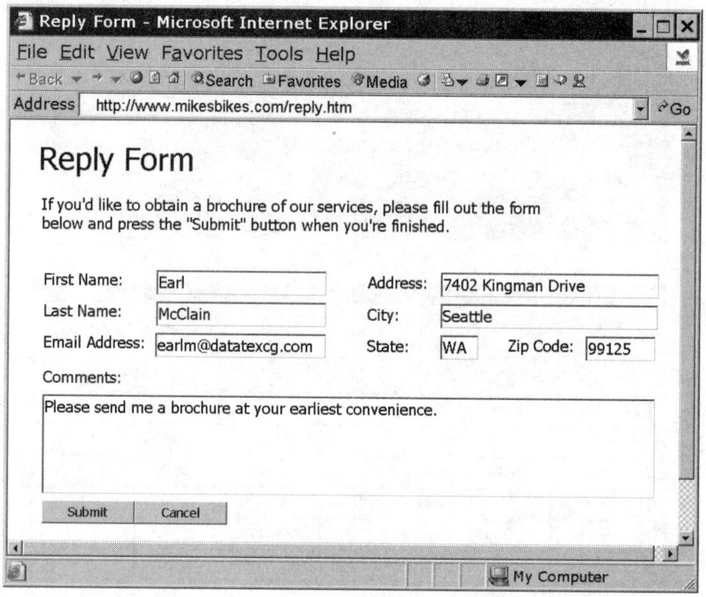

Figure 6.3. *An example of a typical Web-based data-entry screen.*

You can follow the same examination procedure here that you used with the application programs. Take a screen shot of a given Web page, paste it into a word-processing document, indicate the program name and screen capture date, and print it. Continue to review the Web pages and repeat this procedure as appropriate. Once you've printed copies of all the appropriate screen shots, assemble them and store them in a folder for use later in the design process.

Make sure you clearly mark the folders containing the samples you've gathered during your analysis. The small amounts of time you invest to organize your materials pay big dividends when you use those materials during a complex phase of the design process.

Looking at How Information Is Presented

The second step in the analysis process involves reviewing the various ways in which the organization presents its data as information. During this process, you'll review items, such as hand-written documents, computer printouts, screen presentations, and Web pages.

Here are three of the most popular presentation methods that you'll encounter during this process:

1. *Reports.* A report is any document (hand-written, typed, or computer-generated) used to arrange and present data in such a way that it is meaningful to the person or people viewing it. Although using a software program (such as a word processor or spreadsheet) is the standard method of generating a report nowadays, you'll still find a number of reports written by hand or typed on a typewriter. (Yes, a typewriter!)

2. *Screen presentations (a.k.a. slide shows).* This type of presentation incorporates a series of screens that discuss various topics in an organized manner. It is generally created with a program, such

as Microsoft PowerPoint or Lotus Freelance Graphics, and executed on a computer, but it can also be composed of a series of plastic sheets that are displayed on a screen by an overhead projector. (For our purposes, we'll assume that you're reviewing a computer-based screen presentation.)

3. *Web pages.* Many organizations are now making vast amounts of information available via Web pages on their Web sites. A Web page is used much in the same manner as a report, and, indeed, it is really nothing more than a different *type* of report.

Begin this step by identifying and reviewing each report the organization generates from the database, regardless of whether they produce the report by hand or from within a software program. Gather samples of the reports and assemble them in a folder as you did with the items in the previous step. Overall, this task is easier to perform in this step than it was in the previous step because people in the organization are typically familiar with the reports they use. Copies of the reports are usually readily available, and most reports can be reprinted if necessary. Figure 6.4 shows an example of a report written by hand and a report generated from a word-processing program.

Next, review screen presentations that use or incorporate the data in the database. It's unnecessary for you to review *every* presentation, but you do need to review those that have a direct bearing on the data in the database. For example, you don't need to review a presentation on the organization's new product *if it doesn't draw any data* from the database. On the other hand, a presentation on sales statistics that does incorporate data from the database is one that you do need to review.

Once you've identified which presentations you need to review, go through each one carefully and make screen shots of the slides that use

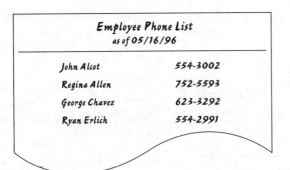

Figure 6.4. *Examples of hand-written and computer-generated reports.*

or incorporate data from the database. Copy the screen shots into a word-processing document, print the document, and then store the document in a folder for later use. (Write the name of the presentation and the date you captured the screen shots on the folder; you may need to refer to it again at a later time.) *Follow this procedure separately for each presentation.* You want to make sure you don't accidentally combine two or more presentations together, because this mistake will inevitably lead to mass confusion and result in one huge mess!

Figure 6.5 shows an example of the type of slides you'll examine during this review.

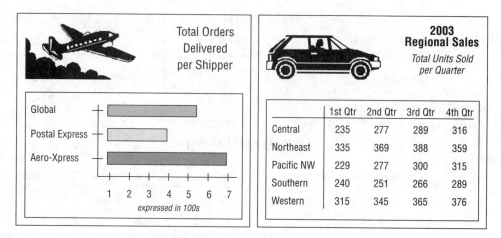

Figure 6.5. *Examples of screen presentation slides.*

Reviewing a presentation is difficult in some cases, and deciding whether or not a slide should be included as a sample is purely a discretionary decision. Therefore, work closely with the person most familiar with the presentation to ensure that you include all appropriate slides in the samples.

Finally, review Web pages that draw information directly from the database. Perform this review in the same manner as the review for the screen presentations. As with the previous review, you need to review those Web pages that have a direct bearing on the data in the database. For example, you *don't* need to review a Web page that provides a history of your organization, but you *do* need to review a Web page that displays regional employee information.

Once you've identified which Web pages you need to review, take a screen shot of each page. Copy the screen shots into a word-processing document, print the document, and then store the document in a folder for later use. (Write the uniform resource locator, or URL, address, and the current date under each screen shot in the document; you may need to refer to a particular Web page again at a later time.)

Figure 6.6 shows an example of a Web page you would examine during this review.

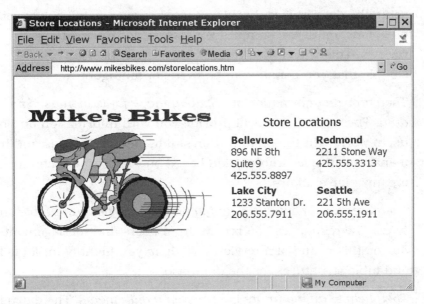

Figure 6.6. *Example of a Web page that presents information from a database.*

Whenever possible, work with the person (or persons) who created and developed the organization's Web site. She can save you a lot of time by directing you to the exact pages you should examine for this review.

Conducting Interviews

Now that you have a general idea of how the organization collects and presents its data, it's time to interview users and management to determine how the organization *uses* its data. Interviews are useful in the analysis phase for these reasons:

- *They provide details about the samples you assembled during the previous reviews.* The discussions you had with users and management during the previous reviews were solely meant to identify (in general terms) how the organization collects and presents the data it uses. In this phase, however, you'll ask specific questions about the samples you assembled during those reviews. This will enable you to clarify the aspects of a specific sample that you consider to be vague or ambiguous.

- *They provide information on the way the organization uses its data.* These interviews will provide you with information on how users work with the organization's data on a daily basis and how management uses information based on that data to manage the organization's affairs.

- *They are instrumental in defining preliminary field and table structures.* The responses you receive from users and management during this round of interviews will help you identify initial field and table structures for the database.

- *They help to define future information requirements.* The discussions you'll have with users and management regarding the organization's future growth will often reveal new information requirements that must be supported by the database.

I cannot overemphasize, and you must not underestimate, the impact interviews have on the final database structure and how important they are to your successful completion of the database-design process. Only full and complete interviews will help you ensure that the database you design fulfills your organization's information requirements.

Basic Interview Techniques

In order for you to conduct successful interviews, you must first learn a few basic interview techniques. I address this issue here by providing you with a set of fundamental techniques that you can use to conduct every interview within the database-design process. These techniques are relatively easy to learn and apply, and they'll enable you to obtain the information you require for the task at hand.

You'll probably execute these techniques in a strict, mechanical fashion as you're just starting to learn them, but you'll apply them more instinctively and intuitively as you conduct further interviews and gain additional experience. Conducting an interview is a skill, and, as with any other skill, you will achieve various degrees of expertise with patience and practice.

Asking Questions

You use both open-ended and closed questions throughout an interview, alternating between each type as the interview progresses; the open-ended questions enable you to focus on specific subjects, and the closed questions allow you to focus on specific details of a certain subject. For instance, start the interview with a few open-ended questions to establish some general subjects for discussion, and then select a subject and ask more specific (closed) questions relating to that subject. You could begin by asking one of the interview participants an open-ended question such as this:

"How would you define the work that you do on a daily basis?"

Most participants will use three or more sentences to answer this type of question. It's perfectly acceptable for a participant to provide you with a long, descriptive response because you can work with this type of response more easily than you can with one that is terse. To illustrate this point, assume the participant responds to your question in this manner:

> "As an account representative, I'm responsible for 10 clients. Each of my clients makes an appointment to come into the showroom to view the merchandise we have to offer for the current season. Part of my job is to answer any questions they have about our merchandise and make recommendations regarding the most popular items. Once they make a decision on the merchandise they'd like to purchase, I write up a sales order for the client. Then I give the sales order to my assistant, who promptly fills the order and sends it to the client."

This is a very good response. The participant not only answered your question, but also provided you with the opportunity to begin asking follow-up questions. His response also suggests several subjects that you can discuss later in the interview.

> ❖ **Note** When you receive a terse response such as "I fill out customer sales orders," you'll have to work a little harder with the participant to obtain the information you need. Terse responses commonly indicate that the participant is just nervous or uncomfortable. In this case, you could put him at ease by discussing an unrelated topic for a few moments, or by allowing him to select a more familiar or comfortable subject.

Identifying Subjects

As you ask each open-ended question, identify the subjects suggested within the response to the question. You can identify subjects by looking for *nouns* within the sentences that make up the response. Subjects are always represented by nouns and identify a person, place, or thing or an event (something that occurs at a given point in time). There are some nouns, however, that represent a *characteristic* of a person, place, or thing or event; you don't need to concern yourself with these just yet. Therefore, make sure you only look for nouns that *specifically* represent a person, place, or thing or event. You can ensure that you account for every subject you need to discuss by marking the nouns with a double-underline as you identify them, as in this example:

> "As an account representative, I'm responsible for 10 clients. Each of my clients makes an appointment to come into the showroom to view the merchandise we have to offer for the current season. Part of my job is to answer any questions they have about our merchandise and make recommendations regarding the most popular items. Once they make a decision on the merchandise they'd like to purchase, I write up a sales order for the client. Then I give the sales order to my assistant, who promptly fills the order and sends it to the client."

After you've identified all of the appropriate nouns within the response, list them on a sheet of paper; this becomes your *list of subjects*. You'll add more subjects to the list as you continue to work through the design process. Compile this list carefully and methodically because you'll use it to generate further discussions as the interview progresses and to help you define tables later in the design process.

Here are subjects that are represented in the previous response:

Account Representative	Job
Appointment	Merchandise
Assistant	Sales Order
Clients	Season
Items	Showroom

You can now use this list as the basis of further questions during the interview.

> ❖ **Note** I refer to this entire procedure as the *subject-identification technique* throughout the remainder of the book.

Verify that the nouns you've underlined are genuine subjects by reviewing the way they're used in the response. For example, "account representative" is a subject suggested by a noun in the first sentence, and you can assume that the subject identifies an *object* (person, place, or thing) by the way the noun is used in the sentence. "Appointment" is another subject suggested by a noun in the second sentence, and you can assume this subject represents an *event* (something that occurs at a given point in time) by the way it is used in the sentence.

Identifying Characteristics

After you've identified the subjects suggested within the response, pick a particular subject and begin to ask follow-up questions related to that subject. You use this line of questioning to obtain as much detailed information as possible about the subject you've selected. Therefore, make your follow-up questions more specific as you progress through this part of the discussion. The nature of your follow-up questions will depend on the responses you receive from the participant. Based on our sample response, for example, you could continue the discussion by asking more specific questions about sales orders, or you could begin an entirely new line of questioning regarding clients. Assume, for now, that you ask the following question to learn more about sales orders:

> "Let's discuss sales orders for a moment. What does it take to complete a sales order for a client?"

Note that this question begins with a statement directing the interview participant to focus on a particular subject. This is a technique you should use to guide your conversation after you've selected a specific subject to discuss. Also note that the question is open-ended; it prompts the participant for details related to the subject you've selected (sales orders) and allows you to establish the focus of the participant's subsequent responses.

Now, assume that the participant gives the following reply:

> "Well, I enter all the client information first, such as the client's name, address, and phone number. Then I enter the items the client wants to purchase. After I've entered all the items, I tally up the totals and I'm done. Oh, I forgot to mention: I enter the client's fax number and shipping address—if they have one."

Analyze this response with the subject-identification technique to determine whether there are subjects suggested within the response. Then add the new subjects to your list of subjects. Remember: List only those nouns that represent person, place, or thing or event.

After you've finished identifying new subjects, begin looking for *details* regarding the subject under discussion. Your objective here is to obtain as many facts about the subject as possible. *Now* you're interested in nouns that represent *characteristics* of a subject—they *describe* particular aspects of that subject. You can identify these nouns quite easily because they are usually in singular form ("phone number," "address"). In contrast, nouns that identify subjects are usually in possessive form ("the *client's* phone number," "the *company's* address").

Try to account for as many characteristics of the subject as possible. Use a single underline to mark a noun that represents a characteristic, as in this example:

> "Well, I enter all the client information first, such as the client's <u>name</u>, <u>address</u>, and <u>phone number</u>. Then I enter the items the client wants to purchase. After I've entered all the items, I tally

up the <u>totals</u> and I'm done. Oh, I forgot to mention that I enter the client's <u>fax number</u> and <u>shipping address</u>—if they have one."

As you identify the appropriate nouns within a response, list them on a sheet of paper; this becomes your *list of characteristics.* You'll add more characteristics to the list as you work through the design process, and you'll use this list later when you're determining the fields for the database. *Use a separate sheet of paper for the list of characteristics. Do not list the subjects and characteristics on the same sheet!* (The reason for keeping them on different lists will become clear when you begin to define tables for the database in Chapter 7.)

Here are the characteristics (shown in alphabetical order) that are represented in the previous response:

Address	Phone Number
Fax Number	Shipping Address
Name	Totals

This constitutes the list of characteristics for the subject under discussion. These characteristics will eventually become fields in the database.

> ❖ **Note** I refer to this entire procedure as the *characteristic-identification technique* throughout the remainder of the book.

Verify that the nouns you've marked with a single underline are genuine characteristics by reviewing the way they're used in the response. For example, "name," is a characteristic suggested by a noun in the first sentence, and you can assume that it describes some aspect of the subject "Client" by the way the noun is used in the sentence. "Shipping address" is another characteristic suggested by a noun in the last sentence, and you can assume that this noun also represents some aspect of the subject "Client" by the way the noun is used in the sentence.

After you've finished discussing a particular subject, move on to the next subject on your subjects list and begin the same pattern of questioning. Start with open-ended questions, identify the subjects suggested in the responses, ask more specific questions as the discussion progresses, and identify as many of the subject's characteristics as possible. Continue this process in an orderly manner until you've discussed every subject on your list.

You should learn the subject-identification technique and the characteristic-identification technique as thoroughly as possible because you'll use them during your interviews with users and management and as you identify fields and tables for the initial database structure. Note that you won't have to incorporate the single and double underlines forever; you'll eventually execute these techniques in your mind as you gain experience and as they become more instinctive and intuitive.

Before You Begin the Interview Process . . .

You can use the techniques you've just learned in this section for both user interviews and management interviews. The only differences between the two sets of interviews lie in the subject matter and the content of the questions.

The interview process involves two sets of discussions: one with users and the other with management. You'll speak to the users first because they represent the "front lines" of the organization. They have the clearest picture of the details connected with the organization's daily operations. Also, the information you gather from the users should help you to understand the answers you receive from management.

Interviewing Users

The first part of the interview process involves conducting user interviews. The interviews focus on these four issues:

1. The types of data users are currently using

2. How users are currently using their data

3. The collection of samples you assembled during the first two steps of the analysis

4. The types of information users require for their daily work

Because these issues are both data-centric and information-centric, you must be certain that you understand and always keep in mind the difference between data and information. Recall from Chapter 3 that *data* are the values you store in the database, and *information* is data that you process in a manner that makes it meaningful and useful to you when you work with it or view it. Keeping these definitions in mind will help ensure that you focus on each issue properly and conduct each segment of the interview successfully.

Reviewing Data Type and Usage

You can usually discuss the first two issues at the same time if you carefully phrase your questions at the beginning of the interview. Your objective for this part of the interview is to identify the types of data the users are currently using and how they use that data in support of the work they do. You'll use this information later in the design process to help define field and table structures. Use the data-collection and data-representation samples to help you formulate questions about the user's data. (However, don't actually discuss the samples just yet; you should deal with them separately.) During this discussion, you'll start with open-ended questions, identify subjects within the responses, and then use specific follow-up questions to identify the characteristics of each subject.

As you begin the interview, ask each participant about the work he or she performs on a daily basis. After the participant provides an overall description of the work he does, ask him to explain his job in more detail. Perhaps he can walk you through the job he performs on a daily basis.

Here's an example of a typical conversation that occurs during this part of the interview:

INTERVIEWER:	"What kind of work do you do on a day-to-day basis?"
PARTICIPANT:	"I accept land-use <u>applications</u> that are submitted by various <u>people</u>, log them in, and set a hearing date with the hearing examiner. I also assist <u>applicants</u> if they have any questions regarding a specific application."
INTERVIEWER:	"Let's talk about the applications for a moment. What types of facts are associated with an application?"
PARTICIPANT:	"There's quite a number, actually. There are facts concerning the type and name of the application, its designation and address, and its location."
INTERVIEWER:	"Tell me about the facts concerning the application's type and name."
PARTICIPANT:	"There are four things we record: the <u>type of application</u>, the <u>name of the subdivision</u>, the <u>purpose</u> of the project, and a <u>description</u> of the project."

Note how the interviewer starts the discussion with an open-ended question. After the participant responds, the interviewer uses the subject-identification technique to identify subjects within the response. The interviewer then chooses a particular subject and uses another open-ended question to focus the participant's attention on that subject.

Because the participant's next response is general in nature, the interviewer focuses on a particular *aspect* of the subject and uses a more specific follow-up question to elicit a detailed response from the participant.

The interviewer can continue to narrow the focus of his questions as the discussion progresses. As the participant responds to each question, the interviewer continues to use the characteristic-identification technique to identify characteristics of the subject that appear in the response. After he's identified all of the subject's characteristics, the interviewer then moves on to the next subject and begins the entire process again. He'll continue in this manner until he's covered his entire list of subjects. You'll go through the same exact process when you act as interviewer.

Reviewing the Samples

The next round of discussions centers on all the samples you assembled earlier in the analysis process. Your objectives during these discussions are to identify how the objects represented by the samples are used, to clarify the aspects of the samples you don't understand, and to assign a description to each sample.

It should be relatively easy for you to talk to participants about the samples now that you have an idea of the data the participants use on a daily basis. Begin the conversation by asking questions about a specific sample. Figure 6.7 shows an example of a data-collection sample you might use as a starting point.

Review your notes from the discussions you held at the beginning of the interview before you ask your first question. You want to determine whether anything you've *already* discussed is relevant to the sample you're about to discuss. In one of the previous discussions, for example, a participant indicated that part of his job is to keep track of all the or-

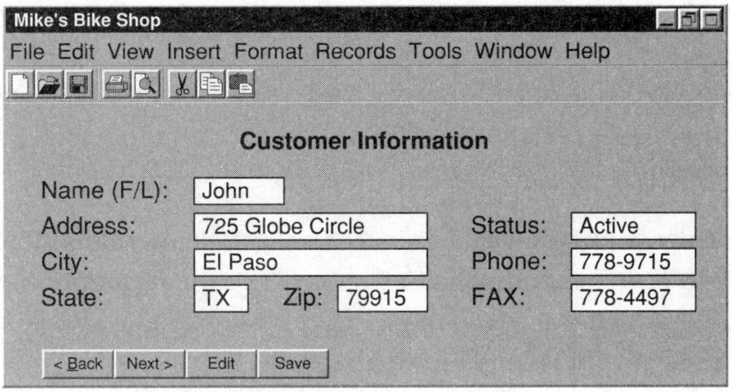

Figure 6.7. *A data-collection sample.*

ganization's customers. Using that statement as a starting point, you could ask him how he uses this particular data-collection sample to perform that task.

> "You mentioned in a previous discussion that you keep track of all the customers. How does this screen help you to carry out that task?"

This is a well-phrased question. It begins with a statement that focuses on a particular subject and then continues by bringing the participant's attention to the sample. The question is open enough to elicit a clear and complete response.

Now, assume the participant provides this response:

> "This screen allows me to enter new customers, as well as modify and maintain all the information we have on existing customers."

If this reply answers the question to your complete satisfaction, use it as the basis for a description of the sample. On the other hand, if the reply does not completely answer the question, continue with an appropriate line of questioning until the participant clearly identifies the purpose and use of the sample. You must supply descriptions for all of your samples because you'll use them again later in the design process.

A sample's description should be succinct, yet clear enough to indicate the sample's purpose and how it is used. Write the description on a slip of paper and attach it to the sample. Here's an example of a description you might use for the sample in Figure 6.7:

     This screen is used to collect and maintain all customer data.

It's necessary for you to understand the sample as completely as possible so that you can write a clear and concise description. If there are aspects of a given sample you don't understand, ask the participant to clarify them for you. For example, assume you're working with the report sample shown in Figure 6.8.

Current Product Inventory

Product ID	Product Description	Category	SRP	Quantity
9001	Shur-Lok U-Lock	Accessories	75.00	
9002	SpeedRite Cyclecomputer		65.00	20
9003	SteelHead Microshell Helmet	Accessories	36.00	33
9004	SureStop 133-MB Brakes	Components	23.50	16

Figure 6.8. *A report sample.*

If you don't know what the abbreviation "SRP" represents, ask someone to tell you what it means. A simple question such as this will often clarify the issue:

> "What do the letters 'SRP' represent in the 'Current Product Inventory' report?"

As you compose descriptions for each of the samples, you might find it difficult to write a description for a *complex* sample. A sample is complex if it represents more than one subject. The sample in Figure 6.8, for example, covers only one subject: products. The sample in Figure 6.9, however, covers at least three subjects: doctor services, nursing services, and patients. You'll often have to work a little harder to determine a complex sample's purpose and use. In some cases, you'll have to use the subject-identification technique to determine what subjects are represented

		Patient Name:	George Edelman
Eastside Medical Clinic 7743 Kingman Dr. Seattle, WA 98032 (206) 555-9982		Patient ID:	10884
		Visit Date: Physician:	05/16/96 Daniel Chavez

Doctors Services	Service Code	Fee	Nursing Services	Service Code	Fee
[X] Consultation	92883	119.00	[ ] R.N. Exam	89327	
[X] EKG	92773	95.00	[ ] Supplies	82372	
[ ] Physical	98377		[ ] Nurse Instruction	88332	
[ ] Ultrasound	97399		[ ] Insurance Report	81368	

Figure 6.9. *An example of a complex report sample.*

within the sample. Once you've identified the subjects, it will be easier for you to clarify the function or functions of the sample. You can then compose a description that gives a clear picture of the sample's purpose.

Let's say you're working with the report sample shown in Figure 6.9 and you have questions regarding the nursing services. You wonder whether the organization is using this report as an indirect means of maintaining a current list of nursing services. A question that elicits a yes or no response from a participant is not going to help you much at all, so you need to use an open-ended question that will elicit a more informative response. You could begin your discussion of this sample with this question:

> "What nursing services do you provide besides those listed in this sample?"

This type of question gives the participant an opportunity to provide you with a detailed response; furthermore, you've given yourself the opportunity to ask follow-up questions as warranted by the participant's reply. To continue the example, say you receive the following answer:

> "We provide various specialized services for the more complex patient. You see only the general services on this report. However, I can show you a complete list of our services that Katherine maintains on her computer."

You can continue with the process of writing the sample's description if this reply clarifies the point in question and you now understand the purpose of this report sample; otherwise, continue asking follow-up questions until everything is explained to your satisfaction.

Reviewing Information Requirements

The final issue you'll discuss with users concerns their information requirements. The objectives of this discussion are to determine whether individual users receive information based on data they don't directly control or maintain, to determine what types of additional information they need, and to determine what types of information they can foresee themselves needing in the future. You'll use the information you gather during this discussion later in the design process to help define and verify field and table structures. You can also use this information as yet another way of determining whether you accidentally overlooked anything during the previous discussions.

Current Information Requirements

Users typically receive the information they use through a variety of reports. Therefore, the best way to begin this discussion is by reviewing the report samples. This time around, though, you're not so concerned with how the reports are used as you are with the data upon which they are based. It's quite common that information on some of the reports a user receives is based on data he does not personally create and maintain. In this situation, you must determine the origin of that data so that you can identify *all* the data used by a user, whether he uses it directly or indirectly.

Select a report from the report samples and work with one of the participants to determine what data is used to produce the report. Ask him if he creates and maintains the data on which the report is based. You can move on to the next sample if he answers yes, but you'll need to identify the origin of the data if he answers no. Here's an example that illustrates this process.

Say you have an assistant named Kendra who is beginning a discussion with a participant named Joyce regarding the report sample shown in Figure 6.10.

As Kendra begins the conversation, Joyce mentions that she works in the telemarketing department. When Kendra first asks about the sample

Customer Phone List

Customer Name	Customer Type	Last Purchase	Phone Number
Alastair Black	Preferred	05/21/96	551-0993
Dave Cunningham	Silver	03/19/96	533-9182
Zachary Ehrlich	Preferred	05/16/96	515-3921
Frank Lerum	Gold	04/12/96	552-3884

Figure 6.10. *A sample report.*

report, Joyce indicates that she receives it every Monday morning. So Kendra asks her the following question:

> "Do you provide the data that's used to generate this report?"

Her next course of action depends on Joyce's response. Kendra can move on to the next sample if Joyce's answer is yes; however, it would be a good idea for Kendra to ask a follow-up question to make certain that Joyce's answer is true.

> "Do you personally enter and maintain this data on a daily basis?"

If Joyce's answer is still yes, Kendra can definitely move on to the next sample.

On the other hand, if Joyce's answer to the original question is no, Kendra will need to ask a few follow-up questions. First, she'll ask Joyce whether she contributes *any* data to the report. If she does, Kendra will then determine what data Joyce specifically submits. Then Kendra will ask whether or not Joyce knows the source of the remaining data.

To continue the example, say Joyce's reply to the original question is no and that the following dialog takes place after her response:

> KENDRA: "Can you tell me, then, if there is any data that you contribute to the report at all?"
>
> JOYCE: "I do supply the customer's name and phone number."
>
> KENDRA: "Then you don't supply the customer type or the last purchase date. Is that correct?"
>
> JOYCE: "Yes."
>
> KENDRA: "Can you tell me who provides this data?"
>
> JOYCE: "I'm not really sure, but . . ."
>
> KENDRA: "Do you have an idea of where these items come from?"
>
> JOYCE: "As a matter of fact, I do. They come from the sales department."
>
> KENDRA: "That sounds good to me. I'll make a note of that on this sample, and then we can move on to the next one."

Note that as the dialog begins, Kendra first tries to determine whether Joyce submits any data at all to the report. When Joyce reveals that she contributes two of the items for the report, Kendra then poses a follow-up question to verify that Joyce is not submitting any of the other data. Finally, Kendra tries to identify the source of the remaining data by asking Joyce if she knows from where the data originates. In this case, it takes only two well-phrased questions to find the answer. If Joyce could not answer the last two questions, Kendra would need to continue her investigation with other participants.

You're sure to obtain all the information you need about your report samples if your discussions progress in the same manner as the preceding dialog. Remember: Follow-up questions are a crucial part of the conversation. You must phrase your questions properly to elicit the types of responses you need from the participants.

Additional Information Requirements

The next subject of discussion is *additional* information requirements. The objective here is to determine whether users require additional information that is not being delivered to them currently. If this is the case, you must identify what additional information they require and then define new data structures to support this extra information later in the design process.

Start this conversation by directing the participants to review the reports they currently receive. Ask them whether there is other information they would like to see in their reports. Next, direct them to discuss the additional information, which reports the information will affect, and the reason they believe the information is necessary. Then determine whether the additional information represents new subjects or new characteristics. If it does, identify each new item and add it to the appropriate list. Finally, review the participants' comments and determine whether there are further issues you need to discuss with them in regard to the reports. Here's an example that illustrates the process.

Say you're beginning this discussion and you've just asked the participants to review the report samples they currently use. One of the participants is reviewing the sample report shown in Figure 6.11.

Current Product Inventory

Product ID	Product Description	Category	SRP	Quantity
9001	Shur-Lok U-Lock	Accessories	75.00	
9002	SpeedRite Cyclecomputer		65.00	20
9003	SteelHead Microshell Helmet	Accessories	36.00	33
9004	SureStop 133-MB Brakes	Components	23.50	16

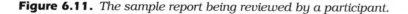

Figure 6.11. *The sample report being reviewed by a participant.*

You now instruct this particular participant to note the additional information she would like to see on the reports and to provide a brief statement indicating why the information is necessary. It doesn't really
matter exactly *how* she makes the notations so long as they are clear
and attached to the report in an obvious manner. In this case, she decides to use large sticky notes as a means of documenting her comments. She's specified two new fields she'd like to add to the report,
along with the reason for their inclusion. She's also suggested possible
locations for the fields by writing their names on the report itself.
Figure 6.12 shows the sample report with her comments.

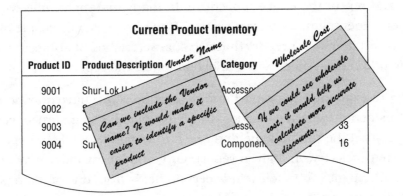

Figure 6.12. *A report sample with a participant's comments.*

Next, determine whether there are *new* subjects or *new* characteristics
represented in the additional information. Examine each report and
apply the subject-identification technique and the characteristic-
identification technique to the comments attached to the report. Here's
an example of how you apply these techniques to the first comment in
Figure 6.12:

> "Can we include the <u>vendor name</u>? It would make it easier to
> identify a specific <u>product</u>."

Here you've identified both a subject and a characteristic. (Note that the subject and characteristic aren't directly related: "vendor name" is a characteristic of a vendor, not of a product. There's no problem here, but you should be aware that this apparent mismatch of subjects and characteristics is typical. You'll address this issue later in the design process.) Now, check your subjects list and characteristics list to determine whether you've already accounted for these items. If you have, move on to the next comment and repeat this procedure.

If you do discover a new subject, add it to your list of subjects and then identify as many of its characteristics as possible. When you're finished, add these items to your list of characteristics, move on to the next comment, and repeat the entire procedure. In many instances, however, you'll only identify new characteristics. Don't be alarmed. People often want to add items to a report that are characteristics of subjects that are *already* represented by the information on the report.

Finally, re-examine each report and determine if you have questions or concerns about the notes participants have made. For instance, you may question the rationale behind one participant's belief that specific fields are necessary on a given report. Or you might wonder why another participant wants to *exclude* certain fields from one of his reports. You definitely want to make sure that the fields he wants to exclude are truly unnecessary and that removing them will not have an adverse effect on the information the report provides to other people. In either case, the inclusion or exclusion of fields will affect the final database structure.

If a report has one or more remarks that are cause for concern, review it with the appropriate participant and settle as many of the issues as you can. You can usually resolve all your concerns with a few simple questions, but in some cases the resolution to certain issues will not become apparent until later in the design process. For example, you might have noticed that certain fields appear on two or more reports. It's difficult to determine if the fields are being unnecessarily duplicated until you begin to define the field and table structures. When you encounter an issue that is difficult to resolve at the present time, make a note of it and put the report aside for later review.

Future Information Requirements

The last subject of discussion concerns *future* information requirements. Your objective here is to identify the information that the participants believe will be necessary for them to receive as the organization evolves. Once you identify these future information requirements, you can ensure that you define the data structures necessary to support that information.

You first need to make sure that every participant has some idea of how the organization is evolving. The nature of the organization's evolution will determine what new information participants will require. If several people are unacquainted with these issues, you'll need to obtain this information from management and then relay it to the participants prior to the discussion. Once everyone is familiar with these matters, you can begin the conversation.

Start the discussion by directing the participants to think about the future evolution of the organization and how it may affect the work they do on a daily basis. You'll often find that some participants are going to have a difficult time envisioning this scenario. When this happens, use questions such as these to help them focus their thoughts:

How will the organization's evolution affect the amount of information you'll need to do your job?

Do you think you'll need additional types of information to carry out your duties effectively as the organization evolves?

How will the evolution of the organization increase the time you spend on your daily tasks?

Can you predict what types (categories, not specific items) of new information you'll need in order to carry out your duties as the organization evolves?

Do you anticipate a need for new information if your duties are increased as a result of the organization's evolution?

Keep in mind that most of the participants' answers will be based on *speculation*. There's no accurate way for them to predict what types of information they'll really need until the organization's evolution occurs. However, if you can anticipate their hypothetical information requirements, you can prepare for them by defining the necessary data structures in advance.

As the participants respond, use the subject-identification technique to identify brand-new subjects and then add them to your list of subjects. Then use the characteristic-identification technique to uncover new details concerning existing or new subjects and add them to your list of characteristics.

You can sketch ideas for new reports or data-entry forms to help participants visualize the types of information they may need in the future. These sketches can then help you identify new subjects or characteristics that the database structure needs to address. If you create several rough drawings of sample reports, be sure to assemble them in a separate, clearly marked folder. Then code each revision so that you can compare it with earlier revisions. Figure 6.13 shows an example of a preliminary design for a future report.

Continue the conversation with users until you're satisfied that you've accounted for as many of the participants' future information require-

1st Quarter Customer Sales Statistics

| | | | Sales Amounts | |
Customer ID	Customer Name	Maximum	Minimum	Average
9001	Stewart Jameson	265.00	23.00	55.00
9002	Shannon McLain	550.00	125.00	70.00
9003	Estela Pundt	250.00	35.00	36.00
9004	Timothy Ennis	325.00	20.00	25.00

Figure 6.13. *An example of a design for a new report.*

ments as possible. When you've completed the discussion, you're ready to conduct interviews with management.

> ❖ **Note** You can use all of the techniques you learned in this section for the management interviews as well. Therefore, the next section is somewhat shorter and more concise.

Interviewing Management

The second part of the interview process involves interviewing management personnel. This round of interviews focuses on these issues:

1. The types of information managers currently receive

2. The types of additional information they need to receive

3. The types of information they foresee themselves needing

4. Their perception of the organization's *overall* information requirements

> ❖ **Note** Throughout the remainder of the book, I use the term *management* to refer to the person or persons controlling or directing the organization.

Reviewing Current Information Requirements

Your objectives during the first part of this interview are to identify the information that management routinely receives and to determine whether it receives reports that are not represented in your group of report samples.

As you begin the interview, ask each participant about the work he performs and the responsibilities associated with his position. A manager typically has a number of issues on his mind, so these questions will help him focus his attention on the matters at hand. His answers will give you some idea of how he might use the information on the reports he receives and will provide you with a perspective on his need for that information.

Next, ask each participant if he uses any of the reports in your collection of report samples. Proceed with the next step if he says he doesn't use any of the reports; otherwise, examine each report and ask him to help you identify other subjects that you might have previously overlooked. Use the subject-identification technique as necessary to aid you in this process. If the manager identifies a new subject, add it to your list of subjects and use the characteristic-identification technique to determine the subject's characteristics. Then add the new characteristics to your list of characteristics. Repeat this entire procedure for each sample report.

Continue the discussion by asking each participant whether he receives reports that are *not* represented in your report samples. If he answers yes, obtain a sample of each new report and review it with the participant. Use the subject-identification technique and the characteristic-identification technique to identify the subjects (and their associated characteristics) represented within the report and then add the subjects and characteristics to their respective lists. Finally, attach a description to the report and add it to your collection of report samples. Repeat this procedure until you've accounted for every new report.

Reviewing Additional Information Requirements

The next subject of discussion concerns management's need for *additional* information. Your objective is to determine whether it requires supplemental information that is currently missing from the reports it receives. If you conclude that this is the case, you must identify that additional information. You'll then define new data structures (as appropriate) to support this information later in the design process. However, you can move on to the next part of the interview if management doesn't require additional information.

You use the same techniques for this discussion as those you used for this segment of the user interviews. Here are the steps you'll follow:

1. Review the report samples with the participants once again and ask them if there is additional information they would like to include in any of the reports.

2. Have the participants note the additional information—including the reasons that they believe it's necessary—on the appropriate reports. Remember that it doesn't matter how the participants make the notations so long as they are clear, noticeable, and are attached to the appropriate report.

3. Identify new subjects or characteristics within the information and add them to the appropriate list.

4. Review the reports and discuss any concerns you have about them with the participants. Once your concerns are resolved, this process is complete.

Reviewing Future Information Requirements

Future information requirements are the next subject of discussion. Your objective here is to determine what information management foresees itself needing in the future. Once you've identified these requirements, you can ensure that there are data structures in place to support this information as the need for it arises.

As you begin the discussion, have the participants consider how the organization is currently evolving. Then ask them how this evolution will affect the information they require to make sound decisions and how it will influence the way they guide or direct the organization. Remember that their answers are going to be based on speculation, as was the case with the similar questions you asked users; there's no way for management to predict its future needs accurately until the organization actually begins to evolve. (It's always a good idea, however, to plan for the future as much as possible.) Use the subject-identification technique and characteristic-identification technique to identify new subjects and characteristics within the participants' responses and then add the new items (if any) to the appropriate lists.

Next, make sketches of any new reports the participants might have in mind. Identify new subjects and characteristics within each report and add them to the appropriate lists. Then assemble these new reports in a clearly marked folder and add it to your collection of samples.

You're ready to move on to the last subject when you've accounted for as many of management's future information requirements as possible.

Reviewing Overall Information Requirements

The last topic of discussion concerns the organization's *overall* information requirements. In management's opinion, what generic class of information does the organization need? Your objective here is to discover whether there is data that the organization needs to maintain that has not been previously discussed in either the user interviews or the management interviews. If you determine that there is such data, you must account for it in the database structure.

Take all of the reports that you've gathered throughout the analysis and interview processes and review them with the participants once more. Then ask the participants to consider the information the reports provide and how they might use that information. (Note that they'll have to make assumptions about how they might use the information from the new reports.) Next, ask participants to determine whether there is information that would be useful or valuable to the organization, but that is not currently being received by *anyone* within the organization. If they determine that there is indeed some new information that the organization could use, go through the normal process of identifying that information and the subjects and characteristics represented within it. Sketch samples of new reports for the information, as appropriate, and add the samples to your existing collection of new reports.

For example, assume that one of the participants has identified a need for demographic information; she believes that it would help the organization identify a more specific target market for its product. None of the existing reports furnishes this information, so you identify exactly what she needs by working with her to create a sketch of a report that will present this information. (She might actually sketch more than one report, but this is neither a problem nor a cause for your concern.) You then use the appropriate techniques to identify and note the subjects and characteristics represented within the report and add it to your existing collection of new reports. Later in the design process, you'll define the data structures necessary to support the new information.

Repeat this procedure until the participants can no longer identify any further information that the organization might find useful or valuable. After you're reasonably confident that you've accounted for all of the organization's information requirements, suspend the interview process and begin the process of compiling the preliminary field list.

It's important for you to understand that you may have to revisit this process, even though you and the participants may believe that you've accounted for all the information the organization could possibly use. You'll commonly identify new information as the database-design process unfolds.

Compiling a Complete List of Fields

The Preliminary Field List

Now that you have completed your analysis of the current database and the interviews with users and management, you can create a *preliminary field list*. This list represents the organization's fundamental data requirements and constitutes the core set of fields that you'll define in the database. You create the preliminary field list using a two-step process.

Step One: Review and Refine the List of Characteristics

The first step involves reviewing and refining the list of characteristics you compiled throughout the analysis and interview process. As you learned in Chapter 3, a *field* represents a characteristic of a particular subject; therefore, each item on your list of characteristics will become a field. Before you transform those characteristics into fields, however, you first need to review the list to identify and remove duplicate characteristics.

During the interviews, you identified various characteristics within each participant's responses, compiling them into a list as the interview progressed. There were probably times when you mistakenly added the same characteristic to the list more than once, or unknowingly referred to the *same* characteristic by two or more different names. As a result, your list of characteristics requires some refinement.

Refining Items with the Same Name

Begin refining your list of characteristics by looking for items with the same name. When you find one or more occurrences of a particular name, determine whether they all represent the same characteristic. Remove all but one occurrence of the name from the list if they do represent the same characteristic; otherwise, determine what each instance of the name represents. You'll often find that a duplicate name represents the *same type* of characteristic as its original counterpart, but should be associated with a different subject than its counterpart. In this case, you rename the duplicate to reflect how it relates to the appropriate subject.

Assume, for example, that the item "Name" appears three times on your list of characteristics. Your first inclination will probably be to remove two of the occurrences because your current objective is to eliminate duplicate characteristics. However, you should determine whether each instance of "Name" represents a distinct characteristic before you remove it. You can easily make this determination by examining your interview notes; this will help you remember when and why you added the item to the list.

After careful examination, you discover that the first occurrence of "Name" represents a characteristic of the subject "Clients," the second, a characteristic of the subject "Employees," and the third, a characteristic of the subject "Contacts." You resolve this duplication by *renaming* each occurrence of "Name" (using the subject as a prefix) to reflect its true meaning. Now you'll have three new characteristics called "Client Name," "Employee Name," and "Contact Name."

Items similar to "Name" commonly appear on a list of characteristics, and you must address them in the same manner. You'll commonly see one or more occurrences of items such as "Address," "City," "State," "Zip Code," and "Phone Number," and you can refer to them collectively as *generic items*. The point here is that you must rename each instance of a generic item to reflect its true relationship to a particular subject, thus ensuring that you have as accurate a field list as possible.

Refining Items Representing the Same Characteristic

Now look for items that represent the *same* characteristic and remove all but one. The idea here is that a given characteristic should appear only once in the list of characteristics. For example, assume that "Product #," "Product No.," and "Product Number" appear on your list of characteristics. It's evident that these items all represent the same characteristic, and you need only one of them on your list. Choose the one that conveys the intended meaning clearly, completely, and unambiguously and remove the remaining items from the list of characteristics. (In this case, the best choice is "Product Number" because it fulfills the previous criteria.)

Ensuring Items Represent Characteristics

Finally, make sure that each item on your list represents a *characteristic*. It's easy to place items accidentally on the list that represents subjects. You can test each item by asking yourself questions such as these:

Can this word be used to describe something?

Does this word represent a component, detail, or piece of some-thing in particular?

Does this word represent a *collection* of things?

Does this word represent something that can be broken down into smaller pieces?

Depending on the item you're working with, some questions are easier to answer than others. When you find that an item represents a subject rather than a characteristic, remove it from the list of characteristics and add it to the list of subjects. Be sure to identify the new subject's characteristics and add them to the existing list of characteristics.

For example, say "Item" appears on your list of characteristics, and you're not quite sure whether it represents a characteristic or a subject. Use the questions above to help you make a determination.

Can "Item" be used to describe something?

Does "Item" represent a component, detail, or piece of something in particular?

You could make a case that "Item" helps to describe a sale inasmuch as it identifies what a customer purchased. On the other hand, you could also say that "Item" isn't a characteristic because it doesn't represent a *singular* aspect of a sale. "Date Sold," for example, represents a singular characteristic of a sale. Leaving the quandary surrounding these ques-tions unresolved, you go on to the next question.

Does "Item" represent a collection of things?

You can answer this question easily by looking at the plural form of the word, which in this case is "Items." If "Items" can be referred to as a collection, it *is* a subject. It's beginning to become clear that "Item" does represent a collection of some sort, and you can make a final determination by asking yourself the last question:

> Does "Items" represent something that can be broken down into smaller pieces?

You can answer this question by determining whether you can identify any characteristics for "Items." If you can, then "Items" definitely represents a subject and you should move it to the list of subjects. You also need to identify its characteristics and add them to your list of characteristics.

Continue with this procedure until you've reviewed and refined the entire list of characteristics to your satisfaction. When you are through, you have your first version of the *preliminary field list*. Now you'll add new items to it and refine it further during the next step.

Step Two: Determine Whether There Are New Characteristics in Any of Your Samples

This step involves an examination of all the samples you gathered throughout the analysis process. Your goal is to determine whether there are characteristics on the samples that need to be added to the preliminary field list.

Begin this step by highlighting every characteristic you find on each sample. Then, examine each characteristic and determine whether it's already on the preliminary field list; cross it out on the sample if it's already on the list. Next, study the remaining characteristics and determine whether any of them has the *same meaning* as an existing field; if it does, cross it out on the sample. (Use the same procedure you used in the first step to make this determination.) Finally, add any highlighted characteristics remaining on the samples to the preliminary field list.

For example, say you're working with the data-collection sample shown in Figure 6.14.

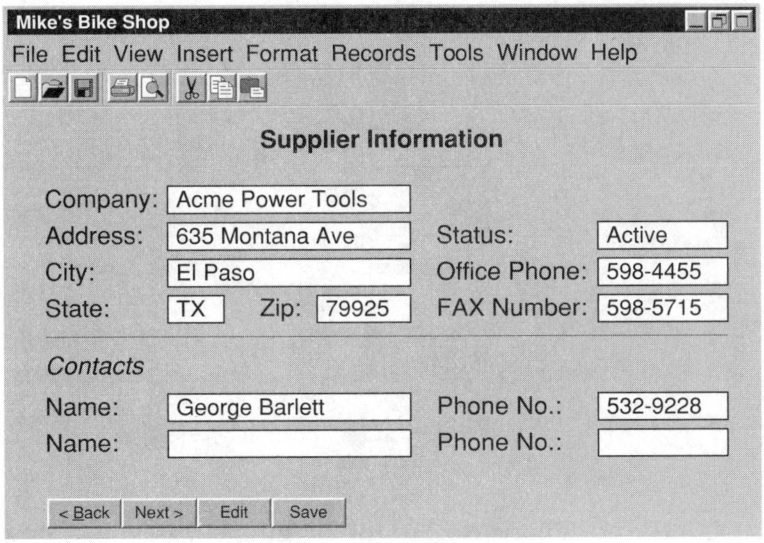

Figure 6.14. *An example of a data-collection sample.*

Highlight each characteristic you find on the sample, as shown in Figure 6.15.

You're likely to find multiple occurrences of various characteristics in some of the samples. As you can see, both "Name" and "Phone No." appear twice on this particular sample. You can cross out the duplicates in this case because they have the same meaning as the original instances.

To continue with the example, say you reviewed the preliminary field list and found that every characteristic on the sample is already on the list with the exception of "Name" and "Phone No." Cross out the existing items on the sample to show that you have accounted for them. Before

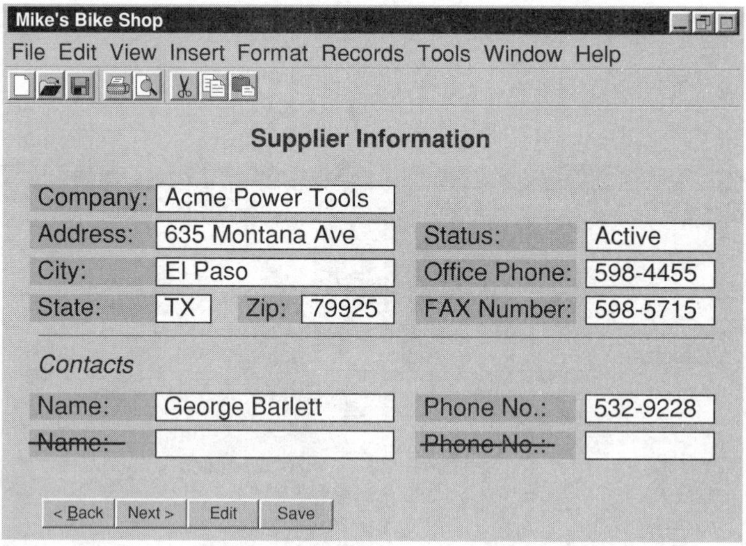

Figure 6.15. *A sample with highlighted characteristics*

you add "Name" and "Phone No." to the preliminary field list, however, make sure that the names of these items properly describe their relationship to the subject represented within the sample. In this case, the two remaining items represent characteristics of a group of people known as "Contacts." Therefore, you rename these characteristics (using the subject as a prefix) as "Contact Name" and "Contact Phone Number," and then add them to the preliminary field list. Repeat this procedure for each sample you've gathered until you've gone through all the samples you've collected. When you're through, you have the *second* version of the preliminary field list.

A Side Note: Value Lists

As you examine the characteristics on a database, spreadsheet, or Web page sample, record on a sheet of paper the name of each characteristic that incorporates a *value list* (also known as an *enumerated list*). This list specifies the acceptable range of values for a particular characteristic and often enforces a given business rule. (You'll learn about business rules in Chapter 11.) For example, say you work for a manufacturing company that uses four specific vendors to deliver its goods to customers across the nation. You could use a value list to ensure that a user selects one of those four vendors to ship a particular order. Figure 6.16 illustrates this example (note SHIP VIA) and also shows two common types of value list.

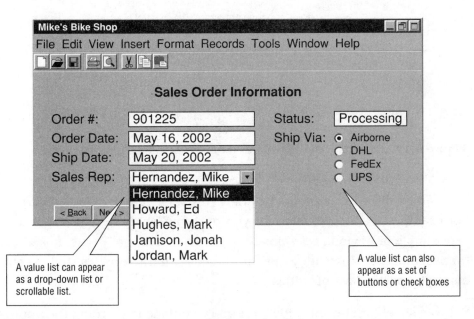

Figure 6.16. *A database screen with two value lists.*

When you record the name of a characteristic that incorporates a value list, also record the values within the list. If the list contains a large number of values, write a brief description of the type of values in the list and (if possible) a minimum and maximum value; otherwise, write down each of the values. Figure 6.17 shows an example of the record you're creating.

Characteristics Incorporating a Value List	
Characteristic	**Value List**
Category	Accessories, Bikes, Clothing, Components, Maintenance, Racks, Wheels
Department	Accessories, Bikes, Clothing, Service,
Sales Rep	The name of every employee within the organization whose position is that of a sales rep.
Ship Via	Airborne, DHL, FedEx, UPS

Figure 6.17. *Recording characteristics that incorporate value lists.*

You can be discerning about the characteristics you choose to record. For example, it's unnecessary for you to record characteristics that accept simple or obvious sets of values, such as "yes/no," "true/false," or "active/inactive." Instead, you should record characteristics that accept distinct, specific sets of values.

Set this sheet (or sheets) aside after you've finished recording the appropriate characteristics. You'll refer to this sheet when you define field specifications for the fields in the database and again when you define business rules.

The Calculated-Field List

There's one final refinement you must make to the preliminary field list before you can consider it complete: You must remove every *calculated field* and place it on a separate list. This new list becomes your *calculated-field list.* Recall from Chapter 3 that a calculated field is one that stores the result of a string concatenation or mathematical expression as its value. You list calculated fields separately because you'll use them in a specific manner later in the design process.

You build the calculated-field list using existing fields from the preliminary field list. Examine the preliminary field list and determine whether there are fields that fit the description of a calculated field. Fields that have names containing words such as "amount," "total," "sum," "average," "minimum," "maximum," and "count" are likely candidates for the calculated-field list. Common names for calculated fields include "Subtotal," "Average Age," "Discount Amount," and "Customer Count." As you identify each calculated field, remove it from the preliminary field list and place it on the calculated-field list. When you've completed your examination of all of the fields in the preliminary field list, you'll have two completely new lists: a *third* version of the preliminary field list and a calculated-field list.

Reviewing Both Lists with Users and Management

Conduct brief interviews with users and management to review the items that appear on the preliminary field list and the calculated-field list. Your objective here is to determine whether there are fields that have been omitted from either list. You can continue with the next step in the design process when everyone is satisfied that the lists are complete; otherwise, identify the fields that are missing and add them to the appropriate list. Once the interviews are complete, you'll have a "final" version of each list.

Be sure you conduct these interviews because the participants' feedback provides you with a means of verifying the fields on both lists. Let me remind you once again to avoid becoming too invested in the idea that these lists are absolutely complete and final. At this point you still may not have identified every field that needs to be included in the database—inadvertently, you're almost sure to miss a few fields—but if you strive to make your lists as complete as you can, the inevitable additions or deletions will be quick and easy to make.

CASE STUDY

You've already defined the mission statement and mission objectives for Mike's new database. Now it's time to perform an analysis, conduct interviews, and compile a preliminary field list.

First, analyze Mike's current database. As you already know, he keeps most of his data on paper; the only exception is the product inventory he maintains in a spreadsheet program. Gather samples of the various papers Mike uses to collect data and a screen shot or printout of the spreadsheet he uses to maintain the product inventory. Assemble these samples together in a folder for later use. For example, Figure 6.18 shows a sample of the index cards Mike uses to collect customer information, along with a screen shot of his spreadsheet program.

Next, identify the methods Mike uses to present information. He and his staff currently produce a variety of reports that present the information they need to conduct their daily affairs. They generate most of the reports using an old typewriter and the rest using a word-processing program on the computer. Gather samples of all the reports and place them in a folder for later use. Figure 6.19 shows a sample report that Mike creates with his typewriter.

Now you're ready to interview Mike's staff. Here are some points to remember as you're conducting the interviews:

1. Identify the types of data staff members are using and how they use that data. Be sure to use the subject-identification technique and the characteristic-identification technique to help you analyze responses and formulate follow-up questions.

Steven Pundt	363-9755
Apartment 2B	
2380 Redbird Lane	
Seattle, WA 98115	
He's primarily interested in mountain bike stuff.	
Keep him abreast of the summer bike tours.	

Mike's Bike Shop - Product Information

File Edit View Insert Format Tools Data Window Help

	A	B	C	D	E
1	Product ID	Product Description	Category	SRP	Qty On Hand
2	9001	Shur-Lok U-Lock	Accessories	75.00	
3	9002	SpeedRite Cyclecomputer		65.00	20
4	9003	SteelHead Microshell Helmet	Accessories	36.00	33
5	9004	SureStop 133-MB Brakes	Components	23.50	16
6	9005	Diablo ATM Mountain Bike	Bikes	1,200.00	
7	9006	UltraVision Helmet Mount Mirrors		7.45	10

Figure 6.18. *A paper-based and a computer-generated sample from Mike's Bikes.*

2. Review all the samples you gathered during the beginning of the analysis process. Determine how each sample is used, write an appropriate description, and attach the description to the sample.

3. Identify the staff's information requirements. Determine what information they're currently using, what additional information they need (remember to use the samples), and what kind of information they believe they'll need as the business evolves.

```
                    Supplier Phone List


Company Name                     Contact Name   Phone Number

ACME Cycle Supplies              George Chavez   633-9910

B & M Bike Supplies              Carol Ortner    527-3817

CycleWorks                       Julia Black     527-0019

Evanstone's Cycle Warehouse Allan Davis          636-9360
```

Figure 6.19. *A report sample from Mike's Bikes.*

During the interview, one of the employees wonders whether she can add a new field to the supplier phone list report. How do you respond? You hand her the report and ask her to attach a note indicating the name of the new field and a brief explanation of why she believes it's necessary. When she's finished, return the sample to the report samples folder. Figure 6.20 shows the report sample with the attached note.

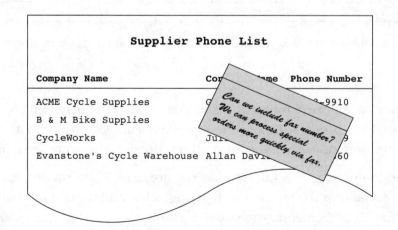

Figure 6.20. *A report sample with attached note suggesting a new field.*

You'll conduct the final interview with Mike. Keep the following points in mind as you speak with him:

1. Identify the reports he currently receives; you need to know what kind of information he uses to make business decisions. If he receives reports that are not represented in your group of report samples, obtain a sample of each report and add it to the group, updating the subject and characteristic lists as needed.

2. Review the group of report samples with him and determine whether he can identify subjects or characteristics that have been overlooked by his staff. Use the appropriate techniques to identify these items and then add them to the appropriate list.

3. Determine whether there is any additional information Mike needs to supplement the information he currently receives.

4. Determine what types of information Mike will need as the business evolves.

As you and Mike discuss his future information needs, he indicates that there is some new information he'd like to receive once the business really gets rolling: He'd like to see total bike sales by manufacturer. He believes this information would help him determine which bikes should be consistently well stocked. Such a report does not currently exist, so have Mike sketch it out on a sheet of paper. Next, identify the subjects and characteristics represented within the report and add them to the appropriate list. Then add the new report to your group of report samples. Figure 6.21 shows the sketch of Mike's new report.

Your analysis is now complete. You've interviewed Mike and his staff, you've gathered all the relevant samples, and you've created a list of subjects and a list of characteristics. A *partial* list of subjects and characteristics is shown in Figure 6.22. All you need to do now is to create your preliminary field list.

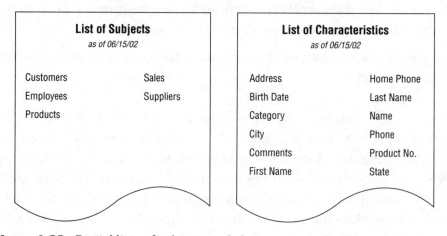

Figure 6.21. *The sketch of Mike's new report.*

List of Subjects
as of 06/15/02

Customers	Sales
Employees	Suppliers
Products	

List of Characteristics
as of 06/15/02

Address	Home Phone
Birth Date	Last Name
Category	Name
City	Phone
Comments	Product No.
First Name	State

Figure 6.22. *Partial lists of subjects and characteristics for Mike's Bikes.*

As you already know, you need to refine the list of characteristics before it can become the first version of the preliminary field list. Remove all duplicate characteristics, delete items that represent the *same* characteristic, and refine those items that have generic names. (Remember the problem with the characteristic called "Name"? If you find such characteristics, now is the time to resolve them.) Next, review all your samples and determine whether they contain characteristics that do not currently appear on the preliminary field list. Add to the list any new characteristics that you find. When you complete these tasks, you have the first version of your preliminary field list.

Now you remove all the calculated fields from the preliminary field list and place them on their own list; this becomes your new calculated-field list. Figure 6.23 shows a *small portion* of your final preliminary field list and calculated-field list.

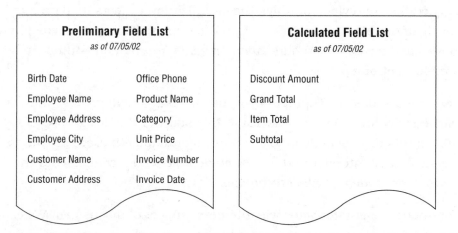

Figure 6.23. *A partial preliminary field list and a calculated-field list.*

❖ **Note** You may have noticed that each list includes a date in the title. It's a good idea to date your lists so that you can maintain a clear history of their development.

Summary

This chapter begins by discussing why you should analyze the organization's current database. You learned that the analysis helps you identify aspects of the current database that will be useful to you when you design the new database. Armed with this information, you can design a database that best suits the organization's needs. Next, we briefly looked at the two types of databases organizations commonly used: *paper-based* databases and *legacy* databases. We ended this discussion by identifying the *three steps used in the analysis process:* reviewing the way data is collected, reviewing the way information is presented, and conducting interviews with the organization's staff.

The chapter continues with a discussion of the review process. You learned how to review the ways the organization collects its data and how to assemble a set of *data-collection* samples. Then you learned how to *review the ways the organization presents information* and how to assemble a set of *report* samples.

Next, we discussed the process you use to *conduct interviews*, and you learned why interviews are useful at this stage of the design process. During this discussion you learned two techniques that are crucial to the success of interviews: the *subject-identification technique* and the *characteristic-identification technique*.

Conducting *user interviews* was the next subject of discussion. We examined the four issues you must address during these interviews, along with the techniques you use to address them. Next, we discussed conducting *management interviews*. Here you learned about the issues and techniques these interviews incorporate.

Finally, we discussed the process of *compiling a list of fields* based on the list of characteristics and the characteristics that appear in the samples. You learned that you decompose the field list into two separate lists: a *preliminary field list* and a *calculated-field list*. The preliminary field list enumerates the organization's fundamental data requirements and establishes the core set of fields you must define in the database. The calculated-field list consists of fields that contain values resulting from string concatenations or mathematical expressions.

Review Questions

1. State two goals of analyzing the current database.

2. True or False: You can adopt the current database structure as the basis for the new structure.

3. What is a *legacy database*?

4. State two steps of the analysis process.

5. Which types of computer software programs should you review during the analysis?

6. Why should you conduct interviews after you gather data-collection and information-presentation samples?

7. How do you use "open" and "closed" questions?

8. What is the *subject-identification technique*?

9. How do you identify specific attributes for a particular subject?

10. True or False: You should interview users and management at the same time.

11. What three basic types of information requirements must you identify?

12. What is the *preliminary field list*?

13. State why each item on this list should have a unique name.

14. What is a *value list*?

15. What are *calculated fields*? What (if anything) should you do about them?

7

Establishing Table Structures

> *It is a capital mistake to theorize*
> *before one has data.*
> —SHERLOCK HOLMES,
> *THE ADVENTURES OF SHERLOCK HOLMES*

Topics Covered in This Chapter

Defining the Preliminary Table List

Defining the Final Table List

Associating Fields with Each Table

Refining the Fields

Refining the Table Structures

Case Study

Summary

Review Questions

Organizations use databases to keep track of various subjects that are important to them. For example, a medical clinic keeps track of, among other things, its patients, doctors, and appointments; an equipment-rental business must maintain data on its customers, equipment, and rental agreements; and a registrar's office is concerned (at the very least) with students, teaching staff, and courses. In every case—and in any other scenario you can imagine—a table within the database represents each subject. Furthermore, each table is composed of *fields*, which represent the characteristics that define or describe the subject of the table. Tables constitute the very foundation of the database, and they guarantee a solid and sound foundation when they are properly designed.

Defining the Preliminary Table List

During this portion of the database-design process, you'll define a *preliminary table list* that you'll use to identify and establish the tables for the new database. You'll use three procedures to develop this list. The first involves using the *preliminary field list*, the second involves using the *list of subjects* you gathered during the interviewing process, and the third involves using the *mission objectives* you defined at the beginning of the database-design process. You'll then move on to build the structure of each table using fields from the preliminary field list.

Identifying Implied Subjects

The process of defining the tables for the database begins with a review of the preliminary field list. Your objective is to identify subjects that are implied by the fields on the list.

You may wonder why you're reviewing the preliminary field list instead of starting with the list of subjects. The list of subjects does seem to be a more intuitive place to start. After all, you've carefully built this list during the interview process, and you've been influenced by the conversations you've had with the users and management. Surely, all of this has helped you identify every subject that needs to be represented in the database. You may be correct, but you could have a minor problem if you're wrong: missing tables.

Studying the fields on the primary field list helps you identify subjects from an *unbiased viewpoint*—you're letting the fields "talk" to you. It's crucial that you now look at this list as objectively as possible—as though you've never seen it before—*without* any of the biases you've as-similated during the interview process. This enables you to see how cer-tain groups of fields suggest specific subjects, some of which may not have been identified during the interview process. You can also use the preliminary field list to verify many of the subjects on the list of sub-jects. Using the preliminary field list in these ways allows you to cross-check your previous work and helps you ensure that the new database structure includes all of the necessary subjects.

As you review the preliminary field list, ask yourself whether a certain set of fields defines or describes a particular subject. Move on to an-other set of fields if nothing readily comes to mind. When you can infer a subject from the field in the list, enter that subject on a new *prelimi-nary table list*. Figure 7.1 shows a partial sample of a preliminary field list and illustrates how a subject can be suggested by a set of fields.

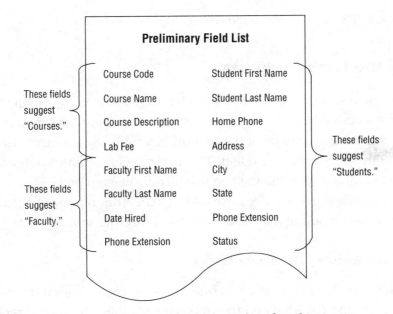

Figure 7.1. *Using the preliminary field list to identify subjects.*

Continue your review until you've scanned all the fields and identified as many subjects as possible. Be sure to add each subject you identify to the preliminary table list. This list will grow as you work with the list of subjects and mission objectives. Figure 7.2 shows an example of the first version of a preliminary table list.

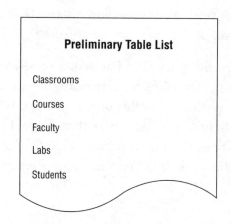

Preliminary Table List

Classrooms

Courses

Faculty

Labs

Students

Figure 7.2. *The first version of the preliminary table list.*

Using the List of Subjects

Now, create a second version of the preliminary table list by merging the list of subjects (created during the interviews with users and management) with the first version of the preliminary table list (compiled by studying the preliminary field list). This new version contains a more complete list of tables. Merging the two lists is a three-step process, which involves resolving duplicate items, resolving items that represent the same subject, and combining the remaining items together into one list.

Step One: Resolve Duplicate Items

Start this step by reviewing and crosschecking each item on the list of subjects against the items on the preliminary table list. Your objective here is to identify *duplicate items*, which are items on the list of subjects that already appear on the preliminary table list. You must be very careful how you resolve the duplicate items that you find. Begin by determining whether the items represent *different* subjects, despite the fact that they share the same name. (Use your interview notes as necessary to help you make the determination.) If they do represent different subjects, rename each item so that it accurately identifies the subject it represents and then add both items to the preliminary table list; otherwise, determine whether they truly represent the same subject. When you determine that both items do represent the same subject, cross out the item on the list of subjects and keep the one that appears on the preliminary table list. Then resume the review until you've examined all of the items on both the list of subjects and the preliminary table list. Let's take a look at an example of this process.

Assume that you're developing a database for an equipment rental business, and you're working with the list of subjects and the preliminary table list shown in Figure 7.3.

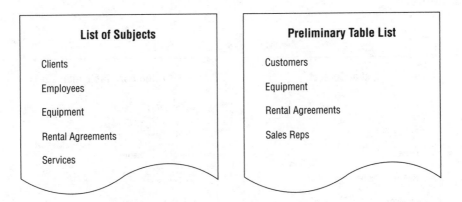

List of Subjects

Clients

Employees

Equipment

Rental Agreements

Services

Preliminary Table List

Customers

Equipment

Rental Agreements

Sales Reps

Figure 7.3. *The list of subjects and the preliminary table list for an equipment rental business.*

As you review these lists, you discover two duplicate items: "Equipment" and "Rental Agreements." These items warrant further examination, so you start with "Equipment" and try to determine whether each occurrence represents a *different* subject. In reviewing your interview notes, you find that "Equipment" on the list of subjects represents items such as tools, appliances, and audiovisual equipment. Then you remember that "Equipment" on the preliminary table list also includes trucks, vans, and trailers. You review your interview notes further and discover that vehicle rentals are treated differently from "regular" equipment rentals. Therefore, each occurrence of "Equipment" *does* represent a different subject. You resolve the duplication by keeping one occurrence of "Equipment" and renaming the other "Vehicles." You then list both items on the preliminary table list.

Now you go through the same process with "Rental Agreements." Fortunately, you discover that both occurrences share exactly the same meaning. The only thing you have to do in this case is cross out "Rental Agreements" on the list of subjects. Now you can continue your review until you've inspected each item on the list of subjects. Figure 7.4 shows the revised list of subjects and the preliminary table list.

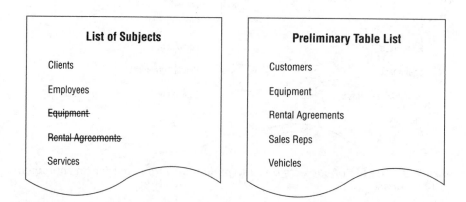

Figure 7.4. *The revised list of subjects and the revised preliminary table list (first view).*

Step Two: Resolve Items That Represent the Same Subject

Your objective during this step of the merge process is to determine whether an item on the list of subjects and an item on the preliminary table list *represent the same subject* even though they have *different* names. When you identify such a set of items, select the name that best represents the subject and use it as the sole identifier for that subject. Then deal with the name in this manner:

- If the name you've selected already appears on the preliminary table list, cross out its counterpart on the list of subjects.

- If the name appears on the list of subjects, *remove* its counterpart on the preliminary table list and *replace* it with the name from the list of subjects.

Repeat this process until you've covered all the items on the list of subjects.

Continuing with the equipment rental business example, assume you've discovered that "Clients" and "Employees" on the list of subjects and "Customers" and "Sales Reps" on the preliminary table list represent (respectively) the same subject (see Figure 7.4). Deciding to deal with "Clients" and "Customers" first, you review your interview notes and determine that "Customers" is the name that best represents both the people and the organizations that rent equipment from the business. You then resolve the duplication by keeping "Customers" and crossing out "Clients." Moving on to the next set of duplicate items, you decide to keep "Employees" and discard "Sales Reps" because you believe that "Employees" best describes those people who are employed by the business, regardless of their position. Figure 7.5 shows a revised version of both lists and the resolution of the duplicate items.

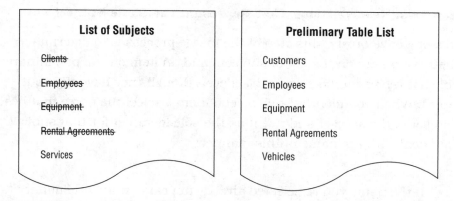

Figure 7.5. *The revised list of subjects and the revised preliminary table list (second view).*

Step Three: Combine the Items on the List of Subjects and the Preliminary Field List

The final step of this process is the easiest of the three. All you do is add the remaining items from the list of subjects to the preliminary table list. Then throw away the list of subjects—you won't need it anymore. The list that remains becomes the second version of the preliminary table list. That's all there is to it! Figure 7.6 shows the second version of

Figure 7.6. *The second version of the preliminary table list.*

the preliminary table list, which is the result of merging the two lists shown in Figure 7.5.

Using the Mission Objectives

In this third and final procedure, you use the mission objectives to determine whether you've overlooked any subjects during the previous two procedures. This is your final opportunity to add tables to the preliminary table list.

Start with the first mission objective, and use the subject-identification technique to identify the subjects represented in that statement. Underline each subject you identify and then crosscheck it against the items on the preliminary table list. Use the same techniques here that you used in the previous procedure.

1. When an item you underlined in a mission objective statement matches an item on the preliminary table list, determine whether the items represent different subjects. If they do, assign an appropriate name to each occurrence and then add each one to the preliminary table list; otherwise, cross out the duplicate item on the mission objective.

2. When an item you underlined in the mission objective statement has a name that is synonymous with the name of an item on the preliminary table list and both items represent the same subject, select the name that best identifies that subject and use it in the preliminary table list.

3. When an item you underlined in the mission objective statement represents a new subject, add it to the preliminary table list.

Repeat these steps until you've worked through all the mission objectives. Here's an example of how you use these techniques to review the mission objectives.

Assume that you're designing a database for a flight training school. You're just starting this particular process, and you've just used the subject-identification technique on the following statement:

We need to maintain data on our <u>pilots</u> and their <u>certifications</u>.

You now crosscheck the subjects you identified in this mission objective against the items in the preliminary table list shown in Figure 7.7.

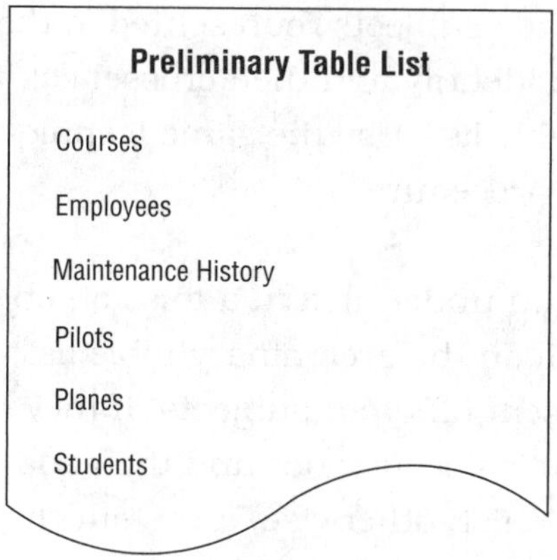

Preliminary Table List

Courses

Employees

Maintenance History

Pilots

Planes

Students

Figure 7.7. *The preliminary table list for a flight training school.*

In this case, you cross out "pilots" in the mission objective statement because it already exists on the preliminary table list and it represents the same subject. You then decide to examine "certifications" further, and, after some careful thought, you make these observations:

1.   It does not appear on the preliminary table list.

2.   It doesn't duplicate any item on the preliminary table list.

3. Its name is not synonymous with any item on the preliminary table list.

4. It doesn't represent the same subject as any other item on the preliminary table list.

These findings indicate that "certifications" is a new item and should be added to the preliminary table list. So, you add it to the preliminary table list and cross it out on the mission objective statement; this shows you that you've already dealt with this particular item. Figure 7.8 shows the revised version of the preliminary table list.

Preliminary Table List

Certifications

Courses

Employees

Maintenance History

Pilots

Planes

Students

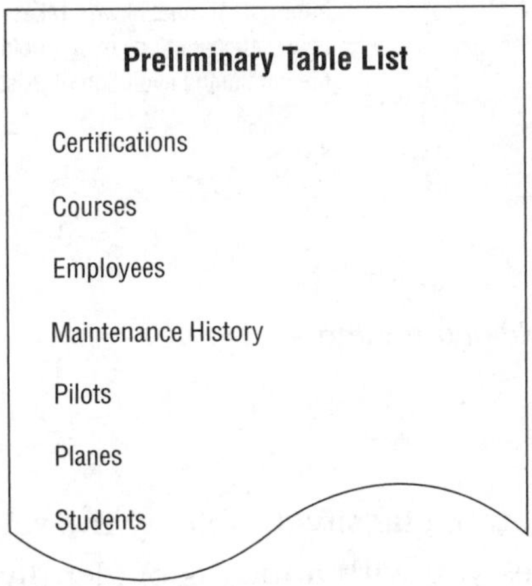

Figure 7.8. *The revised preliminary table list.*

Defining the Final Table List

Your preliminary table list is as complete as it can be at this point, so you'll now transform it into a *final table list*. This new list incorporates two elements that are not currently on the preliminary table list: *table type* and *table description*. Figure 7.9 shows an example of a final table list.

Final Table List

Name	Type	Description
Classrooms	Data	The spaces or areas within a facility reserved for the purpose of conducting class proceedings. Information regarding the physical aspects, on-site resources, and availability of these areas is useful because it allows us to assign classes to the facility that can make the best use of these areas.
Courses	Data	The programs of instruction conducted through courses offered by this institution. Course information must always reflect the addtion of new courses, the deletion of old courses, and the continuing evolution of existing courses.

Figure 7.9. *An example of a final table list.*

A *table type* allows you to classify a table by the role it plays within the database and provides you with a means of identifying tables that function in a similar manner. The table's role determines its type, and there are four table types that you can associate with a given table:

1. A *data table* represents a subject that is important to the organization and is the primary foundation of the information that the database provides. (You'll learn more about data tables later in this chapter.)
2. A *linking table* establishes a link between two tables in a many-to-many relationship. (Chapter 10 covers linking tables in more detail.)

3. A *subset table* contains fields that are related to a particular data table and further describes the data table's subject in a very specific manner. (You'll learn more about subset tables later in this chapter.)

4. A *validation table* contains relatively static data and is a crucial component of data integrity. (Chapter 11 provides further details on this type of table.)

A *table description* provides a clear definition of the subject represented by the table and states why the subject is important to the organization. There are certain guidelines that govern how you create a table description, and you'll learn about them later in this chapter. There is a final task you have to perform before you transform your preliminary table list into the final table list: refining the table names.

Refining the Table Names

Naming a table is a more complex affair than you may realize at the moment. As you learned in Chapter 3, a table represents a single subject; therefore, its name must clearly identify the subject it represents. The following guidelines will help you create table names that are clear, unambiguous, descriptive, and meaningful. They will also help ensure that you name your tables in a consistent manner.

Guidelines for Creating Table Names

- *Create a unique, descriptive name that is meaningful to the entire organization.* Using unique names helps to ensure that each table clearly represents a different subject and that everyone in the organization will understand what the table represents. (If you encounter duplicate table names at this point, resolve the problem using the techniques you learned earlier in this chapter.) Choose names that are descriptive enough to be self-explanatory. "Vehicle

Maintenance" is an example of a good, descriptive name. Defining a unique and descriptive name does take some work on your part, but it's well worth the effort in the long run.

- *Create a name that accurately, clearly, and unambiguously identifies the subject of the table.* Vague or ambiguous names usually indicate that the table represents more than one subject. When you encounter such a name, identify the subjects the table truly represents and then treat each subject as a separate table. "Dates" is a good example of a vague table name. You really don't know what the table represents without referring to its description. For example, assume you're designing a database for an entertainment agency and this table appears in the preliminary table list. Upon seeing this table name, you decide to review your interview notes. You discover that one person says "Dates" represents appointments for client meetings, and another person says it represents booking dates for the agency's stable of entertainers. This table clearly represents two subjects, so you remove "Dates" from the preliminary table list and replace it with two new tables called "Client Meetings" and "Entertainer Schedules."

  Possibly the most vague and ambiguous name you could assign to a table is "Miscellaneous"—it doesn't identify a single subject whatsoever. You might occasionally feel compelled to create a "Miscellaneous" table because you just can't figure out what to do with certain fields on your preliminary field list. When that happens, stop, take a break, and then come back and re-examine those fields. Carefully and methodically apply the design techniques you've learned, and you're sure to determine what to do with the fields after all.

- *Use the minimum number of words necessary to convey the subject of the table.* Everyone in the organization should be able to identify what the table represents without having to read its description. Although your objective is to create a short, succinct table name, avoid using a minimalist approach. "TD_1" is a good example of a name that is exceedingly short. You won't have the slightest idea what this table represents unless you know the meaning of each character in the name. You should also avoid going in the opposite direction as well. "Multiuse Vehicle Maintenance Equipment" is much too long and can easily be shortened to just "Equipment."

- *Do not use words that convey physical characteristics.* Avoid using words such as "file," "record," and "table" in the table name because they add a level of confusion that you don't need. A table name that includes this type of word is very likely to represent more than one subject. Consider the name "Patient Record." On the surface, this may appear to be an acceptable name. You'll realize, however, that there are potential problems with this name when you take some time to think about what a "patient record" is supposed to represent. The name contains a word that you're trying hard to avoid ("record") and it potentially represents three subjects: "patients," "doctors," and "examinations." With this in mind, remove "patients" from the preliminary table list and replace it with three new tables, one for each of the three subjects.

- *Do not use acronyms and abbreviations.* Acronyms are hard to decipher, abbreviations rarely convey the subject of the table, and both violate the first guideline in this list. Take acronyms, for example. Say you're helping an organization revise its database structure and you encounter a table named "SC." How do you know what the table represents without knowing the meaning of the letters themselves? The fact is that you can't easily identify the subject of the table. What's more, you may find that the table means different things to different departments in the organization. So, you decide to conduct a brief interview with some of the staff in order to determine what the letters represent. (Now, this is the scary part.) To your disbelief, you discover that the folks in *personnel* think it stands for "Steering Committees"; the *information systems* staff believes it to be "System Configurations"; and the people in *security* insist that it represents "Security Codes." This example clearly illustrates why you should make every effort to avoid using abbreviations and acronyms in a table name.

- *Do not use proper names or other words that will unduly restrict the data that can be entered into the table.* This guideline will keep you from falling into the trap of creating duplicate table structures. A name such as "Southwest Region Employees," for example, severely restricts the data that you can enter into this table. As the organization grows, how will you deal with employees from other regions? When the organization begins to hire employees in Washington, Oregon, and Idaho, you'll have to create a "Pacific Northwest Region Employees" table, and you'll have to create a "Western Region Employees" table when the organization begins to hire folks in Arizona, Utah, Nevada, and California.

Proper database-design principles dictate that you should not create duplicate structures such as these because they can be quite problematic.

1. Users could have a difficult time retrieving data from all three tables simultaneously.

2. The person maintaining the database would have the added responsibility of ensuring that the tables are always structurally synchronized. If he adds, modifies, or deletes a field in one table, he must take the same action on all the other tables.

3. The person maintaining the database would also have the added responsibility of ensuring synchronized data integrity between the tables. He must be able to guarantee that data is completely and accurately transferred from one table to the other when an employee relocates from one region to another.

- *Do not use a name that implicitly or explicitly identifies more than one subject.* This is one of the most common mistakes you can make with a table name, and it is relatively easy to identify. This type of name typically contains the words "and" or "or" and characters such as the slash (\) or ampersand (&); examples include "Department or Branch" and "Facility\Building." A table with an ambiguous name suggests that you may have not identified the subject clearly or accurately during the analysis and interview processes. You can rectify this problem by reviewing your notes and conducting further analysis and interviews as necessary. Just remember that you must always ensure that each table represents only one subject.

Another name that falls under this category is "Miscellaneous." (Yes, here's that name again!) A moment ago, I said that this name didn't identify a single subject whatsoever; this is a correct and valid assertion. It is also true, however, that the name implicitly identifies more than one subject; you can't specifically identify the subjects because the name is vague and ambiguous. The *Concise Oxford Dictionary, Ninth Edition,* defines the word itself as follows:

Miscellaneous *adj.* 1. of mixed composition or character. 2. of various kinds.

You can clearly see the problems that this name creates, so you should not use it as a table name at all. There are certainly good reasons not to do so.

- *Do use the plural form of the name.* As you know, a table represents a single subject, which can be an object or event. You can take this definition one step further and state that a table represents a *collection* of *similar* objects or events. For example, a sales representative wants to maintain data on *all* of his customers, not just a single one; and a car rental business wants to keep track of *all* its vehicles, not just the blue BMW. Using the plural form of the table name is a sound idea because it makes clear your intention to refer to a collection. Collections, of course, always take the plural ("Boats," not "Boat"). In contrast, words that identify fields are always singular ("Home Phone," not "Home Phones"). Following this rule will make it easy for you to differentiate between table names and field names in any documentation you create for the database. (As you rename your tables, remember that the plural form of some words does not end in *s* or *es*. For instance, the singular and plural forms of "equipment" are exactly the same.)

Use these guidelines to refine each table name on the preliminary table list. When you're finished, this list becomes your final table list and remains so for the duration of the database-design process. Note that the list is "final" only in the sense that you've accounted for all the tables that you identified throughout the entire analysis process. It's very likely that you'll add new tables to this list based on requirements imposed by relationships, data integrity, or other information that you develop.

Indicating the Table Types

As you learned earlier in this chapter, you indicate each table's type on the final table list. Recall that the four classifications you can use to identify the table type are *data, linking, subset,* and *validation.*

When you first create your final table list, every item on the list is a *data* table because it represents a subject that is important to the organization and serves as the primary foundation of the information that the database provides. There will be no *linking* tables or *validation* tables on the list because you have not yet defined relationships or imposed data integrity. (You'll address these issues later in the design process.) The list will not contain *subset* tables because you define them *after* you assign fields to the data tables.

For the moment, designate each table on the final table list as a data table. You'll assign other table types later as the database-design process continues to unfold.

Composing the Table Descriptions

The *table description* is another aspect of a table that you record on the final table list. A table description is crucial because it helps everyone understand why a given table exists and why the organization is concerned with collecting the data for that table. In fact, the description must *explicitly define the table* and *state its importance* to the organization. It doesn't matter whether the definition comes first or you use more than one sentence to convey this information—both the definition and the explanation of the table's importance must be in the description. The table description also provides a means of validating the need for a table—if you are unable to explain why a table is important to the organization, then you need to determine when and how the table was identified and whether it really is necessary at all.

Just as you had guidelines to help define table names, you also have a set of guidelines to help you compose a table description that is focused, concise, unambiguous, and clear.

Guidelines for Composing a Table Description

- *Include a statement that accurately defines the table.* Anyone should easily be able to determine the identity of the table from its description without any confusion or ambiguity. Here's an example of a poor definition for a table named "Suppliers" in a bakery database. As you can see, it's not very accurate.

  > Suppliers—the companies that supply us with ingredients and equipment

What if the bakery receives some of its ingredients from local farmers? The farmers certainly don't qualify as "companies." What type of equipment do these suppliers supply? Cooking utensils? Hand trucks? Delivery racks? Here's a much better definition of suppliers.

> Suppliers—the people and organizations from whom we purchase ingredients and equipment

This statement can be used in the table description as the *table definition*.

- *Include a statement that explains why this table is important to the organization.* A table contains data that is collected, maintained, manipulated, and retrieved by the organization for a *particular* reason. Your statement should explain *why* the data is important to the organization. Keeping in mind that this statement becomes part of your table description, you might be tempted to construct a statement such as this:

> We need the Suppliers table to keep track of the names, addresses, phone numbers, and contact names of all our suppliers.

This statement is inadequate because it emphasizes only *what* needs to be stored in the Suppliers table instead of amplifying *why* the data is important to the business. The next example conveys a better sense of why the information is important.

> Supplier information is vital to the bakery because it allows us to maintain a constant supply of ingredients and ensure that our equipment is always in working order.

This is a more effective statement because it conveys the importance of the data by identifying the services the suppliers provide to the bakery. It also implies that the bakery could run out of ingredients or have a hard time keeping its equipment in top shape without the suppliers' services. This statement now reflects why the table is important to the organization.

- *Compose a description that is clear and succinct.* Avoid the common mistake of restating or rephrasing the table name in your table description, as in this example:

  Student Schedule—the class schedule of the student

Don't be too brief or too verbose. You want to make sure that everyone can identify the table and understand its importance to the organization, but you also want to avoid furnishing too much information. Here's an example of a description that is quite lengthy and provides more information than is necessary:

  Student Schedule—All the classes that a student will attend (including the days, times, and the faculty conducting the class) during the course of the school year. The data in this table is important because it will let the student know the name of the class and when and where he's supposed to be. Also the student will know the duration of the class, as well as the name of the teacher who is teaching the class.

This can be recast more clearly and succinctly as follows:

  Student Schedule—Those classes that the student is scheduled to attend during this school year. The information provided by this table helps the student implement effective time management and enables the school to figure class loads and student loads.

The first sentence in this example provides the definition of the table, and the second sentence states why the table is important to the academic organization.

- *Do not include implementation-specific information in your table description, such as how or where the table is used.* Avoid statements that indicate how you will specifically use this table, or how you will physically access it. This type of information is germane to the database *implementation* process, which is wholly separate from the *database-design* process you're learning in this book. Here is an example of a description containing this type of inappropriate information:

  > Student Schedule—Those classes that the student is scheduled to attend during this school year. This information is used by the registrar and is accessed from the Student Admissions menu in the Registration Program.

- *Do not make the table description for one table dependent upon the table description of another table.* Each table description should be self-explanatory and independent from every other table description; it should be absolutely unnecessary for you to cross-reference one table description against another. This is the type of statement you're trying to avoid:

  > Dependents—the spouse, children, or wards of a given employee. (See description of Employee table for further information.)

  Here's a much better description:

  > Dependents—the spouse, children, or wards of a given employee. This information allows us to make the appropriate tax deductions for the employee, and is necessary for the benefits programs in which the employee is enrolled.

- *Do not use examples in a table description.* An example is a valuable communication tool that helps you convey a particular meaning or concept and is very effective when you use it wisely. But an example depends on supplemental information (and, in some cases, further examples) to complete the idea it's supposed to convey. For instance, just think of the number of examples you would have to use in order to define fully what a table represents. A well-defined description is clear, succinct, and self-explanatory; therefore, it does not require an example to convey its meaning.

Interviewing Users and Management

Now you'll define table descriptions for the tables on the final table list. You'll conduct interviews with both users and management, and enlist their aid in establishing each table's definition and importance to the organization. (This is one of the few times that you'll actually interview both groups together.) Your main objective is to get a consensus on general descriptions for the tables. When your interviews are complete, take your notes and compose final table descriptions, making sure to follow the guidelines outlined above. Then confer with both parties once more to make certain that the descriptions are acceptable and easily understood by all. The final table list is complete when everyone has agreed on the descriptions.

Consider this example: Assume you're developing a database for a local software training organization. Your assistant, John, is conducting an interview with some of the people from the organization. Specifically, he's speaking to Mark from the administration department; Frits, the instructor coordinator; Sara, the vice president of sales; and Caroline, the head of the organization. The dialogue on the next page is a partial transcript of John's interview. John is currently discussing the Students table.

> ❖ **Note** Unlike the interviews you conducted during the analysis and requirements review stages of the design process, you no longer need to involve everyone in the organization. But you will work with a representative group of users and management for the interviews you'll conduct throughout the remainder of the design process.

JOHN: "Okay, let's talk about the Students table. How
            would you describe a 'student'?"

FRITS: "A student is a private individual who comes in for one of
            our classes."

SARA: "That's only partially true. A student can also be an indi-
            vidual that an organization sends to our classes. For ex-
            ample, many of our students come from local banks and
            insurance companies, and those organizations pay for
            the students' tuitions."

MARK: "Yes, you're quite right. I guess we can simply say that a
            student is an individual who comes in for one of our
            classes."

(John makes a note of what Mark just said.)

JOHN: "Good—got it. Does everyone agree with Mark?"

(Everyone nods in approval.)

            "Great. Now, how would you explain to someone why stu-
            dent information is important to this organization?"

CAROLINE: "Without students, we don't have a business!"

FRITS: "If we can keep track of the students who attend our
            classes, we can send them information regarding our
            new classes."

SARA: "Keeping track of this information allows us to keep bill-
            ing and contact information current. This is especially
            true for organizations that send their employees to our
            classes. Training coordinators move on to other posi-
            tions, and we have to know the name of the new person
            we'll be dealing with."

JOHN: "Good point. Does anyone have anything further to add?
            No? Okay, does everyone agree with what has been said
            so far?"

(Everyone once again nods in approval. Because no additional comments are made, John jots down some final notes and moves on to
the next table.)

As you can see, conducting this type of interview is a fairly straightforward affair. Notice how John attempts to get a consensus as he recognizes that no one has anything else to say about the topic at hand. He then makes note of the points that will help him compose the description and moves on to his next topic.

After John has finished conducting the interview, he uses his notes to develop a table description for each table on the final table list. He'll have to interpret and study the participant's responses in order to develop a suitable table description. Based on his examination, John writes the following description:

> Students—those individuals who attend our classes. The information provided by the data in the Students table allows our organization to further promote our classes and supports proper communications with the students.

John then writes a description for each table on the final table list. When he's finished, he'll speak with Mark, Frits, Sara, and Caroline once more to make sure the descriptions are acceptable and that everyone understands them without any difficulty.

Associating Fields with Each Table

In Chapter 3 you learned that tables are composed of fields. During this stage of the database-design process, you'll assign fields to each table on the final table list using fields from your *preliminary field list*.

Assigning fields to a table is a relatively easy process: Determine which fields best represent characteristics of the table's subject and assign them to that table. Repeat this procedure for every table on the final table list. If you think you can use a field or set of fields to represent characteristics of more than one table, then assign them accordingly. You'll discover whether you've assigned the appropriate fields to each table later when you go through the process of refining the table structures.

> ❖ **Note** In the following examples, you'll note that I ask you to use sheets of paper for specific procedures. Using paper helps you avoid the temptation of using an RDBMS program to design your database. I cannot overemphasize or overstate the fact that you should not use the computer at all until the database-design process is complete *unless* you're using some type of *database-design-specific* software, such as Computer-Assisted Software Engineering (CASE) software. By heeding this advice, you will avoid the traps I discuss later in Chapter 14.

Begin this process by taking a sheet of legal paper and laying it in front of you lengthwise from left to right. Write the name of each table (from the final table list) across the top of the paper, starting at the left-hand side; leave enough space between the table names to give you enough room to list lengthy field names underneath them. Repeat this procedure, using as many sheets as you need to account for every table on the list. Continuing with the school database example, Figure 7.10 shows the set of table structures currently under development.

Next, assign fields from the preliminary field list to each table. Determine which fields best describe or define a table's subject and then list these fields underneath the table name. After you've assigned all of the fields you believe to be appropriate for the table, move on to the next table and repeat the process. Continue in this manner until you've assigned fields to all the tables. Figure 7.11 shows a partial set of table structures.

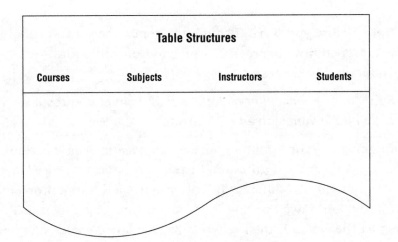

Figure 7.10. *Setting up a sheet for listing table structures.*

	Table Structures		
Classes	**Subjects**	**Instructors**	**Students**
Class Number	Subject Name	Instructor Name	Student Name
Class Name	Subject Description	Instructor SSN	Student SSN
Subject Name	Category	Instructor Address	Student Address
Instructor Name	Credits	Instructor Phone	Student Phone
Room Number		Date Hired	
		Pay Rate	

Figure 7.11. *Listing tables with their associated fields.*

❖ **Note** Before you work through the remainder of the chapter, now is a good time to recall a principle I presented in the Introduction:

Focus on the concept or technique and its intended results, not on the example used to illustrate it.

I bring this to your attention once again because you'll certainly wonder why I created an example in a particular manner. Maybe you've thought of a different or better approach to the problem, and you might have thoroughly valid reasons for using it. But don't let the example mislead you. I've fashioned each example in a specific manner for the sole reason of illustrating the concept or technique at hand. Therefore, study the way that I correct the problems you see in a particular example so that you can use those techniques when you encounter similar problems in your database.

Refining the Fields

Now that you've assigned fields to each table, you'll refine the fields by improving the field names and resolving any structural problems that may exist. Then you'll refine the tables further by establishing that you've assigned the appropriate fields to each table and that the table structures are sound.

Improving the Field Names

As you know, a field represents a characteristic of the subject of the table to which it belongs. You can easily identify the characteristic a field is supposed to represent when that field has an appropriate name. A field name that is ambiguous, vague, or unclear is a sure sign of trouble and suggests that you have not thoroughly identified the purpose of the field.

Earlier in this chapter, you learned a set of guidelines for naming a table. Now you'll learn another set of guidelines that you'll apply to field names. Fortunately, many of them are similar to the guidelines governing table names, so you're already familiar with most of the concepts.

Guidelines for Creating Field Names

- *Create a unique, descriptive name that is meaningful to the entire organization.* A given field name should appear only once in the entire database; the only exception to this rule occurs when the field serves to establish a relationship between two tables. Make certain the name is descriptive enough to convey its meaning accurately to everyone who sees it. (Chapter 10 covers this issue in greater detail.)

- *Create a name that accurately, clearly, and unambiguously identifies the characteristic a field represents.* "Phone Number" is a good example of an inaccurate, ambiguous field name. What kind of phone number does it represent? A home phone? An office phone? A cellular phone? Learn to be specific. If you need to record each of these types of phone numbers, then create "Home Phone," "Work Phone," and "Cellular Phone" fields.

  In Chapter 6, you learned how to resolve generic field names, such as "Address," "City," and "State" by using the *table* name as a prefix for the field name. This produces names such as "*Employee* Address," "*Customer* Address," and "*Supplier* Address." When you have field names such as these, you can abbreviate the prefix (for brevity's sake) by using the first three or four letters of the table name as the revised prefix. This allows you to transform the previous field names into "*Emp*Address," "*Cust*Address," and "*Supp*Address." This technique helps you fulfill not only this guideline, but the previous one as well.

❖ **Note** The degree to which you use prefixes within a table is a matter of style. When a table contains generic field names, some database designers will choose to prefix the generic names only, while others elect to prefix *all* of the field names within the table. Regardless of the prefix method you choose to use, it is very important that you use it consistently throughout the database structure.

I personally prefer to prefix the generic field names only, and I'll follow this preference throughout the remainder of the book.

- *Use the minimum number of words necessary to convey the meaning of the characteristic the field represents.* You want to avoid lengthy field names, but at the same time, you also want to avoid using a single word as a field name if that word is inappropriate. For example, if you're trying to record the date a particular employee joined the organization, "Hired" is too short (and slightly vague) and "Date That the Employee Was Hired" is too long! "Date Hired," however, is a more appropriate name and accurately represents the characteristic the field represents.

- *Do not use acronyms, and use abbreviations judiciously.* Acronyms can be hard to decipher and often lead to misunderstanding. Imagine a field named "CAD_SW." How would you determine what the field represents? On the other hand, you can use abbreviations so long as you use them sparingly and handle them with care. Only use an abbreviation if it supplements or enhances the field name in a positive manner. An abbreviation shouldn't make a field name ambiguous or diminish its meaning.

- *Do not use words that could confuse the meaning of the field name.* A field name that contains redundant words or synonyms can make the name's meaning unclear and subject to misinterpretation. For instance, consider the name "Digital Identification Code Number." "Digital" and "number" are redundant, so you can eliminate either one without diminishing the field name's meaning. Let's assume that you decide to eliminate "digital." You can split the remaining name into two smaller names: "Identification Code" and "Identification Number." These names are often synonymous, and you can easily use either as the final field name. In this situation, just use the name that is most meaningful within the organization.

- *Do not use names that implicitly or explicitly identify more than one characteristic.* These types of names are easy to spot because they typically use the words "and" or "or." Field names that contain a slash (\) or an ampersand (&) are dead giveaways as well. When you encounter a field with a name such as "Area or Location" or "Phone\Fax," identify each characteristic that the name implies, and create a new field for the characteristic. Then test the new field name against these guidelines to ensure that the name is sound.

- *Use the singular form of the name.* A field with a plural name, such as "Skills," implies that it may contain two or more values for a given record, which is not a good idea. (You'll learn more about this later in the chapter.) A field name is singular because it represents a *single* characteristic of the subject of the table to which it belongs. A table name, on the other hand, is plural because it represents a *collection* of similar objects or events. You can distinguish table names from field names quite easily when you use this naming convention.

With these guidelines in mind, review each table and determine whether you can make improvements to any of the field names. When you're finished, you're ready to identify and resolve any problems with the fields. Figure 7.12 shows revisions to the field names of the table structures in Figure 7.11.

Table Structures

Classes	Subjects	Instructors	Students
ClsNumber	SubjName	InstName	StdName
ClsName	SubjDescription	InstSocial Security Number	StdSocial Security Number
SubjName	Category	InstAddress	StdAddress
InstName	Credits	InstPhone	StdPhone
Room Number		Date Hired	
		Pay Rate	

Figure 7.12. *Revised field names.*

In Figure 7.12, "Classes" is shortened to "Cls," "Subjects" is shortened to "Subj," "Instructors" is shortened to "Inst," "Student" is shortened to "Std," and "Social Security Number" replaces "SSN." Remember that abbreviations can be very useful so long as they are meaningful and understood by everyone in the organization. Using proper and appropriate abbreviations will not detract from the meaning of the field name.

❖ **Note** Throughout the remainder of the chapter and the rest of the book, table names within the text appear in all capital letters (such as VENDORS) and field names within the text appear in small capital letters (such as VENDOR ID NUMBER).

Using an Ideal Field to Resolve Anomalies

Although you've carefully identified the fields on your preliminary field list, you may have created a few fields that could prove problematic to the table structure. Poorly defined fields can cause duplicate data and redundant data, and they can be difficult to use. You might find it difficult to determine whether any of the fields in a table is going to cause problems unless you know the warning signs. The best way to identify potentially troublesome fields is to determine whether they comply with the Elements of the Ideal Field. These elements constitute a set of guidelines you can use to create sound field structures and to spot poorly designed fields easily.

Elements of the Ideal Field

- *It represents a distinct characteristic of the subject of the table.* As you know, a table represents a specific subject, which can be an object or event. The ideal field represents a distinct characteristic of that object or event.

- *It contains only a single value.* A field that can potentially store two or more occurrences of the *same* value is known as a *multivalued* field. A multivalued field causes data-redundancy problems (quite obviously) and is difficult to use when you try to edit, delete, or sort the data within it. The ideal field is free of these problems because it contains only a single value.

- *It cannot be deconstructed into smaller components.* A field that can potentially store two or more *distinct* items within a value is known as a *multipart* (or composite) field. Like the multivalued field, this type of field causes problems when you try to edit, delete, or sort the data within it. These problems don't occur with an ideal field because it represents a single, distinct characteristic of the subject of the table to which it belongs. (You'll learn more about multivalued and multipart fields in just a moment.)

- *It does not contain a calculated or concatenated value.* The values of the fields in a table should be mutually independent; a particular field should not have to depend on the values of other fields for its own value. A calculated field, however, *does* depend on the values of other fields for its own value, and therein lies the problem. The calculated field's value *is not updated* when the value of any field participating in the calculation changes. It then becomes the responsibility (and an undesirable burden) of the user or the database application program to update the calculated field when this type of change takes place. This is precisely why you deal with calculated fields separately.

- *It is unique within the entire database structure.* The only duplicate fields that appear in a properly designed database are those that establish relationships between tables. If duplicate fields other than these exist in a table, it is very likely that the table will accumulate unnecessary redundant data and that the data within the duplicate fields will inevitably become inconsistent.

> ❖ **Note** Remember that you're dealing strictly with the *logical* database structure at this point. You might have cause to duplicate specific fields when you *physically* implement the database in an RDBMS program. During that process, however, you're making a conscious decision to duplicate the fields, and you're prepared to deal with the consequences of that decision.

- *It retains a majority of its properties when it appears in more than one table.* A field that establishes a relationship between two tables is a structural component of each table. A majority of the field's properties remain constant in each occurrence of the field. (Chapters 9 and 10 cover this matter in greater detail.)

Although you now know the specific elements of an ideal field, you'll still find it difficult in many instances to identify problematic fields just by looking at their names. Figure 7.13 shows a table structure that helps to illustrate this point. Take a moment and try to determine whether each field complies with the Elements of the Ideal Field or needs to be modified.

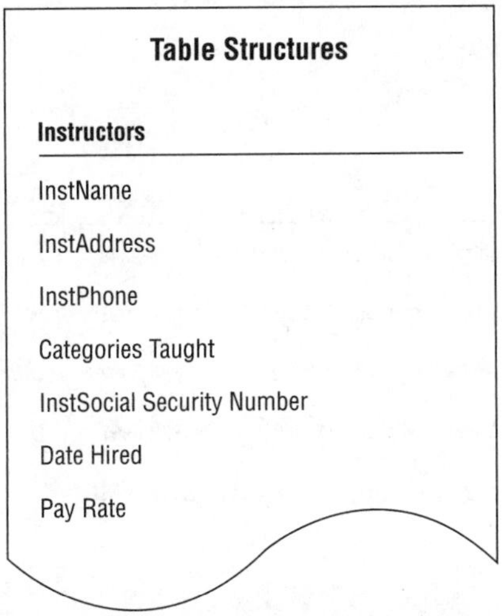

Table Structures

Instructors

InstName

InstAddress

InstPhone

Categories Taught

InstSocial Security Number

Date Hired

Pay Rate

Figure 7.13. *A table containing fields with questionable structures.*

Each field on the list seems to conform to the Elements of the Ideal Field. Examine the list carefully, however, and you'll see that some fields don't really comply with the second and third elements. Three fields have anomalies that will cause problems unless you resolve them: INSTNAME, INSTADDRESS, and CATEGORIES TAUGHT. If you doubt this assertion, you can test it by "loading" the table with sample data. This will quickly reveal anomalies, if any exist, and is the best way to confirm whether a field complies with all of the Elements of the Ideal Field.

You don't have to create a table physically to perform this test. Take a sheet of legal paper and lay it in front of you lengthwise from left to right.

Write the name of each field across the top of the paper, starting from the left-hand side; leave enough space between the field names to allow room for the values you're going to place underneath them. Then enter records into the table by filling in each field with some sample data; be sure the sample data represents the data you're actually going to enter into the database. You need only a few records for the test to work properly. Your sheet of paper should look similar to the one in Figure 7.14.

Instructors

InstName	InstAddress	InstPhone	Categories Taught	<< other fields >>
Kendra Bonnicksen	3131 Mockingbird Lane, Seattle, WA 98157	363-9948	DTP, SS, WP	......
Timothy Ennis	7402 Kingman Drive, Redmond, WA 98115	527-4992	WP, DB, OS	......
Shannon McLain	4141 Lake City Way, Seattle, WA 98136	336-5992	DB, SS	......
Estela Pundt	970 Phoenix Avenue, Bellevue, WA 98046	322-6992	DTP, WP, PG	......

Figure 7.14. *Testing a table with sample data.*

❖ **Note** As I mentioned in Chapter 3, I show only those fields that are most relevant to the discussion at hand and use *<<other fields>>* to represent fields that are inessential to the example.

Now you can easily identify which fields are going to be troublesome unless they are resolved. As you can see, INSTNAME and INSTADDRESS are both multipart fields, and CATEGORIES TAUGHT is a multivalued field. You must resolve these fields before you can refine the table structure.

Resolving Multipart Fields

Working with a multipart field is difficult because its value contains two or more *distinct* items. It's hard to retrieve information from a multipart field, and it's hard to sort or group the records in the table by the field's value. The INSTADDRESS field in Figure 7.14 illustrates these difficulties; you'd certainly have a problem retrieving information for the city of Seattle or sorting information by zip code.

You resolve a multipart field by identifying the distinct items within the field's value and treating each item as an individual field. Accomplish this task by asking yourself a simple question: "What specific items does this field's value represent?" Once you've answered the question and identified the items (as best you can), transform each item into a new field.

In Figure 7.14, the value of the field INSTNAME represents two items: the first name and the last name of an instructor. You resolve this field by creating a new INSTFIRST NAME field and a new INSTLAST NAME field. The value of INSTADDRESS represents four items: the street address, city, state, and zip code of an instructor. You transform these items into fields as well; they will appear in the table as INSTSTREET ADDRESS, INSTCITY, INSTSTATE, and INSTZIPCODE. Figure 7.15 shows the newly revised INSTRUCTORS table.

Instructors

InstFirst Name	InstLast Name	InstStreet Address	InstCity	InstState	InstZipcode	InstPhone	Categories Taught	<< other fields >>
Kendra	Bonnicksen	3131 Mockingbird Lane	Seattle	WA	98157	363-9948	DTP, SS, WP	......
Timothy	Ennis	7402 Kingman Drive	Redmond	WA	98115	527-4992	WP, DB, OS	......
Shannon	McLain	4141 Lake City Way	Seattle	WA	98136	336-5992	DB, SS	......
Estela	Pundt	970 Phoenix Avenue	Bellevue	WA	98046	322-6992	DTP, WP, PG	......

Figure 7.15. *Resolving the multipart fields in the INSTRUCTORS table.*

Some multipart fields are hard to recognize. Take a look at the INSTRU-MENTS table in Figure 7.16. At first glance, the table doesn't seem to contain multipart fields. When you examine the data in the table more closely, however, you'll see that INSTRUMENT ID is actually a multipart field. This field's value represents two distinct items: the category to which the instrument belongs—AMP (amplifier), GUIT (guitar), MFX (multieffects unit), SFX (single-effect unit)—and the instrument's identi-fication number. Clearly, you should deconstruct INSTRUMENT ID into two smaller fields in accordance with the third element of an ideal field. Imagine how difficult it would be for you to update the field's value if the MFX category changed to MFU if you don't do this. You would have to write programming code to parse the value, test for the existence of MFX, and then replace it with MFU if it existed within the parsed value. It's not so much that you *can't* do this, but you would definitely be working harder than necessary, and you shouldn't have to go through this at all if you have a properly designed database.

GUIT = Category ("Guitar")
2201 = Identification Number

Instruments

Instrument ID	Manufacturer	Instrument Description	<< other fields >>
GUIT2201	Fender	Stratocaster	......
MFX3349	Zoom	Player 2100 Multieffects	......
AMP1001	Marshall	JCM 2000 Tube Super Lead	......
AMP5590	Crate	VC60 Pro Tube Amp	......
SFX2227	Dunlop	Cry Baby Wah-Wah	......
AMP2766	Fender	Twin Reverb Reissue	......

Figure 7.16. *An example of a "hidden" multipart field.*

Resolving Multivalued Fields

As you know, a multivalued field can potentially store two or more oc-currences of the *same* value. Fortunately, you'll recognize a multivalued field when you see one. The field's name is often plural and its value al-most invariably contains a number of commas, which serve to separate the various occurrences that exist within the value itself.

Resolving multipart fields is not very hard at all, but resolving multival-ued fields can be a little more difficult and will take some work. A mul-tivalued field has the same fundamental set of problems as a multipart field, as the CATEGORIES TAUGHT field in Figure 7.17 clearly illustrates. For example, you'll have difficultly retrieving information for everyone who teaches a specific category (such as WP), you can't sort the data in any meaningful fashion, and, most important, you don't have room to enter more than four categories. What happens when one or more in-structors teach *five* categories? The only option you'll have is to make the field larger every time you need to enter more values than it will currently allow.

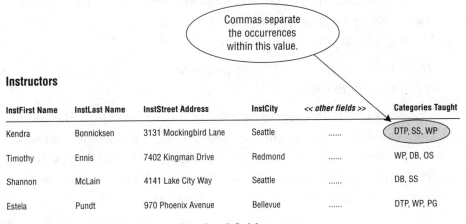

Figure 7.17. *Identifying a multivalued field.*

So how would you resolve this multivalued field? Your first thought may be to create a new field for each value, thus "flattening" the multivalued field into several single-valued fields. Figure 7.18 shows what will happen if you follow through with this idea.

Instructors

InstFirst Name	InstLast Name	InstStreet Address	InstCity	<< *other fields* >>	Category Taught 1	Category Taught 2	Category Taught 3
Kendra	Bonnicksen	3131 Mockingbird Lane	Seattle	......	DTP	SS	WP
Timothy	Ennis	7402 Kingman Drive	Redmond	......	WP	DB	OS
Shannon	McLain	4141 Lake City Way	Seattle	......	DB	SS	
Estela	Pundt	970 Phoenix Avenue	Bellevue	......	DTP	WP	PG

Figure 7.18. *The result of "flattening" the* Categories Taught *field.*

Unfortunately, this is not much of an improvement at all. There are three specific problems that arise from this type of structure:

1. *Retrieving category information will be tedious at best.* A user attempting to find all instructors who teach the WP category must be sure to search for this value within each of the category fields—there is no guarantee that WP is consistently stored in the same field. Failure to do so means that the user runs the risk of overlooking a qualified instructor.

2. *There is no way for the RDBMS program to sort the category data in a meaningful fashion.*

3. *This structure is inherently volatile.* In its current state, the table unnecessarily restricts the number of categories an instructor can teach; you must create additional category fields when you have instructors who teach more than three categories. Adding more category fields just compounds the first two problems.

Realizing that flattening the Categories Taught field won't solve your problem, your next thought is to bring the field into compliance with the second element of an ideal field and declare that it will contain only a single value. Although this is a good impulse and a step in the right direction, it will not resolve the matter completely because it will introduce yet another problem: data redundancy. Figure 7.19 illustrates what happens when you follow through with this particular idea. Note that there is now a single value in the CATEGORIES TAUGHT field for each record in the table.

Instructors

InstFirst Name	InstLast Name	InstStreet Address	InstCity	InstState	InstZipcode	InstPhone	Categories Taught
Kendra	Bonnicksen	3131 Mockingbird Lane	Seattle	WA	98157	363-9948	DTP
Kendra	Bonnicksen	3131 Mockingbird Lane	Seattle	WA	98157	363-9948	SS
Kendra	Bonnicksen	3131 Mockingbird Lane	Seattle	WA	98157	363-9948	WP
Timothy	Ennis	7402 Kingman Drive	Redmond	WA	98115	527-4992	WP
Timothy	Ennis	7402 Kingman Drive	Redmond	WA	98115	527-4992	DB
Timothy	Ennis	7402 Kingman Drive	Redmond	WA	98115	527-4992	OS
Shannon	McLain	4141 Lake City Way	Seattle	WA	98136	336-5992	DB
Shannon	McLain	4141 Lake City Way	Seattle	WA	98136	336-5992	SS
Estela	Pundt	970 Phoenix Avenus	Bellevue	WA	98046	322-6992	DTP
Estela	Pundt	970 Phoenix Avenus	Bellevue	WA	98046	322-6992	WP
Estela	Pundt	970 Phoenix Avenus	Bellevue	WA	98046	322-6992	PG

Figure 7.19. *The result of bringing* CATEGORIES TAUGHT *into compliance with the second element of an ideal field.*

The values in CATEGORIES TAUGHT cause redundant data because you must duplicate a given instructor record *for each category* that the instructor teaches. This redundancy is obviously unacceptable, so you'll have to resolve this problem in some other manner.

You can avoid this situation entirely by using these steps to resolve a multivalued field:

1. Remove the field from the table and use it as the basis for a new table. If necessary, rename the field in accordance with the field name guidelines that you learned earlier in this chapter.

2. Use a field (or set of fields) from the *original* table to relate the original table to the new table; try to select fields that represent the subject of the table as closely as possible. The field(s) you choose will appear in both tables. (You'll learn more about relating tables in Chapter 10.)

3. Assign an appropriate name, type, and description to the new table and add it to the final table list.

These steps form a generic procedure that you can use to resolve any multivalued field you encounter in a table. Now, apply these steps to the CATEGORIES TAUGHT field.

1. Remove the field from the INSTRUCTORS table and use it as the basis of a new table. Because this will now be a *single*-valued field, rename the field CATEGORY TAUGHT.

2. Use INSTFIRST NAME and INSTLAST NAME as the connecting fields that will relate the INSTRUCTORS table to the new table, and add them to the structure of the new table.

3. Give the new table a proper name, compose a suitable description, and add the table to the final table list. (Indicate the table's type as "Data.") Here's one possible name and description you might use for the new table.

    Instructor Categories—the categories of software programs that an instructor is qualified to teach. The information this table provides allows us to make certain that there is an adequate number of instructors for each software category.

Figure 7.20 shows the revised INSTRUCTORS table and the new INSTRUCTOR CATEGORIES table.

Note that the new INSTRUCTOR CATEGORIES table is free from the problems typically associated with multivalued fields because CATEGORY

Instructors

InstFirst Name	InstLast Name	InstStreet Address	InstCity	InstState	InstZipcode	InstPhone
Kendra	Bonnicksen	3131 Mockingbird Lane	Seattle	WA	98157	363-9948
Timothy	Ennis	7402 Kingman Drive	Redmond	WA	98115	527-4992
Shannon	McLain	4141 Lake City Way	Seattle	WA	98136	336-5992
Estela	Pundt	970 Phoenix Avenue	Bellevue	WA	98046	322-6992

Instructor Categories

InstFirst Name	InstLast Name	Category Taught
Kendra	Bonnicksen	DTP
Kendra	Bonnicksen	SS
Kendra	Bonnicksen	WP
Timothy	Ennis	WP
Timothy	Ennis	DB
Timothy	Ennis	OS
Shannon	McLain	DB
Shannon	McLain	SS

Figure 7.20. *Resolving the multivalued field in the INSTRUCTORS table.*

TAUGHT is a *single-value* field. You can easily retrieve information for a particular instructor or category, and you can sort the records in a meaningful manner. Also note that the INSTFIRST NAME and INSTLAST NAME fields retain their names in the new table, making them compliant with the fifth element of an ideal field.

Although the new table contains redundant data, the redundancy is acceptable because it is *minimal*. It's a fact of life that a relational database will always contain some amount of redundant data. Your goal as the database architect is to make certain that it has only an *absolute minimum* amount of redundant data.

Figure 7.21 shows a version of the INSTRUCTORS table that contains *three* multivalued fields:

CATEGORIES TAUGHT—This indicates the categories of classes that an instructor can teach.

MAXIMUM LEVEL TAUGHT—This indicates the maximum skill level that the instructor can teach for a given category.

LANGUAGES SPOKEN—This indicates the foreign languages that an instructor can speak.

Instructors

InstFirst Name	InstLast Name	Campus Phone	Categories Taught	Maximum Level Taught	Languages Spoken
Kendra	Bonnicksen	363-9948	DTP, OS, SS, WP	Intermediate, Basic, Advanced, Basic	French, Spanish
Timothy	Ennis	527-4992	DB, OS, UT, WP	Intermediate, Basic, Basic, Advanced	German, Spanish
Shannon	McLain	336-5992	DB, PG, SS	Advanced, Intermediate, Intermediate	French, German
Estela	Pundt	322-6992	DTP, PG, WP	Basic, Intermediate, Basic	French, Italian, Spanish

Figure 7.21. *A version of the INSTRUCTORS table containing three multivalued fields.*

Your task here seems relatively clear—you're going to use the procedure you've just learned to resolve these multivalued fields. You then notice one small, relatively obscure problem: There is a distinct one-to-one association between values in CATEGORIES TAUGHT and the values in MAXIMUM LEVEL TAUGHT for any given record. You probably wouldn't have noticed this anomaly had you not carefully examined the sample data within these fields. Don't worry; you'll still use the same procedure, but with one minor modification.

You'll occasionally encounter a situation such as this, where some given field (whether single- or multivalued) depends on a particular multivalued field. You can easily fix this problem by including the dependent field in the structure of the new table you build to resolve the multivalued field. Figure 7.22 shows the results of consolidating this technique with the previous one to resolve CATEGORIES TAUGHT. (It shows the resolution of LANGUAGES SPOKEN as well.)

Instructors

InstFirst Name	InstLast Name	Campus Phone
Kendra	Bonnicksen	363-9948
Timothy	Ennis	527-4992
Shannon	McLain	336-5992
Estela	Pundt	322-6992

Instructor Categories

InstFirst Name	InstLast Name	Category Taught	Maximum Level
Kendra	Bonnicksen	DTP	Intermediate
Kendra	Bonnicksen	OS	Advanced
Kendra	Bonnicksen	SS	Basic
Kendra	Bonnicksen	WP	Advanced
Timothy	Ennis	DB	Intermediate
Timothy	Ennis	OS	Basic
Timothy	Ennis	UT	Basic
Timothy	Ennis	WP	Advanced

Instructor Languages

InstFirst Name	InstLast Name	Language Spoken
Kendra	Bonnicksen	French
Kendra	Bonnicksen	Spanish
Timothy	Ennis	German
Timothy	Ennis	Spanish
Shannon	McLain	French
Shannon	McLain	German
Estela	Pundt	French
Estela	Pundt	Italian
Estela	Pundt	Spanish

Figure 7.22. *Resolving the multipart fields in the INSTRUCTORS table.*

The redundancy in the new tables is acceptable because, once again, it is minimal. In Chapter 10, you'll learn how to reduce this type of redundancy even further by relating the tables with primary keys and foreign keys.

Refining the Table Structures

Now that you've refined the fields and made certain that each field is sound, you can begin the process of refining the table structures. Your objective in this phase of the design process is to make sure that you've assigned the appropriate fields to each table and that you've properly defined each table's structure. This process will also reveal whether the tables have anomalies that you need to resolve.

A Word About Redundant Data and Duplicate Fields

You've seen the term *redundant data* used quite often in this chapter. Redundant data was characterized as being unacceptable in many cases, but appropriate in others. In order for you to better understand how to determine when redundant data is acceptable, a definition of the term is in order.

Redundant data is a value that is repeated in a field as a result of the field's participation in relating two tables or as a result of some field or table anomaly. In the first instance, the redundant data is appropriate; by definition, a field used to relate one table to another will contain redundant data. (You'll learn more about this in Chapter 10.) Redundant data is entirely unacceptable in the second instance, however, because it poses problems with data consistency and data integrity; therefore, you should always strive to keep redundant data to an absolute minimum.

A *duplicate field* is a field that appears in two or more tables for any of these reasons:

- It is used to relate a set of tables together.

- It indicates multiple occurrences of a particular type of value.

- There is a perceived need for supplemental information.

The only instance in which a duplicate field is necessary is when it serves to establish a relationship between two tables; it provides the sole means of associating records in the first table with records in the second table. Duplicate fields are unnecessary in all other cases, and you should avoid them because they introduce needless, redundant data.

As you refine each table structure, you'll assess whether to retain a given duplicate field in the table. If the reason for its existence in the table is valid, then you'll keep it; otherwise, you'll remove it. You'll learn how to deal effectively with both redundant data and unnecessary duplicate fields in the following sections.

Using an Ideal Table to Refine Table Structures

Despite your efforts to refine the fields in a table, the table structure itself may contain anomalies that can produce unnecessary redundant data and make it difficult to work with the data in the table. You can identify a potentially problematic table structure by determining whether it complies with the Elements of the Ideal Table. These elements constitute a set of guidelines you can use to create sound table structures and to spot poorly designed tables easily.

Elements of the Ideal Table

- *It represents a single subject, which can be an object or event.* Yes, I know, I've said this a number of times already. The fact of the matter is that I can't overemphasize this point. As long as you guarantee that each of your tables represents a single subject, you greatly reduce the risk of potential data-integrity problems. This element validates the work you've done during the analysis and interview stages of the database-design process, as well as the work you've just recently performed.

- *It has a primary key.* This is important for two reasons: It uniquely identifies each record within a table, and it plays a key role (no pun intended) in establishing table relationships. Additionally, it has specific characteristics that help to implement and enforce various levels of data integrity. If you fail to assign a primary key to each table, you will eventually have data-integrity problems. Chapter 8 covers primary keys in greater detail.

- *It does not contain multipart or multivalued fields.* Theoretically, you should have resolved these issues when you refined the field structures. Nevertheless, it's still a good idea to review the fields one last time to ensure that you've completely removed each and every one of them.

- *It does not contain calculated fields.* Although you might believe that your current table structures are free of calculated fields, you may have accidentally overlooked one or two calculated fields during the field refinement process. This is a good time to review the table structures once more and make certain you remove those calculated fields you may have missed.

- *It does not contain unnecessary duplicate fields.* (Note that this guideline does not apply to fields used to relate a set of tables together, such as those used in the example in Figure 7.22.) One of the hallmarks of a poorly designed table is the inclusion of duplicate fields from other tables. You might feel compelled to add duplicate fields to a table for one of two reasons: to provide reference information or to indicate multiple occurrences of a particular type of value. Duplicate fields such as these raise various difficulties when you work with the data or attempt to retrieve information from the table.

- *It contains only an absolute minimum amount of redundant data.* Remember that a relational database will never be completely free of redundant data. But you can—and should—make certain that each table contains as little redundant data as possible.

Resolving Unnecessary Duplicate Fields

Before you make final modifications to the table structures, you must first remove all unnecessary duplicate fields from the database. You can then refine the tables so that they comply with the Elements of the Ideal Table.

Duplicate fields that serve to provide reference information (also known as *reference fields*) are unnecessary and easy to resolve—you just remove them from the table. Unfortunately, many people believe that a table must contain every field that will appear in the reports they generate from it, so they introduce various duplicate fields into the table as they deem necessary. They assume that the table will then be able to provide all the requisite information for their reports. But they are mistaken, and their action is both unwise and undesirable. Tables containing reference fields exhibit poor design and will have a number of problems, many of which will become increasingly clear as the database-design process unfolds. Reference fields force the user or database application program to ensure that the values in all occurrences of the field are mutually consistent, a process that carries a high risk of error. Figure 7.23 shows an example of a table containing reference fields.

The MANPHONE and WEB SITE fields in the INSTRUMENTS table are reference fields and, by definition, are actually unnecessary duplicate fields. You certainly don't need to include them in this table because they're already part of the MANUFACTURERS table structure; therefore, you can remove them from the INSTRUMENTS table in order to resolve the unnecessary duplication problem. (MANUFACTURER is not a reference field because it currently relates the INSTRUMENTS table to the MANUFACTURERS table.) You'll learn later in Chapter 12 that you can work with fields from the INSTRUMENTS table *and* the MANUFACTURERS table at the same time by combining them within a *view* (virtual table). You can then use this view as the basis for compiling any reports you require.

Instruments

Instrument ID	Instrument Description	Category	Price	Manufacturer	ManPhone	Web Site
2201	Stratocaster	Guitar	$ 799.99	Fender Musical Instruments	596-9690	www.fender.com
3349	Player 2100 Multi-Effects	Multi-Effect Unit	$ 174.99	Samson Technologies Corp.	364-2244	www.samsontech.com
1001	JCM 2000 Tube Super Lead	Amplifier	$ 549.99	Mesa/Boogie	778-6565	www.mesaboogie.com
5590	Crate VC60 Pro Tube Amp	Amplifier	$ 399.99	St. Louis Music, Inc.	738-7563	www.crateamps.com
2227	Cry Baby Wah-Wah	Single-Effect Unit	$ 169.99	Dunlop Manufacturing, Inc.	745-2722	www.jimdunlop.com
2766	Twin Reverb Reissue	Amplifier	$ 1,224.99	Fender Musical Instruments	596-9690	www.fender.com

These fields duplicate the MANPHONE and WEB SITE fields in the MANUFACTURERS table.

Manufacturers

Manufacturer	ManStreet Address	ManCity	ManState	ManZipcode	ManPhone	Web Site
Dunlop Manufacturing, Inc.	PO Box 846	Benicia	CA	94510	745-2722	www.jimdunlop.com
Fender Musical Instruments	8860 E. Chaparral Road	Scottsdale	AZ	85250	596-9690	www.fender.com
Mesa/Boogie	1317 Ross Street	Petaluma	CA	94954	778-6565	www.mesaboogie.com
Samson Technologies Corp.	PO Box 9031	Syosset	NY	11791	364-2244	www.samsontech.com
St. Louis Music, Inc.	1400 Ferguson Avenue	St. Louis	MO	63133	738-7563	www.crateamps.com

Figure 7.23. *Example of a table containing reference fields.*

Duplicate fields that serve to indicate multiple occurrences of the same type of value are unnecessary as well. For example, take a look at the version of the STUDENTS table presented in Figure 7.24.

Students

StdFirst Name	StdLast Name	StdStreet Address	<< other fields >>	Instrument 1	Instrument 2	Instrument 3
Scott	Barker	2904 Madison Ave	......	Guitar	Tenor Sax	
Michael	Chow	7410 Taxco Drive	......	Tenor Sax	Clarinet	Electric Piano
Debbie	McGuire	332 158th Ave SE	......	Drum Set	Bass Guitar	
Angie	Thomson	970 Pine Blvd	......	Guitar	Electric Piano	Snare Drum

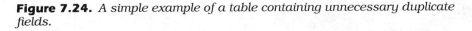

These duplicate fields represent three occurrences of the same type of value.

Figure 7.24. *A simple example of a table containing unnecessary duplicate fields.*

INSTRUMENT 1, INSTRUMENT 2, and INSTRUMENT 3 are duplicate fields that represent multiple occurrences of the *same type* of value. Their purpose in the table is to enable the music department to keep track of the instruments checked out by a given student. Aside from the difficulties these fields pose in retrieving information about a particular instrument, the fields also limit the number of instruments a student can check out. What happens if several students want to check out more than three instruments?

Does this type of field structure look strangely familiar? It should! It's similar to the one back in Figure 7.18. As you've probably already guessed, it's nothing more than a flattened multivalued field. Mind you, the person who created this table probably didn't have a multivalued field in mind (and neither do most folks who create fields such as these), but that is what it truly is.

You already know how to deal with these unnecessary duplicate fields because you know how to resolve multivalued fields. You can easily fix the STUDENTS table by first visualizing the INSTRUMENT 1, INSTRUMENT 2, and INSTRUMENT 3 fields as a singular multivalued field, and then resolving it as you would any multivalued field. Figure 7.25 illustrates this process. The shaded version of the STUDENTS table shows how you visualize the instrument fields as a singular multivalued field. You then resolve the multivalued field by applying the three-step process you learned earlier, which yields the revised STUDENTS table and the new STUDENT INSTRUMENTS table. When you're finished, you'll be able to enter any number of instruments for a particular student. It will then be quite easy for you to retrieve information such as the names of the students who have checked out a guitar, a list of the instruments that are currently checked out by a particular student, and the number of students who have checked out an electric piano.

Students

StdFirst Name	StdLast Name	StdStreet Address	<< other fields >>	Instruments
Scott	Barker	2904 Madison Ave	......	Guitar, Tenor Sax
Michael	Chow	7410 Taxco Drive	......	Tenor Sax, Clarinet, Electric Piano
Debbie	McGuire	332 158th Ave SE	......	Drum Set, Bass Guitar
Angie	Thomson	970 Pine Blvd	......	Guitar, Electric Piano, Snare Drum

Students

StdFirst Name	StdLast Name	StdStreet Address	<< other fields >>
Scott	Barker	2904 Madison Ave	......
Michael	Chow	7410 Taxco Drive	......
Debbie	McGuire	332 158th Ave SE	......
Angie	Thomson	970 Pine Blvd	......

Student Instruments

StudFirst Name	StudLast Name	Instrument
Scott	Barker	Guitar
Scott	Barker	Tenor Sax
Michael	Chow	Tenor Sax
Michael	Chow	Clarinet
Michael	Chow	Electric Piano
Debbie	McGuire	Drum Set
Debbie	McGuire	Bass Guitar

Figure 7.25. *Resolving a simple set of unnecessary duplicate fields.*

In some instances, a table can contain two or more *sets* of duplicate fields that represent multiple occurrences of the same type of value. Figure 7.26 shows a slightly different version of the STUDENTS table shown in Figure 7.24; this version contains *two* sets of duplicate fields. You may be thinking at this very moment, "Why is he saying there are *two* sets of duplicate fields when I clearly see *three*?" Contrary to what you may think, INSTRUMENT 1/CHECKOUT DATE 1, for example, does not constitute a set of duplicate fields. Quite the opposite—INSTRUMENT 1/INSTRUMENT 2/INSTRUMENT 3 constitute the first set of duplicate fields, and CHECKOUT DATE 1/CHECKOUT DATE 2/CHECKOUT DATE 3 constitute the second set of duplicate fields.

Students

StdFirst Name	StdLast Name	<< *other fields* >>	Instrument 1	Checkout Date 1	Instrument 2	Checkout Date 2	Instrument 3	Checkout Date 3
Scott	Barker	......	Guitar	09/26/01	Tenor Sax	09/28/01		
Michael	Chow	......	Tenor Sax	09/26/01	Clarinet	10/03/01	Electric Piano	10/16/01
Debbie	McGuire	......	Drum Set	11/14/01	Bass Guitar	11/20/01		
Angie	Thomson	......	Guitar	11/14/01	Electric Piano	11/14/01	Snare Drum	12/05/01

Figure 7.26. *Example of a table with multiple sets of duplicate fields.*

You've probably realized that these two sets of duplicate fields are actually two flattened multivalued fields and that you can resolve them in the same manner as in the previous example. The only other issue that you must be concerned with is the distinct one-to-one association between an instrument and a checkout date. This won't be a problem, however, because you've dealt with this type of scenario before. If you visualize one multivalued field called INSTRUMENTS and another called CHECKOUT DATE, you'll see that the overall table structure is quite similar to the one in Figure 7.21. (There's a one-to-one association between the CATEGORIES TAUGHT and MAXIMUM LEVEL TAUGHT fields.)

Figure 7.27 illustrates how you can fix this table. As before, the shaded version of the STUDENTS table shows how you visualize the instrument and checkout date fields as singular multivalued fields. You then resolve the multivalued fields by applying the three-step process you learned earlier, yielding the revised STUDENTS table and the new STUDENT INSTRUMENTS table.

Students

StdFirst Name	StdLast Name	<< other fields >>	Instruments	Checkout Dates
Scott	Barker	......	Guitar, Tenor Sax	09/26/01, 09/28/01
Michael	Chow	......	Tenor Sax, Clarinet, Electric Piano	09/28/01, 10/03/01, 10/16/01
Debbie	McGuire	......	Drum Set, Bass Guitar	11/14/01, 11/20/01
Angie	Thomson	......	Guitar, Electric Piano, Snare Durm	11/14/01, 11/14/01, 12/05/01

Students

StdFirst Name	StdLast Name	StdStreet Address	<< other fields >>
Scott	Barker	2904 Madison Ave	......
Michael	Chow	7410 Taxco Drive	......
Debbie	McGuire	332 158th Ave SE	......
Angie	Thomson	970 Pine Blvd	......

Student Instruments

StudFirst Name	StudLast Name	Instrument	Checkout Date
Scott	Barker	Guitar	09/26/01
Scott	Barker	Tenor Sax	09/28/01
Michael	Chow	Tenor Sax	09/28/01
Michael	Chow	Clarinet	10/03/01
Michael	Chow	Electric Piano	10/16/01
Debbie	McGuire	Drum Set	11/14/01
Debbie	McGuire	Bass Guitar	11/20/01

Figure 7.27. *Resolving the multiple sets of duplicate fields in the STUDENTS table.*

Now that you're familiar with the Elements of the Ideal Table, review your table structures and refine them as necessary. When you're in doubt about a particular table, sketch its structure on a piece of paper and load it with sample data. You'll then be able to resolve the anomalies revealed by the data.

Establishing Subset Tables

As you refine the structures of your tables, you may find that some of the fields in a particular table do not always contain values. This situation will not affect your ability to retrieve information from the table, but it can indicate that the table might need further refinement. Consider the structure of the INVENTORY table in Figure 7.28.

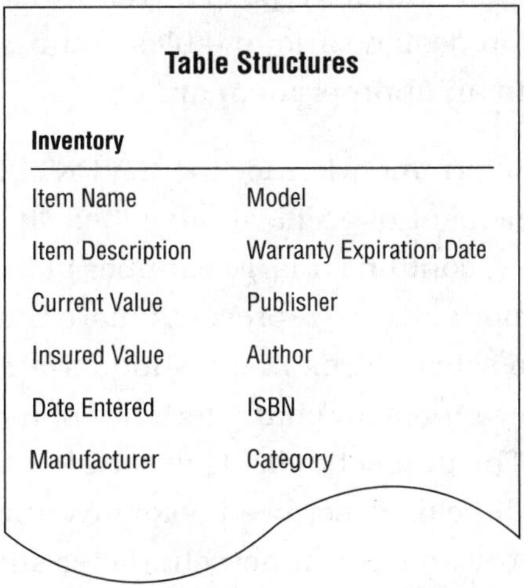

Table Structures

Inventory

Item Name	Model
Item Description	Warranty Expiration Date
Current Value	Publisher
Insured Value	Author
Date Entered	ISBN
Manufacturer	Category

Figure 7.28. *Structure of an office inventory table.*

In this scenario, the table contains data about various items in a person's office, such as office furniture, office equipment (computers, faxes, and so forth), and books. It's inevitable that the values of several fields in many of the records will be blank. For example, a book will not have a MANUFACTURER, MODEL, or WARRANTY EXPIRATION DATE, and a fax machine will not have an AUTHOR, PUBLISHER, ISBN, or CATEGORY. This doesn't pose a problem from a *physical* viewpoint (limited hard-disk space isn't the critical issue it was in years past), but it can pose a *perceptual* problem. Users (and management, for that matter) get fairly nervous when they see a lot of blank values in a table. Is the data missing? Did someone forget to make entries into these fields? Has someone mistakenly deleted the data? Did the computer accidentally destroy the original values? (Yes, the urban myth, "The computer did it!" still lives on.) The more important question is this: If you were adhering to the Elements of the Ideal Table as you were creating this table, how did you arrive at this particular structure?

Fortunately, this is just another type of structural anomaly that occasionally occurs as you design various tables. Your task now is to learn how to deal with it in an appropriate manner.

The first step is to determine whether the INVENTORY table truly complies with the first element of an ideal table (i.e., "It represents a single subject"). A table that contains a large number of blank values in its fields usually—but not always—represents more than one subject. Think about the two sets of fields in question for a moment, and you'll soon realize that they represent characteristics of *two distinct aspects* of the table's subject. The first set of fields describes equipment inventory, and the second set of fields describes books inventory; furthermore, both types of inventory share common characteristics, such as ITEM NAME, ITEM DESCRIPTION, and CURRENT VALUE. In essence, "Equipment" and "Books" are subjects that are dependent upon the INVENTORY table for their very existence; neither describes a completely distinct object or event. As a result, they are *subordinate subjects*, and you'll create a *subset* table for each of them.

Just as a data table represents a distinct subject, a subset table represents a subordinate subject of a particular data table. The subset table contains fields that are germane to the subordinate subject it represents, and it also includes a field (or fields) from the data table that serves to relate the data table to the subset table. It's important to note that a subset table *does not* contain fields that represent characteristics common to both it and the data table; these fields must remain in the data table.

Now that you've determined that the INVENTORY table describes three subjects (it doesn't matter that two of them are subordinate subjects), you must bring it into compliance with the first element of an ideal table by removing the fields in question. You then use the fields as the basis for two new subset tables, one for each subordinate subject. Here are the steps you follow to accomplish these tasks:

1. Use the MANUFACTURER, MODEL, and WARRANTY EXPIRATION DATE fields to create a new subset table called EQUIPMENT.

2. Use the PUBLISHER, AUTHOR, ISBN, and CATEGORY fields to create a new subset table called BOOKS.

3. Add ITEM NAME to both tables; this field will relate each subset table to the data table.

4. Compose a suitable description for both subset tables and add them to the final table list. Indicate each table's type as "Subset."

Figure 7.29 shows the new subset table structures.

Take a moment to review your table structures once more. You may discover that you've created subset tables without knowing it. Tables that have *almost* identical structures are commonly subset tables; there are usually only a few unique fields that distinguish one table from the other. For example, consider the two partial table structures in Figure 7.30. Each table represents a distinct aspect of the *same* subject.

Both of these tables represent employees, but each represents a *specific type* of employee. Notice, however, that there are generic fields common

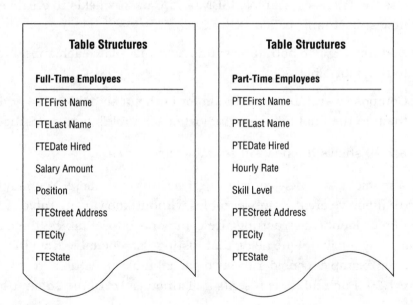

Table Structures

Inventory	Equipment	Books
Item Name	Item Name	Item Name
Item Description	Manufacturer	Publisher
Current Value	Model	Author
Insured Value	Warranty Expiration Date	ISBN
Date Entered		Category

Figure 7.29. *The new subset table structures.*

Table Structures

Full-Time Employees

FTEFirst Name

FTELast Name

FTEDate Hired

Salary Amount

Position

FTEStreet Address

FTECity

FTEState

Table Structures

Part-Time Employees

PTEFirst Name

PTELast Name

PTEDate Hired

Hourly Rate

Skill Level

PTEStreet Address

PTECity

PTEState

Figure 7.30. *Previously unidentified subset tables.*

to both tables: first name, last name, date hired, street address, city, and state. These fields are duplicated unnecessarily, so you'll need to refine the table structures to resolve this problem.

Refining Previously Unidentified Subset Tables

When you identify subset tables such as these, you can refine them using these steps:

1. Remove all the fields that the subset tables have in common and use them as the basis for a new *data* table.

2. Identify what subject the new data table represents, and then give the table an appropriate name.

3. Make sure that the subset tables represent subordinate subjects of the data table and modify the subset table names as necessary.

4. Compose a suitable description for the data table and then add it to the final table list. Indicate the table type as "Data."

Figure 7.31 shows the results of using these steps on the FULL-TIME EMPLOYEES and PART-TIME EMPLOYEES tables.

At this point, all of your table structures should be in pretty good shape. You will need to refine them even further, however, as you learn about primary keys, foreign keys, relationships, and business rules.

CASE STUDY

You're now going to define the *preliminary table list* for Mike's Bikes. As you know, the first thing you need to do is review the preliminary field list to determine what subjects you can infer from the fields on the list. Figure 7.32 shows a *partial* sample of that list.

Table Structures

Employees	Full-Time Employees	Part-Time Employees
EmpFirst Name	EmpFirst Name	EmpFirst Name
EmpLast Name	EmpLast Name	EmpLast Name
Date Hired	Salary Amount	Hourly Rate
EmpStreet Address	Position	Skill Level
EmpCity		
EmpState		

Figure 7.31. *The results of refining the subset tables.*

Preliminary Field List
as of 07/05/96

Birth Date	Office Phone
Employee Name	Product Name
Employee Address	Category
Employee City	Unit Price
Customer Name	Invoice Number
Customer Address	Invoice Date

Figure 7.32. *The preliminary field list for Mike's Bikes.*

After carefully reviewing the entire preliminary field list, you determine that the fields on the list suggest these subjects: customers, employees, invoices, products, and vendors. You then compile these items into the first version of your *preliminary table list*.

Now you create a *second* version of the list by merging the current preliminary table list with the *list of subjects* you created during the analysis process. Keep the following steps in mind as you merge the two lists together:

1. *Resolve items that are duplicated on both lists.* Remember that a single item can appear on both lists yet represent *different* subjects. When you identify such items, use the appropriate techniques to resolve this problem.

2. *Resolve items that represent the same subject but have different names.* You want to ensure that only *one* table represents a particular subject.

3. *Combine the remaining items together into one list.* The combined list becomes the *second* version of the preliminary table list.

After following these steps, your preliminary table list should look similar to the one shown in Figure 7.33.

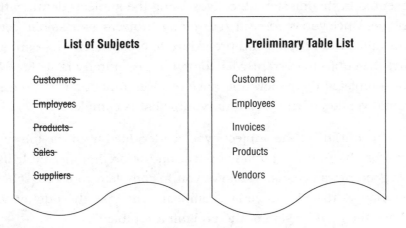

Figure 7.33. *The second version of the preliminary table list.*

You cross out "Customers," "Employees," and "Products" on the list of subjects because they represent the same subjects as their counterparts on the preliminary table list. The SALES table has no counterpart on the preliminary table list, but it does represent the *same* subject as "Invoices." "Invoices" is most meaningful to Mike and his staff, however, so you use it on the preliminary table list instead of "Sales." A similar situation exists between "Suppliers" and "Vendors"; Mike selects "Vendors" as the name to appear on the preliminary table list, so you cross out "Suppliers."

> ❖ **Note** Selecting a name that best represents the subject of the table is an arbitrary task. A good rule to follow is to use the name that is *most* meaningful to everyone in the organization.

Now you'll work toward the final version of the preliminary table list. Use the mission objectives you created at the beginning of the database-design process to determine whether there are subjects you may have overlooked during the previous two procedures. Identify each subject represented in the mission objectives using the subject-identification technique. Once you've identified as many subjects as possible, you can use the steps from the second procedure to crosscheck these subjects against the subjects currently listed on the preliminary table list. When you've completed the review and have resolved any duplicate items, your final version of the preliminary table list is complete.

As it turns out, *all* of the subjects you've identified from the mission objectives for Mike's Bikes already appear on the preliminary table list. This is good news because it allows you to complete your crosscheck quite easily. Satisfied that you've completed the task thoroughly, you now have the final version of the preliminary table list.

Now that the preliminary table list is complete, you're ready to transform it into a *final table list*. Keep these steps in mind as you begin this process:

1. *Refine the table names.* Use the *appropriate* guidelines to ensure that each table name is clear, unambiguous, descriptive, and meaningful.

2. *Compose a suitable description for each table.* Make certain that the table description explicitly defines the table and states its importance to the organization. Use the pertinent guidelines to create each table description.

3. *Indicate the table's type.* Remember that a table can be classified in one of four ways—*data, linking, subset,* or *validation*. At this point, all of your tables are *data* tables.

Figure 7.34 shows a *partial* example of the final table list for Mike's Bikes.

Final Table List

Name	Type	Description
Customers	Data	The people who purchase the products we have to offer. Keeping track of our customers allows us to promote our business and obtain valuable feedback in assessing the quality of our customer service.
Employees	Data	The people who work for our company in various capacities. This information is important for tax purposes, health benefits, and work-related issues.

Figure 7.34. *A partial listing of the final table list for Mike's Bikes.*

The next order of business is to associate fields from the preliminary field list with each table in the final table list. Make certain you select the fields that best represent characteristics of each table's subject; each field should define or describe a particular aspect of the subject. Figure 7.35 shows a *partial* example of the table structures for Mike's Bikes.

Table Structures

Customers	Employees	Invoices	Products
Customer First Name	Employee Name	Invoice Number	Product Name
Customer Last Name	Employee Address	Invoice Date	Product Description
Customer Phone	Employee Phone	Employee Name	Category
Customer Address	SSN	Customer Last Name	Wholesale Price
Status	Date Hired	Customer First Name	Retail Price
	Position	Customer Phone	Quantity

Figure 7.35. *A partial listing of the table structures for Mike's Bikes.*

Now you refine the fields. Remember to follow these steps as you work with each field:

1. *Improve the field name.* Use the appropriate guidelines to ensure that each field name is as clear, unambiguous, and descriptive as possible.

2. *Determine whether the field complies with the Elements of the Ideal Field.* Make certain you check for multipart and multivalued fields. As you learned earlier, they can cause a number of problems within a table.

As you review the fields, you decide to abbreviate some of the field names in the CUSTOMERS, EMPLOYEES, and INVOICES tables, shortening CUSTOMER to Cust and EMPLOYEE to Emp. You also decide that the field name Quantity (in the PRODUCTS table) does not completely describe the characteristic it represents, so you change it to Quantity On Hand. The phone fields in the CUSTOMERS and EMPLOYEES tables suffer the same problem, so you change them to CustHome Phone and EmpHome Phone respectively. Furthermore, you change SSN to Social Security Number so that the field name is absolutely unambiguous.

Further investigation of the fields reveals that almost all of them comply with the Elements of the Ideal Field. The only exceptions are the address fields in the CUSTOMERS and EMPLOYEES tables, and the Employee Name fields in the EMPLOYEES and INVOICES tables. After ascertaining that you can decompose each address field into four individual items—street address, city, state, and zip code—you transform these items into fields and add them to the CUSTOMERS and EMPLOYEES tables. Similarly, you notice that the Employee Name field represents two items—first name and last name—and you make the appropriate adjustments to that field in the EMPLOYEES and INVOICES tables.

Figure 7.36 shows the result of all the changes you've made to the fields.

Your final task is to refine the table structures. Make certain that you have assigned the appropriate fields to each table and that you have properly defined each table. Remember to follow these steps as you work with each table:

1. *Resolve unnecessary duplicate fields.* When you create new tables as a result of resolving duplicate fields, make sure you properly identify them and add them to the final table list.

2. *Determine whether each table complies with the Elements of the Ideal Table.* Make certain you resolve all the anomalies you identify in the fields or within the table structure as a whole.

3. *Establish subset tables as appropriate.* Make certain you properly identify these tables and add them to the final table list as well.

Table Structures

Customers	Employees	Invoices	Products
CustFirst Name	EmpFirst Name	Invoice Number	Product Name
CustLast Name	EmpLast Name	Invoice Date	Product Description
CustHome Phone	EmpHome Phone	EmpFirst Name	Category
CustStreet Address	Social Security Number	EmpLast Name	Wholesale Price
CustCity	EmpStreet Address	CustFirst Name	Retail Price
CustState	EmpCity	CustLast Name	Quantity On Hand
CustZipcode	EmpState	CustHome Phone	

Figure 7.36. *Refinements to the fields in the table structures.*

As you complete your review of the tables, you determine that all of them conform to the Elements of the Ideal Table with the exception of the INVOICES table. The only problem with this table is that it contains an unnecessary duplicate field: CustHome Phone. You can remove this field from the table, however, because it provides only reference information.

As you work with the PRODUCTS table, you notice that there are fields you might be able to remove and then use as the basis for a subset table. So you review the table once again. Figure 7.37 shows the PRODUCTS table structure you're currently examining. (This is an expanded version of the table structure shown in Figure 7.36.)

Your assumption proves correct. You determine that certain fields describe a service, and you can construe a service as being a different type of product. A service is similar to a product in that it has a name, description, and category, but it is different inasmuch as it has a type, materials charge, and service charge. With this in mind, you create a

Table Structures

Products

Product Name	Service Name
Product Description	Service Description
Category	Service Category
Wholesale Price	Service Type
Retail Price	Materials Charge
Quantity On Hand	Service Charge

Figure 7.37. *The PRODUCTS table structure (expanded version).*

new subset table called SERVICES, make the appropriate modifications to the PRODUCTS table, and use the PRODUCT NAME field to relate the two tables to each other. You then add the suitable listing for the SERVICES table to the final table list. Figure 7.38 shows the revised PRODUCTS table and the new SERVICES subset table.

Table Structures

Products	**Services**
Product Name	Product Name
Product Description	Service Type
Category	Materials Charge
Wholesale Price	Service Charge
Retail Price	
Quantity On Hand	

Figure 7.38. *The new PRODUCTS and SERVICES tables.*

Summary

We opened the chapter with a discussion of the *preliminary table list*. This list constitutes the initial table structures for the new database. You learned how to develop this list using the preliminary field list, the list of subjects, and the mission objectives, all of which you compiled during the analysis phase of the database-design process.

Next we discussed the procedure for transforming the preliminary table list into a *final table list*, which contains the name, type, and description of each table in the database. You learned a set of *guidelines for creating table names*, and another set of *guidelines for composing table descriptions*. We then worked on creating table names that are unambiguous, descriptive, and meaningful and descriptions that explicitly define tables, as well as stating their importance to the organization. You also learned that enlisting the help of users and management is crucial to the process of developing well-defined table descriptions. Table descriptions must be suitable and easily understood by everyone in the organization.

We then discussed the process of associating fields with each table on the final table list. Here you learned how to build a structure for a given table using fields from the preliminary field list that best represent characteristics of the table's subject.

Refining fields was the next subject of discussion, and you learned a set of guidelines for creating field names that will help you ensure that they are clear, descriptive, and meaningful. You also learned about the Elements of the Ideal Field. Now you know that you can resolve anomalies in a field by determining whether it complies with these elements. We then discussed how to resolve *multipart* and *multivalued* fields. You learned that decomposing multipart fields yields new fields, whereas decomposing multivalued fields yields new tables.

The chapter closes with a discussion of refining table structures. You learned to identify the Elements of the Ideal Table, and you now know that you can ferret out a problem in table structure by determining whether a table complies with these elements. We then discussed *unnecessary duplicate fields*, and you now know that they appear in a table for two reasons: to supply reference information or to represent different occurrences of the same type of value. You then learned how to resolve duplicate fields to eliminate the problems they present.

The final discussion centered on the topic of *subset tables*. As you now know, a subset table represents a *subordinate subject* of a particular data table, and there is a distinct relationship between the subset table and the data table. You also know that you can explicitly create subset tables. You then learned that you may have unknowingly created subset tables earlier in the database-design process and that you need to look for subset tables you have not previously identified. When you identify a subset table, you refine it and add it to the final table list.

Review Questions

1.   How do you identify and establish tables for the new database?

2.   Why do you use the preliminary field list to help you define tables for the database?

3.   What action do you take when an item on the list of subjects and a differently named item on the preliminary table list both represent the same subject?

4.   What information does the *final table list* provide?

5.   State three guidelines for creating table names.

6.   State two guidelines for composing table descriptions.

7.   How do you assign fields to a table on the *final table list*?

8.   State three guidelines for creating field names.

9.   What two problems can poorly designed fields cause?

10.   What can you use to resolve field anomalies?

11.   State three of the Elements of the Ideal Field.

12.   Under what condition is redundant data acceptable?

13.   In general terms, what three steps do you follow to resolve a multi-valued field?

14.   When is it necessary to use a duplicate field in a table?

15.   How can you refine table structures?

16.   State three of the Elements of the Ideal Table.

17.   What is a subset table?

8

Keys

A fact in itself is nothing. It is valuable only for the idea attached to it, or for the proof which it furnishes.
—CLAUDE BERNARD

Topics Covered in This Chapter

Why Keys Are Important

Establishing Keys for Each Table

Table-Level Integrity

Reviewing the Initial Table Structures

Case Study

Summary

Review Questions

By now you've identified all the subjects that the database will track and defined the table structures that will represent those subjects. Furthermore, you've put the structures through a screening process to control their makeup and quality. In this next stage of the database-design process, you'll begin the task of assigning *keys* to each table. You'll soon learn that there are different types of keys, and each plays a particular role within the database structure. All but one key is assigned during this stage; you'll assign the remaining key later (in Chapter 10) as you establish relationships between tables.

Why Keys Are Important

Keys are crucial to a table structure for the following reasons:

- *They ensure that each record in a table is precisely identified.* As you already know, a table represents a singular collection of similar objects or events. (For example, a CLASSES table represents a *collection* of classes, not just a single class.) The complete set of records within the table constitutes the collection, and each record represents a unique instance of the table's subject within that collection. You must have some means of accurately identifying each instance, and a key is the device that allows you to do so.

- *They help establish and enforce various types of integrity.* Keys are a major component of table-level integrity and relationship-level integrity. For instance, they enable you to ensure that a table has unique records and that the fields you use to establish a relationship between a pair of tables always contain matching values.

- *They serve to establish table relationships.* As you'll learn in Chapter 10, you'll use keys to establish a relationship between a pair of tables.

Always make certain that you define the appropriate keys for each table. Doing so will help you guarantee that the table structures are sound, that redundant data within each table is minimal, and that the relationships between tables are solid.

Establishing Keys for Each Table

Your next task is to establish keys for each table in the database. There are four main types of keys: *candidate, primary, foreign,* and *non-keys*. A key's type determines its function within the table.

Candidate Keys

The first type of key you establish for a table is the *candidate* key, which is a field or set of fields that uniquely identifies a single instance of the table's subject. Each table must have *at least one* candidate key. You'll eventually examine the table's pool of available candidate keys and designate one of them as the official primary key for the table.

Before you can designate a field as a candidate key, you must make certain it complies with *all* of the Elements of a Candidate Key. These elements constitute a set of guidelines you can use to determine whether the field is fit to serve as a candidate key. You cannot designate a field as a candidate key if it fails to conform to *any* of these elements.

Elements of a Candidate Key

- *It cannot be a multipart field.* You've seen the problems with multipart fields, so you know that using one as an identifier is a bad idea.

- *It must contain unique values.* This element helps you guard against duplicating a given record within the table. Duplicate records are just as bad as duplicate fields, and you must avoid them at all costs.

- *It cannot contain null values.* As you already know, a null value represents the *absence* of a value. There's absolutely no way a candidate key field can identify a given record if its value is null.

- *Its value cannot cause a breach of the organization's security or privacy rules.* Values such as passwords and Social Security Numbers are not suitable for use as a candidate key.

- *Its value is not optional in whole or in part.* A value that is optional implies that it may be null at some point. You can infer, then, that an optional value automatically violates the previous element and is, therefore, unacceptable. (This caveat is especially applicable when you want to use two or more fields as a candidate key.)

- *It comprises a minimum number of fields necessary to define uniqueness.* You can use a combination of fields (treated as a single unit) to serve as a candidate key, so long as each field contributes to defining a unique value. Try to use as few fields as possible, however, because overly complex candidate keys can ultimately prove to be difficult to work with and difficult to understand.

- *Its values must uniquely and exclusively identify each record in the table.* This element helps you guard against duplicate records and ensures that you can accurately reference any of the table's records from other tables in the database.

- *Its value must exclusively identify the value of each field within a given record.* This element ensures that the table's candidate keys provide the only means of identifying each field value within the record. (You'll learn more about this particular element in the section on primary keys.)

- *Its value can be modified only in rare or extreme cases.* You should never change the value of a candidate key unless you have an absolute and compelling reason to do so. A field is likely to have difficulty conforming to the previous elements if you can change its value arbitrarily.

Establishing a candidate key for a table is quite simple: Look for a field or set of fields that conforms to all of the Elements of a Candidate Key. You'll probably be able to define more than one candidate key for a given table. Loading a table with sample data will give you the means to identify potential candidate keys accurately. (You used this same technique in the previous chapter.)

See if you can identify any candidate keys for the table in Figure 8.1.

Employees

Employee ID	Social Security Number	EmpFirst Name	EmpLast Name	EmpStreet Address	EmpCity	EmpState	EmpZipcode	EmpHome Phone
1000	856-91-9938	Kendra	Bonnicksen	1204 Bryant Road	Seattle	WA	98157	363-9948
1001	886-11-2231	Katherine	Erlich	101 C Street, Apt. 32	Bellevue	WA	98046	322-6992
1002	901-48-0039	Timothy	Ennis	7402 Kingman Drive	Redmond	WA	98115	527-4992
1003	816-93-1299	Shannon	McLain	4141 Lake City Way	Seattle	WA	98136	336-5992
1004	978-02-1129	Susan	McLain	2100 Mineola Avenue	Seattle	WA	98115	572-9948
1005	955-92-5583	Estela	Pundt	101 C Street, Apt. 32	Bellevue	WA	98046	322-6992
1006	801-22-1734	Timothy	Sherman	66 NE 120th	Bothell	WA	98216	522-3232

Figure 8.1. *Are there any candidate keys in this table?*

You probably identified EMPLOYEE ID, SOCIAL SECURITY NUMBER, EMPLAST NAME, EMPFIRST NAME *and* EMPLAST NAME, EMPZIPCODE, and EMPHOME PHONE as potential candidate keys. But you'll need to examine these fields more closely to determine which ones are truly eligible to become candidate keys. Remember that you must automatically disregard any field(s) failing to conform to even *one* of the Elements of a Candidate Key.

Upon close examination, you can draw the following conclusions:

- *EMPLOYEE ID is eligible.* This field conforms to every element of a candidate key.

- *SOCIAL SECURITY NUMBER is ineligible because it could contain null values and will most likely compromise the organization's privacy rules.* Contrary to what the sample data shows, this field could contain a null value. For example, there are many people working in the United States who do not have Social Security numbers because they are citizens of other countries.

❖ **Note** Despite its widespread use in many types of databases, I would strongly recommend that you refrain from using SOCIAL SECURITY NUMBER as a candidate key (or a primary key, for that matter) in any of your database structures. In many instances, it doesn't conform to the Elements of a Candidate Key. You can learn some very interesting facts about Social Security numbers (which will shed some light on why they make poor candidate/primary keys) by visiting the Social Security Adminstration's Web site at http://www.ssa.gov.

- *EMPLAST NAME is ineligible because it can contain duplicate values.* As you've learned, the values of a candidate key must be unique. In this case there can be more than one occurrence of a particular last name.

- *EMPFIRST NAME and EMPLAST NAME are eligible.* The combined values of both fields will supply a unique identifier for a given record. Although multiple occurrences of a particular first name or last name will occur, the combination of a given first name and last name will always be unique. (Some of you are probably saying, "This is not necessarily always true." You're absolutely right. Don't worry; we'll address this issue shortly.)

- *EMPZIPCODE is ineligible because it can contain duplicate values.* Many people live in the same zip code area, so the values in EMPZIPCODE cannot possibly be unique.

- *EMPHOME PHONE is ineligible because it can contain duplicate values and is subject to change.* This field will contain duplicate values for either of these reasons:

  1. One or more family members work for the organization.

  2. One or more people share a residence that contains a single phone line.

You can confidently state that the EMPLOYEES table has two candidate keys: EMPLOYEE ID and the combination of EMPFIRST NAME and EMPLAST NAME.

Mark candidate keys in your table structures by writing the letters "CK" next to the name of each field you designate as a candidate key. A candidate key composed of two or more fields is known as a *composite candidate key*, and you'll write "CCK" next to the names of the fields that make up the key. When you have two or more composite candidate keys, use a number within the mark to distinguish one from another. If you had two composite candidate keys, for example, you would mark one as "CCK1" and the other as "CCK2."

Apply this technique to the candidate keys for the EMPLOYEES table in Figure 8.1. Figure 8.2 shows how your structure should look when you've completed this task.

Table Structures

Employees

Employee ID	*CK*
Social Security Number	
EmpFirst Name	*CCK*
EmpLast Name	*CCK*
EmpStreet Address	
EmpCity	
EmpState	
EmpZipcode	
EmpHome Phone	

Figure 8.2. *Marking candidate keys in the EMPLOYEES table structure.*

Now, try to identify as many candidate keys as you can for the PARTS table in Figure 8.3.

Parts

Part Name	Model Number	Manufacturer Name	Retail Price
Shimka XT Cranks	XT-113	Shimka Incorporated	199.95
Faust Brake Levers	BL / 45	Faust USA	53.79
MiniMite Pump		MiniMite	35.00
Hobo Fanny Pack		Hobo Bike Company	59.00
Diablo Bike Pedals	Mtn-A26	Diablo Sports	129.50
Shimka Truing Stand	SP-100		37.95
Faust Brake Levers	BL / 60	Faust USA	79.95

Figure 8.3. *Can you identify any candidate keys in the PARTS table?*

At first glance, you may believe that PART NAME, MODEL NUMBER, the combination of PART NAME and MODEL NUMBER, and the combination of MANUFACTURER and PART NAME are potential candidate keys. After investigating this theory, however, you come up with the following results:

- *PART NAME is ineligible because it can contain duplicate values.* A given part name will be duplicated when the part is manufactured in several models. For example, this is the case with Faust Brake Levers.

- *MODEL NUMBER is ineligible because it can contain null values.* A candidate key value must exist for each record in the table. As you can see, some parts do not have a model number.

- *PART NAME and MODEL NUMBER are ineligible because either field can contain null values.* The simple fact that MODEL NUMBER can contain null values instantly disqualifies this combination of fields.

- *MANUFACTURER and PART NAME are ineligible because the values for these fields seem to be optional.* Recall that a candidate key value cannot be optional in whole or in part. In this instance, you can infer that entering the manufacturer name is optional when it appears as a component of the part name; therefore, you cannot designate this combination of fields as a candidate key.

It's evident that you don't have a single field or set of fields that qualifies as a candidate key for the PARTS table. This is a problem because each table must have at least *one* candidate key. Fortunately, there is a solution.

Artificial Candidate Keys

When you determine that a table does not contain a candidate key, you can create and use an *artificial* (or *surrogate*) candidate key. (It's artificial in the sense that it didn't occur "naturally" in the table; you have to manufacture it.) You establish an artificial candidate key by creating a new field that conforms to all of the Elements of a Candidate Key and then adding it to the table; this field becomes the official candidate key.

You can now solve the problem in the PARTS table. Create an artificial candidate key called PART NUMBER and assign it to the table. (The new field will automatically conform to the Elements of a Candidate Key because you're creating it from scratch.) Figure 8.4 shows the revised structure of the PARTS table.

When you've established an artificial candidate key for a table, mark the field name with a "CK" in the table structure, just as you did for the EMPLOYEES table in the previous example.

You may also choose to create an artificial candidate key when it would be a stronger (and thus, more appropriate) candidate key than any of the existing candidate keys. Assume you're working on an EMPLOYEES table and you determine that the only available candidate key is the combination of the EMPFIRST NAME and EMPLAST NAME fields. Although this may be a valid candidate key, using a single-field candidate key might

Parts

Part Number	Part Name	Model Number	Manufacturer Name	Retail Price
41000	Shimka XT Cranks	XT-113	Shimka Incorporated	199.95
41001	Faust Brake Levers	BL / 45	Faust USA	53.79
41002	MiniMite Pump		MiniMite	35.00
41003	Hobo Fanny Pack		Hobo Bike Company	59.00
41004	Diablo Bike Pedals	Mtn-A26	Diablo Sports	129.50
41005	Shimka Truing Stand	SP-100		37.95
41006	Faust Brake Levers	BL / 60	Faust USA	79.95

Figure 8.4. *The PARTS table with the artificial candidate key PART NUMBER.*

prove more efficient and may identify the subject of the table more easily. Let's say that everyone in the organization is accustomed to using a unique identification number rather than a name as a means of identifying an employee. In this instance, you can choose to create a new field named EMPLOYEE ID and use it as an artificial candidate key. This is an absolutely acceptable practice—do this without hesitation or reservation if you believe it's appropriate.

❖ **Note** I commonly create an ID field (such as EMPLOYEE ID, VENDOR ID, DEPARTMENT ID, CATEGORY ID, and so on) and use it as an artificial candidate key. It always conforms to the Elements of a Candidate Key, makes a great primary key (eventually), and, as you'll see in Chapter 10, makes the process of establishing table relationships much easier.

Review the candidate keys you've selected and make absolutely certain that they thoroughly comply with the Elements of a Candidate Key. Don't be surprised if you discover that one of them is not a candidate key after all—incorrectly identifying a field as a candidate key happens occasionally. When this does occur, just remove the "CK" designator from the field name in the table structure. Deleting a candidate key won't pose a problem as long as the table has more than one candidate key. If you discover, however, that the only candidate key you identified for the table is *not* a candidate key, you *must* establish an artificial candidate key for the table. After you've defined the new candidate key, remember to mark its name with a "CK" in the table structure.

Primary Keys

By now, you've established all the candidate keys that seem appropriate for every table. Your next task is to establish a *primary* key for each table, which is the most important key of all.

- A *primary key field* exclusively identifies the table throughout the database structure and helps establish relationships with other tables. (You'll learn more about this in Chapter 10.)

- A *primary key value* uniquely identifies a given record within a table and exclusively represents that record throughout the entire database. It also helps to guard against duplicate records.

A primary key must conform to the exact same elements as a candidate key. This requirement is easy to fulfill because you select a primary key from a table's pool of available candidate keys. The process of selecting a primary key is somewhat similar to that of a presidential election. Every four years, several people run for the office of president of the United States. These individuals are known as "candidates" and they have all of the qualifications required to become president. A national election is held, and a single individual from the pool of available presidential candidates is elected to serve as the country's official president. Similarly, you identify each qualified candidate key in the table, run your own election, and select one of them to become the official primary key of the table. You've already identified the candidates, so now it's election time!

Assuming that there is no other marginal preference, here are a couple of guidelines you can use to select an appropriate primary key:

1. *If you have a simple (single-field) candidate key and a composite candidate key, choose the simple candidate key.* It's always best to use a candidate key that contains the least number of fields.

2. *Choose a candidate key that incorporates part of the table name within its own name.* For example, a candidate key with a name such as SALES INVOICE NUMBER is a good choice for the SALES INVOICES table.

Examine the candidate keys and choose one to serve as the primary key for the table. The choice is largely arbitrary—you can choose the one that you believe most accurately identifies the table's subject or the one that is the most meaningful to everyone in the organization. For example, consider the EMPLOYEES table again in Figure 8.5.

Either of the candidate keys you identified within the table could serve as the primary key. You might decide to choose EMPLOYEE ID if everyone in the organization is accustomed to using this number as a means of identifying employees in items such as tax forms and employee benefits programs. The candidate key you ultimately choose becomes the primary key of the table and is governed by the Elements of a Primary Key. These elements are exactly the same as those for the candidate key, and you should enforce them to the letter. For the sake of clarity, here are the Elements of a Primary Key:

Elements of a Primary Key

- It cannot be a multipart field.
- It must contain unique values.
- It cannot contain null values.

- Its value cannot cause a breach of the organization's security or privacy rules.

- Its value is not optional in whole or in part.

- It comprises a minimum number of fields necessary to define uniqueness.

- Its values must uniquely and exclusively identify each record in the table.

- Its value must exclusively identify the value of each field within a given record.

- Its value can be modified only in rare or extreme cases.

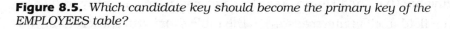

Table Structures

Employees

Employee ID	CK
Social Security Number	
EmpFirst Name	CCK
EmpLast Name	CCK
EmpStreet Address	
EmpCity	
EmpState	
EmpZipcode	
EmpHome Phone	

Figure 8.5. *Which candidate key should become the primary key of the EMPLOYEES table?*

Before you finalize your selection of a primary key, it is imperative that you make absolutely certain that the primary key fully complies with this particular element:

- Its value must exclusively identify the value of each field within a given record.

Each field value in a given record should be unique throughout the entire database (unless it is participating in establishing a relationship between a pair of tables) and should have *only one* exclusive means of identification—the specific primary key value for that record.

You can determine whether a primary key fully complies with this element by following these steps:

1.   Load the table with sample data.

2.   Select a record for test purposes and note the current primary key value.

3.   Examine the value of the first field (the one immediately after the primary key) and ask yourself this question:

     Does this primary key value *exclusively* identify the current value of *<fieldname>*?

     a.   If the answer is yes, move to the next field and repeat the question.

     b.   If the answer is no, *remove the field from the table*, move to the next field and repeat the question.

4.   Continue this procedure until you've examined every field value in the record.

A field value that the primary key *does not* exclusively identify indicates that the field itself is *unnecessary* to the table's structure; therefore, you should remove the field and reconfirm that the table complies with the Elements of the Ideal Table. You can then add the field you just removed to another table structure, if appropriate, or you can discard it completely because it is truly unnecessary.

Here's an example of how you might apply this technique to the partial table structure in Figure 8.6. (Note that INVOICE NUMBER is the primary key of the table.)

Sales Invoices

Invoice Number	Invoice Date	CustFirst Name	CustLast Name	EmpFirst Name	EmpLast Name	EmpHome Phone
13000	06/15/02	Frank	DeSoto	Estela	Pundt	363-9948
13001	06/15/02	Gregory	Mattson	Katherine	Erlich	322-6992
13002	06/15/02	Caroline	Coie	Kendra	Bonnicksen	527-4992
13003	06/16/02	David	Cunningham	Kendra	Bonnicksen	336-5992
13004	06/16/02	Caroline	Coie	Shannon	McLain	572-9948
13005	06/17/02	Frank	DeSoto	Estela	Pundt	322-6992

Figure 8.6. *Does the primary key exclusively identify the value of each field in this table?*

First, you load the table with sample data. You then select a record for test purposes—we'll use the third record for this example—and note the value of the primary key (13002). Now, pose the question above for each field value in the record.

> Does this primary key value *exclusively* identify the current value of . . .

INVOICE DATE?   Yes, it does. This invoice number will always identify the specific date that the invoice was created.

CUSTFIRST NAME?   Yes, it does. This invoice number will always identify the specific first name of the particular customer who made this purchase.

CUSTLAST NAME?	Yes, it does. This invoice number will always identify the specific last name of the particular customer who made this purchase.
EMPFIRST NAME?	Yes, it does. This invoice number will always identify the specific first name of the particular employee who served the customer for this sale.
EMPLAST NAME?	Yes, it does. This invoice number will always identify the specific last name of the particular employee who served the customer for this sale.
EMPHOME PHONE?	*No*, it doesn't! The invoice number *indirectly* identifies the employee's home phone number via the employee's name. In fact, it is the *current value* of both EMPFIRST NAME and EMPLAST NAME that exclusively identifies the value of EMPHOME PHONE— change the employee's name and you *must* change the phone number as well. You should now remove EMPHOME PHONE from the table for two reasons: The primary key does not exclusively identify its current value and (as you've probably already ascertained) it is an unnecessary field. As it turns out, you can discard this field completely because it is already part of the EMPLOYEES table structure.

After you've removed the unnecessary fields you identified during this test, examine the revised table structure and make sure it complies with the Elements of the Ideal Table.

The primary key should now exclusively identify the values of the remaining fields in the table. This means that the primary key is truly sound and you can designate it as the official primary key for the table. Remove the "CK" next to the field name in the table structure and replace it with a "PK." (A primary key composed of two or more fields is known as a *composite primary key,* and you mark it with the letters

"CPK.") Figure 8.7 shows the revised structure of the SALES INVOICE table with INVOICE NUMBER as its primary key.

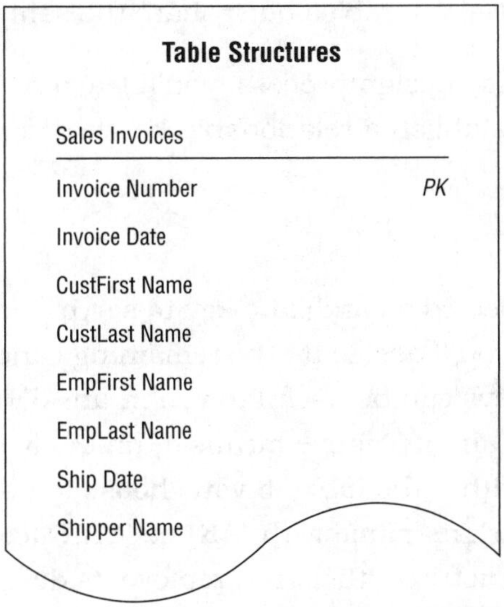

Table Structures

Sales Invoices
_____

Invoice Number   *PK*

Invoice Date

CustFirst Name

CustLast Name

EmpFirst Name

EmpLast Name

Ship Date

Shipper Name

Figure 8.7. *The revised SALES INVOICES table with its new primary key.*

As you create a primary key for each table in the database, keep these two rules in mind:

Rules for Establishing a Primary Key

1. *Each table must have one—and only one—primary key.* Because the primary key *must* conform to each of the elements that govern it, only one primary key is necessary for a particular table.

2. *Each primary key within the database must be unique—no two tables should have the same primary key unless one of them is a subset table.* You learned at the beginning of this section that the primary key exclusively identifies a table throughout the database structure; therefore, each table must have its own *unique* primary

key in order to avoid any possible confusion or ambiguity concerning the table's identity. A subset table is excluded from this rule because it represents a more specific version of a particular data table's subject—both tables *must* share the same primary key.

Later in the database-design process, you'll learn how to use the primary key to help establish a relationship between a pair of tables.

Alternate Keys

Now that you've selected a candidate key to serve as the primary key for a particular table, you'll designate the remaining candidate keys as *alternate* keys. These keys can be useful to you in an RDBMS program because they provide an alternative means of uniquely identifying a particular record within the table. If you choose to use an alternate key in this manner, mark its name with "AK" or "CAK" (composite alternate key) in the table structure; otherwise, remove its designation as an alternate key and simply return it to the status of a normal field. You won't be concerned with alternate keys for the remainder of the database-design process, but you will work with them once again as you implement the database in an RDBMS program. (Implementing and using alternate keys in RDBMS programs is beyond the scope of this work—our only objective here is to designate them as appropriate. This is in line with the focus of the book, which is the logical design of a database.)

Figure 8.8 shows the final structure for the EMPLOYEES table with the proper designation for both the primary key and the alternate keys.

Non-keys

A *non-key* is a field that does not serve as a *candidate*, *primary*, *alternate*, or *foreign* key. Its sole purpose is to represent a characteristic of the table's subject, and its value is determined by the primary key.

Table Structures

Employees

Employee ID	*PK*
Social Security Number	
EmpFirst Name	*CAK*
EmpLast Name	*CAK*
EmpStreet Address	
EmpCity	
EmpState	
EmpZipcode	
EmpHome Phone	

Figure 8.8. *The EMPLOYEES table with designated primary and alternate keys.*

There is no particular designation for a non-key, so you don't need to mark it in the table structure.

Table-Level Integrity

This type of integrity is a major component of overall data integrity, and it ensures the following:

- There are no duplicate records in a table.

- The primary key exclusively identifies each record in a table.

- Every primary key value is unique.

- Primary key values are not null.

You began establishing table-level integrity when you defined a primary key for each table and ensured its enforcement by making absolutely certain that each primary key fully complied with the Elements of a Primary Key. In the next chapter, you'll enhance the table's integrity further as you establish *field specifications* for each field within the table.

Reviewing the Initial Table Structures

Now that the fundamental table definitions are complete, you need to conduct interviews with users and management to review the work you've done so far. This set of interviews is fairly straightforward and should be relatively easy to conduct.

During these interviews, you will accomplish these tasks:

- *Ensure that the appropriate subjects are represented in the database.* Although it's highly unlikely that an important subject is missing at this stage of the database-design process, it can happen. When it does happen, identify the subject, use the proper techniques to transform it into a table, and develop it to the same degree as the other tables in the database.

- *Make certain that the table names and table descriptions are suitable and meaningful to everyone.* When a name or description appears to be confusing or ambiguous to several people in the organization, work with them to clarify the item as much as possible. It's common for some table names and descriptions to improve during the interview process.

- *Make certain that the field names are suitable and meaningful to everyone.* Selecting field names typically generates a great deal of discussion, especially when there is an existing database in place. You'll commonly find people who customarily refer to a particular field by a certain name because "that's what it's called on my screen." When you change a field name—you have good reasons for doing so—you must diplomatically explain to these folks that you renamed the field so that it conforms to the standards imposed by the new database. You can also tell them that the field can appear with the more familiar name once the database is implemented in an RDBMS program. What you've said is true; many RDBMSs allow you to use one name for the field's physical definition and another name for display purposes. This feature, however, does not change, reduce, or negate the need for you to follow the guidelines for creating field names that you learned in Chapter 7.

- *Verify that all the appropriate fields are assigned to each table.* This is your best opportunity to make certain that all of the necessary characteristics pertaining to the subject of the table are in place. You'll commonly discover that you accidentally overlooked one or two characteristics earlier in the design process. When this happens, identify the characteristics, use the appropriate techniques to transform them into fields, and follow all the necessary steps to add them to the table.

When you've completed the interviews, you'll move to the next phase of the database-design process and establish *field specifications* for every field in the database.

CASE STUDY

It's now time to establish keys for each table in the Mike's Bikes database. As you know, your first order of business is to establish candidate keys for each table. Let's say you decide to start with the CUSTOMERS table in Figure 8.9.

As you review each field, you try to determine whether it conforms to the Elements of a Candidate Key. You determine that STATUS, CUSTHOME PHONE, and the combination of CUSTFIRST NAME and CUSTLAST NAME are potential candidate keys, but you're not quite certain whether any of

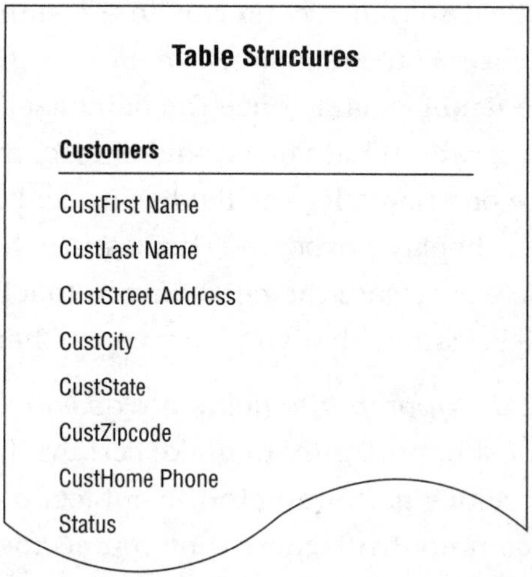

Figure 8.9. *The CUSTOMERS table structure in the Mike's Bikes database.*

them will completely conform to all of the elements. So you decide to test the keys by loading the table with sample data as shown in Figure 8.10.

Customers

CustFirst Name	CustLast Name	CustStreet Address	CustCity	CustState	CustZipcode	CustHome Phone	Status
Bridget	Berlin	2121 NE 35th	Bellevue	WA	98004	422-4982	Valued
Phillip	Bradley	101 9th Avenue	Kent	WA	98126	322-1178	
Kel	Brigan	7525 Taxco Lane	Redmond	WA	98225	363-9360	Valued
Barbara	Carmichael	7525 Taxco Lane	Redmond	WA	98225	363-9360	Preferred
Daniel	Chavez	750 Pike Street	Bothell	WA	98001	441-3987	Valued
Daniel	Chavez	301 N Main	Seattle	WA	98115	365-7199	
Sandi	Cooper	115 Pine Place	Seattle	WA	98026	332-0499	Preferred

Figure 8.10. *Testing candidate keys in the CUSTOMERS table.*

Always remember that a field must comply with *all* of the Elements of a Candidate Key in order to qualify as a candidate key. You must immediately disqualify the field if it does not fulfill this requirement.

As you examine the table, you draw these conclusions:

- *Status is ineligible because it will probably contain duplicate values.* As business grows, Mike is going to have many "Valued" customers.

- *CustHome Phone is ineligible because it will probably contain duplicate values.* The sample data reveals that two customers can live in the same residence and have the same phone number.

- *CustFirst Name and CustLast Name are ineligible because they will probably contain duplicate values.* The sample data reveals that the combination of first name and last name can represent more than one distinct customer.

These findings convince you to establish an artificial candidate key for this table. You then create a field called CUSTOMER ID, confirm that it complies with the requirements for a candidate key, and add the new field to the table structure with the appropriate designation.

Figure 8.11 shows the revised structure of the CUSTOMERS table.

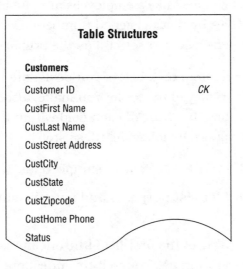

Figure 8.11. *The CUSTOMERS table with the new artificial candidate key, CUSTOMER ID.*

Now you'll repeat this procedure for each table in the database. Remember to make certain that every table has at least *one* candidate key.

The next order of business is to establish a primary key for each table. As you know, you select the primary key for a particular table from the table's pool of available candidate keys. Here are a few points to keep in mind when you're choosing a primary key for a table with more than one candidate key:

- Choose a simple (single-field) candidate key over a composite candidate key.

- If possible, pick a candidate key that has the table name incorporated into its own name.

- Select the candidate key that best identifies the subject of the table or is most meaningful to everyone in the organization.

You begin by working with the EMPLOYEES table in Figure 8.12. As you review the candidate keys, you decide that EMPLOYEE NUMBER is a much better choice for a primary key than the combination of EMPFIRST NAME and EMPLAST NAME because Mike's employees are already accustomed to identifying themselves by their assigned numbers. Using EMPLOYEE NUMBER makes perfect sense, so you select it as the primary key for the table.

Now you perform one final task before you designate EMPLOYEE NUMBER as the official primary key of the table: You make absolutely certain that it exclusively identifies the value of each field within a given record. So, you test EMPLOYEE NUMBER by following these steps:

1. Load the EMPLOYEES table with sample data.

2. Select a record for test purposes and note the current value of EMPLOYEE NUMBER.

3. Examine the value of the first field (the one immediately after EMPLOYEE NUMBER) and ask yourself this question:

Table Structures

Employees

Employee Number	CK
Social Security Number	
EmpFirst Name	CCK
EmpLast Name	CCK
EmpStreet Address	
EmpCity	
EmpState	
EmpZipcode	
EmpHome Phone	

Figure 8.12. *The EMPLOYEES table structure in the Mike's Bikes database.*

Does this primary key value *exclusively* identify the current value of *<fieldname>*?

a.   If the answer is yes, move to the next field and repeat the question.

b.   If the answer is no, *remove the field from the table*, move to the next field and repeat the question. (Be sure to determine whether you can add the field you just removed to another table structure, if appropriate, or discard it completely because it is truly unnecessary.)

4.   Continue this procedure until you've examined every field value in the record.

You know that you'll have to remove any field containing a value that EMPLOYEE NUMBER *does not* exclusively identify. EMPLOYEE NUMBER does exclusively identify the value of each field in the test record, however, so you use it as the official primary key for the EMPLOYEES table and mark its name with the letters "PK" in the table structure. You then repeat this process with the rest of the tables in Mike's new database until every table has a primary key.

Remember to keep these rules in mind as you establish primary keys for each table:

- Each table must have one—and only one—primary key.

- Each primary key within the database should be unique—no two tables should have the same primary key (unless one of them is a subset table).

As you work through the tables in Mike's database, you remember that the SERVICES table is a subset table. You created it during the previous stage of the design process (in Chapter 7), and it represents a more specific version of the subject represented by the PRODUCTS table. The PRODUCT NAME field is what currently relates the PRODUCTS table to the SERVICES subset table. You now know, however, that a subset table *must* have the same primary key as the table to which it is related, so you'll use PRODUCT NUMBER (the primary key of the PRODUCTS table) as the primary key of the SERVICES table. Figure 8.13 shows the PRODUCTS and SERVICES tables with their primary keys.

The last order of business is to conduct interviews with Mike and his staff and review all the work you've performed on the tables in the database. As you conduct these interviews, make certain you check the following:

- That the appropriate subjects are represented in the database

- That the table names and descriptions are suitable and meaningful to everyone

- That the field names are suitable and meaningful to everyone

- That all the appropriate fields are assigned to each table

Table Structures

Products		Services	
Product Number	*PK*	Product Number	*PK*
Product Name		Service Type	
Product Description		Materials Charge	
Category		Service Charge	
Wholesale Price			
Retail Price			
Quantity On Hand			

Figure 8.13. *Establishing the primary key for the SERVICES subset table.*

By the end of the interview, everyone agrees that the tables are in good form and that all the subjects with which they are concerned are represented in the database. Only one minor point came up during the discussions: Mike wants to add a CALL PRIORITY field to the VENDORS table. There are instances in which more than one vendor supplies a particular product, and Mike wants to create a way to indicate which vendor he should call first if that product is unexpectedly out of stock. So, you add the new field to the VENDORS table and bring the interview to a close.

Summary

The chapter opened with a discussion of the importance of *keys*. You learned that there are different types of keys, and each type plays a different role within the database. Each key performs a particular function, such as uniquely identifying records, establishing various types of integrity, and establishing relationships between tables. You now know that you can guarantee sound table structure by making certain that the appropriate keys are established for each table.

We then discussed the process of establishing keys for each table. We began by identifying the four main types of keys: *candidate*, *primary*, *foreign*, and *non-keys*. First, we looked at the process of establishing candidate keys for each table. You learned about the Elements of a Candidate Key and how to make certain that a field (or set of fields) complies with these elements. Then you learned that you can create and use an artificial candidate key when none of the fields in a table can serve as a candidate key or when a new field would make a stronger candidate key than any of the existing candidate key fields.

The chapter continued with a discussion of *primary keys*. You learned that you select a primary key from a table's pool of candidate keys and that the primary key is governed by a set of specific elements. We then covered a set of guidelines that help you determine which candidate key to use as a primary key. Next, you learned how to ensure that the chosen primary key exclusively identifies a given record and its set of field values. When the primary key does not exclusively identify a particular field value, you know that you must remove the field from the table in order to ensure the table's structural integrity. You also know that each table must have a single, unique primary key.

You then learned that you designate any remaining candidate keys as *alternate keys*. These keys will be most useful to you when you implement the database in an RDBMS program because they provide an alternate means of identifying a given record. We then discussed the *non-key* field, which is any field not designated as a candidate, primary, alternate, or foreign key. You now know that a non-key field represents a characteristic of the table's subject and that the primary key exclusively identifies its value.

Table-level integrity was the next subject of discussion, and you learned that it is established through the use of primary keys and enforced by the Elements of a Primary Key.

The chapter closed with some guidance on conducting further *interviews* with users and management. You now know that these interviews provide you with a means of reviewing the work you have performed on the tables and help you to verify and validate the current database structure.

Review Questions

1. State the three reasons why keys are important.

2. What are the four main types of *keys*?

3. What is the purpose of a *candidate key*?

4. State four items of the *Elements of a Candidate Key*.

5. True or False: A candidate key can be composed of more than one field.

6. Can a table have more than one candidate key?

7. What is an *artificial* candidate key?

8. What is the most important key you assign to a table?

9. Why is this key important?

10. How do you establish a *primary key*?

11. State four items of the *Elements of a Primary Key*.

12. What must you do before you finalize your selection of a primary key?

13. What is an *alternate key*?

14. What do you ensure by establishing table-level integrity?

15. Why should you review the initial table structures?

Field Specifications

It has long been an axiom of mine that the little things are infinitely the most important.
—SHERLOCK HOLMES,
THE ADVENTURES OF SHERLOCK HOLMES

Topics Covered in This Chapter

Why Field Specifications Are Important

Field-Level Integrity

Anatomy of a Field Specification

Using Unique, Generic, and Replica Field Specifications

Defining Field Specifications for Each Field in the Database

Case Study

Summary

Review Questions

Fields are the bedrock of the database. They represent characteristics of the subjects that are important to an organization. Fields store the data that the organization uses as the basis of information—information that is vital to its daily operations, success, and future growth. Despite their inherent value, fields are still the most overlooked, underutilized, and neglected assets of the organization! Frequently, little or no time is spent ensuring the structural and logical integrity of the fields in the database.

Much is said and written about data integrity, but little is *done* about it. Many people believe that keeping an eye on their data-entry personnel and having a "foolproof" user interface for the database will greatly minimize potential data-related problems. This superficial approach to data integrity commonly stems from an incorrect belief that proper data integrity takes too much time to establish. It's important to note, however, that the people who don't have time to establish data integrity usually spend a large amount of time fixing their improperly designed databases—typically spending up to three times as long as it would have taken them to design the database properly in the first place!

In this chapter, you'll learn how to establish data integrity by defining *field specifications* for each field in the database. First, you'll learn about the three sets of elements that compose a field specification; then you'll learn how to conduct interviews with users and management to enlist their help in defining the specifications for the fields.

Why Field Specifications Are Important

Despite what you may have heard, the time it takes to establish field specifications for each field in the database is an *investment* toward building consistent data and quality information—you *are not* wasting time whatsoever by performing this process. In fact, you'll waste *more* time in the end if you only partially perform this process or neglect it entirely. Shirking this duty means you're bound to encounter (and suffer from) inconsistent and erroneous data and inaccurate information.

There are several reasons why field specifications are crucial:

- *Field specifications help establish and enforce field-level integrity.* Implementing these specifications enables you to guarantee that the data in each field is consistent and valid.

- *Defining field specifications for each field enhances overall data integrity.* Remember that field-level integrity is one of the four components of overall data integrity. Field-level integrity enhances (to some extent) the table-level integrity you established in the previous stage of the design process. (This will become apparent when you work with the logical elements of the field specification.)

- *Defining field specifications compels you to acquire a complete understanding of the nature and purpose of the data in the database.* Understanding the data means that you can judge whether the data is truly necessary and important to the organization, and you can learn how to use it to your best advantage.

- *Field specifications constitute the "data dictionary" of the database.* Each field specification stores data on the characteristics of a particular field within the database. The complete set of specifications you establish for all of the fields in the database composes a literal dictionary of the database's structure. This data dictionary is particularly useful when you implement your database in an RDBMS—you can use it as a guide for creating the fields and setting their fundamental properties. These specifications will also help you determine what type of data-entry and data-validation procedures you need to implement within any user-interface application you create for the database.

Keep in mind that the levels of consistency, quality, and accuracy of the data in the database (and information retrieved from that data) are in direct proportion to the degree that you complete these specifications. It is paramount that you establish each field specification completely if your organization depends heavily on the information you retrieve from the database.

Field-Level Integrity

A field attains *field-level integrity* after you've defined a complete set of field specifications for the field. Field-level integrity warrants the following:

- The identity and purpose of a field is clear, and all of the tables in which it appears are properly identified.

- Field definitions are consistent throughout the database.

- The values of a field are consistent and valid.

- The types of modifications, comparisons, and operations that can be applied to the values in the field are clearly identified.

You can guarantee that a field structure is sound and optimally designed when it has a complete set of field specifications and fully conforms to the Elements of the Ideal Field. In fact, ensuring that the field complies with the Elements of the Ideal Field makes defining a set of specifications a relatively easy task.

If you've had any lingering doubt about a particular field's conformance to the Elements of the Ideal Field, now is a good time to review that field once more. If you determine that it is *not* in conformance, use the appropriate techniques to resolve the problem and make the proper adjustments to the table; otherwise, you can begin the process of defining field specifications for each field in the database. Here are the Elements of the Ideal Field once again for your convenience.

Elements of the Ideal Field

- It represents a distinct characteristic of the subject of the table.

- It contains only a single value.

- It cannot be deconstructed into smaller components.

- It does not contain a calculated or concatenated value.

- It is unique within the entire database structure.

- It retains a majority of its characteristics when it appears in more than one table.

Anatomy of a Field Specification

A field specification incorporates various elements that define every attribute of a field. All of the elements within the specification are categorized as *general elements*, *physical elements*, or *logical elements*. These element categories enable you to focus on a distinct aspect of the field as you're defining the specification, and they provide a way for you to find a particular element quite easily.

Here are the elements within each category:

- *General Elements:* Field Name, Parent Table, Label, Specification Type, Source Specification, Shared By, Alias(es), Description

- *Physical Elements:* Data Type, Length, Decimal Places, Character Support, Input Mask, Display Format

- *Logical Elements:* Key Type, Key Structure, Uniqueness, Null Support, Values Entered By, Required Value, Default Value, Range of Values, Edit Rule, Comparisons Allowed, Operations Allowed

Figure 9.1 shows an example of a Field Specifications sheet. We'll use this sheet (or various portions of it) as we work on field specification examples throughout the remainder of the book.

General Elements

Items under the General Elements category represent the most fundamental attributes of the field. They provide information on the field's purpose, the name of the table(s) in which the field appears, and the pseudonyms the field assumes under certain circumstances.

Field Name

This is the set of *absolute minimal* words that uniquely identifies a particular field throughout the database. You created and refined field names earlier in the database-design process (see Chapter 7), so you'll just take each name and use it as the setting for this element.

FIELD SPECIFICATIONS

General Elements

Field Name:	**Specification Type:** ☐ Unique ☐ Generic ☐ Replica
Parent Table:	**Source Specification:**
Label:	

Shared By:

Alias(es):

Description:

Physical Elements

Data Type:	**Character Support:**
Length:	☐ Letters (A–Z) ☐ Keyboard (. , / $ # %)
Decimal Places:	☐ Numbers (0–9) ☐ Special (© ® ™ ∑ π)

Input Mask:

Display Format:

Logical Elements

Key Type:	☐ Non	☐ Primary	**Edit Rule:**
	☐ Foreign	☐ Alternate	☐ Enter Now, Edits Allowed
Key Structure:	☐ Simple	☐ Composite	☐ Enter Now, Edits Not Allowed
Uniqueness:	☐ Non-unique	☐ Unique	☐ Enter Later, Edits Allowed
Null Support:	☐ Nulls Allowed	☐ No Nulls	☐ Enter Later, Edits Not Allowed
Values Entered By:	☐ User	☐ System	☐ Not Determined At This Time
Required Value:	☐ No	☐ Yes	

Default Value:

Range of Values:

Comparisons Allowed:

☐ Same Field	☐ All	☐ =	☐ >	☐ >=	☐ ≠	☐ <	☐ <=
☐ Other Fields	☐ All	☐ =	☐ >	☐ >=	☐ ≠	☐ <	☐ <=
☐ Value Expression	☐ All	☐ =	☐ >	☐ >=	☐ ≠	☐ <	☐ <=

Operations Allowed:

☐ Same Field	☐ All	☐ +	☐ −	☐ x	☐ ÷	☐ Concatenation
☐ Other Fields	☐ All	☐ +	☐ −	☐ x	☐ ÷	☐ Concatenation
☐ Value Expression	☐ All	☐ +	☐ −	☐ x	☐ ÷	☐ Concatenation

Figure 9.1. *Field Specifications sheet.*

Parent Table

The table that incorporates a given field within its structure is known as the field's *parent table*. This is the only table in which the field will appear *unless* the field is participating in establishing a relationship. (You'll learn more about this exception in Chapter 10.) For example, STUDENTS is the parent table of the STUDFIRST NAME field.

Label

This is an alternate name (typically a shorter form of the field name) by which you can identify the field within an end-user application interface that you create for the database. For example, you might use QTY ON HAND as a label for a field named QUANTITY ON HAND because many people in the organization are already accustomed to this particular name. Labels can be particularly useful when you want to conserve space on a data-entry screen or squeeze more fields into a particular report.

Avoid the temptation of using the label as the official field name within the table structure; otherwise, you make it possible for someone to misinterpret or incorrectly identify the field. Always use the most precise and accurate name as the official field name and then use the label (judiciously, of course) within your end-user interface applications. This will enable you to make a distinction between the two at all times.

Specification Type

The elements you set for a given field depend upon the type of specification you define for the field. You can define a specification in three ways:

1. *Unique.* This is the default specification for all fields except those that serve as a template for other fields or those that participate within a table relationship as foreign keys. You can incorporate all but the Source Specification element for this type of specification, and the element settings you establish will apply only to the field indicated in the Field Name element.

2. *Generic.* This specification serves as a template for other field specifications and helps you ensure consistent definitions for fields that have the same *general* meaning. For example, you could create this type of specification for a generic STATE field and then use it as the basis for every other STATE field in the database. Fields such as CUSTSTATE, EMPSTATE, and VENDSTATE all have the same meaning (they represent a state within the United States), but there is enough of an obvious distinction between them to require that they remain separate fields. (If you recall, you learned about generic fields in Chapter 6 when you were developing the preliminary field list and in Chapter 7 when you were working with the Elements of the Ideal Field.)

    A *generic* specification requires you to use a nonspecific field name and element settings that are as broad and general as possible. You can, however, incorporate any element except Parent Table, Label, Shared By, Alias(es), and Source Specification.

3. *Replica.* This is the default specification for a field based on a *generic* field or a field that serves as a foreign key within a table relationship, and it draws a majority of its element settings from an existing specification. You can incorporate elements that were not already incorporated by the source specification, and you can alter any element settings drawn from the source specification.

You'll learn how to define each type of specification in the section "Using Unique, Generic, and Replica Field Specifications" later in the chapter.

Source Specification

This element is set only on a *Replica* specification and indicates the name of the specific field specification upon which the current specification is based. (You'll see a good example of this element in the next section as well.)

Shared By

This element indicates the names of other tables that share this field. The only table names that should appear here are those that have an explicit relationship to the field's parent table. For example, assume you have a data table called EMPLOYEES that is related to two subset tables called PART-TIME EMPLOYEES and FULL-TIME EMPLOYEES via a field called EMPLOYEE ID NUMBER. As you create a field specification for EMPLOYEE ID NUMBER, you would use "PART-TIME EMPLOYEES, FULL-TIME EMPLOYEES" as the setting for this element.

Alias(es)

This is a name (or set of names) that you use for the field in very *rare* circumstances. One instance in which you would use an alias is when there *must* be two occurrences of the field in the *same* table. Let's assume that an organization is accustomed to identifying its employees by unique values within an EMPLOYEE ID NUMBER field. Now, consider the SUBSIDIARIES table structure in Figure 9.2 (this is a *partial* structure only).

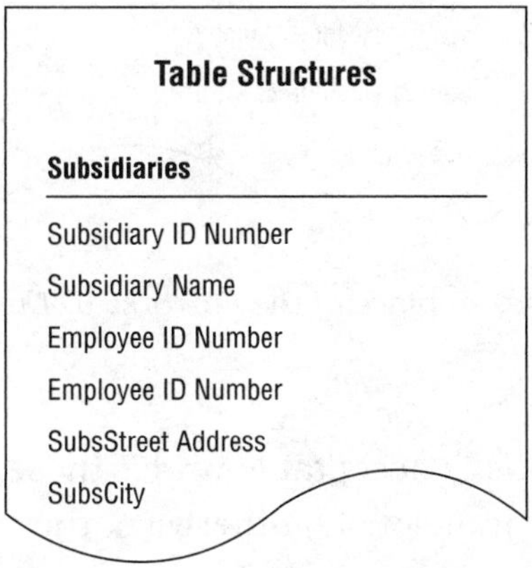

Table Structures

Subsidiaries

Subsidiary ID Number

Subsidiary Name

Employee ID Number

Employee ID Number

SubsStreet Address

SubsCity

Figure 9.2. *A table requiring two occurrences of the same field.*

In this instance, each subsidiary has a president and a vice president. Both of these individuals *must* be represented in the table because of their positions within the subsidiary organization, so there are two EMPLOYEE ID NUMBER fields in the table structure. Proper database design, however, dictates that there can only be *one* occurrence of this field within the table; there is an obvious problem here. The only solution is to use an alias for one or both occurrences of the EMPLOYEE ID NUMBER field. For instance, you could (for sake of clarity) use PRESIDENT ID as an alias for the first occurrence of EMPLOYEE ID NUMBER and VICE PRESIDENT ID as an alias for the second occurrence of EMPLOYEE ID NUMBER. With the aliases in place, both employees are properly represented within the table. Figure 9.3 shows the revised table structure.

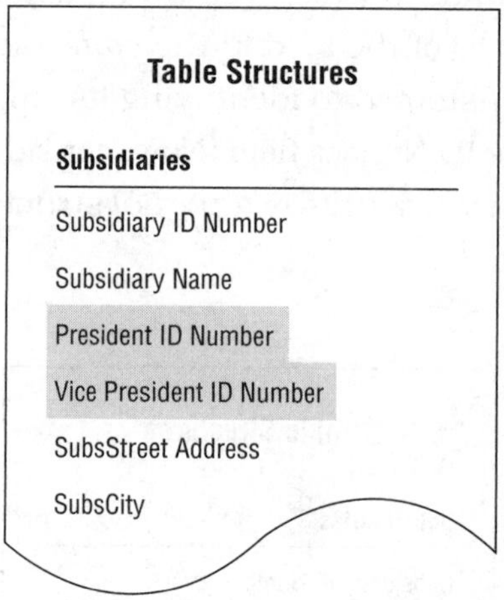

Table Structures

Subsidiaries

Subsidiary ID Number

Subsidiary Name

President ID Number

Vice President ID Number

SubsStreet Address

SubsCity

Figure 9.3. *Using aliases in place of the EMPLOYEE ID NUMBER fields.*

Although using an alias is acceptable under these circumstances, you should use them very judiciously; otherwise, they can become difficult to manage and maintain, eventually conceal or disguise the true meaning of the original fields, and cause you to misunderstand what the data actually represents. This issue will become even clearer when you begin to establish table relationships.

Description

This is a complete interpretation of the field. Composing a field description is extremely beneficial because it forces you (and everyone in the organization) to think carefully about the nature of the data that will be stored in the field. You can be relatively sure that the field requires further refinement if you have difficultly composing a suitable description.

Earlier in the database-design process, you learned a set of guidelines for composing a table description. Similarly, there is a set of guidelines that governs how you compose a proper field description.

Guidelines for Composing a Field Description

- *Use a statement that accurately identifies the field and clearly states its purpose.* The description should supplement the field name in terms of defining what the field represents. It should also state the field's role within the table or its relationship to the table's subject. Here's an example of such a description:

  CustCity—the metropolitan area in which a customer resides or conducts business. This is an integral component of a customer's complete address.

- *Write a clear and succinct statement.* The description should be free of confusing sentences or ambiguous phrases. Although the description should be as complete as possible, use the minimum number of words necessary to convey the required information. As you've seen with table descriptions, verbose statements are difficult to read and understand.

- *Refrain from restating or rephrasing the field name.* Neither of these practices does anything to illuminate the identity or purpose of the field. Remember that the purpose of a description is to provide a complete interpretation of the field. Here's an example of a poor description:

> CustLast Name—the last name of a customer.

A description is far more useful when you write it in this manner:

> CustLast Name—the surname of a customer, whether original or by marriage, that we use in all formal communications and correspondence with that customer.

- *Avoid using technical jargon, acronyms, or abbreviations.* Although some people within the organization will understand these types of idioms, its better for you to use terminology that everyone understands. Remember that a description must be as clear as possible to *anyone* who reads it. For example, you should avoid this type of statement:

> Employee ID Number—a unique number used to identify an employee within the organization. It is a component of the SSP.

  The problem with this description is that there is no inherent way to determine the meaning of the acronym SSP. You could resolve this problem by spelling out the complete term, but it would be better for you to restate the purpose of the field.

- *Do not include implementation-specific information.* There's no reason to include the fact that a given field appears on a particular data-entry screen or is used within a specific piece of programming code. This type of information is more appropriate for the implementation phase of the overall database-development process.

- *Do not make this description dependent upon the description of another field.* Each description should be as complete as possible and independent of every other description in the database. *Interdependent* descriptions introduce unnecessary confusion and can inadvertently obscure the field's true identity and purpose. Avoid using a description such as this:

> Item Reorder Level—minimum number of items that must exist for a particular product. (See description for Quantity On Hand).

- *Do not use examples.* As you learned in Chapter 7, using examples in a description is a bad idea because they depend on supplemental information to convey their full meaning. You can ensure that a description is clear and succinct by keeping it absolutely free of examples.

Figure 9.4 shows the General Elements section of a Field Specifications sheet for an EMPLOYEE ID NUMBER field.

General Elements					
Field Name:	Employee ID Number	**Specification Type:**	[X] Unique	☐ Generic	☐ Replica
Parent Table:	Employees	**Source**			
Label:	Employee #	**Specification:**			
Shared By:	Full-Time Employees, Part-Time Employees, Customers				
Alias(es):					
Description:	A unique number used to identify each employee within our organization. It is assigned during the first day of employee orientation and remains with the employee throughout the duration of his or her employment.				

Figure 9.4. *The General Elements category for an EMPLOYEE ID NUMBER field.*

Physical Elements

This category pertains to the structure of a field. Its elements are expressed in general terms because each RDBMS program implements them in a slightly different manner. Establishing these elements during this phase of the design process helps you ensure consistent field definitions throughout the database and reduces the time it will take you to implement the field structures in an RDBMS program.

Data Type

This element indicates the nature of the data that the field stores.

In Chapter 1, you learned that Structured Query Language, or SQL, is the standard language used to create, modify, maintain, and query relational databases. SQL is actually a fully documented standard set forth jointly by the American National Standards Institute (ANSI) and the International Organization for Standardization (ISO). Although the current version of the standard (as of this writing) is SQL/3, most major RDBMS programs implement much of the previous version, SQL/92.

The SQL standard defines seven major data types, and each data type has one or more uniquely named variations. Here's a brief definition of each data type.

Character	This data type stores a fixed- or varying-length character string of one or more printable characters. A fixed-length Character data type is known as CHARACTER or CHAR, and a varying-length Character data type is known as CHARACTER VARYING, CHAR VARYING, or VARCHAR.
National Character	This data type is the same as the Character data type, but it can also store characters from foreign-language character sets. A fixed-length National Character data type is known as NATIONAL CHARACTER, NATIONAL CHAR, and NCHAR, and a varying-length National Character data type is known as NA-

	TIONAL CHARACTER VARYING, NATIONAL CHAR VARYING, and NCHAR VARYING.
Bit	This data type stores strings of binary number sequences, such as digitized images and sound waves. This data type is often referred to as BIT or BIT VARYING.
Exact Numeric	This data type stores whole numbers and numbers with decimal places. Most RDBMS programs implement an Exact Numeric as NUMERIC, DECIMAL (DEC), INTEGER (INT), and SMALLINT, and each variation determines the range of values that the field will accept.
Approximate Numeric	This data type stores numbers with decimal places and exponential numbers. Most RDBMS programs implement an Approximate Numeric as FLOAT, REAL, and DOUBLE PRECISION, and each variation determines the range of values that the field will accept.
DateTime	This data type is commonly known as TIMESTAMP in most RDBMS programs, and it stores dates, times, and combinations of both. Note that the implementation of this data type varies widely among RDBMS programs, so you must make absolutely certain that you refer to the RDBMS's documentation to determine how the RDBMS handles dates and times.
Interval	This data type stores the quantity of time between two DateTime values, expressed either as year, month, year/month day, time, or day/time. Most major database systems do not yet support this data type, so you needn't worry about it for now.

Many RDBMS programs provide additional data types beyond those specified by the standard, which are known as *extended data types*. Examples of extended data types include MONEY/CURRENCY, BOOLEAN (for True or False values), SERIAL/ROWID (for unique row identifiers), and BYTE/BLOB (for unstructured binary data).

I've presented the SQL standard data types because you will encounter them (or variations thereof) in practically every RDBMS program. I have not provided much detail on these data types, however, because they are not implemented consistently across all RDBMS programs; you must consult your RDBMS's documentation to determine which data types the RDBMS supports and how the RDBMS implements them.

You can use any of the SQL data types (except *Interval*) as the setting for the Data Type element of a given specification. Due to their inconsistent implementation, however, I recommend that you use one of the following *general* data types as the setting for this element instead.

Alphanumeric This data type stores any combination of letters, numbers, keyboard characters, or special characters. Keyboard characters include the comma, dollar sign, exclamation mark, percentage sign, and period. Special characters include the copyright symbol, the trademark symbol, and the symbol for pi.

Numeric This data type stores only whole numbers and real numbers. It will not accept numbers with leading zeroes (e.g., 0000234) because they are not genuine numbers.

DateTime This data type stores dates, times, or a combination of both.

These data types are quite suitable for indicating the nature of the data that the field stores, and they are certainly much easier for users and management to understand. Using general data types will help you avoid unnecessary confusion, especially when you're reviewing the specification with users and management.

❖ **Note** I use these general data types as the basis for all further data type references and examples throughout the remainder of the book.

Length

This element specifies the total number of characters that a user can enter for any given field value. The RDBMS program you use to implement the database will determine the maximum number of characters you can set for this element. Although you can theoretically set the Length element for any data type, you should be aware that some RDBMS programs do not allow you to specify a length for a numeric field. Instead, the RDBMS program sets the length of a numeric field based on the *type* of number the field stores, such as an integer, a long integer, or a real number.

Decimal Places

This denotes the number of digits to the *right* of the decimal point in a real number. The number of digits determines the real number's precision. For example, many businesses require that all currency values have four digits of precision to the right of the decimal point.

Character Support

This element indicates the type of characters that a user can enter into a given field value. Setting and enforcing this element helps you ensure that the user cannot introduce meaningless data into the field, thus enhancing *field-level integrity*.

Let's say you're working with a CustState field and its data type is alphanumeric. This data type is appropriate for the field because it allows a user to incorporate letters as part of a given field value. But it also allows him to use numbers, keyboard characters, and extended characters, which means that he can enter a meaningless value into the field—there are no state names or state abbreviations that contain characters other than letters. You solve this problem by using the Character Support element to define the characters that the user can incorporate within a field value. (I address the issue of a *valid* combination of letters in the "Logical Elements" section.)

You can choose to include or exclude any of the following types of characters:

- *Letters*—all letters of the alphabet *including* foreign language letters such as é and ñ.

- *Numbers*—0 through 9.

- *Keyboard characters*—any standard character other than letters and numbers, such as asterisk, ampersand, bracket, caret, comma, equals sign, exclamation point, parenthesis, percent sign, period, pound sign, question mark, quote, semicolon, slash, or vertical bar. Note that the Field Specifications sheet includes examples of the characters that belong to this category.

- *Special characters*—any character that you can produce only through specific combinations of standard keys and the CTRL, ALT, and SHIFT keys, or with the aid of a special software program. Characters in this category include complex mathematical symbols, the copyright symbol, fractions, the symbol for pi, and the trademark symbol. The Field Specifications sheet includes examples of these characters as well.

Input Mask

This element specifies the manner in which a user should enter data into the field. For example, there are many ways to enter a date, such as "01/01/02," "01-01-02," and "01-Jan-2002." Using an input mask helps you ensure that a user enters values into the field consistently and (in this case) prevents confusion over the meaning of the date sequence.

RDBMS programs implement input masks in various ways, so you should use a relatively generic setting for this element. (You can assign multiple input masks, if appropriate.) For example, you could use "mm/dd/yy" as the input mask for a date field. This mask indicates the sequence of the date components (month, day, year), the structure of the date (two numbers per component, e.g., 05/16/02), and the date component separator (the slash).

Display Format

This element governs the appearance of a field's value when it is displayed on a screen or printed within a document. A display format enables you to present the field value in a more meaningful or readable fashion than the manner in which it was entered. For example, "03/13/88" might be the way you enter a given date, but "March 13, 1988" is much easier to read and comprehend.

Use a generic setting for this element, just as you did with the Input Mask; RDBMS programs implement display formats in various ways as well. For example, you can use "Month Day, Year" as a display format for a DATE HIRED field. You can also use a complete sentence to indicate a display format, such as the one in this example of a display format setting for a COMPANY NAME field.

Each word should start with a capital letter.

Figure 9.5 shows the Physical Elements section of a Field Specifications sheet for an EMPLOYEE ID NUMBER field.

Physical Elements		
Data Type: Numeric	**Character Support:**	
Length: 4	☐ Letters (A–Z)	☐ Keyboard (. , / $ # %)
Decimal Places: 0	☒ Numbers (0–9)	☐ Special (© ® ™ Σ π)
Input Mask: ####		
Display Format: 0000		

Figure 9.5. *The Physical Elements category for an* EMPLOYEE ID NUMBER *field.*

Logical Elements

This category pertains mainly to the values within a field. Its elements govern matters such as whether each value should be unique, when a value should be entered, whether a value can be edited, and the types of comparisons and operations that can be performed on each value. Setting these elements helps you establish and enforce a large part of field-level integrity.

Key Type

This element designates a field's role within a table, which you identified as you were establishing a primary key for the table. As you already know, a field can serve as a non-key, a primary key, or an alternate key. In Chapter 10, you'll learn all about *foreign* keys and when to designate a field as a foreign key on the Field Specifications sheet.

Key Structure

This element denotes whether a field designated as a primary key is acting as a simple (single-field) primary key or as part of a composite (multifield) primary key.

Uniqueness

This element indicates whether a field's values are unique. You set it as "Unique" when the *Key Type* element is set to "Primary"; otherwise, you'll typically set this element as "Non-unique."

When you work with a *non-key* field, think about how its values are going to be used so that you can determine whether they should be unique. Consider the DEPARTMENTS table structure in Figure 9.6.

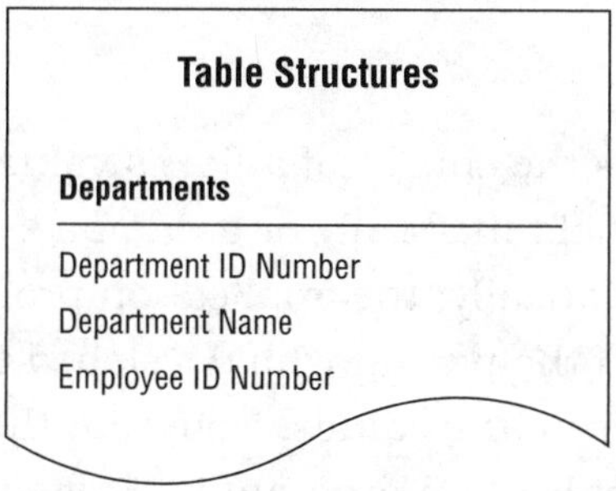

Table Structures

Departments

Department ID Number
Department Name
Employee ID Number

Figure 9.6. *Should the values of* EMPLOYEE ID NUMBER *be unique?*

In this example, the EMPLOYEE ID NUMBER field identifies the person who manages a particular department. Assuming that a person is allowed to manage only one department at any given time, the values in this field should be unique; therefore, you should set the Uniqueness element for this field as "Unique."

Null Support

This specifies whether a field accepts null values. "No Nulls" is the setting you'll commonly use for this element, especially when a field serves as a primary key or an alternate key, or when the field's Required Value element is set to "Yes." You can set this element to "Nulls Allowed," however, when there is a valid reason for a field to accept null values. A CUSTCOUNTY field, for example, must accept nulls because a customer may not know the name of the county in which she lives. (Of course, it will no longer be null once she supplies the county name.)

Remember that a null does not represent a blank—it represents a *missing* or *unknown* value. Users commonly make the mistake of using a blank to represent a *meaningful* value, such as "None," "Not Applicable," "No Response," and "Not Wanted." If these values are valid for a particular field, then make sure you include them in the Range of Values element for the field. Above all, use nulls judiciously and *do not* use blanks!

Values Entered By

This element indicates the source of a field's values. Either a user will enter values into the field manually or a database application program will enter them automatically; the application program can provide values for the field only if the person who developed the program provided a means for it to generate the values. Note that the setting that represents the database application program is "System."

Required Value

This denotes whether a user is required to enter a value for a field. Although you'll typically set this element to "No" for most of the fields in a table, you *must* set it to "Yes" when the field serves as the primary key. You may also need to set Required Value to "Yes" for a field such as CustZipcode—a letter or package you send to a given customer must include a zip code in order for the Postal Service to handle it properly and accurately.

Default Value

This is a value that a user can enter into a field when a more appropriate value is not yet available and nulls are disallowed. Use a default value very judiciously, and only if it is *meaningful*. For example, "WA" is a meaningful default value for a CustState field when the vast majority of your customers live in Washington state. Conversely, "01/01/96" is not a good default value for a Date Hired field because it is a completely arbitrary value that has no real meaning.

Range of Values

This element specifies every possible valid value for a field. You can set this element in various ways, such as with a lower and upper limit (1,000 to 9,999) or with a specific list of values ("WA," "OR," "ID," "MT"). There are three categories under which you can establish a range of values:

1. *General—a complete collection of every possible value for this field.* For example, the general range of values for a CustState field might include all valid abbreviations for every state in the United States.

2. *Integrity specific—a collection of values based on the field's role within a table relationship.* (You'll learn all about this category in Chapter 10.)

3. *Business specific—a collection of values generated by a particular business requirement.* Organizations commonly have various requirements that limit the range of values for a field. In an organization that conducts its business strictly in the Pacific Northwest, for example, the valid range of values for a CustState field are "WA," "OR," "ID," and "MT." (You'll learn more about this category in Chapter 11.)

You're concerned only with the *general* range of values during this stage of the database-design process, and you'll revisit the Range of Values element later when you establish table relationships and business rules.

It's important to note that "Other" and "Miscellaneous" are two values that you *do not* want to set within any category of the Range of Values element. Both values are nonspecific and absolutely meaningless within this context and are a sign of mental laziness in that their very presence indicates a need to review the field for possible refinement. You can avoid unnecessary confusion and potential problems by refraining from using these values.

Edit Rule

This element designates at what point a user can enter a value into a field and whether he can modify that value. You set this element to one of these four options:

1. *Enter Now, Edits Allowed.* A user *must* enter a value for this field when she creates a new record in the field's parent table. She can then edit the value at any time.

2. *Enter Later, Edits Allowed.* A user *has the option* of entering a value for this field when he creates a new record in the field's parent table. This does not imply in any way that the field's value can be null for all time; the user must enter a value for this field *at some point* in the near future. After he's entered the value, he can then edit it at any time.

3. *Enter Now, Edits Not Allowed.* A user *must* enter a value for this field when she creates a new record in the field's parent table, but she *cannot* edit it at any time whatsoever.

4. *Enter Later, Edits Not Allowed.* A user *has the option* of entering a value for this field when he creates a new record in the field's parent table. This does not imply in any way that the field's value can be null for all time; the user must enter a value for this field *at some point* in the near future. After he's entered the value, he *cannot* edit it at any time whatsoever.

You should use a default value when you set the Edit Rule element to the second or fourth option; this will keep the field's value from being null until such time that the user enters an appropriate value.

Comparisons Allowed

This indicates the types of comparisons a user can apply to a given field value when he's retrieving information from the field. There are six types of comparisons: equal to (=), not equal to (≠), greater than (>), less than (<), greater than or equal to (>=), and less than or equal to (<=). This element also indicates whether a user can compare a given field value to any of the following:

- Another value within the same field. When a field serves as a primary key, this option applies to the values of related foreign key fields. (You'll learn more about this in the next chapter.)

- A value of another field within the parent table or from some other table in the database.

- A value expression, which is some form of operation involving field values, literal values, or a combination of both. It returns a single value that you can then use for the comparison: (RETAIL PRICE − 2.50) is an example of a value expression.

Controlling the types of comparisons a user can apply to the field's values enables you to keep him from making meaningless comparisons. Let's say that he's working with an EMPLOYEE ID NUMBER field based on a numeric data type. Unless you indicate otherwise, he can make a comparison such as this one:

Is an Employee ID Number in the Employees table *greater than or equal to* an Employee ID Number in the Part-Time Employees table?

Although a "greater than or equal to" comparison is generally acceptable in a numeric field, it is not appropriate in this instance; there is no valid reason for him to make this type of comparison.

Similarly, it would be pointless for him to make a comparison between a given EMPLOYEE ID NUMBER value and the value of another numeric field within the EMPLOYEES table or some other table within the database; therefore, a comparison such as this is invalid:

> Is an Employee ID Number in the Employees table *greater than or equal to* a Quantity On Hand in the Products table?

It is both suitable and reasonable, however, for him to make a comparison between a given EMPLOYEE ID NUMBER value within the EMPLOYEES table and another EMPLOYEE ID NUMBER value within a related data table or related subset table. This comparison, then, is a valid one:

> Is an Employee ID Number in the Employees table *equal to* an Employee ID Number in the Part-Time Employees table?"

There are instances when it is perfectly suitable for the user to compare a particular value of one field to the value of a completely different field. For example, it is totally logical for him to make the following comparison between a DATE SHIPPED field and a DATE ORDERED field:

> Is the current value of Date Shipped *greater than or equal to* the current value of Date Ordered?

It's fortunate that he can make this type of comparison—he certainly doesn't want the value of DATE SHIPPED to be earlier than the value of DATE ORDERED!

As you set the Comparisons Allowed element for a given field, think about how you're going to use the field's values so that you can designate the appropriate comparisons. It's very likely that you'll review this element later in the design process when you establish table relationships and define business rules.

Operations Allowed

This element specifies the types of operations that a user can perform on the field's values. There are five types of operations: addition (+), subtraction (–), multiplication (×), division (÷), and concatenation. (Obviously, any combination of these operations is valid as well.) This element also indicates whether an operation can incorporate any of the following:

- Another value within the same field

- A value from another field within the parent table or from some other table in the database

- The result of a value expression (which, as you recall, is itself some form of operation involving field values, literal values, or a combination of both, that returns a single value)

You can prevent the user from defining meaningless operations by limiting the types of operations that he can perform on the field's values. Let's consider the EMPLOYEE ID NUMBER, DATE SHIPPED, and DATE ORDERED fields once again. There is no reason for the user to perform mathematical operations on a pair of EMPLOYEE ID NUMBER values within the EMPLOYEES table, nor is there any reason for him to perform such operations using a given EMPLOYEE ID NUMBER value and some other numeric field's value. In the case of the DATE SHIPPED field, however, it *is* suitable to perform some of these operations using a given DATE SHIPPED value and the value of some other appropriate date field within the database. For example, the user might need to subtract DATE ORDERED from DATE SHIPPED to determine the time that elapsed between the date that the customer placed the order and the date that the items within the order were shipped to the customer.

As you set the Operations Allowed element for a given field, think about how you're going to use the field's values so that you can designate the appropriate operations. It's very likely that you'll review this element later in the design process as you define business rules.

Figure 9.7 shows the Logical Elements section of a Field Specifications sheet for an EMPLOYEE ID NUMBER field.

Logical Elements				
Key Type:	☐ Non	☒ Primary	**Edit Rule:**	
	☐ Foreign	☐ Alternate	☐ Enter Now, Edits Allowed	
Key Structure:	☒ Simple	☐ Composite	☒ Enter Now, Edits Not Allowed	
Uniqueness:	☐ Non-unique	☒ Unique	☐ Enter Later, Edits Allowed	
Null Support:	☐ Nulls Allowed	☒ No Nulls	☐ Enter Later, Edits Not Allowed	
Values Entered By:	☐ User	☒ System	☐ Not Determined At This Time	
Required Value:	☐ No	☒ Yes		
Default Value:				
Range of Values:	1000–9999			

Comparisons Allowed:

		All	=	>	>=	≠	<	<=
☒	Same Field	☐	☒	☐	☐	☐	☐	☐
☐	Other Fields	☐	☐	☐	☐	☐	☐	☐
☒	Value Expression	☐	☒	☐	☐	☐	☐	☐

Operations Allowed:

		All	+	−	x	÷	Concatenation
☐	Same Field	☐	☐	☐	☐	☐	☐
☐	Other Fields	☐	☐	☐	☐	☐	☐
☐	Value Expression	☐	☐	☐	☐	☐	☐

Figure 9.7. *The Logical Elements category for an EMPLOYEE ID NUMBER field.*

Using Unique, Generic, and Replica Field Specifications

Earlier in this chapter, you learned that you could define a specification as *Unique, Generic,* or *Replica.* You can ensure that you define the appropriate type of specification for a given field by following these simple guidelines:

- Use a *Unique* specification for any field that will appear only once within the entire database or for a field that serves as a *primary key*.

- Use a *Generic* specification for a field that serves as a template for other fields within the database. Remember to use a nonspecific field name and element settings that are as broad and general as possible.

- Use a *Replica* specification for a field that you base on a given generic field or for a field that serves as a foreign key within a table relationship.

Figure 9.8 shows the complete Unique field specification for a VENDOR ID NUMBER field.

Here are a few things to note about this specification:

1. This field also appears in the PRODUCTS table, as indicated by the Shared By general element. This is both reasonable and necessary because each product must be associated with a specific vendor. (You'll learn more about this type of issue in the next chapter.)

2. Examine the settings for the Uniqueness, Null Support, Required Value, and Edit Rule logical elements. They are set in this manner because the Key Type element is set to "Primary." You should, in fact, use these element settings for any field that serves as a primary key.

3. The Comparisons Allowed logical element is set to "Same Field—Equals" so that a user can compare VENDOR ID NUMBER values in the VENDORS table to VENDOR ID NUMBER values in the PRODUCTS table.

4. The Comparisons Allowed logical element is also set to "Value Expression—Equals" so that a user can compare VENDOR ID NUMBER values to some arbitrary numeric value.

Figure 9.9 shows the complete Generic field specification for a generic STATE field.

FIELD SPECIFICATIONS

General Elements

Field Name:	Vendor ID Number	**Specification Type:**	[X] Unique [ ] Generic [ ] Replica
Parent Table:	Vendors	**Source Specification:**	
Label:	Vendor #		
Shared By:	Products		
Alias(es):			

Description: A unique number used to identify each vendor that supplies our organization with goods or services. It is assigned when we place the first order for such goods or services with the vendor.

Physical Elements

Data Type:	Numeric	**Character Support:**
Length:	6	[ ] Letters (A–Z) [ ] Keyboard (. , / $ # %)
Decimal Places:	0	[X] Numbers (0–9) [ ] Special (© ® ™ ∑ π)
Input Mask:	######	
Display Format:	000000	

Logical Elements

Key Type:	[ ] Non	[X] Primary	**Edit Rule:**
	[ ] Foreign	[ ] Alternate	[ ] Enter Now, Edits Allowed
Key Structure:	[X] Simple	[ ] Composite	[X] Enter Now, Edits Not Allowed
Uniqueness:	[ ] Non-unique	[X] Unique	[ ] Enter Later, Edits Allowed
Null Support:	[ ] Nulls Allowed	[X] No Nulls	[ ] Enter Later, Edits Not Allowed
Values Entered By:	[ ] User	[X] System	[ ] Not Determined At This Time
Required Value:	[ ] No	[X] Yes	
Default Value:			

Range of Values: 100000–200000

Comparisons Allowed:

[X] Same Field	[ ] All	[X] =	[ ] >	[ ] >=	[ ] ≠	[ ] <	[ ] <=
[ ] Other Fields	[ ] All	[ ] =	[ ] >	[ ] >=	[ ] ≠	[ ] <	[ ] <=
[X] Value Expression	[ ] All	[X] =	[ ] >	[ ] >=	[ ] ≠	[ ] <	[ ] <=

Operations Allowed:

[ ] Same Field	[ ] All	[ ] +	[ ] −	[ ] x	[ ] ÷	[ ] Concatenation
[ ] Other Fields	[ ] All	[ ] +	[ ] −	[ ] x	[ ] ÷	[ ] Concatenation
[ ] Value Expression	[ ] All	[ ] +	[ ] −	[ ] x	[ ] ÷	[ ] Concatenation

Figure 9.8. *Unique field specification for the* VENDOR ID NUMBER *field.*

FIELD SPECIFICATIONS

General Elements

Field Name: State	**Specification Type:** ☐ Unique ☒ Generic ☐ Replica
Parent Table:	**Source Specification:** State
Label: State	
Shared By:	
Alias(es):	
Description: A state or territory within the United States in which a person, organization, or institution resides or conducts business.	

Physical Elements

		Character Support:	
Data Type:	Alphanumeric		
Length:	2	☒ Letters (A–Z)	☐ Keyboard (. , / $ # %)
Decimal Places:	None	☐ Numbers (0–9)	☐ Special (© ® ™ Σ π)
Input Mask:	AA		
Display Format:	Both letters should be capitalized.		

Logical Elements

Key Type:	☒ Non	☐ Primary	**Edit Rule:**
	☐ Foreign	☐ Alternate	☒ Enter Now, Edits Allowed
Key Structure:	☐ Simple	☐ Composite	☐ Enter Now, Edits Not Allowed
Uniqueness:	☒ Non-unique	☐ Unique	☐ Enter Later, Edits Allowed
Null Support:	☐ Nulls Allowed	☒ No Nulls	☐ Enter Later, Edits Not Allowed
Values Entered By:	☒ User	☐ System	☐ Not Determined At This Time
Required Value:	☐ No	☒ Yes	

Default Value:

Range of Values: All state abbreviations recognized by the United States Postal Service.

Comparisons Allowed:

	All	=	>	>=	≠	<	<=
☐ Same Field	☐	☐	☐	☐	☐	☐	☐
☐ Other Fields	☐	☐	☐	☐	☐	☐	☐
☒ Value Expression	☐	☒	☐	☐	☐	☐	☐

Operations Allowed:

	All	+	–	x	÷	Concatenation
☐ Same Field	☐	☐	☐	☐	☐	☐
☒ Other Fields	☐	☐	☐	☐	☐	☒
☒ Value Expression	☐	☐	☐	☐	☐	☒

Figure 9.9. *Generic field specification for a generic* STATE *field.*

Take note of these particular items:

1. The description is very general, as it should be for this type of specification.

2. The setting of the Display Format physical element is in the form of an instruction. This demonstrates that you have a great deal of flexibility in the way you set this element.

3. The Range of Values logical element is appropriately broad.

4. The Comparisons Allowed logical element is set to "Value Expression—Equals" so that a user can compare STATE values to some arbitrary two-character alphanumeric value.

5. The Operations Allowed logical element is set to "Other Fields—Concatenation" so that a user can concatenate a given STATE value to the value of some other alphanumeric field.

6. The Operations Allowed logical element is also set to "Value Expression—Concatenation" so that a user can concatenate a given STATE value to some arbitrary alphanumeric value.

This field (and its specification) now serves as a template for all other state fields you create in the database. For example, you can create a VENDSTATE field based on the generic STATE field. You'll define a Replica specification for the VENDSTATE field that is based on the STATE field's Generic specification. Although the VENDSTATE field's Replica specification draws its initial element settings from the STATE field's Generic specification, you can modify any of the Replica specification's element settings so that you can completely customize them for the VENDSTATE field. Figure 9.10 shows the customized Replica field specifications for the VENDSTATE field.

Here are a few things to note about this specification:

1. The field name (VENDSTATE) accurately denotes what the field represents.

2. The label ("State") is what the user will see on visual displays and printed documents.

FIELD SPECIFICATIONS

General Elements

Field Name:	VendState	Specification Type:	☐ Unique ☐ Generic ☒ Replica
Parent Table:	Vendors	Source Specification:	State
Label:	State		

Shared By:

Alias(es):

Description: The state in which the vendor's headquarters are located. This data is a component of the vendor's overall mailing address.

Physical Elements

Data Type:	Alphanumeric	**Character Support:**
Length:	2	☒ Letters (A–Z) ☐ Keyboard (. , / $ # %)
Decimal Places:	None	☐ Numbers (0–9) ☐ Special (© ® ™ Σ π)
Input Mask:	AA	
Display Format:	Both letters should be capitalized.	

Logical Elements

Key Type:	☒ Non	☐ Primary	**Edit Rule:**
	☐ Foreign	☐ Alternate	☒ Enter Now, Edits Allowed
Key Structure:	☐ Simple	☐ Composite	☐ Enter Now, Edits Not Allowed
Uniqueness:	☒ Non-unique	☐ Unique	☐ Enter Later, Edits Allowed
Null Support:	☐ Nulls Allowed	☒ No Nulls	☐ Enter Later, Edits Not Allowed
Values Entered By:	☒ User	☐ System	☐ Not Determined At This Time
Required Value:	☐ No	☒ Yes	
Default Value:	WA		

Range of Values: CA, ID, MT, OR, WA

Comparisons Allowed:

		All	=	>	>=	≠	<	<=
☐ Same Field		☐	☐	☐	☐	☐	☐	☐
☐ Other Fields		☐	☐	☐	☐	☐	☐	☐
☒ Value Expression		☐	☒	☐	☐	☐	☐	☐

Operations Allowed:

		All	+	−	x	÷	Concatenation
☐ Same Field		☐	☐	☐	☐	☐	☐
☒ Other Fields		☐	☐	☐	☐	☐	☒
☒ Value Expression		☐	☐	☐	☐	☐	☒

Figure 9.10. *Customized Replica field specification for the* VEND STATE *field.*

3. The Source Specification general element properly references the generic STATE field's specification.

4. The Description element is now specific to this field. Recall that the description is more general in the source specification.

5. A default value has been set for this field; there is no such value in the source specification.

6. The Range of Values element is now specific to this field; it was much broader in the source specification.

In the next chapter, you'll learn how to define a Replica field specification for a field that serves as a foreign key.

Defining Field Specifications for Each Field in the Database

Now that you have all the necessary fields assigned to each table and you understand the various elements within a field specification, you can begin the process of defining a field specification for each field in the database. It will take you a considerable amount of time to complete this process, but remember that you're working diligently to establish field-level integrity by ensuring that the data is consistent, valid, and as free from errors as possible. All your hard work will pay great dividends because the information you retrieve from the database will always be timely and accurate, and you will have a reliable set of structural blueprints you can use when you implement the database in an RDBMS program.

You can ensure that the specifications are as complete and accurate as possible by working with both users and management to define them. They can provide insights into the data and can be of special assistance in refining the specification's logical elements. You don't have to speak with *everyone* in the organization, but you do want to assemble and meet with a representative number of people who are very familiar with the data and how it is used. Schedule as many meetings as are necessary (or possible) to complete the interview process, and take the time you need to be as thorough as you can. Above all, *do not* rush through this phase! Doing so just diminishes the benefits of your overall efforts and increases your chances of making unnecessary mistakes.

The best strategy for this task is to define as many of the specifications as you can (as completely as possible) and then work with the participants to complete the rest. As you work with a field's specifications, use your best judgment to define the settings for each element. Don't worry if your settings seem slightly incorrect or if you have difficulty providing settings for some of the elements—you're going to review them with the participants anyway. After you've defined specifications for all of the fields that are familiar to you, begin meeting with the participants to work on specifications for the remaining fields.

Your first order of business during the *initial* meeting is to explain the various elements within a field specification and make sure that everyone understands them as much as possible. Providing the participants with a brief and succinct education on the specification's elements gives them the knowledge they need to help you define a specification properly. (In subsequent meetings, just review the elements to make certain that everyone remembers what they represent.)

Next, review all of the specifications you've defined and ask the participants whether the settings for the elements are suitable and correct. In some cases, the participants will reveal new information about a field that will affect that field's specification. For example, a participant may remember (prompted by some topic in the discussion) that there is a specific set of values that has always been used for a particular field; therefore, you set the field's Range of Values element to reflect this new information. Make sure that you examine each part of the specification and then move on to the next specification when the participants have no further suggestions for refinement. Repeat this process for each specification.

Now, work with the participants on the specifications you were unable to define or complete. Try to work with the people who are *most* familiar with the fields under discussion because they are likely to know what settings should be used for the Logical Elements category. Identify the appropriate element settings for each field and mark them on the Field Specifications sheet. After you've defined specifications for every field in the database, the entire process is complete.

The design of the new database is now close to completion. In the next chapter, you'll learn how to establish *relationships* between the tables in the database. Relationships are important because they allow a view to draw data from multiple tables simultaneously.

CASE STUDY

Now that you have all the appropriate fields assigned to the tables in the Mike's Bikes database, it's time to define field specifications for each field. Before you meet with Mike and his staff, you define as many field specifications as you can. None of the tables are unusual in any way, and the fields are pretty straightforward, so you have little difficulty in defining the specifications. Figure 9.11 shows the specification for the PRODUCT DESCRIPTION field in the PRODUCTS table.

Now you meet with Mike and his staff to discuss the field specifications you've defined. No one seems to have problems with any of the specifications; everyone confirms that all of the element settings seem suitable and correct. You do have a question, however, regarding the CATEGORY field in the PRODUCTS table: You want to know the appropriate setting for the Range of Values element. The response to your question is mixed—no one seems to know the complete list of categories that are

FIELD SPECIFICATIONS

General Elements

Field Name:	Product Description	**Specification Type:**	[X] Unique	[ ] Generic	[ ] Replica
Parent Table:	Products	**Source Specification:**			
Label:	Description				
Shared By:					
Alias(es):					

Description: A statement that provides pertinent details about the product. This information is useful to our sales and promotion efforts and is provided to our customers by means of various promotional materials.

Physical Elements

		Character Support:	
Data Type:	Alphanumeric		
Length:	180	[X] Letters (A–Z)	[X] Keyboard (. , / $ # %)
Decimal Places:	None	[X] Numbers (0–9)	[X] Special (© ® ™ Σ π)
Input Mask:			
Display Format:			

Logical Elements

Key Type:	[X] Non	[ ] Primary	**Edit Rule:**
	[ ] Foreign	[ ] Alternate	[X] Enter Now, Edits Allowed
Key Structure:	[ ] Simple	[ ] Composite	[ ] Enter Now, Edits Not Allowed
Uniqueness:	[ ] Non-unique	[X] Unique	[ ] Enter Later, Edits Allowed
Null Support:	[ ] Nulls Allowed	[X] No Nulls	[ ] Enter Later, Edits Not Allowed
Values Entered By:	[X] User	[ ] System	[ ] Not Determined At This Time
Required Value:	[ ] No	[X] Yes	

Default Value:

Range of Values:

Comparisons Allowed:

[ ] Same Field	[ ] All	[ ] =	[ ] >	[ ] >=	[ ] ≠	[ ] <	[ ] <=
[ ] Other Fields	[ ] All	[ ] =	[ ] >	[ ] >=	[ ] ≠	[ ] <	[ ] <=
[ ] Value Expression	[ ] All	[ ] =	[ ] >	[ ] >=	[ ] ≠	[ ] <	[ ] <=

Operations Allowed:

[ ] Same Field	[ ] All	[ ] +	[ ] –	[ ] x	[ ] ÷	[ ] Concatenation
[ ] Other Fields	[ ] All	[ ] +	[ ] –	[ ] x	[ ] ÷	[ ] Concatenation
[ ] Value Expression	[ ] All	[ ] +	[ ] –	[ ] x	[ ] ÷	[ ] Concatenation

Figure 9.11. *Field specification for the* PRODUCT DESCRIPTION *field.*

valid for the field, so you decide to specify a general range of values for now. Figure 9.12 shows the revised logical elements for the CATEGORY field.

Logical Elements

Key Type:	[X] Non	[ ] Primary	**Edit Rule:**
	[ ] Foreign	[ ] Alternate	[X] Enter Now, Edits Allowed
Key Structure:	[ ] Simple	[ ] Composite	[ ] Enter Now, Edits Not Allowed
Uniqueness:	[X] Non-unique	[ ] Unique	[ ] Enter Later, Edits Allowed
Null Support:	[ ] Nulls Allowed	[X] No Nulls	[ ] Enter Later, Edits Not Allowed
Values Entered By:	[X] User	[ ] System	[ ] Not Determined At This Time
Required Value:	[ ] No	[X] Yes	

Default Value:

Range of Values: Any valid internal or external product category.

Comparisons Allowed:

	All	=	>	>=	≠	<	<=
[ ] Same Field	[ ]	[ ]	[ ]	[ ]	[ ]	[ ]	[ ]
[ ] Other Fields	[ ]	[ ]	[ ]	[ ]	[ ]	[ ]	[ ]
[X] Value Expression	[ ]	[X]	[ ]	[ ]	[ ]	[ ]	[ ]

Operations Allowed:

	All	+	−	x	÷	Concatenation
[ ] Same Field	[ ]	[ ]	[ ]	[ ]	[ ]	[ ]
[X] Other Fields	[ ]	[ ]	[ ]	[ ]	[ ]	[X]
[X] Value Expression	[ ]	[ ]	[ ]	[ ]	[ ]	[X]

Figure 9.12. *The logical elements for the* CATEGORY *field in the PRODUCTS table.*

You'll revisit this field (and its elements) again when you establish business rules for the database. With this problem solved, your meeting—as well as the process of establishing field specifications—is complete.

Summary

The chapter opened with an explanation of why field specifications are important and the benefits you derive from defining them. You learned that defining specifications helps you establish and enforce *field-level integrity*, enhances overall data integrity, and compels you to acquire a complete understanding of the nature and purpose of the data in the database. This level of understanding enables you to leverage the data to your best advantage.

Next, we discussed the anatomy of a field specification. You're now familiar with the three categories of elements within the specification and the sheet you use to record them. We then discussed each category and its elements in detail. As you now know, the *General Elements* category represents the most basic attributes of the field. During this discussion, you learned a set of guidelines that will help you compose a good field description. You also learned that you could define three types of specifications, thus enabling you to establish and maintain consistent field definitions. We examined the *Physical Elements* category next, and you learned that it pertains to the structure of the field. The *Logical Elements* category was the last topic of discussion in this section. You now know that it mainly pertains to a field's values and that it includes elements such as Key Type, Null Support, Range of Values, Edit Rule, Comparisons Allowed, and Operations Allowed.

We then discussed how to use each type of specification, and you learned a set of guidelines that will help you determine which one to define for a given field. You also examined samples of the specifications, and you know how they differ.

The chapter ended with a discussion of defining field specifications for each field. Here you learned that the best way to ensure complete and accurate specifications is to work with users and management to define them. You should first define as many specifications as you can and then work with the staff to define specifications for the remaining fields. You also learned that you could work with staff to refine the specifications you initially defined.

Review Questions

1. State two major reasons why *field specifications* are important.

2. What do you gain by establishing *field-level integrity*?

3. What are the three categories of elements in a field specification?

4. Name the three types of specifications.

5. Why is it beneficial for you to compose a proper field description?

6. What does the Data Type element indicate?

7. What does the Character Support element indicate?

8. What is the purpose of the Display Format element?

9. What types of keys are indicated on a field specification?

10. True or False: A null represents a blank value.

11. What is the significance of the Range of Values element?

12. What is the purpose of an Edit Rule?

13. What is the purpose of the Comparisons Allowed element?

14. What is a *value expression*?

15. When do you use a generic specification?

10

Table Relationships

There is no substitute for the comfort supplied by the
utterly taken-for-granted relationship.
—IRIS MURDOCH

Topics Covered in This Chapter

Why Relationships Are Important

Types of Relationships

Identifying Existing Relationships

Establishing Each Relationship

Refining All Foreign Keys

Establishing Relationship Characteristics

Relationship-Level Integrity

Case Study

Summary

Review Questions

You learned in Chapter 3 that a *relationship* exists between two tables when you can in some way associate the records of the first table with those of the second. You also learned that each relationship has three distinct characteristics: the type of relationship that exists between the tables, the manner in which each participates, and the degree to which each table participates.

In this chapter, I'll discuss these topics in more detail. You'll first learn how to identify and establish the relationships between the tables in a database and then how to set each relationship's characteristics. You'll also learn how to diagram tables and relationships, which will enable you to create a graphic representation of the entire database structure.

Why Relationships Are Important

A relationship is an important component of a relational database.

- *It establishes a connection between a pair of tables that are logically related to each other.* A pair of tables is logically related via the data each contains. For example, consider the tables in Figure 10.1.

Students

Student ID	StudFirst Name	StudLast Name	<< other fields >>
60001	Zachary	Ehrlich	......
60002	Susan	McLain	......
60003	Joe	Rosales	......
60004	Michael	Chow	......
60005	Angie	Thompson	......

Student Instruments

Student ID	Instrument ID	Checkout Date
60002	1000	09/26/01
60001	1002	09/28/01
60003	1010	09/28/01
60003	1013	09/28/01
60003	1011	09/28/01
60001	1022	10/02/01
60001	1021	10/02/01

Figure 10.1. *A pair of logically related tables.*

A logical relationship exists between the data in the STUDENTS table and the data in the STUDENT INSTRUMENTS table. A student can check out one or more instruments during the course of a school year, so a record in the STUDENTS table (representing the student) can be related to one or more records in the STUDENT INSTRUMENTS table (representing the particular instruments the student checks out).

- *It helps to further refine table structures and minimize redundant data.* As you establish a relationship between a pair of tables, you will inevitably make minor modifications to the table structures. These refinements will make the structures more efficient and minimize any redundant data that the tables may contain.

- *It is the mechanism that enables you to draw data from multiple tables simultaneously.* In Chapter 12, you'll learn how a relationship enables you to construct a view using fields from two or more related tables.

A properly defined relationship ensures relationship-level integrity, which guarantees that the relationship itself is reliable and sound. (Recall that relationship-level integrity is a component of overall data integrity.) You can take advantage of the many benefits a relational database provides only when you establish each relationship carefully and properly. Failure to do so means that you'll have a hard and tedious time working with data from multiple tables, and you'll certanly encounter problems when you try to insert, update, or delete records in related tables. You'll learn more about these types of problems later as the design process unfolds.

Types of Relationships

Before you begin to establish relationships between tables in the database, you must know what *types of relationships* can exist between a given pair of tables. Knowing how to identify them properly is an invaluable skill for designing a database successfully.

There are three specific types of relationships that can exist between a pair of tables: *one-to-one*, *one-to-many*, and *many-to-many*. The tables participate in *only one* type of relationship at any given time. (You'll rarely need to change the type of relationship between a pair of tables. Only major changes in either of the table's structures could cause you to change the relationship.)

❖ **Note** The discussion for each type of relationship begins with a generic example of the relationship. Learning how to visualize a relationship generically enables you to understand the principle behind the relationship itself. Once you understand how and why the relationship works, you'll be able to determine whether it exists between a given pair of tables quite easily.

Each discussion also includes an example of how to diagram the relationship. I provide special instructions pertaining to the diagramming process where appropriate and explain the symbols incorporated within the diagram as necessary. This allows you to learn the diagramming method at a reasonable pace and keeps you from having to memorize the entire set of diagram symbols all at once.

Figure 10.2 shows the first symbols you will use to diagram a table relationship.

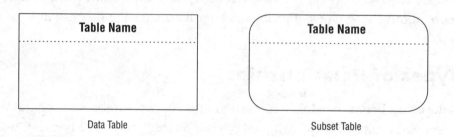

Figure 10.2. *Diagramming symbols for a data table and a subset table.*

One-to-One Relationships

A pair of tables bears a *one-to-one* relationship when a single record in the first table is related to *only one* record in the second table, and a single record in the second table is related to *only one* record in the first table. Figure 10.3 shows a generic example of a one-to-one relationship.

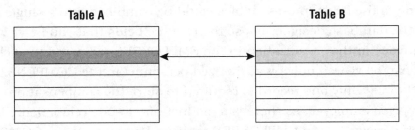

Figure 10.3. *A generic example of a one-to-one relationship.*

As you can see, a single record in TABLE A is related to only one record in TABLE B, and a single record in TABLE B is related to only one record in TABLE A. A one-to-one relationship usually (but not always) involves a *subset* table. Figure 10.4 shows an example of a typical one-to-one relationship that you might find in a database for an organization's human resources department. This example also illustrates a situation where neither of the tables is a subset table.

Employees

EmpID	EmpFirst Name	EmpLast Name	Home Phone	<< other fields >>
100	Zachary	Erlich	553-3992	......
101	Susan	McLain	790-3992	......
102	Joe	Rosales	551-4993	......

Compensation

EmpID	Hourly Rate	Commission Rate	<< other fields >>
100	25.00	5.0%	......
101	19.75	3.5%	......
102	22.50	5.0%	......

Figure 10.4. *A typical example of a one-to-one relationship.*

Although the fields in these tables could be combined into a single table, the database designer chose to place the fields that can be viewed by anyone in the organization in the EMPLOYEES table and the fields that can be viewed only by authorized personnel in the COMPENSATION table. Only one record is required to store the compensation data for a given employee, so there is a distinct one-to-one relationship between a record in the EMPLOYEES table and a record in the COMPENSATION table.

A one-to-one relationship usually (but not always) involves a *subset* table. (Indeed, neither of the tables in Figure 10.4 is a subset table.) Figure 10.5 shows a generic example of how you create a relationship diagram for a one-to-one relationship.

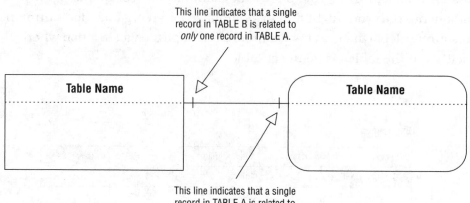

This line indicates that a single
record in TABLE B is related to
only one record in TABLE A.

Table Name   Table Name

This line indicates that a single
record in TABLE A is related to
only one record in TABLE B,

Figure 10.5. *Diagramming a one-to-one relationship.*

The line that appears between the tables in the diagram indicates the type of relationship, and there is a particular line that you use for each type. Later in this chapter, you'll learn how to modify the line to show the characteristics of the relationship as well. Figure 10.6 shows the relationship diagram for the EMPLOYEES and COMPENSATION tables in Figure 10.4. (Note that a Data Table symbol represents each table.)

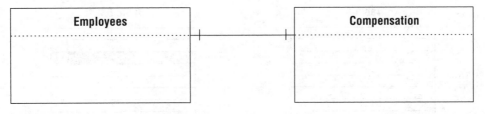

Figure 10.6. *The relationship diagram for the EMPLOYEES and COMPENSATION tables.*

One-to-Many Relationships

A *one-to-many* relationship exists between a pair of tables when a single record in the first table can be related to one or more records in the second table, but a single record in the second table can be related to *only one* record in the first table. Let's look at a generic example of this type of relationship.

Say you're working with two tables, TABLE A and TABLE B, that have a one-to-many relationship between them. Because of the relationship, a single record in TABLE A can be related to one or more records in TABLE B. Figure 10.7 shows the relationship from the perspective of TABLE A.

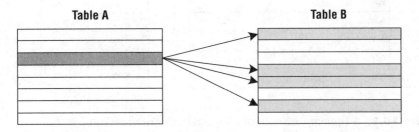

Figure 10.7. *A one-to-many relationship from the perspective of TABLE A.*

Conversely, a single record in the TABLE B can be related to *only* one record in TABLE A. Figure 10.8 shows the relationship from the perspective of TABLE B.

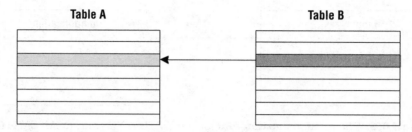

Figure 10.8. *A one-to-many relationship from the perspective of TABLE B.*

This is by far the most common relationship that exists between a pair of tables in a database, and it is the easiest to identify. It is crucial from a data-integrity standpoint because it helps to eliminate duplicate data and to keep redundant data to an absolute minimum. Figure 10.9 shows a common example of a one-to-many relationship that you might find in a database for a video rental store.

Customers

Customer ID	CustFirst Name	CustLast Name	<< other fields >>
9001	Paul	Litwin	......
9002	Alison	Balter	......
9003	Andy	Baron	......
9004	Chris	Kunicki	......
9005	Mary	Chipman	......

Customer Rentals

Customer ID	Video ID	Checkout Date
9002	80115	09/26/01
9001	64558	09/28/01
9003	10202	09/28/01
9003	11354	09/28/01
9003	78422	10/02/01
9005	30556	09/26/01
9004	20655	10/05/01

Figure 10.9. *A typical example of a one-to-many relationship.*

A customer can check out any number of videos, so a single record in the CUSTOMERS table can be related to one or more records in the CUSTOMER RENTALS table. A single video, however, is associated with only one customer at any given time, so a single record in the CUS-

TOMER RENTALS table is related to only one record in the CUSTOM-ERS table.

Figure 10.10 shows a generic example of how you create a relationship diagram for a one-to-many relationship.

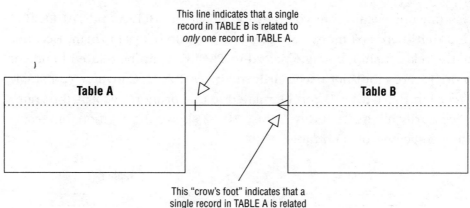

Figure 10.10. *Diagramming a one-to-many relationship.*

Note that the crow's foot symbol is always located next to the table on the "many" side of the relationship. Figure 10.11 shows the relationship diagram for the CUSTOMERS and CUSTOMER RENTALS tables in Figure 10.9.

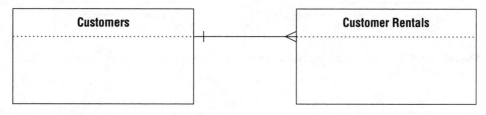

Figure 10.11. *The relationship diagram for the CUSTOMERS and CUSTOMER RENTALS tables.*

Many-to-Many Relationships

A pair of tables bears a *many-to-many* relationship when a single record in the first table can be related to one or more records in the second table *and* a single record in the second table can be related to one or more records in the first table.

Assume once again that you're working with TABLE A and TABLE B and that there is a many-to-many relationship between them. Because of the relationship, a single record in TABLE A can be related to one or more records (but not necessarily all) in TABLE B. Conversely, a single record in the TABLE B can be related to one or more records (but not necessarily all) in TABLE A. Figure 10.12 shows the relationship from the perspective of each table.

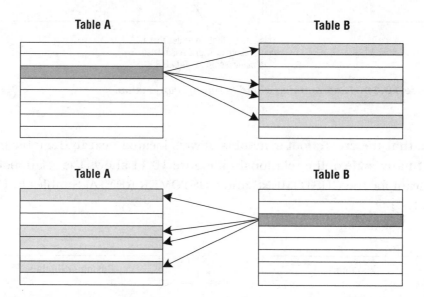

Figure 10.12. *A many-to-many relationship from the perspective of both TABLE A and TABLE B.*

This is the second most common relationship that exists between a pair of tables in a database. It can be a little more difficult to identify than a one-to-many relationship, so you must be sure to examine the tables carefully. Figure 10.13 shows a typical example of a many-to-many relationship that you might find in a school database, which happens to be a classic example of this type of relationship (no pun intended!).

Students

Student ID	StudFirst Name	StudLast Name	StudStreet Address	StudCity	StudState	StudZipcode	<< other fields >>
60001	Zachary	Erlich	1204 Bryant Road	Seattle	WA	98125	....
60002	Susan	McLain	101 C Street, Apt. 32	Redmond	WA	98052	....
60003	Joe	Rosales	201 Cherry Lane SE	Redmond	WA	98073	....
60004	Diana	Barlet	4141 Lake City Way	Woodinville	WA	98072	....
60005	Tom	Wickerath	2100 Mineola Avenue	Bellevue	WA	98006	....

Classes

Class ID	Class Name	Class Category	Credits	Instructor ID	Classroom	<< other fields >>
900001	Advanced Calculus	Math	5	220087	2201	....
900002	Advanced Music Theory	Music	3	220039	7012	....
900003	American History	History	5	220148	3305	....
900004	Computers in Business	Computer Science	2	220387	5115	....
900005	Computers in Society	Computer Science	2	220387	5117	....
900006	Introduction to Biology	Biology	5	220498	3112	....
900007	Introduction to Database Design	Computer Science	5	220516	5105	....
900008	Introduction to Physics	Physics	4	220087	2205	....
900009	Introduction to Political Science	Political Science	5	220337	3308	....

Figure 10.13. *A typical example of a many-to-many relationship.*

A student can attend one or more classes during a school year, so a single record in the STUDENTS table can be related to one or more records in the CLASSES table. Conversely, one or more students will attend a given class, so a single record in the CLASSES table can be related to one or more records in the STUDENTS table.

Figure 10.14 shows a generic example of how you create a relationship diagram for a many-to-many relationship.

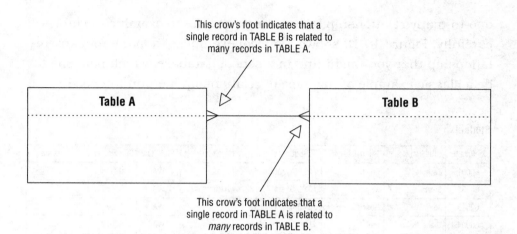

Figure 10.14. *Diagramming a many-to-many relationship.*

In this case, there is a crow's foot symbol located next to *each* table. Figure 10.15 shows the relationship diagram for the STUDENTS and CLASSES tables in Figure 10.13.

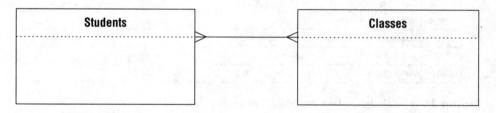

Figure 10.15. *The relationship diagram for the STUDENTS and CLASSES tables.*

Problems with Many-to-Many Relationships

A many-to-many relationship has an inherent peculiarity that you must address before you can effectively use the data from the tables involved in the relationship. The issue is this: How do you *easily* associate records from the first table with records in the second table in order to establish the relationship? This is an important question because you'll encounter problems such as these if you do not establish the relationship properly:

- It will be tedious and somewhat difficult to retrieve information from one of the tables.

- One of the tables will contain a large amount of redundant data.

- Duplicate data will exist within both tables.

- It will be difficult for you to insert, update, and delete data.

There are two common methods that novice and inexperienced developers use in a futile attempt to address this situation. I'll demonstrate how you might apply these methods using the STUDENTS and CLASSES tables in Figure 10.16 as examples.

Table Structures

Students		Classes	
Student ID	PK	Class ID	PK
StudFirst Name		Class Name	
StudLast Name		Class Category	
StudStreet Address		Credits	
StudCity		Instructor ID	
StudState		Classroom	
StudZipcode		Class Description	
StudHome Phone		Catalog Code	
StudEmail Address			
Social Security Number			

Figure 10.16. *Structures of the STUDENTS and CLASSES tables.*

> ❖ **Note** As this example unfolds, keep in mind that every many-to-many relationship you encounter will exhibit these same issues.

As you can see, there is no actual connection between the two tables, so you have no way of associating records in one table with records in the other table. The first method you might use to attempt to establish a connection involves taking a field from one table and incorporating it a given number of times within the other table. (This approach usually appeals to people who are accustomed to working with spreadsheets.) For example, you could take the STUDENT ID field from the STUDENTS table and incorporate it within the CLASSES table structure, creating as many copies of the field as you need to represent the maximum number of students that could attend any class. Figure 10.17 shows the revised version of the CLASSES table structure.

Table Structures

Classes

Class ID	PK	Student ID 1	Student ID 9	Student ID 17
Class Name		Student ID 2	Student ID 10	Student ID 18
Class Category		Student ID 3	Student ID 11	Student ID 19
Credits		Student ID 4	Student ID 12	Student ID 20
Instructor ID		Student ID 5	Student ID 13	Student ID 21
Classroom		Student ID 6	Student ID 14	Student ID 22
Class Description		Student ID 7	Student ID 15	Student ID 23
Catalog Code		Student ID 8	Student ID 16	Student ID 24

Figure 10.17. *Incorporating STUDENT ID fields within the CLASSES table structure.*

This structure is likely to be problematic, so you might try taking the CLASS ID field from the CLASSES table and incorporating it within the STUDENTS table structure instead. Figure 10.18 shows the revised version of the STUDENTS table structure.

Table Structures

Students

Student ID	*PK*	Class ID 1
StudFirst Name		Class ID 2
StudLast Name		Class ID 3
StudStreet Address		Class ID 4
StudCity		Class ID 5
StudState		Class ID 6
StudZipcode		Class ID 7
StudHome Phone		Class ID 8
StudEmail Address		
Social Security Number		

Figure 10.18. *Incorporating CLASS ID fields within the STUDENTS table structure.*

Do these structures look (vaguely) familiar? They should. All you've done using this method is introduce a "flattened" multivalued field into the table structure. In doing so, you've also introduced the problems associated with a multivalued field. (If necessary, review Chapter 7.) Although you know how to resolve a multivalued field, this is not a good or proper way to establish the relationship.

The second method you might attempt to use is simply a variation of the first method. In this case, you take one or more fields from one table and incorporate a *single instance of each field* within the other table. For example, you could take the CLASS ID, CLASS NAME, and INSTRUCTOR ID fields from the CLASSES table and incorporate them into the STUDENTS table in order to identify the classes in which a student is currently enrolled. This may seem to be a distinct improvement over the first method, but you'll see that there are problems that arise from such modifications when you load the revised STUDENTS table with sample data.

Figure 10.19 clearly illustrates the problems you'll encounter using this method.

Students

Student ID	Student First Name	Student Last Name	Class ID	Class Name	Instructor ID	<< other fields >>
60001	Zachary	Erlich	900009	Introduction to Political Science	220087	......
60001	Zachary	Erlich	900002	Advanced Music Theory	220039	......
60001	Zachary	Erlich	900003	American History	220148	......
60001	Zachary	Erlich	900004	Computers in Business	220121	......
60002	Susan	McLain	900009	Introduction to Political Science	220087	......
60002	Susan	McLain	900002	Advanced Music Theory	220039	......
60002	Susan	McLain	900006	Introduction to Biology	220117	......
60003	Joe	Rosales	900004	Computers in Business	220121	......
60003	Joe	Rosales	900001	Advanced Calculus	220101	......
60003	Joe	Rosales	900008	Introduction to Physics	220075	......
60004	Diana	Barlet	900007	Introduction to Database Design	220120	......

Figure 10.19. *The revised STUDENTS table with sample data.*

- *The table contains unnecessary duplicate fields.* You learned all about unnecessary duplicate fields and the problems they pose back in Chapter 7, so you know that using them here is not a good idea. Besides, it is very likely that the CLASS NAME and IN- STRUCTOR ID fields are not appropriate in the STUDENTS table— the CLASS ID field identifies the class sufficiently, and it is really all you need to identify the classes a student is taking.

- *There is a large amount of redundant data.* Even if you remove the CLASS NAME and INSTRUCTOR ID fields from the STUDENTS table, the CLASS ID field will still produce a lot of redundant data.

- *It is difficult to insert a new record.* If you enter a record in the STUDENTS table for a new class (instead of entering it in the CLASSES table) without also entering student data, the fields pertaining to the student will be null—including the primary key of the STUDENTS table (STUDENT ID). This will automatically trigger a violation of the Elements of a Primary Key because the primary key *cannot* be null; therefore, you cannot insert the record into the table until you can provide a proper primary key value.

- *It is difficult to delete a record.* This is especially true if the only data about a new class has been recorded in the particular student record you want to delete. Note the record for Diana Barlet, for example. If Diana decides not to attend any classes this year and you delete her record, you will lose the data for the "Introduction to Database Design" class. That might not create a serious problem—unless someone neglected to enter the data about this class into the CLASSES table as well. Once you delete Diana's record, you'll have to re-enter all of the data for the class in the CLASSES table.

Fortunately, you will not have to worry about any of these problems because you're going to learn the *proper* way to establish a many-to-many relationship.

Self-Referencing Relationships

This particular type of relationship *does not* exist between a pair of tables, which is why it isn't mentioned at the beginning of this section. It is instead a relationship that exists *between the records within a table*. Ironically, you'll still regard this throughout the design process as a table relationship.

A table bears a *self-referencing* relationship (also known as a *recursive* relationship) to itself when a given record in the table is related to other records within the table. Similar to its dual-table counterpart, a self-referencing relationship can be one-to-one, one-to-many, or many-to-many.

One-to-One

A *self-referencing one-to-one* relationship exists when a given record in the table can be related to only one other record within the table. The MEMBERS table in Figure 10.20 is an example of a table with this type of relationship. In this case, a given member can sponsor only one other member within the organization; the SPONSOR ID field stores the member identification number of the member acting as a sponsor. Note that Susan McLain is Tom Wickerath's sponsor.

Members

Member ID	MbrFirst Name	MbrLast Name	Sponsor ID	<< other fields >>
1001	Zachary	Erlich		......
1002	Susan	McLain	1001	......
1003	Joe	Rosales		......
1004	Diana	Barlet	1003	......
1005	Tom	Wickerath	1002	......

Figure 10.20. *Example of a self-referencing one-to-one relationship.*

Figure 10.21 shows how you diagram this type of relationship.

One-to-Many

A table bears a *self-referencing one-to-many* relationship to itself when a given record in the table can be related to one or more other records within the table. Figure 10.22 shows an example in which a given customer can refer other customers to the organization. The REFERRED BY

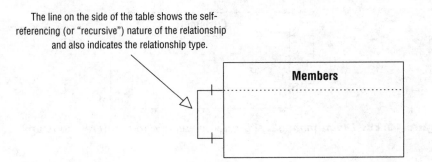

The line on the side of the table shows the self-referencing (or "recursive") nature of the relationship and also indicates the relationship type.

Members

Figure 10.21. *Diagramming a self-referencing one-to-one relationship.*

field stores the customer identification number of the customer making the referral. Note that Paul Litwin referred both Andy Baron and Mary Chipman.

Customers

Customer ID	CustFirst Name	CustLast Name	Referred By	<< other fields >>
9001	Paul	Litwin		......
9002	Alison	Balter		......
9003	Andy	Baron	9001	......
9004	Chris	Kunicki	9003	......
9005	Mary	Chipman	9001	......

Figure 10.22. *Example of a self-referencing one-to-many relationship.*

Figure 10.23 shows how you diagram a self-referencing one-to-many relationship.

Many-to-Many

A *self-referencing many-to-many* relationship exists when a given record in the table can be related to one or more other records within the table and one or more records can themselves be related to the given record.

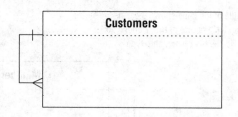

Figure 10.23. *Diagramming a self-referencing one-to-many relationship.*

This may sound somewhat confusing at first, but the example in Figure 10.24 should help clarify the matter.

Parts

Part ID	Part Name	<< other fields >>
701	Top Clamp	......
702	Bottom Clamp	......
703	Fastening Bolt	......
704	Clamp Assembly	......
705	Saddle	......
706	Seatpost	......
707	Seat Assembly	......
708	Body Tube	......
709	Front Fork Tube	......
710	Rear Stay Tube	......
711	Frame Assembly	......

Figure 10.24. *Example of a self-referencing many-to-many relationship.*

In this case, a particular part can comprise several different component parts, *and* it can itself be a component of other parts. For example, a clamp assembly (Part ID 704) is composed of a fastening bolt (Part ID 703), a bottom clamp (Part ID 702), and a top clamp (Part ID 701). Additionally, the clamp assembly is itself a component of a seat assembly (Part ID 707) and a frame assembly (Part ID 711). Figure 10.25 shows how you diagram this type of relationship.

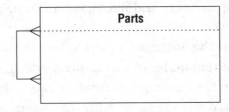

Figure 10.25. *Diagramming a self-referencing many-to-many relationship.*

❖ **Note** Before you begin to work through the examples in the remainder of the chapter, now is a good time to remember a principle I presented in the introduction:

> Focus on the concept or technique and its intended results, *not on the example used to illustrate it.*

There are, without a doubt, any number of ways in which you can relate the tables in these examples (and in the case study as well), depending on each table's role within a given database. The manner in which I use the examples here is not important; what is important are the techniques I use to identify and establish relationships between tables. Once you learn these techniques, you can identify and establish relationships for any pair of tables within any context you may encounter.

Now that you've learned about the various types of table relationships, your next task is to *identify* the relationships that currently exist among the tables in the database.

Identifying Existing Relationships

When you were composing the table descriptions earlier in the database-design process (back in Chapter 7, to be exact), you assembled a representative group of users and management to help you with that task. These people were also designated as representatives of the organization and granted the authority to aid in the decision-making process throughout the remainder of the database-design process. (At least, this is the current assumption for the sake of discussion and example.) Now you'll arrange meetings with this group once again so that they can help you identify existing table relationships. These folks can provide valuable input because they are likely to have a good perspective on how various subjects (or tables) are related. Although their perceptions of the manner in which these subjects are related may not always be complete or accurate, their contributions will still be useful in identifying most of the relationships.

Begin the process of identifying relationships by creating a matrix of all the tables in your database. (You can do this on a sheet of paper, a white board, or a spreadsheet program.) For example, assume you're working with these tables:

BUILDINGS   FACULTY   STUDENTS

CLASSES   ROOMS

COMPENSATION   STAFF

List each of the tables across the top of the matrix, and then again down the left-hand side of the matrix; make certain the table names are in the same order. Figure 10.26 illustrates how the matrix should appear.

Select a table on the left as a starting point and determine whether it has a relationship with any of the tables listed across the top, working your way through the matrix as you do so. (It doesn't matter whether you work your way across the top or down the side. Just make sure you work consistently, as it will make the task much easier.)

Keep in mind that you're looking for *direct* relationships only—there must be a specific connection between tables participating in the rela-

	Buildings	Classes	Compensation	Faculty	Rooms	Staff	Students
Buildings							
Classes							
Compensation							
Faculty							
Rooms							
Staff							
Students							

Figure 10.26. *Setting up a table matrix to help identify existing relationships.*

tionship. For example, the CLASSES table has a direct relationship to the STUDENTS table because one or more students can attend a given class. Conversely, the CLASSES table has an *indirect* relationship to the STAFF table via the FACULTY table; it is a *faculty* member that teaches a class, not a staff member. (You don't have to worry about indirect relationships just yet.)

As you work with a pair of tables, ask the participants questions about the records in each table. Your goal is to determine the relationship between a single record in one table to one or more records in the other table, and vice versa. (Remember that each record represents a single instance of the subject represented by the table.) When you get to a point where you're examining the same table on both sides of the matrix, try to determine the relationship between a given record in the table to one or more other records within the table.

There are two types of questions you can ask:

1. *Associative.* This is a simple and straightforward type of question that you can generically phrase as follows: Can a single record in (name of first table) be associated with one or more records in

(name of second table)? Considering the matrix in Figure 10.26, you might ask an associative question such as this:

> Can a single record in CLASSES be associated with one or more records in BUILDINGS?

You can use this type of question to determine whether a table has a self-referencing relationship by making two minor modifications to the question itself: Can a single (*singular form of the table name*) be associated with one or more (*plural form of the table name*)? For example, here's a question you might pose for the STAFF table:

> Can a single staff member be associated with one or more other staff members?

2. *Contextual.* This type of question contrasts a single instance of the subject represented by the first table against multiple instances of the subject represented by the second table. There are two categories within this type of question: *ownership-oriented* and *action-oriented.*

  a. Ownership-oriented questions include words or phrases such as "own," "has," "is part of," and "contain." Here's an example of this type of question:

  > Can a single order *contain* one or more products?

  You can use this question to test for a self-referencing relationship by making the same modifications you made to the associative question. Here's an example of a question you might pose for a PARTS table:

  > Can a single part *contain* one or more other parts?

  b. Action-oriented questions incorporate action verbs such as "make," "visit," "place," "teach," and "attend." Here's an example of this type of question:

> Does a single flight instructor *teach* one or more types of classes?

As you may have already guessed, you can use this question to test for a self-referencing relationship as well by making the same modifications:

> Does a single staff member *manage* one or more other staff members?

Use the type of question you believe to be the most appropriate for the pair of tables you're working with. As you work down the list of tables in the matrix, you'll eventually realize that you're asking questions about a given pair of tables twice—once from the perspective of the first table and then again from the perspective of the second table. The answers to both of these questions will identify the type of relationship that exists between the tables.

Continuing with the example, assume that you've decided to start with the CLASSES table and this is your first question:

> Is a single class held in one or more buildings?

The answer to this question will reveal the type of relationship that exists between these tables *from the perspective of the CLASSES table*. If you receive the following answer, then a one-to-one relationship exists between these tables:

> A single class is held in only one building.

If you receive this answer, however, then a *one-to-many* relationship exists between the two tables:

> A single class may be held in more than one building.

Once you've identified the relationship, indicate the relationship type in the box located at the junction of the CLASSES table row (on the left) and the BUILDINGS table column (on the top). You can use the following shorthand symbols for the relationship types:

1:1—one-to-one

1:N—one-to-many

M:N—many-to-many

> ❖ **Note** You won't need the many-to-many shorthand symbol at this point, but I've included it here for completeness.

Figure 10.27 shows how the table matrix looks after you've finished identifying relationships for the CLASSES table. Remember that the relationships indicated here are *from the perspective of the CLASSES table*.

	Buildings	Classes	Compensation	Faculty	Rooms	Staff	Students
Buildings							
Classes	1:1			1:N	1:1		1:N
Compensation							
Faculty							
Rooms							
Staff							
Students							

Figure 10.27. *Completed table-matrix entries for the CLASSES table.*

You've probably noticed that some of the junction boxes are empty; this is perfectly acceptable. It's unnecessary for you to enter anything into the junction box if there is no relationship between the tables at either end of the junction.

Now you repeat this process for each table on the left-hand side of the matrix. Remember that you can start with any table. Let's assume that you decide to continue with the BUILDINGS table, and you're attempting to identify the relationship between it and the CLASSES table. Yes, I know you've covered this once already, but in this case you're identifying the relationship *from the perspective of the* BUILDINGS *table*. Let's now assume that you ask this question:

Does a single building provide space for more than one class?

If the answer is yes, then a one-to-many relationship exists between these tables; otherwise, it's a one-to-one relationship. Once you've identified the relationship, indicate the relationship type in the box located at the junction of the BUILDINGS table row (on the left) and the CLASSES table column (on the top). Figure 10.28 shows the revised table matrix with your entries for the BUILDINGS table.

	Buildings	Classes	Compensation	Faculty	Rooms	Staff	Students
Buildings		**1:N**			**1:N**		
Classes	1:1			1:N	1:1		1:N
Compensation							
Faculty							
Rooms							
Staff							
Students							

Figure 10.28. *Completed table-matrix entries for the BUILDINGS table.*

You've just seen two examples of how to identify a relationship between a distinct pair of tables, so let's take a look at how you identify a self-referencing relationship for a single table. Assume you're working with the STAFF table, and you're now at the junction between the STAFF table on the left and the STAFF table on the top. Using the techniques you learned earlier in this section, you might pose a question such as this:

> Can a single staff member be associated with one or more other staff members?

As with the earlier examples, the answer will indicate the type of relationship. Say you received this answer:

> Yes, a given staff member can be the spouse of another staff member.

This indicates (rather obviously) that a self-referencing *one-to-one* relationship exists for the STAFF table. But assume you received this answer instead:

> Yes, a single staff member can manage several other staff members.

You probably quickly realized that this answer indicates that a self-referencing *one-to-many* relationship exists for the STAFF table. Identifying these two types of relationships is a relatively easy task; identifying a self-referencing many-to-many relationship can be slightly more difficult.

This is the type of question you must ask in order to determine whether a table has a self-referencing many-to-many relationship: Can a single (*singular form of the table name*) be associated with one or more other (*plural form of the table name*), and can any of *those* (*plural form of the table name*) then be associated with yet one or more other (*plural form of the table name*)? For example, here's a question you might pose for the STAFF table:

> Can a single staff member be associated with one or more other staff members, and can any one of *those* staff members then be associated with one or more other staff members?

An answer such as the following (or one very similar to it) indicates that the STAFF table has a self-referencing many-to-many relationship:

> Yes, a given staff member can manage several other staff members, and any one of those folks can then supervise one or more other staff members.

Once you've identified the *type* of self-referencing relationship that exists for the table, you indicate it in the table matrix as you would any other relationship.

Relationships will often differ from one perspective to the other, and you must know how to determine what type of relationship officially exists between each pair of tables on the matrix. You make this determination using the following set of formulas; each formula corresponds to a particular relationship type definition. (I've provided the definitions as a point of reference.)

1:1 + 1:1 = **1:1**   A pair of tables bears a *one-to-one* relationship when a single record in the first table is related to *only one* record in the second table, and a single record in the second table is related to *only one* record in the first table.

1:N + 1:1 = **1:N**   A *one-to-many* relationship exists between a pair of tables when a single record in the first table can be related to one or more records in the second table, but a single record in the second table can be related to *only one* record in the first table.

1:N + 1:N = **M:N**   A pair of tables bears a *many-to-many* relationship when a single record in the first table can be related to one or more records in the second table *and* a single record in the second table can be related to one or more records in the first table.

Here is the specific procedure you'll use to identify the official relationship between a pair of tables in the matrix. (It incorporates the relationship formulas above.) Let's first look at a generic version of the procedure.

1. Select a pair of tables and note the entry at the junction between the first table and the second table.

2. Locate the second table on the same side of the matrix you're working on and note the entry at the junction between it and the first table on the opposite side of the matrix.

3. Apply the appropriate formula to the two entries and identify the official relationship between the tables.

4. Diagram the relationship in the appropriate manner.

5. Cross out both entries on the matrix.

Now, let's take a look at how you apply this procedure to a pair of tables in the matrix. (In this example, you're working down the left-hand side of the matrix.)

1. Assume you've selected the BUILDINGS and CLASSES tables. You note that the entry at the junction between BUILDINGS and CLASSES is 1:N.

2. Now you proceed down the left-hand side of the matrix until you locate the CLASSES table and then note that the entry at the junction between the CLASSES and BUILDINGS table is 1:1.

3. Using these entries with the appropriate formula, you determine that the official relationship between the BUILDINGS and CLASSES tables is 1:N. (1:N + 1:1 = 1:N)

4. You create a one-to-many relationship diagram for the BUILDINGS and CLASSES tables.

5. You cross out the entries on the matrix.

Figure 10.29 shows the results of your work.

	Buildings	Classes	Compensation	Faculty	Rooms	Staff	Students
Buildings		~~1:N~~				1:N	
Classes	~~1:1~~			1:N	1:1		1:N
Compensation						1:1	
Faculty		1:N				1:1	
Rooms	1:1	1:N					
Staff			1:1	1:1		1:N	
Students		1:N					

Figure 10.29. *Identifying the official relationship between the BUILDINGS and CLASSES tables.*

Note that the relationship diagram is built from the perspective of the BUILDINGS table. This is due to the fact that the BUILDINGS table is on the "one" side of the relationship. When you create a simple diagram such as this, I recommend that you always show the "one" side of the relationship on the left and the "many" side on the right. Following this practice will make your diagrams easy to read and help ensure that you create them in a consistent manner. (This practice is unnecessary, however, when you create a complex diagram showing the relationships between several tables.)

At the very least, you should include each table's primary key in the diagram. Doing so will prove to be a valuable visual aid when you begin to *establish* the relationships. You could go so far as to display each table's complete structure (as you see in Figure 10.30), assuming you have space on the diagram. Displaying the structures in this manner often helps to reinforce the decision you've made regarding the type of relationship that exists between the tables. (I use both types of diagrams throughout the remainder of the book.)

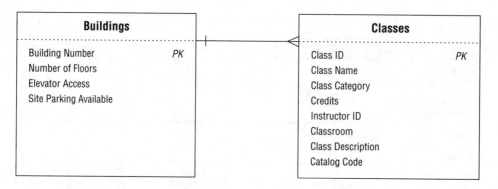

Figure 10.30. *Displaying each table's structure in a relationship diagram.*

> ❖ **Note** You'll occasionally find it difficult to identify the exact relationship between a given pair of tables. When this happens, just load the tables with some sample data. This usually helps to reveal the type of relationship that exists between the tables.

It's worth mentioning that this procedure is much easier and shorter when you work with a table that has a self-referencing relationship, such as the STAFF table. As Figure 10.31 illustrates, all you have to do here is diagram the relationship and cross out the entry on the matrix.

Continue this procedure until you've eliminated all of the entries on the matrix. When you've finished identifying the official relationships among the tables in the database, you can then go through the process of *establishing* each relationship in the appropriate manner.

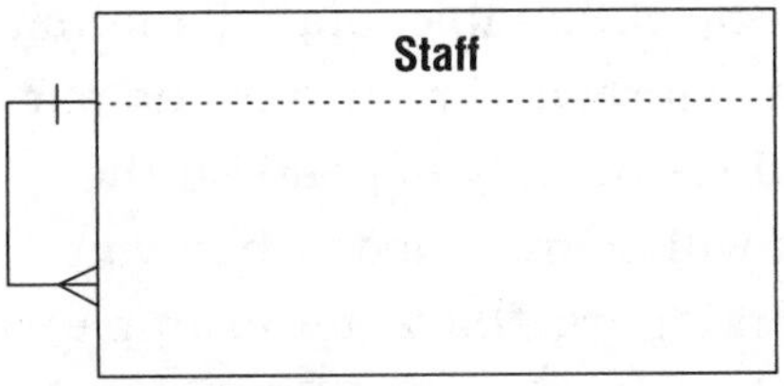

	Buildings	Classes	Compensation	Faculty	Rooms	**Staff**	Students
Buildings		~~1:N~~			1:N		
Classes	~~1:1~~			1:N	1:1		1:N
Compensation						1:1	
Faculty		1:N				1:1	
Rooms	1:1	1:N					
Staff			1:1	1:1		~~1:N~~	
Students		1:N					

Figure 10.31. *Working with a self-referencing relationship.*

Establishing Each Relationship

This process involves defining an explicit logical connection between a pair of related tables. The type of relationship that exists between the tables determines the manner in which you define the connection.

One-to-One and One-to-Many Relationships

You use a *primary key* and a *foreign key* to establish the connection between tables participating in a one-to-one or one-to-many relationship. (You'll learn the definition of a foreign key in just a moment.)

The One-to-One Relationship

In this type of relationship, one table serves as a parent table and the other serves as a child table. A record must exist in the parent table *before* you can enter a related record in the child table; stated another way, a record in the child table *must* have a related record in the parent table. The roles you assign to the tables usually depend on the subjects they represent, although there will be instances when you can assign the roles rather arbitrarily. In Figure 10.32, for example, you would most likely assign the parent role to the STAFF table and the child role to the COMPENSATION table. This is a reasonable assumption because it would be completely illogical to have a record in the COMPENSATION table that is not related to a record in the STAFF table.

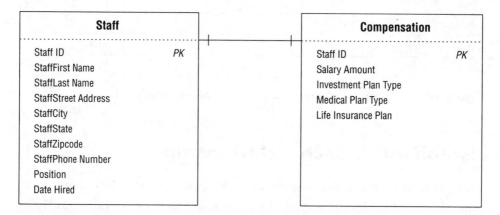

Figure 10.32. *Which table would you pick as the parent table?*

In the case where one of the tables is a *subset* table, you will *usually* assign the child role to the subset table. There are instances, however, when you can assign the parent role to the subset table.

You establish a one-to-one relationship by taking a copy of the parent table's primary key and incorporating it within the structure of the child table, where it then becomes a *foreign key*. (The term *foreign key* is derived from the fact that the child table already has a primary key of its own, and the primary key you are introducing from the parent table is "foreign" to the child table.) In most one-to-one relationships, however, the foreign key *also* serves as the child table's *primary* key.

Figure 10.33 illustrates how you would establish the relationship between the STAFF and FACULTY tables. STAFF is the parent table in this case because a record in the FACULTY table *must* be related to a record in the STAFF table; faculty members are drawn from the school's staff. If you were to follow the procedure you just learned, you would take a copy of the STAFF table's primary key and incorporate it as a foreign key in the FACULTY table. This is unnecessary, however, because FACULTY is already a properly defined subset table. (Recall that a subset table and the data table from which it was derived must share the same primary key. You learned how to define a subset table in Chapter 7 and how to establish its primary key in Chapter 8.)

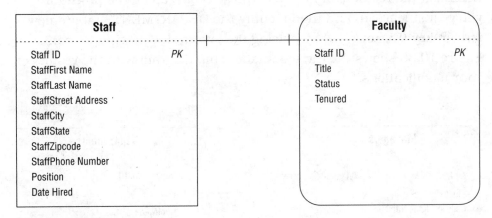

Figure 10.33. *Establishing the one-to-one relationship between the STAFF and FACULTY tables.*

Figure 10.34 shows a slightly different example of a one-to-one relationship. Assume that MANAGERS is a subset table of EMPLOYEES, but has a direct relationship to DEPARTMENTS—a single manager is associated with only one department, and a single department is associated with only one manager. Further assume that MANAGERS is the parent table and

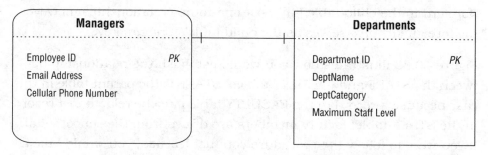

Figure 10.34. *A one-to-one relationship with a subset table in the parent role.*

DEPARTMENTS is the child table. (This is a good example of a scenario in which you can choose the roles rather arbitrarily. It's also an instance of when a subset table plays the parent role within the relationship.)

Establish the relationship between these tables using the procedure you've just learned, and then identify the DEPARTMENTS table's new foreign key (EMPLOYEE ID) by placing the letters "FK" next to its name. Figure 10.35 shows the revised relationship diagram with the results of your modifications.

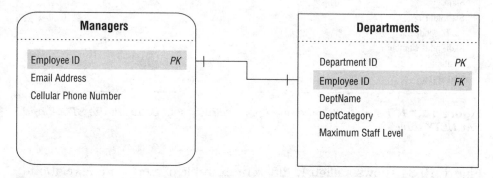

Figure 10.35. *Establishing the relationship between the MANAGERS and DEPARTMENTS tables.*

As long as you can visualize this process generically, you'll be able to establish any one-to-one relationship you encounter.

❖ **Note** Many database designers will use MANAGER ID as the primary key name in the MANAGERS table and the foreign key name in the DEPARTMENTS table. I choose to use EMPLOYEE ID instead for these reasons:

- MANAGERS is a subset of the EMPLOYEES table, so it shares the same primary key (EMPLOYEE ID).
- It keeps the field in conformance with the Elements of the Ideal Field. (*It retains a majority of its characteristics when it appears in more than one table.*)
- It keeps the field in conformance with the Elements of a Foreign Key. (You'll learn about foreign keys later in this chapter.)
- It removes any possible ambiguity or doubt about the true nature of a foreign key. (I'll explain this in more detail during the discussion of the Elements of a Foreign Key.)

There is no absolute right or wrong way to do this—in the end, the approach you use is simply a matter of style. Once you decide which approach you want to use, however, make certain you use it consistently.

There is a small change in the way you'll diagram the relationships from this point forward. You should now use the primary key as the beginning point and the foreign key as the end point of the relationship line. (The only exception will be when you're diagramming the relationship between a subset table and its parent data table.) Making this minor modification will help you visualize the relationships more clearly and make it easier to identify the fields that establish the relationship.

The One-to-Many Relationship

The technique you use to establish a one-to-many relationship is similar to the one you used to establish a one-to-one relationship. You simply take a copy of the primary key from the table on the "one" side of the relationship and incorporate it within the table structure on the "many" side, where it then becomes a foreign key. For example, consider the one-to-many relationship between the BUILDINGS and ROOMS tables shown in Figure 10.36.

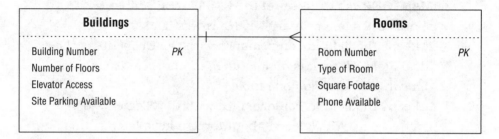

Figure 10.36. *The existing one-to-many relationship between the BUILDINGS and ROOMS tables.*

The relationship between these two tables is such that a single building can contain one or more rooms, but a single room is contained within only one building. Using the procedure above, you establish this relationship by taking a copy of the primary key (BUILDING NUMBER) from the BUILDINGS table and incorporating it as a foreign key within the ROOMS table. Now, revise the relationship diagram and make the same type of adjustments as you did with the diagram for the one-to-one relationship. Your revised diagram should look like the one in Figure 10.37. (Note that the *middle* line of the crow's foot symbol is the significant connection point—it should point directly to the foreign key.)

Resolving Multivalued Fields—Revisited

Back in Chapter 7 you learned how to resolve a multivalued field by using this generic procedure:

1. Remove the field from the table and use it as the basis for a new table. If necessary, rename the field in accordance with the field naming guidelines that you learned earlier in this chapter.

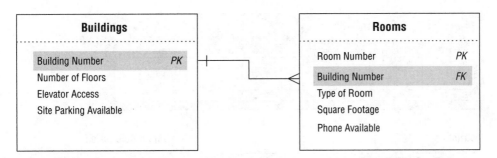

Figure 10.37. *Establishing the one-to-many relationship between the BUILDINGS and ROOMS tables.*

2. Use a field (or set of fields) from the *original* table to relate the original table to the new table; try to select fields that represent the subject of the table as closely as possible. The field(s) you choose will appear in both tables.

3. Assign an appropriate name, type, and description to the new table and add it to the final table list.

You used this procedure to resolve a multivalued field called CATEGORIES TAUGHT in an INSTRUCTORS table. Figure 10.38 shows the original version of the table and the results of applying the procedure.

There's one final fact about a multivalued field that you need to learn: An inherent one-to-many relationship exists between a given set of values within a multivalued field and the record in which they reside. You'll see this when you examine the original INSTRUCTORS table in Figure 10.38. A single instructor (such as Kendra Bonnicksen) can teach one or more categories (DTP, SS, WP)—this holds true for every record in the table.

When you properly resolve the multivalued field, the tables produced by the procedure inherit the relationship. This is clearly the case with the revised INSTRUCTORS and new INSTRUCTOR CATEGORIES tables. You can now establish this one-to-many relationship as you would any

Instructors

InstFirst Name	InstLast Name	InstStreet Address	InstCity	<< other fields >>	*Categories Taught*
Kendra	Bonnicksen	3131 Mockingbird Lane	Seattle	......	DTP, SS, WP
Timothy	Ennis	7402 Kingman Drive	Redmond	......	WP, DB, OS
Shannon	McLain	4141 Lake City Way	Seattle	......	DB, SS
Estela	Pundt	970 Phoenix Avenue	Bellevue	......	DTP, WP, PG

Instructors

InstFirst Name	InstLast Name	InstStreet Address	InstCity	<< other fields >>
Kendra	Bonnicksen	3131 Mockingbird Lane	Seattle	......
Timothy	Ennis	7402 Kingman Drive	Redmond	......
Shannon	McLain	4141 Lake City Way	Seattle	......
Estela	Pundt	970 Phoenix Avenue	Bellevue	......

Instructor Categories

InstFirst Name	InstLast Name	Category Taught
Kendra	Bonnicksen	DTP
Kendra	Bonnicksen	SS
Kendra	Bonnicksen	WP
Timothy	Ennis	WP
Timothy	Ennis	DB
Timothy	Ennis	OS
Shannon	McLain	DB
Shannon	McLain	SS

Figure 10.38. *The original resolution of the* CATEGORIES TAUGHT *multivalued field.*

other. (Of course, this assumes that you've assigned a primary key to the INSTRUCTORS table.) Figure 10.39 shows the results of properly establishing this relationship.

Instructors

Instructor ID	InstFirst Name	InstLast Name	InstStreet Address	InstCity	<< other fields >>
60001	Kendra	Bonnicksen	3131 Mockingbird Lane	Seattle	......
60002	Timothy	Ennis	7402 Kingman Drive	Redmond	......
60003	Shannon	McLain	4141 Lake City Way	Seattle	......
60004	Estela	Pundt	970 Phoenix Avenue	Bellevue	......

Instructor Categories

Instructor ID	Category Taught
60001	DTP
60001	SS
60001	WP
60002	WP
60002	DB
60002	OS
60003	DB
60003	SS

Figure 10.39. *Establishing the one-to-many relationship between the* INSTRUCTORS *and* INSTRUCTOR CATEGORIES *tables.*

The INSTRUCTOR ID field in the INSTRUCTOR CATEGORIES table serves as a foreign key and helps to establish the one-to-many relationship between the INSTRUCTORS and INSTRUCTOR CATEGORIES tables.

INSTRUCTOR ID is also part of the composite primary key for the INSTRUC-TOR CATEGORIES table; a given combination of INSTRUCTOR ID and CATE-GORY TAUGHT values uniquely identifies a specific record in the table.

The Many-to-Many Relationship

You establish a many-to-many relationship with a *linking* table. This is a new table that you'll create using the following three-step procedure.

1. Define the linking table by taking copies of the primary key from each table in the relationship and using those keys to form the structure of the table. These fields will serve two distinct purposes within the linking table: Together they constitute the table's *composite primary key*, and each is a unique foreign key that helps to establish a relationship between its parent table and the linking table.

2. Give the linking table a name that represents the nature of the relationship between the two tables. For example, if you're establishing a many-to-many relationship between a PILOTS table and a CERTIFICATIONS table, you might choose to call the linking table PILOT CERTIFICATIONS.

3. Add the linking table to the *final table list* and make the proper entries for "Table Type" and "Table Description."

Figure 10.40 shows how you establish the many-to-many relationship between the STUDENTS and CLASSES tables. (Note the new diagram symbol used to represent a linking table.)

> ❖ **Note** You could have used STUDENT SCHEDULES or CLASS SCHEDULES as the name of the linking table; STUDENT CLASSES just happens to be my personal preference. The point to remember is that you should use a name that makes the most sense to you or to the organization.

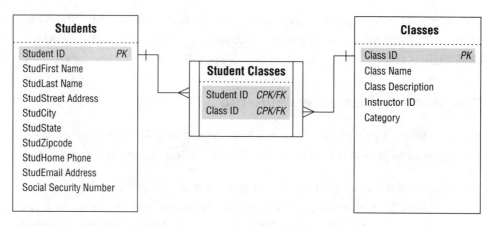

Figure 10.40. *Establishing the many-to-many relationship between the STUDENTS and CLASSES tables.*

Creating a linking table produces a few noteworthy results.

- *The original many-to-many relationship has been dissolved because there is no longer a direct relationship between the STUDENTS and CLASSES tables.* The original relationship has been replaced by *two* one-to-many relationships: one between STUDENTS and STUDENT CLASSES and another between CLASSES and STUDENT CLASSES. In the first relationship, a single record in STUDENTS can be associated with one or more records in STUDENT CLASSES, but a single record in STUDENT CLASSES table can be associated with only one record in STUDENTS. In the second relationship, a single record in the CLASSES table can be associated with one or more records in STUDENT CLASSES, but a single record in STUDENT CLASSES can be associated with only one record in CLASSES.

- *The STUDENT CLASSES linking table contains two foreign keys.* STUDENT ID and CLASS ID are both copies of the primary keys from the STUDENTS and CLASSES tables respectively; therefore, each is a foreign key by definition. As such, they help to establish the relationship between their parent tables and the linking table.

- *The STUDENT CLASSES linking table has a composite primary key composed of the STUDENT ID and CLASS ID fields.* Except in rare instances, a linking table always contains a composite primary key. (This rule applies to the database's logical design only. There are various reasons why you might break this rule when you transform the logical design into a physical design, but this is a discussion that is beyond the scope of this book.) It's important to note that you'll occasionally have to add more fields to the linking table in order to guarantee a unique primary key value. For example, assume the school decides to record student schedules for every term of the school year (fall, winter, and spring). You would have to add a new field, perhaps called TERM, and designate it as part of the composite primary key. This would enable you to enter another instance of a given student and class into the table, but for a different term; a student may need to retake a class during the *spring* term because he failed the class in the *fall* term.

- *The linking table helps to keep redundant data to an absolute minimum.* There is no superfluous data in this table at all. In fact, the main advantage of this table structure is that it allows you to enter as few or as many classes for a single student as is necessary. Later in the database-design process, you'll learn how to create views to draw the data from these tables together in order to present it as meaningful information.

- *The name of the linking table reflects the purpose of the relationship it helps establish.* The data stored in the STUDENT CLASSES table represents a student and the classes in which he or she is enrolled.

As you work with many-to-many relationships, there will be instances in which you will need to *add* fields to the linking table in order to reduce data redundancy and further refine structures of the tables participating in the relationship. For example, assume you're working on a new database with a colleague and he's just brought the ORDERS and PRODUCTS tables in Figure 10.41 to your attention.

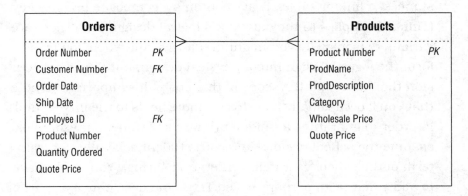

Figure 10.41. *Is there a problem with either of these tables?*

You note that there's a many-to-many relationship between the tables and then realize that your colleague tried to establish this relationship by taking a copy of the PRODUCT NUMBER and QUOTE PRICE fields from the PRODUCTS table and incorporating them into the ORDERS table. He thought that this was the best way to associate various products with a particular order. The presence of these fields in the ORDERS table, however, produces a large amount of redundant data. Figure 10.42 illustrates this problem quite clearly.

You can enter only one product number, quantity ordered, and quote price for any given record; therefore, you'll have to enter a new record into the table for each item a customer places on his order. Customer number 9001, for example, included eight items on an order he made on May 16, so there are *eight records* in the table for this order alone.

Based on what you've learned earlier in this chapter, you know that this is an improper way to establish this relationship. You also know

Orders

Order Number	Customer Number	Order Date	<< other fields >>	Product Number	Quantity Ordered	Quote Price
1000	9001	05/16/02	......	410001	4	8.95
1000	9001	05/16/02	......	410004	12	3.75
1000	9001	05/16/02	......	410005	6	5.99
1000	9001	05/16/02	......	410007	5	6.50
1000	9001	05/16/02	......	410011	5	6.50
1000	9001	05/16/02	......	410015	11	4.45
1000	9001	05/16/02	......	410021	2	31.50
1000	9001	05/16/02	......	410029	8	5.00
1001	9012	05/16/02	......	410011	5	6.50
1001	9012	05/16/02	......	410015	3	4.00
1001	9012	05/16/02	......	410022	12	6.35

Figure 10.42. *Redundant data caused by an improperly established many-to-many relationship.*

that you can establish the relationship properly by creating and using a linking table. So you remove the PRODUCT NUMBER field from the ORDERS table, establish the relationship in the appropriate manner, and revise the relationship diagram. Figure 10.43 shows the results of your work.

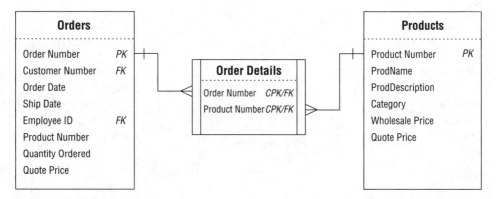

Figure 10.43. *Properly establishing the many-to-many relationship between the ORDERS and PRODUCTS tables.*

You've eliminated the redundant data in the ORDERS table, but you still have two minor problems.

1. The QUOTE PRICE and QUANTITY ORDERED fields are no longer appropriate for the ORDERS table; the ORDERS table's primary key does not exclusively identify their values, and they bear no relationship to any of the remaining fields in the table. They do, however, relate to a particular PRODUCT NUMBER that's part of a given order within the ORDER DETAILS table.

2. You have duplicate data because there are two copies of the QUOTE PRICE field: one in the ORDERS table and another in the PRODUCTS table.

So you resolve the first problem by removing the QUOTE PRICE and QUANTITY ORDERED fields from the ORDERS table and incorporating them within the ORDER DETAILS table. You then resolve the second problem by deleting the QUOTE PRICE field from the PRODUCTS table; it makes more sense to associate a quote price with a product as it's being ordered. Finally, you modify the relationship diagram to reflect the changes you made to the structures. Figure 10.44 shows your revised diagram.

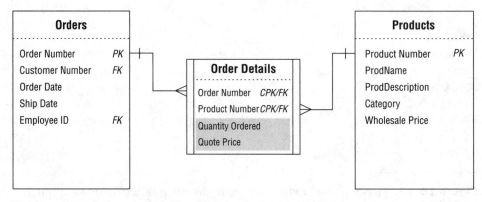

Figure 10.44. *The revised ORDER DETAILS linking table.*

When you establish a many-to-many relationship between a pair of tables, make certain you check each table and determine whether there are any fields that you should transfer to the linking table. When in doubt, load all the tables with sample data; this will usually reveal any potential problems.

> ❖ **Note** You won't encounter this problem very often if you faithfully follow the design process you've learned thus far. It will typically arise, however, when you're trying to incorporate a pair of tables from an existing or legacy database and you haven't taken the time to refine their structures properly. You'll also encounter this problem when you work with someone who has little or no database-design experience.

Self-Referencing Relationships

Establishing a self-referencing relationship will be a relatively simple task now that you know how to establish a relationship between a pair of tables.

One-to-One and One-to-Many

You use a primary key and a foreign key to establish these self-referencing relationships, just as you do with their dual-table counterparts. The difference here, however, is that the foreign key will reside in the same table as the primary key to which it refers. You'll often find that the foreign key is already part of the table's structure. If the foreign key does not already exist, you'll simply create one.

Let's revisit the MEMBERS table example from Figure 10.20. Recall that this table has a self-referencing one-to-one relationship because a given member can sponsor only one other member within the organization;

the Sᴘᴏɴsᴏʀ ID field stores the member identification number of the member acting as a sponsor. Because the Sᴘᴏɴsᴏʀ ID field draws its values exclusively from the Mᴇᴍʙᴇʀ ID field, it acts as the foreign key for the relationship. You establish the relationship by officially designating the Sᴘᴏɴsᴏʀ ID field as the foreign key and noting it as such in the relationship diagram. Figure 10.45 shows the revised relationship diagram for the MEMBERS table.

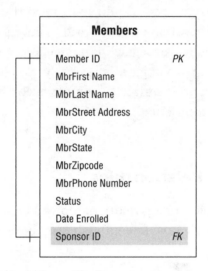

Figure 10.45. *Establishing the self-referencing one-to-one relationship for the MEMBERS table.*

Now, consider the STAFF table example in Figure 10.46. You may remember that this table has a self-referencing one-to-many relationship because a single staff member can manage one or more other staff members.

There is currently no means of associating a given staff member to other staff members within the table; therefore, you must create a new field that will act as the foreign key and enable you to establish the relationship. Let's assume you create a new foreign key field called Mᴀɴᴀɢᴇʀ ID

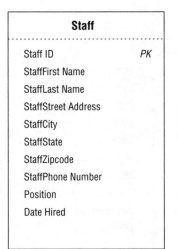

Staff

Staff ID	*PK*
StaffFirst Name	
StaffLast Name	
StaffStreet Address	
StaffCity	
StaffState	
StaffZipcode	
StaffPhone Number	
Position	
Date Hired	

Figure 10.46. *The current structure of the STAFF table.*

that will draw its values exclusively from the STAFF ID field. You now establish the relationship by officially designating MANAGER ID as the foreign key and notating it as such in the relationship diagram. Figure 10.47 shows the revised relationship diagram for the STAFF table.

You probably noticed that the "one" side of the relationship line points to the MANAGER ID field and the "many" side of the line points to the STAFF ID field. This is perfectly acceptable because a manager will manage one or more staff members, but a given staff member reports to only one manager. (As you may have intuitively guessed, the "one" side of the line commonly points to the primary key and the "many" side to the foreign key.)

As you work with self-referencing one-to-one and one-to-many relationships, take a moment and examine each table's structure carefully. You'll occasionally find that you can (or may need to) modify and improve the existing structure in order to *eliminate* the relationship. I know what you're wondering: "But why would I want to do that?"

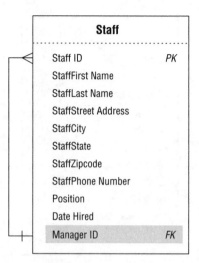

Figure 10.47. *The revised STAFF table with the new MANAGER ID foreign key.*

Retrieving information from tables with these types of relationships can be tedious and somewhat difficult. (A discussion of the reasons for this is, unfortunately, outside the scope of this work.) Additionally, the very presence of the relationship can indicate the need for new field and table structures.

Consider the STAFF table once again. Does it occur to you that if there is a need to track staff members who are managers, there could be a need to track the departments they manage? If this is true, then there must be other facets of the departments that you need to track in the database. You should now conduct a quick interview with the appropriate staff members to answer these questions and then take the appropriate action based on their responses.

Let's assume you were right and the organization does want to track departmental data. Figure 10.48 shows one possible approach you might use to accomplish this task.

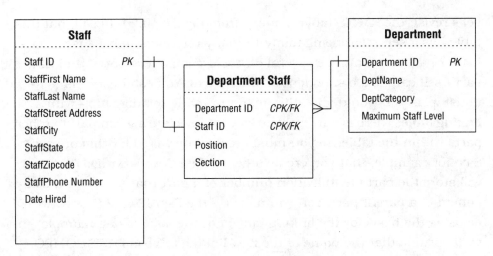

Figure 10.48. *Results of eliminating the self-referencing relationship and adding new structures to track departmental data.*

These new structures and relationships enable you to track the data efficiently and will provide a wide variety of information about the departments. (You will, of course, ensure that the new fields and tables conform to the various design elements that you've learned thus far.)

It's important to note that self-referencing relationships do have their place within a well-designed database. You should be vigilant, however, and make certain that each self-referencing relationship does indeed serve a useful purpose.

The Many-to-Many Relationship

You use a linking table to establish this type of self-referencing relationship, just as you do with its dual-table counterpart. Establishing this relationship is slightly different in that the fields you use to build the linking table come from the same parent table.

Let's revisit the PARTS table example from Figure 10.24. Recall that this table has a self-referencing many-to-many relationship because a particular part can comprise several different component parts, and that part itself can be a component of other parts. You establish this relationship as you would any other many-to-many relationship—with a linking table. There is currently no way to associate a given part to other parts within the table, so you must create a new field for this purpose. Say, for example, that you create a field called Component ID. This field will store the part identification number of a part that serves as a component of a parent part. You can now use the Part ID and Component ID fields as the basis for the linking table. For the sake of our example, we'll assume that the name of the new linking table is PART COMPONENTS. Once you've created and named the linking table, be sure to revise the relationship diagram for the PARTS table. Figure 10.49 shows the results of your work.

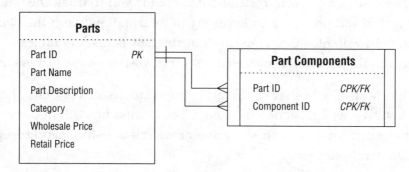

Figure 10.49. *Establishing the self-referencing many-to-many relationship for the PARTS table.*

As you can see, the PARTS table now has two distinct one-to-many relationships with the PART COMPONENTS table. The first relationship is established via the Part ID field and the second relationship is established via the Component ID field. Figure 10.50 illustrates how these re-

Parts

Part ID	Part Name	<< other fields >>
701	Top Clamp	......
702	Bottom Clamp	......
703	Fastening Bolt	......
704	Clamp Assembly	......
705	Saddle	......
706	Seatpost	......
707	Seat Assembly	......
708	Body Tube	......
709	Front Fork Tube	......
710	Rear Stay Tube	......
711	Frame Assembly	......

Part Components

Part ID	Component ID
704	701
704	702
704	703
707	704
707	705
707	706
711	704
711	708
711	709
711	710

Figure 10.50. *Data relationships between the PARTS and PART COMPONENTS tables.*

lationships work. Note that a clamp assembly (Part ID 704) contains three components and is itself a component of a seat assembly (Part ID 707) and a frame assembly (Part ID 711).

Now, use the techniques you've just learned to establish all of the relationships you've identified among the tables in the database. Make absolutely certain you create a diagram for each relationship—you're going to add new information to these diagrams as the design process further unfolds.

Reviewing the Structure of Each Table

Review all of the table structures after you've established the relationships between tables. Remember that you made modifications to the existing table structures and created several new table structures as you established the relationships; therefore, you want to make certain that each table conforms to the Elements of the Ideal Table.

Elements of the Ideal Table

- It represents a single subject, which can be an object or event.

- It has a primary key.

- It does not contain multipart or multivalued fields.

- It does not contain calculated fields.

- It does not contain unnecessary duplicate fields.

- It contains only an absolute minimum amount of redundant data.

When you determine that a table does not comply with the Elements of the Ideal Table, identify the problem and make the necessary modifications. Then, take the table through the appropriate stages of the database-design process until you return to this point. You shouldn't encounter any problems with the tables if you've been following proper procedures thus far.

Refining All Foreign Keys

You now know that a primary key becomes a foreign key when you use it to establish a relationship between a pair of tables in a one-to-one or one-to-many relationship. As with any other key that you've worked with so far, a foreign key must comply with a specific set of elements. These elements are collectively known as the Elements of a Foreign Key.

Elements of a Foreign Key

- *It has the same name as the primary key from which it was copied.* You should adhere to this rule unless there is an absolutely compelling reason not to do so. (Review the discussion of the Alias field specification element in Chapter 9. It provides an example of an occasion when you might decide to break this rule.) Consider the relationship diagram in Figure 10.51, and note that the for-

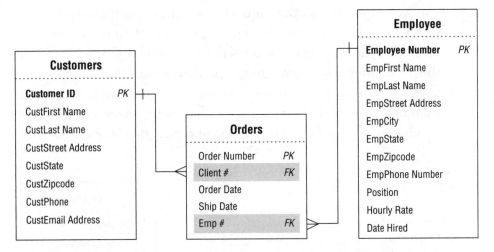

Figure 10.51. *Primary keys and foreign keys with mismatched names.*

eign keys have different names than the primary keys to which they refer.

The fact that the names are different poses a problem because you can't be sure that the foreign keys are truly valid and actually refer to the primary keys. Is EMP # truly equivalent to EMPLOYEE NUMBER? Is "Emp" really a shortened version of "Employee," or does it mean something else? Why did someone choose to use CLIENT # in the ORDERS table instead of CUSTOMER ID? Is there any difference between the two? Do they store the same type of data? These are questions you must answer before you can do anything else with these tables and their respective relationships.

You could make a relatively reasonable argument that the names are close enough to assume that the foreign keys are indeed valid. If there's any doubt, you could test your assumption by loading the tables with sample data. You really shouldn't have to take the time to do this, however. Imagine having to do this for 15 or 20 relationships; the amount of wasted time adds up.

You won't have to ask these questions or perform these tests at all when you adhere to this element. Figure 10.52 shows a revised version of the diagram that uses the proper foreign key names. In this case, there is no ambiguity and little doubt that the foreign keys are appropriate. You can examine this diagram nine months from now and, with a quick glance, confidently ascertain the type of relationships between the tables and how they're established.

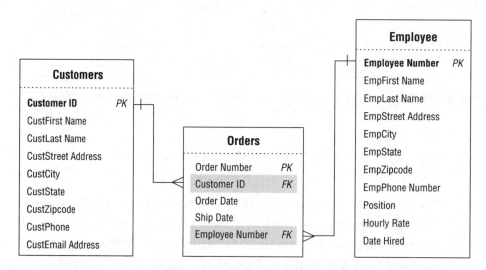

Figure 10.52. *Foreign keys that comply with the first element of a foreign key.*

❖ **Note** I encounter this issue quite often when I'm asked to analyze certain types of database problems. In many cases, the foreign keys are either completely inappropriate or manifest serious data-integrity and relationship-integrity problems. Once I identify the appropriate foreign keys (or revise the existing ones) and ensure that they comply with this particular element, a number of problems disappear.

The only time I can justify and approve of using a different name for the foreign key field is when I establish a *self-referencing* relationship for a given table. This is reasonable because the primary key and foreign key both reside within the table (in most cases), and each must have a unique name.

- *It uses a replica of the field specifications for the primary key from which it was copied.* This supports the sixth element of an ideal field, which you learned in Chapter 7 ("It retains a majority of its properties when it appears in more than one table"). A foreign key, however, has a few settings in both the General Elements and Logical Elements categories that are slightly different from those of its parent primary key.

There are four elements in the General Elements category that you will modify when you define a field specification for a foreign key.

a. *Specification Type.* Because a foreign key is based on an existing primary key, it inherits a *replica* of the primary key's field specifications; therefore, you designate the foreign key's specification type as "Replica." This designation helps you ensure that your foreign key specifications are consistent, and reminds you to keep this specification synchronized with the primary key's specification.

b. *Parent Table.* The name of the *foreign key's* parent table goes here.

c. *Source Specification.* This is where you indicate the name of the parent primary key. (Make certain you include the name of the primary key's parent table as well; this will make it easier for you to find the primary key's specification should you want to compare it to the foreign key's specification.)

d. *Description.* Compose a description that indicates the foreign key's purpose within the table.Figure 10.53 shows an example of these modifications for an EMPLOYEE ID NUMBER field serving as a foreign key in an ORDERS table.

General Elements			
Field Name:	Employee ID Number	**Specification Type:**	☐ Unique ☐ Generic ☒ Replica
Parent Table:	Orders	**Source Specification:**	
Label:	Employee #	Employee ID Number from the EMPLOYEES table.	
Shared By:			
Alias(es):			
Description:	The identification number of an employee within our organization. The values in this field enable us to identify and keep track of the employees who place orders for our customers.		

Figure 10.53. *General Elements for the EMPLOYEE ID NUMBER foreign key field in the ORDERS table.*

You'll also adjust five elements in the Logical Elements category for the foreign key field specification.

a. *Key Type.* Set this element to "Foreign." This is a rather obvious change, but one that you can accidentally overlook if you're not careful.

b. *Uniqueness.* You designate this element as "Non-unique" because you want to be able to associate a single foreign key value with any number of records in the parent table. In terms of our example, you want to be able to associate a specific employee with any number of orders. If you set this to "Unique" instead, you could associate a given employee with one order only, which would greatly limit his or her sales potential! (In the case of a *one-to-one* relationship, however, you'll designate this element as "Unique" because you want to associate a single foreign key value in the child table with *only one* record in the parent table.)

c. *Values Entered By.* Unlike the parent primary key, you (or a user) will enter values into the foreign key; therefore, you set this element to "User."

d. *Range of Values.* You must set this element in such a way that you (or a user) can enter only existing values from the parent primary key. (You'll learn more about this and see a good example in just a moment.)

e. *Edit Rule.* You normally set this to "Enter Now, Edits Allowed," although there might be instances (such as when the foreign key comes from a validation table) when you can set this to "Enter Later, Edits Allowed." Allowing edits of foreign key values enables you to fix mistakes. For example, you might have mistakenly entered employee ID number "100" for a given order when you meant to enter "110."

Figure 10.54 shows an example of these modifications for the EMPLOYEE ID NUMBER foreign key field. (Note the setting for the Range of Values—this is one good way to set this element.)

In order for you to see the significance of these modifications, Figure 10.55 shows the Logical Elements category from the *Source Specification.* (Recall that this element is in the General Elements category; see Figure 10.53.)

- *It draws its values from the primary key to which it refers.* By definition, a foreign key's range of values is limited to existing values

Logical Elements

Key Type:	☐ Non	☐ Primary	**Edit Rule:**
	☒ Foreign	☐ Alternate	☒ Enter Now, Edits Allowed
Key Structure:	☒ Simple	☐ Composite	☐ Enter Now, Edits Not Allowed
Uniqueness:	☒ Non-unique	☐ Unique	☐ Enter Later, Edits Allowed
Null Support:	☐ Nulls Allowed	☒ No Nulls	☐ Enter Later, Edits Not Allowed
Values Entered By:	☒ User	☐ System	☐ Not Determined At This Time
Required Value:	☐ No	☒ Yes	

Default Value:

Range of Values: | Any existing Employee ID Number in the EMPLOYEES table.

Comparisons Allowed:

☒	Same Field	☐ All	☒ =	☐ >	☐ >=	☐ ≠	☐ <	☐ <=
☐	Other Fields	☐ All	☐ =	☐ >	☐ >=	☐ ≠	☐ <	☐ <=
☒	Value Expression	☐ All	☒ =	☐ >	☐ >=	☐ ≠	☐ <	☐ <=

Operations Allowed:

		All	+	−	x	÷	Concatenation
☐	Same Field	☐ All	☐ +	☐ −	☐ x	☐ ÷	☐ Concatenation
☐	Other Fields	☐ All	☐ +	☐ −	☐ x	☐ ÷	☐ Concatenation
☐	Value Expression	☐ All	☐ +	☐ −	☐ x	☐ ÷	☐ Concatenation

Figure 10.54. *Logical Elements for the EMPLOYEE ID NUMBER foreign key field in the ORDERS table.*

of the primary key to which it refers. For example, you cannot enter an invalid EMPLOYEE ID NUMBER into the ORDERS table. Any EMPLOYEE ID NUMBER you enter into the ORDERS table must first exist as an EMPLOYEE ID NUMBER in the EMPLOYEES table. This ensures consistency among the values of both fields in both tables and helps to establish relationship-level integrity.

Review the foreign keys in each table to make certain that they conform to the Elements of a Foreign Key, and make the appropriate modifications to those that fail to do so. You really shouldn't encounter any problems if you've been faithfully following the design process up to this point.

Logical Elements											

Key Type: ☐ Non ☒ Primary

☐ Foreign ☐ Alternate

Edit Rule:

☐ Enter Now, Edits Allowed

☒ Enter Now, Edits Not Allowed

☐ Enter Later, Edits Allowed

☐ Enter Later, Edits Not Allowed

☐ Not Determined At This Time

Key Structure: ☒ Simple ☐ Composite

Uniqueness: ☐ Non-unique ☒ Unique

Null Support: ☐ Nulls Allowed ☒ No Nulls

Values Entered By: ☐ User ☒ System

Required Value: ☐ No ☒ Yes

Default Value:

Range of Values: 1000–9999

Comparisons Allowed:

☒ Same Field   ☐ All ☒ = ☐ > ☐ >= ☐ ≠ ☐ < ☐ <=

☐ Other Fields   ☐ All ☐ = ☐ > ☐ >= ☐ ≠ ☐ < ☐ <=

☒ Value Expression   ☐ All ☒ = ☐ > ☐ >= ☐ ≠ ☐ < ☐ <=

Operations Allowed:

☐ Same Field   ☐ All ☐ + ☐ − ☐ x ☐ ÷ ☐ Concatenation

☐ Other Fields   ☐ All ☐ + ☐ − ☐ x ☐ ÷ ☐ Concatenation

☐ Value Expression   ☐ All ☐ + ☐ − ☐ x ☐ ÷ ☐ Concatenation

Figure 10.55. *Logical Elements for the* EMPLOYEE ID NUMBER *primary key field in the EMPLOYEES table.*

Establishing Relationship Characteristics

Now you'll establish the characteristics of each relationship. These characteristics indicate what will occur when you delete a record, the type of participation each table bears within the relationship, and to what degree each table participates in the relationship.

Defining a Deletion Rule for Each Relationship

The first characteristic you'll establish for the relationship is a *deletion rule.* This rule determines what your RDBMS should do when you place a request to delete a given record in the parent table of the relationship. Deletion rules are crucial to relationship-level integrity because they help guard against *orphaned* records, which are records in the child table that have no relationship whatsoever to any records in the parent table.

These are the five types of deletion rules you can define and the actions the RDBMS should take when a given rule is in force:

1. *Deny.* The RDBMS will not delete the record in the parent table, but will instead keep the record and designate it as "inactive."

2. *Restrict.* The RDBMS will not delete the record in the parent table if related records exist in the child table. You must have the RDBMS delete *all* of the related records in the child table *before* you can have it delete the record in the parent table.

3. *Cascade.* The RDBMS will take two specific actions: It will delete the record in the parent table, and *it will also automatically delete* all related records in the child table.

4. *Nullify.* The RDBMS will delete the record in the parent table and will then update the foreign key values of related records in the child table to *null.* If you are going to use this deletion rule, you must modify the foreign key's field specifications and set the Null Support logical element to "Nulls Allowed."

5. *Set Default.* The RDBMS will delete the record in the parent table and will then update the foreign key values of related records in the child table to the current Default Value logical element setting in the foreign key's field specifications. Obviously, you must have a setting for the Default Value element in order to use this rule.

Use a Restrict deletion rule as a matter of course and the other rules as appropriate. The best way to determine which deletion rule is appropriate for a given relationship is to examine the relationship diagram. Consider the diagram in Figure 10.56.

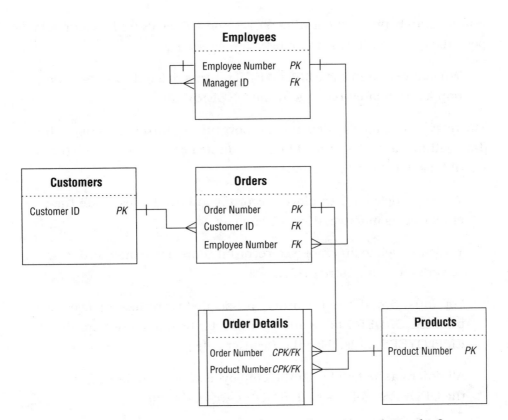

Figure 10.56. *What deletion rule is appropriate for a given relationship?*

Select a relationship, look at the diagram, and pose the following question:

> When a record in the (*name of parent table*) table is deleted, what should happen to related records in the (*name of child table*) table?

Here the question is framed in a generic manner so that you can understand the premise behind it. When you pose this question for a pair of tables in a particular relationship, substitute the phrases within the parentheses with the appropriate table names. If you're working with the relationship between the EMPLOYEES and ORDERS table, you could pose the question in this manner:

> When a record in the EMPLOYEES table is deleted, what should happen to related records in the ORDERS table?

The answer you receive depends on how the organization is using the data within the tables and will usually indicate which deletion rule you should use for the relationship.

> You can't delete an employee record; you have to designate the employee as inactive. (Use a Deny rule.)

> You can't delete an employee record if there are related order records. (Use a Restrict rule.)

> You must first delete the orders associated with the employee from the ORDERS table and then delete the employee from the EMPLOYEES table. (Use the Restrict rule.)

> All orders associated with the employee must be deleted from the ORDERS table as well. (Use the Cascade rule.)

> The employee number for all orders associated with the employee must be deleted. (Use a Nullify rule.)

> The employee number for all orders associated with the employee must be reset to the lead salesperson's employee number. (Use a Set Default rule.)

If you (or the people you're working with) cannot easily provide an answer, make note of the relationship and continue with another relationship. You'll revisit all of these relationships when you establish business rules for the database later in Chapter 11. For now, let's assume you received the first reply and you're going to use a Deny rule for the relationship.

Once you've identified the type of deletion rule you want to use for the relationship, designate the rule on the relationship diagram. Use (D) for Deny, (R) for Restrict, (C) for Cascade, (N) for Nullify, and (S) for Set Default. Place the designation *under* the connection line of the *parent* table. Figure 10.57 shows the revised relationship diagram for the EMPLOYEES and ORDERS tables.

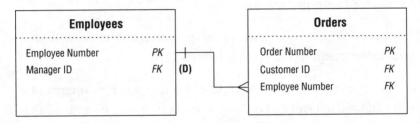

Figure 10.57. *Designating a Restrict deletion rule for the relationship between the EMPLOYEES and ORDERS tables.*

You always set the deletion rule from the perspective of the parent table because it is the more important of the two tables within the relationship. Deleting a record in the parent table will always have some effect on related records in the child table, but deleting a record in the child table will have no effect on the related record in the parent table. (There is a specific circumstance in which you might want to establish a Restrict deletion rule for the child table, and you'll learn about it in Chapter 11.)

The question you use to determine the deletion rule for a self-referencing relationship is just slightly different from the one you just used for a dual-table relationship.

> When a record in the (*name of parent table*) table is deleted, what should happen to the foreign key values of the other records that were related to it?

If you're working with the self-referencing relationship for the EMPLOY-EES table, you could pose the question in this manner:

> When a record in the EMPLOYEES table is deleted, what should happen to the foreign key values of the other records that were related to it?

Once again, the reply will usually indicate which deletion rule you should use for the relationship.

> You can't delete a record for an employee who's currently managing other employees. (Use a Restrict rule.)

> If the employee you want to delete is a manager, you cannot delete his record until you assign the employees he manages to a different manager. (Use the Restrict rule.)

> If the employee whose record you want to delete is a manager, the MANAGER ID must be deleted from the record of every employee he currently manages. (Use a Nullify rule.)

> If the employee whose record you want to delete is a manager, the MANAGER ID must be reset to the senior manager's employee number in the record of every employee he currently manages. (Use a Set Default rule.)

> ❖ **Note** The Cascade rule is notably absent from this example because it doesn't apply to the relationship at all; you don't want to fire employees just because their manager is leaving the organization. This rule is still a viable option in some instances, so do keep it in mind when you're establishing deletion rules for other self-referencing relationships.

Say that you received the fourth reply and have determined that you're going to use a Set Default deletion rule for the relationship. You now complete the process by designating the rule on the relationship diagram. Figure 10.58 shows the results of your work.

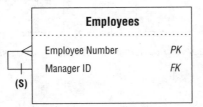

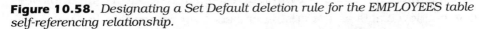

Figure 10.58. *Designating a Set Default deletion rule for the EMPLOYEES table self-referencing relationship.*

Identifying the Type of Participation for Each Table

When you establish a relationship between a pair of tables, each table participates in a particular manner. The *type of participation* you assign to a given table determines whether a record must exist in that table before you can enter records into the related table. There are two types of participation:

1. *Mandatory.* There must be *at least* one record in this table before you can enter any records into the related table.

2. *Optional.* There is no requirement for *any* records to exist in this table before you can enter records into the related table.

You'll commonly determine the type of participation for most tables later when you're defining business rules, although you can quite often establish the type of participation for tables in relationships where the type of participation for each table is obvious, is a result of common sense, or is in accordance with some particular set of standards. For example, consider the one-to-many relationship between the EMPLOYEES and CUSTOMERS tables in Figure 10.59. (These are slightly different versions of the tables in Figure 10.56.)

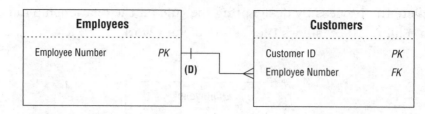

Figure 10.59. *What type of participation should you assign to each table?*

Assume that each customer must be assigned to a particular employee. This employee acts as the customer's account representative and takes care of all transactions and communications between the organization and that customer. Although each customer *must* be associated with a particular employee, a given employee does not have to be associated with any customer at all. Many employees perform other functions within the organization that do not require customer interaction.

This scenario neither implies nor defines any special circumstances, but does indicate the manner in which the organization conducts this part of its business. As such, you can infer the following:

- *You should designate a Mandatory type of participation for the EM-PLOYEES table.* This ensures that there is at least one employee for you to assign to a given customer.

- *You should designate an optional type of participation for the CUS-TOMERS table.* This allows you to enter any person employed by the organization.

Once you've determined the type of participation for each table within the relationship, designate each table's participation on the relationship diagram. Use a vertical line to represent a Mandatory type of participation and a circle to represent an optional type of participation. Figure 10.60 shows the revised relationship diagram for the EMPLOYEES and CUSTOMERS tables and also demonstrates how you indicate

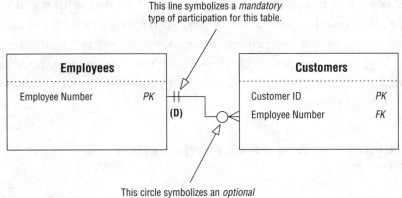

This line symbolizes a *mandatory*
type of participation for this table.

This circle symbolizes an *optional*
type of participation for this table.

Figure 10.60. *Designating the type of participation for the EMPLOYEES and CUSTOMERS tables.*

each type of participation. Note that you place the symbol representing the type of participation *outside* of the symbol that represents the type of relationship.

The type of participation also applies to a self-referencing relationship, although in a slightly different manner. Because of the nature of a self-referencing relationship, you designate the type of participation *for the primary key and foreign key fields* in the table. Figure 10.61 shows a revised relationship diagram for the STAFF table you worked with earlier in this chapter.

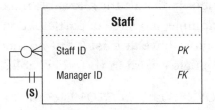

Figure 10.61. *Designating the type of particpation for the primary and foreign keys of the STAFF table.*

In this case, you must have at least one staff member with a valid staff identification number (the primary key) who can serve as a manager. Conversely, you need not provide a manager identification number (the foreign key) for a brand-new staff member; this person may have just been hired earlier today and has not yet been assigned to a particular department or project.

Identifying the Degree of Participation for Each Table

Now that you've determined how each table will participate within the relationship, you must determine the degree to which each table will participate. The *degree of participation* indicates the minimum number of records that a given table *must have* associated with a single record in the related table and the maximum number of records that the table *is allowed to have* associated with a single record in the related table. The factors you use to determine the *degree* of participation—obvious circumstances, common sense, or conformance to some set of standards—are the same as those you used to determine the *type* of participation. You'll commonly identify the degree of participation for some tables now and revisit the remaining tables when you define business rules for the database.

You use two numbers separated by a comma and enclosed within parentheses to represent the degree of participation for a given table. The first number indicates the required minimum number of related records and the second number indicates the allowable maximum number of related records. For example, a degree of participation such as (2,11) indicates that the table must have at least 2 but no more than 11 of its records related to a single record in the other table.

Consider the EMPLOYEES and CUSTOMERS tables once again. There is a one-to-many relationship between these tables, which means that a given customer can be associated with only one employee and a given employee can be associated with any number of customers. (Yes, I know; this is the obvious part.) Assume, however, that your organization has just instituted a new policy that focuses sharply on quality customer service. In order to ensure that each account representative can deliver the level of service the organization requires, the policy stipulates that he cannot be assigned to more than 15 customers at the same time. Based on this scenario, you can infer that the degree of participation for the EMPLOYEES table is (1,1) and the degree of participation for the CUSTOMERS table is (0,15).

Once you've identified the degree of participation for a particular table, add the information to the relationship diagram. Designate the degree of participation *over* the connection line of the appropriate table. Figure 10.62 shows the revised relationship diagram for the EMPLOYEES and CUSTOMERS tables.

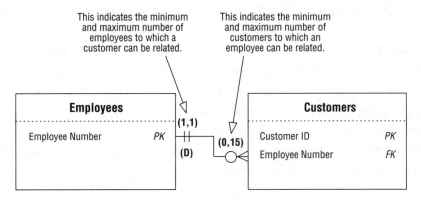

Figure 10.62. *Designating the degree of participation for the EMPLOYEES and CUSTOMERS tables.*

The degree of participation also applies to a self-referencing relationship, although you designate it for *the primary key and foreign key fields* in the table, just as you did with the type of participation. Figure 10.63 shows an updated version of the relationship diagram for the STAFF table that includes the degree of participation information.

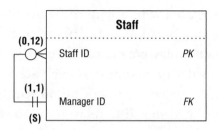

Figure 10.63. *Designating the degree of participation for the primary and foreign keys of the STAFF table.*

STAFF ID has a degree of participation of (0,12) because a manager can manage up to 12 staff members; a new manager who hasn't yet been assigned to a department or project will have no (or 0) staff members to manage. The degree of participation for MANAGER ID is (1,1) because a given staff member is managed by only one manager.

You can designate an *unlimited* degree of participation for any table in a dual-table relationship or key field in a self-referencing relationship by using an "N" in place of the second number. For example, the ORDERS table in Figure 10.64 has an unlimited degree of participation. Although a new customer may have not yet placed an order, you will allow him to place as many orders as he wishes. Imagine the impact on your organization's business if you limited each customer to 35 orders! Your organization would soon be out of business, unless it could continually and consistently acquire new customers.

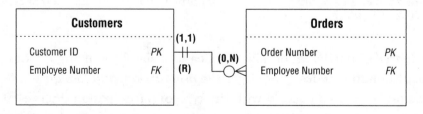

Figure 10.64. *Designating an unlimited degree of participation for the ORDERS table.*

Your task now is to set the relationship characteristics for every relationship you've established thus far. As you complete work on a given relationship, be sure to update the relationship diagram so that it reflects the results of your work.

Verifying Table Relationships with Users and Management

The very last order of business is to verify the relationships. You can perform this task relatively easily by using the following checklist:

1. Make sure that you've properly identified each relationship.

2. Make certain that you've properly established each relationship.

3. Make certain that each foreign key complies with the Elements of a Foreign Key.

4. Make sure that you've established an appropriate deletion rule for each relationship.

5. Make certain that you've identified the proper type of participation for each table within a dual-table relationship and for the appropriate key fields in a self-referencing relationship.

6. Make certain that you've identified the proper degree of participation for each table within a dual-table relationship and for the appropriate key fields in a self-referencing relationship.

If all the relationships check out and everyone you're working with agrees to this assessment, you can be confident that the relationships are sound and ready to be incorporated into views.

A Final Note

The degree to which you can easily implement these three relationship characteristics depends greatly upon your RDBMS. Most RDBMSs do not fully or inherently support all of the characteristics, but they do provide some *basic* support for the deletion rule and type of participation. In most cases, however, you can use SQL and programming code to implement these characteristics for any relationship in your database.

Relationship-Level Integrity

A relationship attains *relationship-level integrity* after you've verified that it is properly established and its characteristics are suitably set. Relationship-level integrity warrants the following:

- *The connection between the two tables (or key fields) in a relationship is sound.* You accomplished this by using primary and foreign key fields to establish a one-to-one or a one-to-many relationship and a linking table to establish a many-to-many relationship.

- *You can insert new records into each table in a meaningful manner.* You ensured this by designating the appropriate type of participation for each table (or key field) within the relationship.

- *You can delete an existing record without producing any adverse effects.* You guaranteed this by assigning an appropriate deletion rule for the relationship.

- *There is a meaningful limit to the number of records that can be interrelated within the relationship.* You implemented this by designating the appropriate degree of participation for each table (or key field) within the relationship.

As you know, relationship-level integrity is the third component of overall data integrity. (The first is table-level integrity and the second is field-level integrity.) You'll establish the final component of overall data integrity in the next chapter when you learn how to establish business rules for the database.

CASE STUDY

It's now time to identify the relationships that exist for the tables that appear on the final table list for Mike's Bikes. You've assigned your assistant, Zachary, to this part of the design process, and he's currently working with these tables:

CUSTOMERS

EMPLOYEES

INVOICES

PRODUCTS

VENDORS

Zachary's first order of business is to identify the relationships that currently exist between the tables. He decides to meet only with Mike because there are few tables in this database, and he figures that Mike should be familiar enough with the tables to help him verify the relationships.

Before Zachary meets with Mike, he creates a table matrix and identifies as many relationships as possible. Figure 10.65 shows his completed matrix.

	Customers	Employees	Invoices	Products	Vendors
Customers			1:N		
Employees			1:N		
Invoices	1:1	1:1		1:N	
Products			1:N		?
Vendors				?	

Figure 10.65. *Identifying the relationships among the tables in the Mike's Bikes database.*

Zachary then studies the table matrix closely and uses the appropriate formula to determine the true relationship between each pair of tables. Here is what he's discovered so far:

CUSTOMERS and INVOICES bear a one-to-many relationship.
(1:1 + 1:N = 1:N)

EMPLOYEES and INVOICES bear a one-to-many relationship.
(1:1 + 1:N = 1:N)

PRODUCTS and INVOICES bear a many-to-many relationship.
(1:N + 1:N = M:N)

Now he diagrams the relationships, places them in a folder, and heads to Starbucks for his meeting with Mike.

At the meeting, Mike and Zachary work on verifying the relationships. They both determine that the three relationships are indeed correct, and then Zachary brings Mike's attention to the PRODUCTS and VENDORS tables. He's not quite sure about the relationship between them, so he discusses the matter with Mike.

ZACHARY: "I wanted to ask you about the relationship between the PRODUCTS and VENDORS tables. Can a single product be associated with one or more vendors?"

MIKE: "Yes, in a manner of speaking. What I mean is that a single type of product—such as a bike lock—*can* be associated with one or more vendors. But I give each lock its own product number and treat it as a distinct item, regardless of the vendor who supplies it. Now, if the true meaning of your question is whether a single *record* in the PRODUCTS table can be associated with one or more records in the VENDORS table, then the answer is no because each record in the PRODUCTS table contains a reference to *only one* vendor in the VENDORS table."

ZACHARY: "I thought as much. In that case, there's a one-to-many relationship between the VENDORS and PRODUCTS tables. I automatically figured that a single vendor could be associated with many products in the PRODUCTS table."

Zachary now diagrams the one-to-many relationship between the VENDORS and PRODUCTS tables and continues with the next step.

He establishes each one-to-many relationship by taking a copy of the primary key from the parent table and incorporating it within the structure of the child table (where it serves as a foreign key) and then revises the relationship diagram accordingly. Figure 10.66 shows one of his revised diagrams.

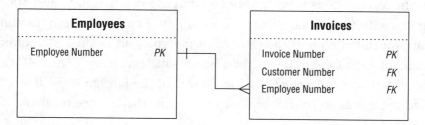

Figure 10.66. *The relationship diagram for the EMPLOYEES and INVOICES tables.*

Now Zachary establishes the many-to-many relationship between the INVOICES and PRODUCTS tables by creating a new linking table called INVOICE PRODUCTS. He bases the new table on the INVOICE NUMBER field from the INVOICES table and the PRODUCT NUMBER field from the PRODUCTS table. Figure 10.67 shows the revised relationship diagram for these tables.

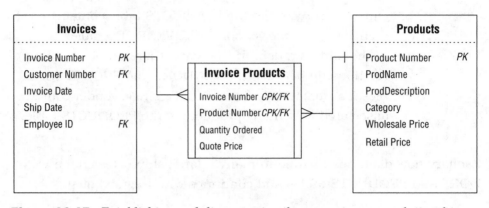

Figure 10.67. *Establishing and diagramming the many-to-many relationship between the INVOICES and PRODUCTS tables.*

Zachary reviews each table structure to ensure that it conforms to the Elements of the Ideal Table. Fortunately, he doesn't have to make any modifications because all of the table structures are sound. He now refines the foreign keys in each table by making certain that each one complies with the Elements of a Foreign Key. Finally, Zachary modifies the appropriate items in the General Elements and Logical Elements sections of each foreign key's Field Specifications sheet. Figure 10.68 shows the modifications he's made for one of the foreign keys. (I've highlighted the changes so that you can recognize them more easily.)

Zachary's next task is to establish the appropriate relationship characteristics for each relationship. He begins by defining a deletion rule for each relationship and then identifies both the type of participation and the degree of participation for each table within the relationship. He completes his task by designating these characteristics on the relationship diagram. Figure 10.69 shows one of the completed diagrams.

Mike and Zachary review and verify all the relationships one last time. They agree that everything is complete, so they celebrate with a couple of Mocha Brèves.

General Elements

Field Name:	Customer Number	Specification Type:	☐ Unique	☐ Generic	☒ Replica
Parent Table:	Invoices	**Source Specification:**			
Label:		Customer Number from the CUSTOMERS table.			
Shared By:					
Alias(es):					

Description: The identification number of a given customer. The values in this field enable us to identify and keep track of the customers who place orders for the products we provide.

Logical Elements

Key Type:	☐ Non	☐ Primary	Edit Rule:
	☒ Foreign	☐ Alternate	☒ Enter Now, Edits Allowed
Key Structure:	☒ Simple	☐ Composite	☐ Enter Now, Edits Not Allowed
Uniqueness:	☒ Non-unique	☐ Unique	☐ Enter Later, Edits Allowed
Null Support:	☐ Nulls Allowed	☒ No Nulls	☐ Enter Later, Edits Not Allowed
Values Entered By:	☒ User	☐ System	☐ Not Determined At This Time
Required Value:	☐ No	☒ Yes	

Default Value:

Range of Values: Any existing Customer Number in the CUSTOMERS table.

Comparisons Allowed:

☒ Same Field	☐ All	☒ =	☐ >	☐ >=	☐ ≠	☐ <	☐ <=
☐ Other Fields	☐ All	☐ =	☐ >	☐ >=	☐ ≠	☐ <	☐ <=
☒ Value Expression	☐ All	☒ =	☐ >	☐ >=	☐ ≠	☐ <	☐ <=

Operations Allowed:

☐ Same Field	☐ All	☐ +	☐ −	☐ x	☐ ÷	☐ Concatenation
☐ Other Fields	☐ All	☐ +	☐ −	☐ x	☐ ÷	☐ Concatenation
☐ Value Expression	☐ All	☐ +	☐ −	☐ x	☐ ÷	☐ Concatenation

Figure 10.68. *The General Elements and Logical Elements sections of the Field Specifications sheet for the* CUSTOMER *ID foreign key field in the INVOICES table.*

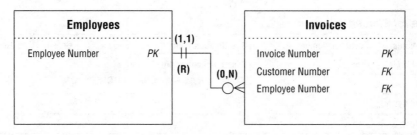

Figure 10.69. *The completed relationship diagram for the EMPLOYEES and INVOICES tables.*

Summary

We opened this chapter with a discussion of the three types of relationships that can exist between a particular pair of tables—*one-to-one, one-to-many,* and *many-to-many*. You now know that the one-to-many relationship is the most common type of dual-table relationship and that the many-to-many relationship gives rise to problems that must be resolved. You then learned about a *self-referencing relationship*, which is a type of relationship that occurs between the records within a given table. It is similar to a dual-table relationship in that it can be one-to-one, one-to-many, or many-to-many.

Next, we discussed how to *identify* the relationships that exist among the tables in a database. First you learned how to construct and use a *table matrix*, and then you learned how to use *associative* and *contextual* questions to help you identify a given relationship. We then discussed three formulas you could use to determine the true relationship that exists between the tables in a dual-table relationship or between the records in a self-referencing relationship.

The chapter continued with a discussion of how relationships are *established*. You learned that one-to-one and one-to-many relationships are established by using *primary keys* and *foreign keys*, and that many-to-many relationships are established using *linking tables*. We then briefly revisited *multivalued fields*, and you learned how to use a proper one-to-many relationship to resolve a multivalued field more efficiently. Next, we discussed self-referencing relationships, and you now know that you establish them in a very similar manner to dual-table relationships. You then learned that you must review all of the table structures and ensure that they still conform to the Elements of the Ideal Table.

Foreign keys were the next topic of discussion, and you learned that every foreign key must comply with the Elements of a Foreign Key. You now know that it can be very important for a foreign key to share the same name as its parent primary key, that you must modify certain elements of a field specification for a field that serves as a foreign key, and that a foreign key must draw its values from the parent primary key.

We then discussed relationship characteristics. You learned how to define a *deletion rule* for a relationship and that there are four ways you can define it. Next, you learned how to identify the *type of participation* and *degree of participation* for each table within a dual-table relationship and for each key field in a self-referencing relationship. As you now know, you can designate the type of participation as *Mandatory* or *Optional*. You also know that the degree of participation gauges the minimum and maximum number of interrelated records that can exist within a given relationship. Finally, you learned that you must verify the relationships with users and management and that you can use a checklist to accomplish this task.

The chapter closed with a look at *relationship-level integrity*. You learned that a relationship attains this type of integrity after you've verified that it is properly established and its characteristics are suitably set.

Review Questions

1. State two major reasons why a *relationship* is important.

2. Name the *three types* of relationships.

3. Which relationship will pose the most problems?

4. State two problems you could possibly encounter with a many-to-many relationship.

5. What is a *self-referencing relationship*?

6. How do you begin the process of *identifying* the relationships among the tables in the database?

7. What are the *two types of questions* you can ask to help you identify existing relationships?

8. What *shorthand symbol* do you use to designate a one-to-many relationship in the *table matrix*?

9. How do you determine what type of relationship officially exists between each pair of tables in the matrix?

10. How do you *establish* a one-to-many relationship?

11. True or False: Retrieving information from tables with a self-referencing relationship can be tedious and somewhat difficult.

12. How do you establish a self-referencing many-to-many relationship?

13. How do you *refine* the foreign keys in the database?

14. What two element categories must you modify for a foreign key's field specification?

15. What is the function of a *deletion rule*?

16. What two *types of participation* can you designate for a table?

17. What does the *degree of participation* indicate?

18. When does a relationship attain *relationship-level integrity*?

11

Business Rules

You are remembered for the rules you break.
—General Douglas MacArthur

Topics Covered in This Chapter

Throughout the database-design process, you've performed tasks that helped to establish various levels of data integrity. You've established table-level integrity, field-level integrity, and relationship-level integrity thus far. In doing so, you've ensured that the table and field structures are sound, that data entered into the fields will be consistent and basically valid, and that relationships are meaningful and properly established. In this chapter you'll learn how to establish the final component of overall data integrity: *business rules*.

What Are Business Rules?

A *business rule* is a statement that imposes some form of constraint on a specific aspect of the database, such as the elements within a field specification for a particular field or the characteristics of a given relationship. You base a business rule on the way the organization perceives and uses its data, which you determine from the manner in which the organization functions or conducts its business.

An important aspect of any design process is making choices. In database design, for example, you must choose which data to store in the database; you would not necessarily want or need to store every last piece of data the organization might *possibly* use. The data you finally choose to store and how you decide to store it will be determined by the way the organization uses its data. A hospital may wish to store times of various events to the second, whereas a warehouse requires only the date for any given event.

To guide these and other choices you'll be required to make during the database-design process (and later, when you implement the database in an RDBMS), you need a formal statement of the organization's business rules. These rules will influence a wide variety of database issues, such as the data you collect and store, the manner in which you define and establish relationships, the types of information that the database can provide, and the very security and confidentiality of the data itself. It is next to impossible to create a generic set of business rules that could apply to two or more organizations. Each organization has its own data and information requirements, and each has its own unique way of conducting its business; therefore, every organization needs its own specific set of business rules.

The following statement is an example of a typical business rule:

A Ship Date cannot be prior to an Order Date for any given order.

This particular business rule imposes a constraint on the Range of Values element of the field specifications for a SHIP DATE field. It will help ensure that the value of SHIP DATE is meaningful within the context of a sales order. Without this constraint, you could enter any date into the field (including one prior to the ORDER DATE), making the SHIP DATE field's value absolutely meaningless. The business rule is what makes the SHIP DATE field's value contextually meaningful.

Because business rules depend on the manner in which an organization perceives and uses its data, it is quite possible that a particular rule can be used by several organizations, but for completely *different* reasons.

For example, say that the music department at Bel Air High School is known far and wide for the quality of musicianship it develops in its student musicians. The students are able to attain this level of musicianship because they're encouraged to focus their musical studies and restrict themselves to learning no more than two instruments. In another part of town, the music department at Lake City High School (a private school) also imbues its student musicians with a high quality of musicianship by helping the students focus their musical studies. The students at this school, however, are restricted to learning no more than two instruments due to school policy; the school's inventory of musical instruments is very limited.

Coincidentally, both schools are in the process of designing their own database. In each case, the school will use the database to support its daily operations and administrative functions. It so happens that each database contains the tables shown in Figure 11.1.

Both schools are at the same stage of the database-design process and are currently establishing business rules. As it turns out, each school is using the following business rule in their respective databases:

> A student cannot have more than two instruments checked out at the same time.

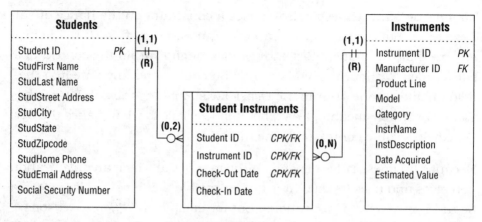

Figure 11.1. *Tables from the Bel Air High School and Lake City High School databases.*

This business rule applies to the *degree of participation* between the STUDENTS table and STUDENT INSTRUMENTS table. In this instance, a single record in the STUDENTS table cannot be associated with more than two records in the STUDENT INSTRUMENTS table where the value of CHECK-IN DATE for each record is null; a null value in the CHECK-IN DATE field indicates that the instrument is still in the student's possession.

The rule *does* apply to both schools, yet each school requires it for a different reason. Bel Air High School requires the rule because of the manner in which its music program has been established, whereas Lake City High School requires the constraint because of the physical limitations of its instrument inventory. The fact that both schools developed an identical rule is pure coincidence. This example illustrates both that a business rule is, indeed, based on the way an organization functions or conducts its business and why every organization must have its own specific set of business rules.

The example also illustrates another issue: You cannot establish constraints imposed by certain business rules, such as this one, within the logical design of the database. For instance, there is no clear way for you to indicate that the CHECK-IN DATE values must be tested in order to determine whether a student can check out another instrument. You must instead address and establish the constraint *outside* of the logical design of the database. How do you determine whether you can properly represent a given constraint within this process? You do so by identifying the *type* of business rule you're defining.

Types of Business Rules

There are two major types of business rules: *database oriented* and *application oriented*. Both types of business rules impose some form of constraint and help enforce and maintain overall data integrity, but they differ with regard to where and how they are established.

Database oriented business rules impose constraints that you can establish within the *logical* design of the database. You implement a given constraint by modifying various field specification elements, relationship characteristics, or a combination of the two. The statement from which you derive the constraint is a database oriented business rule if you can *meaningfully* and *clearly* establish the constraint by either of these means. For example, say you have a VENDORS table and define the following business rule for the VENDSTATE field in that table:

> We conduct business exclusively with vendors from the Pacific Northwest.

This business rule limits the values that you can enter into the VENDSTATE field to WA, OR, ID, and MT. You can establish the business rule's constraint in a meaningful manner by modifying the Range of Values element in the field specifications for the VENDSTATE field. Figure 11.2 shows the modification.

Application oriented business rules impose constraints that you *cannot* establish within the logical design of the database. You must instead es-

Logical Elements

Key Type:	☒ Non	☐ Primary	**Edit Rule:**
	☐ Foreign	☐ Alternate	☒ Enter Now, Edits Allowed
Key Structure:	☐ Simple	☐ Composite	☐ Enter Now, Edits Not Allowed
Uniqueness:	☒ Non-unique	☐ Unique	☐ Enter Later, Edits Allowed
Null Support:	☐ Nulls Allowed	☒ No Nulls	☐ Enter Later, Edits Not Allowed
Values Entered By:	☒ User	☐ System	☐ Not Determined At This Time
Required Value:	☐ No	☒ Yes	
Default Value:	None		
Range of Values:	ID, MT, OR, WA		

Comparisons Allowed:

☒ Same Field	☐ All	☒ =	☐ >	☐ >=	☐ ≠	☐ <	☐ <=
☐ Other Fields	☐ All	☐ =	☐ >	☐ >=	☐ ≠	☐ <	☐ <=
☐ Value Expression	☐ All	☐ =	☐ >	☐ >=	☐ ≠	☐ <	☐ <=

Operations Allowed:

☐ Same Field	☐ All	☐ +	☐ –	☐ x	☐ ÷	☐ Concatenation
☐ Other Fields	☐ All	☐ +	☐ –	☐ x	☐ ÷	☐ Concatenation
☐ Value Expression	☐ All	☐ +	☐ –	☐ x	☐ ÷	☐ Concatenation

Figure 11.2. *Implementing a constraint imposed by a database oriented business rule.*

tablish them within the *physical* design of the database or within the design of a *database application*, where they will be more applicable and meaningful. (I use the term *database application* here to refer to a program written in some RDBMS software that allows people in the organization to use the database easily and to perform tasks related to their daily work activities.)

Here is an example of a typical application oriented business rule:

> A customer with a "Preferred" status receives a 15% discount on all purchases.

This business rule determines the amount of discount applied to a customer's purchases, based on a particular status. You cannot establish this constraint meaningfully in the logical design for two reasons: There is no field in which to store the discount amount (the amount is a result of a calculation, and calculated fields are not allowed in a table), and there is no way to indicate the criterion used—the customer's status—to determine the discount. This is a rule that you must establish within the *physical* design of the database or the design of the *database application*.

❖ **Note** The manner in which you actually define and establish application oriented business rules is a topic that is beyond the scope of this book. Some RDBMSs provide tools that allow you to implement common application oriented business rules relatively easily; most RDBMSs will require you to write programming code to implement and enforce these rules.

Although both types of business rules are important, you'll focus on database oriented business rules during this stage of the database-design process.

❖ **Note** Throughout the remainder of the book, I'll refer to database oriented business rules simply as *business rules*.

Categories of Business Rules

It will be easier for you to understand and define business rules if you divide them into two distinct categories: *field specific* and *relationship specific*.

Field Specific Business Rules

Business rules under this category impose constraints on the elements of a field specification for a particular field. The number of elements a given rule affects depends on the manner in which you define that rule. For example, this rule only affects one element:

> Order dates are to be displayed in long form, such as "January 10, 2003."

This rule affects the Display Format element of the Order Date field in an ORDERS table. You establish this rule by modifying the Display Format element of the field specifications for the Order Date field to indicate the manner in which the date should be displayed.

Here's a rule that affects more than one element:

> We must be able to store a zip code for our Canadian customers.

This rule affects the Data Type, Character Support, and Display Format elements of the field specifications for the CustZipcode field in a CUSTOMERS table. Canadian zip codes include letters, so you must make the following modifications to these elements in order to impose the constraints defined by this rule:

1. Change the Data Type setting to "Alphanumeric."

2. Include "Letters" under the Character Support element.

3. Modify the Display Format element to ensure that the letters in Canadian zip codes will be capitalized.

Figure 11.3 shows the modified Physical Elements section of CustZipcode's field specifications.

Relationship Specific Business Rules

These types of business rules impose constraints that affect the characteristics of a relationship. For instance, assume you're working with the tables and relationships in Figure 11.4.

Physical Elements			
Data Type:	Alphanumeric	**Character Support:**	
Length:	6	☒ Letters (A–Z)	☐ Keyboard (. , / $ # %)
Decimal Places:	Not Applicable	☒ Numbers (0–9)	☐ Special (© ® ™ Σ π)
Input Mask:	Not Applicable		
Display Format:	Uppercase letters where applicable.		

Figure 11.3. *Establishing a field specific business rule for* CUSTZIPCODE.

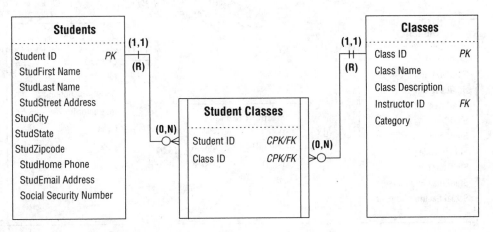

Figure 11.4. *Tables and relationships from a school database.*

Say you determine that there must be a limit to the number of students for each class and you define the following business rule:

> Each class must have a minimum of 5 students, but cannot have more than 20.

This business rule affects the *degree of participation* between the CLASSES and STUDENT CLASSES tables. You enforce the constraint this rule defines by modifying the relationship diagram to show that a single record in the CLASSES table *must* be related to at least 5—but no more than 20—records in the STUDENT CLASSES table. (Depending on your point of view, you could also infer from this business rule that the type of participation for the STUDENT CLASSES table is now mandatory. You can enter a new class or keep an existing class in the CLASSES table if and only if there are at least five students registered for that class.) Figure 11.5 shows the modification you must make to the diagram in order to establish the business rule.

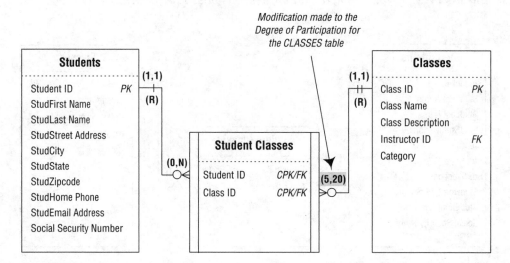

Figure 11.5. *Establishing a relationship specific business rule.*

Defining and Establishing Business Rules

You'll define and establish business rules for the database during this stage of the design process. Remember that you must base these rules on the manner in which your organization perceives and uses its data, which (as you well know) will depend on the way the organization functions or conducts its business. The best approach to this task is to define and establish the field specific business rules first, followed by the relationship specific business rules. This approach helps you to remain focused on the type of rule you're defining. It also keeps you from jumping back and forth between different types of business rules, which can often lead to confusion and some amount of frustration.

Working with Users and Management

Once again, you'll work with the representative group of users and management. Schedule new meetings with them so that you can work together to define and establish the appropriate business rules for the database. Working as a group enables you to make certain that the constraints imposed by the business rules you define are meaningful and that there is no confusion or ambiguity as to the necessity of imposing each constraint. If you or anyone in the group has some doubt about a constraint, you can discuss the effect it will have on the field or relationship involved and the advantages and disadvantages of imposing the constraint. Then, you can decide whether to keep the rule or disregard it completely based on the results of your discussion.

Defining and Establishing Field Specific Business Rules

Begin the process of establishing business rules for the database by working on field specific rules. You define and establish each rule using these steps:

1. Select a table.

2. Review each field and determine whether it requires any constraints.

3. Define the necessary business rules for the field.

4. Establish the rules by modifying the appropriate field specification elements.

5. Determine what actions test the rule.

6. Record the rule on a Business Rule Specifications sheet.

Let's now take a look at each step in greater detail.

Step 1: Select a Table

It doesn't matter which table you start with because you'll eventually apply this procedure to every table within the database. If you choose a table with a familiar structure, however, you can focus a little more on learning the steps within the procedure. This extra effort will pay dividends when you begin to work with tables containing fields that bear closer attention and examination.

Think about the subject the table represents and then pose these questions:

> How does the organization use information based on or related to this subject?

> What relationships does this table have to itself or to other tables in the database?

When necessary, consult the final table list and read the description for this table, and refer to any relationship diagrams that incorporate this table. The answers to these questions will be useful to you while you're defining rules for this table, and focusing on the table in this manner prepares you for the next step.

Step 2: Review Each Field and Determine Whether It Requires Any Constraints

Examine the Field Specifications sheet for each field and determine whether you should apply a constraint to any of its elements. Keep the questions from Step 1 in mind as you review a given specification sheet, and then pose this question:

> Based on how the table is used within the database, is a constraint necessary for any element within this specification?

If the answer is no, move on to the next field; otherwise, go on to the next step. For example, assume you're working with the CustCounty field in a CUSTOMERS table and you have just posed the question about the need for a constraint. (Figure 11.6 shows the current Logical Elements category for this field.)

Logical Elements								
Key Type:	[X] Non	[ ] Primary		**Edit Rule:**				
	[ ] Foreign	[ ] Alternate		[ ] Enter Now, Edits Allowed				
Key Structure:	[ ] Simple	[ ] Composite		[ ] Enter Now, Edits Not Allowed				
Uniqueness:	[X] Non-unique	[ ] Unique		[X] Enter Later, Edits Allowed				
Null Support:	[X] Nulls Allowed	[ ] No Nulls		[ ] Enter Later, Edits Not Allowed				
Values Entered By:	[X] User	[ ] System		[ ] Not Determined At This Time				
Required Value:	[X] No	[ ] Yes						
Default Value:	None							
Range of Values:	King, Kitsap							

Comparisons Allowed:

	All	=	>	>=	≠	<	<=
[ ] Same Field	[ ] All	[ ] =	[ ] >	[ ] >=	[ ] ≠	[ ] <	[ ] <=
[ ] Other Fields	[ ] All	[ ] =	[ ] >	[ ] >=	[ ] ≠	[ ] <	[ ] <=
[X] Value Expression	[ ] All	[X] =	[ ] >	[ ] >=	[ ] ≠	[ ] <	[ ] <=

Operations Allowed:

	All	+	−	x	÷	Concatenation
[ ] Same Field	[ ] All	[ ] +	[ ] −	[ ] x	[ ] ÷	[ ] Concatenation
[X] Other Fields	[ ] All	[ ] +	[ ] −	[ ] x	[ ] ÷	[X] Concatenation
[X] Value Expression	[ ] All	[ ] +	[ ] −	[ ] x	[ ] ÷	[X] Concatenation

Figure 11.6. *Current settings for the Logical Elements category of the* Cust-County *field.*

You should move on to the next step if you receive an answer such as this:

> "Well, the boss wants to begin tracking our customers by county, so we must make certain we record a county for every customer. In fact, we've just added Pierce County and Snohomish County to our sales region, so it'll be *imperative* that the county names get recorded."

This response clearly is a yes, so you will go on to define business rules for this field in the next step.

Step 3: Define the Necessary Business Rules for the Field

You define the appropriate business rules for the CustCounty field by identifying the constraints implied by the response in Step 2. Then you transform each constraint into a rule.

The response in Step 2 suggests two possible constraints that you should impose upon the CustCounty field: A county name is required for each customer, and the range of values for this field is limited to four specific counties (the two currently on the field specification and the two new counties indicated in the response). Here are two statements you might use to begin transforming these constraints into business rules:

A county must be associated with each customer.

The only counties that can be entered into this field are King, Kitsap, Pierce, and Snohomish.

Once you've defined the appropriate business rules, you can move on to Step 4.

Step 4: Establish the Rules by Modifying the Appropriate Field Specification Elements

Establish each business rule you defined in Step 3 by modifying the appropriate elements on the Field Specifications sheet. (Remember that some rules may affect more than one element.) First, however, you must identify which elements of the field specifications the rule affects. For example, consider the first business rule you defined for the CustCounty field in Step 3:

A county must be associated with each customer.

You can deduce that the rule affects the Required Value, Null Support, and Edit Rule elements because it explicitly states that a county "must be associated" with a customer. Now you can make the appropriate modifications to these elements. In this particular case, you'll set Required Value to "Yes," Null Support to "No Nulls," and Edit Rule to "Enter Now, Edits Allowed."

As you can see, it's important for you to examine each business rule very carefully in order to determine which field specification elements it's going to affect. When you first begin to define business rules, it's best to have a Field Specifications sheet handy so that you can refer to it as necessary. Many of the elements will come to mind more easily as you become more experienced at establishing business rules.

Now, consider the next business rule in the example:

> The only counties that can be entered into this field are King, Kitsap, Pierce, and Snohomish.

This business rule affects the Range of Values element, and you'll now revise its setting to "King, Kitsap, Pierce, and Snohomish." Figure 11.7 shows the revised Logical Elements category of the Field Specifications sheet for the CustCounty field.

Step 5: Determine What Actions Test the Rule

The constraint the business rule imposes is tested when you attempt to perform one of three actions: *inserting* a record into the table or an entry into a field, *deleting* a record from the table or a value within a field, or *updating* a field's value. Now that you've established a business rule and understand the constraint it will impose, determine what actions test the rule by identifying when a violation of the rule is most likely to occur. You can make this a relatively easy task by asking yourself the following questions:

> Will this rule be violated if I enter a new record into this table?
>
> Will this rule be violated if I *do not* enter a new record into this table?
>
> Will this rule be violated if I delete a record from this table?

Logical Elements

Key Type:	[X] Non	[ ] Primary	Edit Rule:
	[ ] Foreign	[ ] Alternate	[X] Enter Now, Edits Allowed
Key Structure:	[ ] Simple	[ ] Composite	[ ] Enter Now, Edits Not Allowed
Uniqueness:	[X] Non-unique	[ ] Unique	[ ] Enter Later, Edits Allowed
Null Support:	[ ] Nulls Allowed	[X] No Nulls	[ ] Enter Later, Edits Not Allowed
Values Entered By:	[X] User	[ ] System	[ ] Not Determined At This Time
Required Value:	[ ] No	[X] Yes	
Default Value:	None		

| Range of Values: | King, Kitsap, Pierce, Snohomish |

Comparisons Allowed:

		All	=	>	>=	≠	<	<=
[ ]	Same Field	[ ] All	[ ] =	[ ] >	[ ] >=	[ ] ≠	[ ] <	[ ] <=
[ ]	Other Fields	[ ] All	[ ] =	[ ] >	[ ] >=	[ ] ≠	[ ] <	[ ] <=
[X]	Value Expression	[ ] All	[X] =	[ ] >	[ ] >=	[ ] ≠	[ ] <	[ ] <=

Operations Allowed:

		All	+	–	x	÷	Concatenation
[ ]	Same Field	[ ] All	[ ] +	[ ] –	[ ] x	[ ] ÷	[ ] Concatenation
[X]	Other Fields	[ ] All	[ ] +	[ ] –	[ ] x	[ ] ÷	[X] Concatenation
[X]	Value Expression	[ ] All	[ ] +	[ ] –	[ ] x	[ ] ÷	[X] Concatenation

Figure 11.7. *Revised settings for the Logical Elements category of the* CUST-COUNTY *field.*

Will this rule be violated if I enter a value into this field?

Will this rule be violated if I *do not* enter a value into this field?

Will this rule be violated if I update the value of this field?

Will this rule be violated if I delete the value of this field?

Once you've determined which actions will trigger a violation of the rule, make note of them; you'll use them in the next step. This information will also help you to establish this rule in the most effective manner possible when you implement the database in your RDBMS.

In this case, the business rule for the CustCounty field will be tested when you try to *insert* a value into the field because the value must be within a specific range of values. The rule will also be tested when you try to *delete* a value in the field because the value cannot be null.

Step 6: Record the Rule on a Business Rule Specifications Sheet

You can document a given business rule for future reference by filling out a Business Rule Specifications sheet. This is something you should do for every rule, regardless of its type or category. The Business Rule Specifications sheet provides three advantages:

1. *It allows you to document every database oriented business rule.* This helps you ensure that you have appropriately defined and properly established each rule.

2. *It allows you to document every application oriented business rule.* Although you cannot *establish* this type of rule within the logical design of the database, you can at least indicate its basic elements. The information you document for this type of business rule will prove invaluable to you when you implement the database within your RDBMS or when you create the application program that people will use to work with the database.

3. *It provides a standard method for recording all business rules.* Business rules are easier to track and maintain if you record them in a consistent manner. Using a uniform format also makes it easier for you to troubleshoot business rules; every aspect of the rule appears on the specification sheet.

The Business Rule Specifications sheet contains the following items:

- *Statement.* This is the text of the business rule itself. It should be clear and succinct and should convey the required constraints without any confusion or ambiguity. Here's an example of a well-framed statement:

    A booking agent cannot be assigned to more than 25 entertainers.

- *Constraint.* This is a brief explanation of how the constraint applies to the tables and fields. For instance, you can use the following explanation for the constraint imposed by the business rule in the preceding example:

  > A single record in the AGENTS table can be associated with no more than 25 records in the ENTERTAINERS table.

- *Type.* Here is where you indicate whether the rule is database oriented or application oriented.

- *Category.* This is where you indicate whether the rule is field specific or relationship specific.

- *Test on.* Here is where you indicate which actions (insert, delete, update) will test the constraint the business rule imposes.

- *Structures Affected.* Depending on the type of business rule, the constraint will affect either a field or a relationship. This is where you designate the name of the field(s) the rule will affect or the name of the table(s) involved in the relationship that the rule affects.

- *Field Elements Affected.* A business rule that pertains to a field can affect one or more elements of that field's specifications. This is where you indicate the elements the rule affects.

- *Relationship Characteristics Affected.* A business rule that pertains to a relationship will affect one or more of the relationship's characteristics. Here is where you indicate the characteristics that the rule affects.

- *Action Taken.* Here you indicate the modifications you've made to the elements of a field specification or to a relationship diagram. It is very important that the statement you enter here be as clear and unambiguous as possible. Should a problem occur as a result of enforcing this business rule, this statement serves as accurate documentation of the steps you have taken to establish the rule. You can use this statement to make certain that these steps were actually carried out and that the rule has been properly established.

Now, fill out a Business Rule Specifications sheet for the rule you established in Step 4. Figure 11.8 shows a completed Business Rule Specifications sheet that documents the business rules you established for the CustCounty field.

Defining and Establishing Relationship Specific Business Rules

After defining and establishing *field specific* business rules, the next order of business is to tackle *relationship specific* business rules. The procedure for performing this task involves the following steps:

1. Select a relationship.

2. Review the relationship and determine whether it requires any constraints.

3. Define the necessary business rules for the relationship.

4. Establish the rule by modifying the appropriate relationship characteristics.

5. Determine what actions will test the rule.

6. Record the rule on a Business Rule Specifications sheet.

As you can see, this procedure is similar to the one you used for field specific business rules. Now, let's take a look at each step in more detail.

> ❖ **Note** You can apply this entire procedure to both self-referencing and dual-table relationships. I've based the remainder of the discussion on a dual-table relationship, however, because it is the type of relationship you are likely to work with the majority of the time.

BUSINESS RULE SPECIFICATIONS

Rule Information

Statement: A county must be associated with each customer.

Constraint: An entry must be made into the CustCounty field; it cannot be Null.

Type: [X] Database Oriented   **Category:**   [X] Field Specific   **Test On:**   [X] Insert   [ ] Update

[ ] Application Oriented   [ ] Relationship Specific   [X] Delete

Structures Affected

Field Names: CUST COUNTY

Table Names:

Field Elements Affected

Physical Elements

[ ] Data Type	[ ] Decimal Places	[ ] Input Mask
[ ] Length	[ ] Character Support	[ ] Display Format

Logical Elements

[ ] Key Type	[ ] Values Entered By	[ ] Comparisons Allowed
[ ] Key Structure	[X] Required Value	[ ] Operations Allowed
[ ] Uniqueness	[ ] Default Value	[X] Edit Rule
[X] Null Support	[ ] Range of Values	

Relationship Characteristics Affected

[ ] Deletion Rule	[ ] Type of Participation	[ ] Degree of Participation

Action Taken

Required Value was set to "Yes," Null Support was set to "No Nulls," and Edit Rule was set to "Enter Now, Edits Allowed."

Figure 11.8. *An example of a Business Rule Specifications sheet.*

Step 1: Select a Relationship

Which relationship you choose is a relatively trivial matter because you'll eventually apply this procedure to *every* relationship anyway. Once you select a specific relationship, review its relationship diagram. Then think about what the tables represent and why they are related and pose the following questions:

What kind of information do these tables provide?

Why is the relationship between these two tables important?

The answer to these questions will help you define any necessary business rules for the relationship, and keeping them in mind will prepare you for the next step.

Step 2: Review the Relationship and Determine Whether It Requires Any Constraints

Briefly review each relationship characteristic and keep its current setting in mind. Then examine the relationship as a whole and determine whether it requires some form of constraint. As you review the relationship, remember the answers to the questions you posed in Step 1. You now pose a question such as this to help you determine whether a constraint is necessary:

Is there a need to impose some type of limitation on this relationship based on the way the organization functions or conducts its business?

If the answer is yes, then go to the next step; otherwise, review the next relationship and perform this step once again. For example, assume you're designing a database for a small dance studio, and you're working with the relationship between the INSTRUCTORS and INSTRUCTOR CLASSES tables in Figure 11.9.

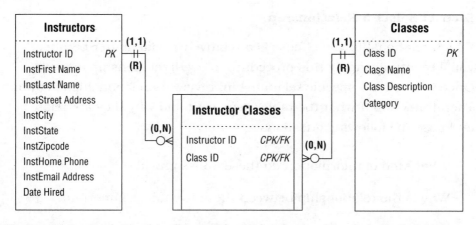

Figure 11.9. *A relationship diagram for tables from a dance studio database.*

Now, pose a question to help you determine whether the relationship requires a constraint.

> Is there a need to impose some type of limitation on this relationship based on the way the dance studio functions or conducts its business?

Move to the next step if you receive an answer such as this:

> Yes, there is. We require all instructors to teach at least one class. We limit them, however, to teaching no more than eight classes.

You'll use this response as the basis of a business rule in the next step.

Step 3: Define the Necessary Business Rules for the Relationship

Next, define an appropriate business rule based on the response you received in Step 2. Identify the constraint the response implies and then transform it into a business rule. For example, you can infer two constraints from the response: The minimum number of classes an instructor can teach is one, and the maximum number is eight. Transform these constraints into a business rule by composing a statement such as this one:

> An instructor must teach one class, but no more than eight classes.

After you've defined the rule, continue with the next step.

Step 4: Establish the Rule by Modifying the Appropriate Relationship Characteristics

Establish the business rule you just defined by modifying the appropriate characteristics in the relationship diagram. Before you make any modifications, consider the business rule statement once again and identify which relationship characteristics the rule affects.

> An instructor must teach one class, but no more than eight classes.

The constraint affects the number of classes an instructor can teach, so you modify the degree of participation characteristic of the INSTRUCTOR CLASSES table by setting it to "(1,8)." This rule also affects the type of participation characteristic of the INSTRUCTOR CLASSES table. You must set the table's type of participation to "Mandatory" because a single record in the INSTRUCTORS table *must* be associated with at least one record in the INSTRUCTOR CLASSES table. Figure 11.10 shows the revised relationship diagram with your modifications.

Step 5: Determine What Actions Will Test the Rule

As you know, the constraint the business rule imposes is tested when you attempt to insert, delete, or update a table record or field value. Now that you've established the business rule and understand how it affects

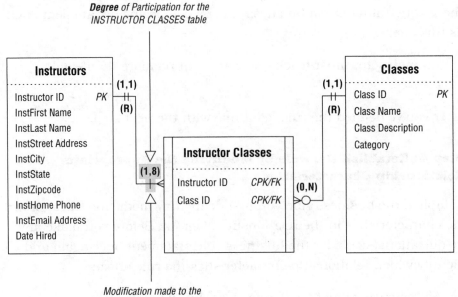

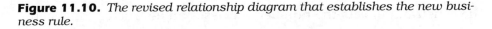

Figure 11.10. *The revised relationship diagram that establishes the new business rule.*

the relationship, determine what actions test the rule by identifying when a violation of the rule is most likely to occur. Use the following questions to help you make your decision:

Are there circumstances under which this rule will be violated if I enter a new record into this table?

Will this rule be violated if I *do not* enter a new record into this table?

Will this rule be violated if I delete a record from this table?

Once you've determined which actions will trigger a violation of the rule, make note of them; you'll use them in the next step. This information will also help you to establish this rule in the most effective manner possible when you implement the database in your RDBMS.

Here's an important point to note: When you determine that a rule will be violated when you attempt to *delete* a record, then you must alter the current deletion rule for the relationship accordingly or add a new deletion rule to the relationship.

You learned in Chapter 10 that you don't need to worry about deleting records in the *child* table of a relationship because there can be no adverse effects from doing so. We must now amend this assertion by stating that an exception occurs when deleting a record in the child table would violate a required business rule. You handle this exception by establishing a Restrict deletion rule for the child table. *Make absolutely certain* that you keep this in mind as you're determining when a rule will be tested.

The new business rule for the dance studio database will be tested when you attempt to *insert* a record into the INSTRUCTOR CLASSES table; you can associate a maximum of only eight records with a particular instructor. The rule will also be tested when you attempt to *delete* a record from the INSTRUCTOR CLASSES table; each instructor *must* be associated with at least one class. As a result, you must establish a Restrict deletion rule for this table. Figure 11.11 shows the modifications you've made to this relationship's diagram.

Step 6: Record the Rule on a Business Rule Specifications Sheet

Finally, fill out a Business Rule Specifications sheet for the business rule you established in Step 4. Figure 11.12 shows the completed Business Rule Specifications sheet for your new rule.

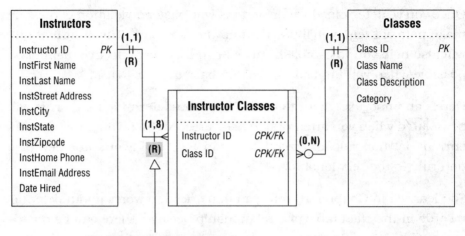

New **Restrict** deletion rule added for
the INSTRUCTOR CLASSES table

Figure 11.11. *Establishing a Restrict deletion rule for the INSTRUCTOR
CLASSES table to support the new business rule.*

Validation Tables

As you define field specific business rules, there will be instances in
which a rule imposes a constraint that defines a *distinct set* of valid values for a given field's range of values. (This obviously affects the field's
Range of Values element in its field specification.) This set of values
commonly comprises a relatively fixed number of entries, and the values
themselves will rarely change. If the number of entries is rather high,
however, you might discover that it's going to be slightly difficult for you
to implement this rule. For example, you'll probably run out of room
very quickly when you attempt to enumerate each of the values within
the Range of Values element on the Field Specifications sheet, and implementing the entire set of values within the RDBMS could prove to be
somewhat complicated. You can avoid problems such as these by storing all of the values in a *validation table*.

BUSINESS RULE SPECIFICATIONS

Rule Information

Statement: An instructor must teach one class, but no more than eight (8) classes.

Constraint: The participation of INSTRUCTORS within the relationship is Mandatory. Also, a single record in INSTRUCTORS can be related to only eight (8) records in INSTRUCTOR CLASSES.

Type: [X] Database Oriented **Category:** [ ] Field Specific **Test On:** [X] Insert [ ] Update
[ ] Application Oriented [X] Relationship Specific [X] Delete

Structures Affected

Field Names:

Table Names: INSTRUCTORS, INSTRUCTOR CLASSES

Field Elements Affected

Physical Elements

[ ] Data Type	[ ] Decimal Places	[ ] Input Mask
[ ] Length	[ ] Character Support	[ ] Display Format

Logical Elements

[ ] Key Type	[ ] Values Entered By	[ ] Comparisons Allowed
[ ] Key Structure	[ ] Required Value	[ ] Operations Allowed
[ ] Uniqueness	[ ] Default Value	[ ] Edit Rule
[ ] Null Support	[ ] Range of Values	

Relationship Characteristics Affected

[X] Deletion Rule [X] Type of Participation [X] Degree of Participation

Action Taken

The type of participation for the INSTRUCTOR CLASSES table was changed to Mandatory.
The degree of participation for the INSTRUCTORS CLASSES table was changed to (1,8).
A new Restrict deletion rule was added to the relationship for the INSTRUCTOR CLASSES table.

Figure 11.12. *The completed Business Rule Specifications sheet for the new business rule.*

What Are Validation Tables?

As you learned in Chapter 3, a *validation table* (also known as a *lookup table*) stores data that you specifically use to implement data integrity. You won't often insert, update, or delete any records within the table once you populate the table with the data you require. Validation tables usually (but not always) comprise two fields: The first acts as the primary key and is what you'll use to help you enforce data integrity, and the second is simply a non-key field that stores a set of values required by some other field in the database. Figure 11.13 shows two examples of validation tables.

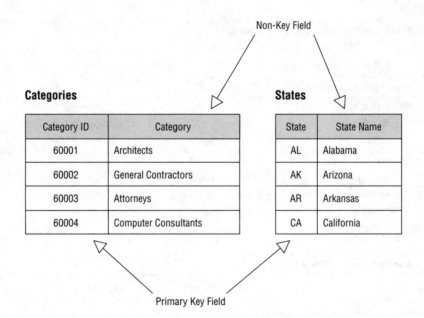

Figure 11.13. *Examples of validation tables.*

In this section, you'll learn how to use the primary key field to help enforce a business rule. You'll learn how to use the non-key field later in Chapter 12.

Using Validation Tables to Support Business Rules

When a business rule limits a field's range of values, you can enforce the constraint by using a validation table; the field will then draw its values from an appropriate field in the validation table. Establishing this type of rule involves two steps: defining a relationship between the parent table of the field affected by the rule and the validation table and making a modification to the Range of Values element of the field specifications for the affected field in the parent table.

For example, assume you're working with the SuppState field of a SUPPLIERS table, and you've defined the following business rule:

> Any supplier we use must be based in one of the 11 contiguous Western states, Alaska, or Hawaii.

You can see that this rule imposes a constraint on the SuppState field's range of values, limiting them to AK, AZ, CA, CO, HI, ID, MT, NM, NV, OR, UT, WA, and WY. (According to the rule, you can't use a supplier based in some other state.) The easiest and most efficient way to establish this rule is to store these values in a validation table called STATES and then use the validation table as the source of the SuppState field's range of values.

Consider the tables in Figure 11.14. (Note the new symbol that is used to represent a validation table.) The SUPPLIERS table stores all the requisite data on the SUPPLIERS engaged by the organization, and the STATES table is a new validation table that will store the names and abbreviations of the specified STATES.

Your first order of business (no pun intended) is to establish a relationship between these tables. As you can see, there is a one-to-many relationship between them—a single record in STATES can be associated with one or more records in SUPPLIERS, but a single record in SUPPLIERS will be associated with only *one* record in STATES. You already know that you establish a one-to-many relationship by taking a copy of

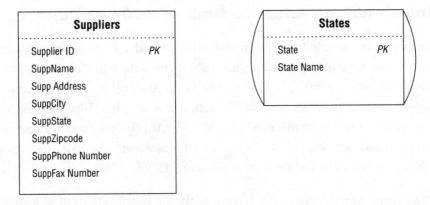

Figure 11.14. *The SUPPLIERS table and the STATES validation table.*

the parent table's primary key and incorporating it within the structure of the child table where it becomes a foreign key. Although the SUPPLIERS table already has a field named SuppState, you'll replace it with the State field from the STATES validation table. (This is a reasonable modification because it is in accordance with the Elements of the Ideal Field and is consistent with the manner in which you establish one-to-many relationships.) Figure 11.15 shows the new relationship diagram for these two tables.

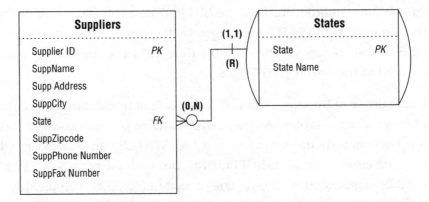

Figure 11.15. *A relationship diagram for the SUPPLIERS and STATES tables.*

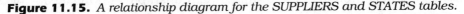

Now that the STATE field is a foreign key in the SUPPLIERS table, make certain that it conforms to the Elements of a Foreign Key (as outlined in Chapter 10) and set its field specification in the appropriate manner. Then set the relationship's characteristics in this manner:

- *Deletion Rule.* Define a Restrict deletion rule for this relationship. You *do not* want to delete a state in the STATES table that is being referenced by records in the SUPPLIERS table.

- *Type of Participation.* Designate an Optional type of participation for the SUPPLIERS table and a Mandatory type of participation for the STATES table. Although it's unnecessary for the SUPPLIERS table to contain any records before you can enter a new record in the STATES table, there must be *at least* one record in the STATES table before you can enter records into the SUPPLIERS table.

- *Degree of Participation.* Assign a (1,1) degree of participation for the STATES table; as you already know, there must be at least one record in the STATES table before you can enter records into the SUPPLIERS table. Assign a (0,N) degree of participation for the SUPPLIERS table; any number of records in this table can be associated with a particular record in the STATES table.

Next, modify the Range of Values element of the field specification for the STATE field in the SUPPLIERS table using a setting such as this:

Any value within the STATE field of the STATES table.

Figure 11.16 shows the settings you've made within the Logical Elements category of the Field Specifications sheet for this field.

Now you must decide which actions test the rule. When you use a validation table to enforce a business rule, you typically want to test the rule when a user attempts to *insert* a new value into the field or *update* an existing value within the field. In either case, a violation will occur when the user attempts to enter a value that does not exist in the validation table.

Logical Elements

Key Type:	☐ Non	☐ Primary	**Edit Rule:**
	☒ Foreign	☐ Alternate	☒ Enter Now, Edits Allowed
Key Structure:	☐ Simple	☐ Composite	☐ Enter Now, Edits Not Allowed
Uniqueness:	☒ Non-unique	☐ Unique	☐ Enter Later, Edits Allowed
Null Support:	☐ Nulls Allowed	☒ No Nulls	☐ Enter Later, Edits Not Allowed
Values Entered By:	☒ User	☐ System	☐ Not Determined At This Time
Required Value:	☐ No	☒ Yes	
Default Value:	None		
Range of Values:	Any value within the State field of the STATES table		

Comparisons Allowed:

☒ Same Field	☐ All	☒ =	☐ >	☐ >=	☐ ≠	☐ <	☐ <=
☐ Other Fields	☐ All	☐ =	☐ >	☐ >=	☐ ≠	☐ <	☐ <=
☒ Value Expression	☐ All	☒ =	☐ >	☐ >=	☐ ≠	☐ <	☐ <=

Operations Allowed:

☐ Same Field	☐ All	☐ +	☐ −	☐ x	☐ ÷	☐ Concatenation
☐ Other Fields	☐ All	☐ +	☐ −	☐ x	☐ ÷	☐ Concatenation
☐ Value Expression	☐ All	☐ +	☐ −	☐ x	☐ ÷	☐ Concatenation

Figure 11.16. *Setting the Logical Elements category for the STATE foreign key field in the SUPPLIERS table.*

Finally, fill out a Business Rule Specifications sheet for the business rule you've just established. Be sure to indicate the modifications you've made to *both* the field and the new relationship. Figure 11.17 shows the completed Business Rule Specifications sheet for your new rule.

Reviewing the Business Rule Specifications Sheets

After you've established the business rules you believe to be appropriate, review their specifications sheets. Carefully examine each specification sheet and make certain that you've properly established the rule and

---

BUSINESS RULE SPECIFICATIONS

Rule Information

Statement: Any supplier we use must be based in one the eleven (11) contiguous Western states, Alaska, or Hawaii.

Constraint: Entries for the State field in the SUPPLIERS table are limited to existing values of the State field in the STATES table.

Type: ☒ Database Oriented   **Category:** ☒ Field Specific   **Test On:** ☒ Insert   ☒ Update
☐ Application Oriented   ☐ Relationship Specific   ☐ Delete

Structures Affected

Field Names: STATE

Table Names: SUPPLIERS, STATES

Field Elements Affected

Physical Elements

☐ Data Type   ☐ Decimal Places   ☐ Input Mask
☐ Length   ☐ Character Support   ☐ Display Format

Logical Elements

☐ Key Type   ☐ Values Entered By   ☐ Comparisons Allowed
☐ Key Structure   ☐ Required Value   ☐ Operations Allowed
☐ Uniqueness   ☐ Default Value   ☐ Edit Rule
☐ Null Support   ☒ Range of Values

Relationship Characteristics Affected

☒ Deletion Rule   ☒ Type of Participation   ☒ Degree of Participation

Action Taken

The Range of Values was set to "Any value within the State field of the STATES table."
The type of participation for each table was changed: STATES is Mandatory; SUPPLIERS is Optional.
The degree of participation for each table was changed: SUPPLIERS is (0,N); STATES is (1,1).
A Restrict deletion rule was defined for the relationship between SUPPLIERS and STATES.

Figure 11.17. *A completed Business Rule Specifications sheet for the new business rule.*

that you've clearly marked all of the appropriate areas on the sheet. If you find an error, make the necessary modifications and review it once more. Repeat this process until you've reviewed every business rule.

Business rules are an important component of the database. They contribute to overall data integrity and impose integrity constraints that are specific to the organization. As you've seen, these rules help to ensure the validity and consistency of the data according to the manner in which the organization functions or conducts its business. Additionally, these rules will eventually influence the manner in which you implement the database within your RDBMS and how you design and develop end-user application programs for the database.

It's important to understand that you will revisit these rules quite often. As you review the final structure, for example, you may determine that additional business rules are necessary. You may discover that some of the rules will not provide the results you had initially envisioned, so you'll need to modify them. It's also possible for you to determine that some of the rules aren't necessary after all. (In this instance, be absolutely sure to examine the rules carefully *before* you remove them.)

Keep in mind that the business rules you define now are bound to require modifications in the future; you will most likely need to *add* business rules in due course because of changes in the way the organization functions or conducts its business. The need to modify existing business rules or develop new ones is quite normal—the organization inevitably grows and matures, and so does the manner in which it acts upon or reacts to external forces. These forces affect the manner in which the organization perceives and uses its data, which, in turn, changes the nature of the organization's business-rule requirements.

The task of defining and establishing business rules is—as are so many other tasks within the database-design process—ongoing. Don't be discouraged if you have to perform this task several times. Your efforts will pay great dividends in the long run.

CASE STUDY

Now it's time to establish business rules for Mike's database. You schedule a meeting with Mike and his staff to review the tables and relationships in their database. The first order of business is to define and establish field specific business rules.

You start the process by reviewing the PRODUCTS table. As you examine each field, you determine whether it requires any constraints. When you come upon the CATEGORY field, you remember that there was some question regarding its range of values. (Refer to the Case Study in Chapter 9.) You discuss this issue once again with Mike and his staff, and you finally come to a consensus on a distinct list of categories. Mike then decides that the values for the CATEGORY field should be limited to those on this list to make certain that the staff does not arbitrarily invent new categories. Based on Mike's decision, you define an appropriate business rule to establish the constraint.

> Invalid product categories are not allowed.

There are a number of items in the list of possible categories, so you decide that the best way to establish this rule is to use a validation table. You create a new table called CATEGORIES and then establish a relationship between it and the PRODUCTS table. Next, you diagram the relationship and set the relationship's characteristics in the appropriate manner. Figure 11.18 shows the results of your work.

Here are the settings you used for the relationship's characteristics:

- There is a Restrict deletion rule for the relationship.

- The CATEGORIES table has a *mandatory* type of participation.

- The PRODUCTS table has an *optional* type of participation.

- The CATEGORIES table has a (1,1) degree of participation.

- The PRODUCTS table has a (0,N) degree of participation.

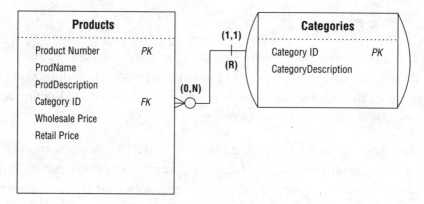

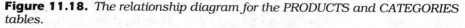

Figure 11.18. *The relationship diagram for the PRODUCTS and CATEGORIES tables.*

Remember that by establishing this relationship, you've replaced the existing CATEGORY field in the PRODUCTS table with a copy of the CATEGORY ID field from the new CATEGORIES table. You must now make certain that the CATEGORY ID field in the PRODUCTS table conforms to the Elements of a Foreign Key and then make the appropriate modifications to its field specification. Finally, set the field's Range of Values element to something such as this:

Any value within the CATEGORY ID field in the CATEGORIES table

Figure 11.19 shows the settings you've made to the Logical Elements category of the field specifications for the CATEGORY ID field in the PRODUCTS table.

Now you must decide when the rule should be tested. As you already know, you typically want to test a rule established with a validation table if the user attempts to insert a value into the field or update an existing value within the field.

Finally, you complete a Business Rule Specifications sheet for this new business rule. This specification sheet will reflect the modifications

Logical Elements

Key Type:	[ ] Non	[ ] Primary	**Edit Rule:**
	[X] Foreign	[ ] Alternate	[X] Enter Now, Edits Allowed
Key Structure:	[X] Simple	[ ] Composite	[ ] Enter Now, Edits Not Allowed
Uniqueness:	[X] Non-unique	[ ] Unique	[ ] Enter Later, Edits Allowed
Null Support:	[ ] Nulls Allowed	[X] No Nulls	[ ] Enter Later, Edits Not Allowed
Values Entered By:	[X] User	[ ] System	[ ] Not Determined At This Time
Required Value:	[ ] No	[X] Yes	
Default Value:	None		
Range of Values:	Any value within the Category ID field in the CATEGORIES table		

Comparisons Allowed:

[X] Same Field	[ ] All	[X] =	[ ] >	[ ] >=	[ ] ≠	[ ] <	[ ] <=
[ ] Other Fields	[ ] All	[ ] =	[ ] >	[ ] >=	[ ] ≠	[ ] <	[ ] <=
[X] Value Expression	[ ] All	[X] =	[ ] >	[ ] >=	[ ] ≠	[ ] <	[ ] <=

Operations Allowed:

[ ] Same Field	[ ] All	[ ] +	[ ] −	[ ] x	[ ] ÷	[ ] Concatenation
[ ] Other Fields	[ ] All	[ ] +	[ ] −	[ ] x	[ ] ÷	[X] Concatenation
[ ] Value Expression	[ ] All	[ ] +	[ ] −	[ ] x	[ ] ÷	[X] Concatenation

Figure 11.19. *Logical Elements settings for the* Category *ID foreign key field in the PRODUCTS table.*

you've made to the field specifications for the Category ID field, as well as the characteristics of the relationship between the CATEGORIES and PRODUCTS tables. Figure 11.20 shows the completed Business Rule Specifications sheet.

You repeat this process for the remaining fields in this table and for the fields in the remaining tables. After you're finished, you move on to the next task.

The next order of business is to establish relationship specific business rules. You begin by reviewing the relationship between the EMPLOYEES and INVOICES tables, and you review the relationship diagram to determine whether the relationship requires any constraints. Everything

BUSINESS RULE SPECIFICATIONS

Rule Information

Statement: Invalid product categories are not allowed.

Constraint: Entries for the Category ID field in the CATEGORIES table are limited to existing values of the Category ID field in the CATEGORIES table.

Type: [X] Database Oriented   **Category:** [X] Field Specific   **Test On:** [X] Insert   [X] Update
     [ ] Application Oriented   [ ] Relationship Specific   [ ] Delete

Structures Affected

Field Names: CATEGORY ID

Table Names: PRODUCTS, CATEGORIES

Field Elements Affected

Physical Elements

[ ] Data Type	[ ] Decimal Places	[ ] Input Mask
[ ] Length	[ ] Character Support	[ ] Display Format

Logical Elements

[ ] Key Type	[ ] Values Entered By	[ ] Comparisons Allowed
[ ] Key Structure	[ ] Required Value	[ ] Operations Allowed
[ ] Uniqueness	[ ] Default Value	[ ] Edit Rule
[ ] Null Support	[X] Range of Values	

Relationship Characteristics Affected

[X] Deletion Rule   [X] Type of Participation   [X] Degree of Participation

Action Taken

The Range of Values was set to "Any value within the Category ID field of the CATEGORIES table."
The type of participation for each table was changed: PRODUCTS is Optional; CATEGORIES is Mandatory.
The degree of participation for each table was changed: PRODUCTS is (0,N); CATEGORIES is (1,1).
A Restrict deletion rule was defined for the relationship between PRODUCTS and CATEGORIES.

Figure 11.20. *The completed Business Rule Specifications sheet for the new business rule.*

seems to be in order, so you move to the relationship between the VEN-
DORS and PRODUCTS tables. Figure 11.21 shows the relationship diagram for these tables.

As you and Mike discuss whether you should impose any constraints
on this relationship, Mike determines that there should be a constraint
on the PRODUCTS table. He wants to make sure that every vendor in
the VENDORS table is associated with *at least* one product; he figures
that it's unnecessary to keep data on a vendor who's not supplying him
with any products. So you define the following business rule for this
constraint:

   Every vendor must supply at least one product.

Now you establish the rule by modifying the appropriate relationship
characteristics. You begin by designating a Mandatory type of participation and assigning a (1,N) degree of participation to the PRODUCTS table. You then define a Restrict deletion rule for the relationship based
on the PRODUCTS table; this will keep you from accidentally deleting
the only product associated with a given vendor. Figure 11.22 shows the
results of your modifications.

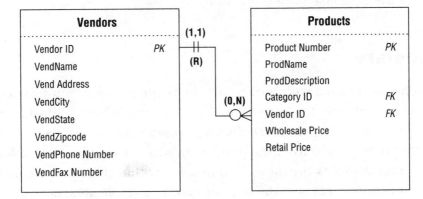

Figure 11.21. *The relationship diagram for the VENDORS and PRODUCTS
tables.*

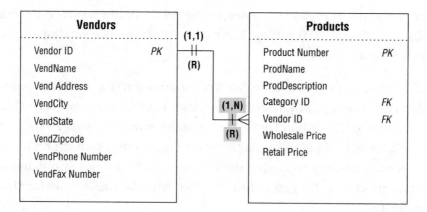

Figure 11.22. *The revised relationship diagram for the VENDORS and PROD-UCTS tables.*

You already know that this type of business rule will be tested when a user attempts to insert a record into or delete a record from the PROD-UCTS table, so you complete this process by filling out a Business Rule Specifications sheet for this rule. Figure 11.23 shows the completed specification sheet.

Now you repeat this process for the remaining relationships. When you're finished, the process is complete and you're ready for the next stage of the database-design process.

Summary

This chapter opened with a definition of *business rules*. You learned that a business rule is a constraint imposed on a field or a relationship that is based on the way the organization perceives and uses its data and that it is derived from the manner in which the organization functions or conducts its business. You now know that there are two major types of business rules: *database oriented* and *application oriented*. Although our focus here is on database oriented business rules, you

BUSINESS RULE SPECIFICATIONS

Rule Information

Statement: Every vendor must supply at least one product.

Constraint: A single record in the VENDORS table must be associated with at least one record in the PRODUCTS table.

Type: [X] Database Oriented   Category: [X] Field Specific   Test On: [X] Insert   [ ] Update
     [ ] Application Oriented   [ ] Relationship Specific   [X] Delete

Structures Affected

Field Names:

Table Names: VENDORS, PRODUCTS

Field Elements Affected

Physical Elements

[ ] Data Type	[ ] Decimal Places	[ ] Input Mask
[ ] Length	[ ] Character Support	[ ] Display Format

Logical Elements

[ ] Key Type	[ ] Values Entered By	[ ] Comparisons Allowed
[ ] Key Structure	[ ] Required Value	[ ] Operations Allowed
[ ] Uniqueness	[ ] Default Value	[ ] Edit Rule
[ ] Null Support	[ ] Range of Values	

Relationship Characteristics Affected

[X] Deletion Rule   [X] Type of Participation   [X] Degree of Participation

Action Taken

The type of participation for PRODUCTS was changed to Mandatory.
The degree of participation for PRODUCTS was changed to (1,N).
A Restrict deletion rule was defined for the PRODUCTS table.

Figure 11.23. *A completed Business Rule Specifications sheet.*

know that you can at least record the basic elements of application oriented business rules for use later in the implementation process.

You then learned that database oriented business rules are divided into two categories: *field specific* business rules, which affect the elements of a field specification for a particular field; and *relationship specific* business rules, which affect the characteristics of a relationship.

The chapter continued with a discussion of defining and establishing business rules. Here you learned that you work with users and management to define the business rules required by the organization. You also learned that it is best to establish the field specific business rules first, followed by the relationship specific business rules.

Next, you learned the steps necessary to define and establish each type of business rule. You now know that, in general, you work with a field or relationship, review the field or relationship in light of the rule to determine whether any constraints are necessary, define the appropriate business rule, establish the rule by modifying the appropriate field specification elements or relationship characteristics, decide which actions test the rule, and then complete a Business Rule Specifications sheet for the rule.

The chapter continued with a discussion of the elements of the Business Rule Specifications sheet, and how each element on the sheet is defined. As you now know, using Business Rule Specifications sheets allows you to document all of your rules and provides you with a standard method for recording and reviewing them.

We closed the chapter by discussing *validation tables*. You learned that you can create and use a validation table to support a business rule that limits the range of values for a particular field. In this manner, the validation table helps to enforce data integrity. You also learned that you need to establish new relationships when you use validation tables and that these relationships have the same types of characteristics as any other types of relationships in the database.

Review Questions

1. What is a *business rule*?

2. Name the two major types of business rules.

3. Can you establish *application oriented* business rules within the logical design of the database?

4. What are the two categories of *database oriented* business rules?

5. What is a *field specific business rule*?

6. When is a business rule tested?

7. How do you document a business rule?

8. State two advantages a Business Rule Specifications sheet provides.

9. What is the purpose of the *Action Taken* section of a Business Rule Specifications sheet?

10. What is the purpose of a *validation table*?

11. What is the typical structure of a validation table?

12. What is the association between a business rule and a validation table?

13. Why should you review all of your completed Business Rule Specifications sheets?

12

Views

There is no object on earth which cannot be
looked at from a cosmic point of view.
—FYODOR MIKHAYLOVICH DOSTOYEVSKY

Topics Covered in This Chapter

What Are Views?

Anatomy of a View

Determining and Defining Views

Case Study

Summary

Review Questions

What Are Views?

As you learned in Chapter 3, a *view* is a *virtual table* composed of fields from one or more tables in the database; it can also include fields from other views. The tables and views that comprise a given view are known as the view's *base tables*. A view is "virtual" because it draws data from base tables rather than storing data on its own. In fact, the only information about a view that is stored in the database is its structure; the RDBMS rebuilds and "repopulates" the view every time you access the view in some manner. Many major RDBMS programs support views, but some (such as Microsoft Access) refer to them as *saved queries*. Your specific RDBMS program will determine whether you refer to this object as a query or a view.

❖ **Note** Although every major database vendor supports the view I've just described, several vendors are now supporting what is known as an *indexed* (or *materialized*) view. An indexed view is different from a regular view in that it does store data, and its fields can be indexed to improve the speed at which the RDBMS processes the view's data. A full discussion of indexed views is beyond the scope of this book because it is a vendor-specific implementation issue. However, you should research this topic further if you are working with a client/server or mainframe RDBMS program.

Views enable you to see the information in your database from many different aspects, providing you with a great amount of flexibility when you work with your data. You can create views in a variety of ways, and they are especially useful when you base them on multiple related tables.

There are several reasons why you should define and use views in your database.

- *You can use them to work with data from multiple tables simultaneously.* During the database-design process, you established relationships between various pairs of tables bearing one-to-many or many-to-many relationships to each other. (Recall that you resolved the many-to-many relationships via linking tables.) A view provides the mechanism that allows you to work with data from two or more related tables simultaneously.

- *They reflect the most current information.* Because the RDBMS rebuilds and repopulates the view every time you access it, the information displayed by the view exhibits the most recent changes to the data in its base tables.

- *You can customize them to the specific needs of an individual or group of individuals.* You can build a view to suit any set of requirements, such as providing the data for a particular report or providing a means of examining specific information that is common to several departments within an organization.

- *You can use them to help enforce data integrity.* You can define a *validation view* that works in the same manner as a validation table—its purpose is to provide a valid range of values for a given field in the database.

- *You can use them for security or confidentiality purposes.* You can determine what data is available to a particular user or group of users by defining a view on select fields from the view's base tables.

Define your views carefully and skillfully, and they will become a valuable asset after you've implemented the database within your RDBMS.

Anatomy of a View

There are three types of views (*data, aggregate, validation*) that you can define as you design the logical structure of the database and two types of views (*materialized* and *partitioned*) that you can define as you implement your database within an RDBMS. The ability to define the latter two types of views and the manner in which you do so are highly dependent upon your RDBMS, so they are beyond the scope of this book. We will, therefore, focus our attention on the first three types of views.

Data View

You use this type of view to examine and manipulate data from a single base table or multiple base tables.

Single-Table Data View

Although you *could* use all of the fields from the base table to build this type of view, you'll usually just use selected fields. (Building a view using all of the base table's fields would simply produce a virtual copy of the base table.) For example, say you want to make a list of employee names and phone numbers available to everyone in the organization. You can construct an EMPLOYEE PHONE LIST view based on the EMPLOYEES table using just the EMPLOYEE ID, EMPFIRST NAME, EMPLAST NAME, and EMP-PHONE NUMBER fields. Figure 12.1 shows a diagram of this particular view. (Note the new symbol used to indicate a view.)

Figure 12.1. *The EMPLOYEE PHONE LIST view.*

Your RDBMS will rebuild and repopulate the EMPLOYEE PHONE LIST view each time you access it, and the view will reflect the latest changes you've made to the data in the EMPLOYEES table. Figure 12.2 shows how an RDBMS will typically display the data within a view. Note that the view's appearance is quite similar to that of a table; this is yet another reason why a view is known as a "virtual table."

Employee Phone List

Employee ID	EmpFirst Name	EmpLast Name	EmpPhone Number
100	Zachary	Erlich	553-3992
101	Susan	McLain	790-3992
102	Joe	Rosales	551-4993
103	Alastair	Black	227-4992
104	Katie	Christian	525-2993
105	Diana	Barlet	248-4953

Figure 12.2. *Information from the EMPLOYEE PHONE LIST view.*

You can modify the data within a single-table data view at any time, and the modifications you make will flow through the view and into the base table. Keep in mind, however, that field specifications and business rules will determine what types of modifications you can make to the data. For example, you won't be able to delete a last name in the EMPLOYEE PHONE LIST view if the Null Support element of the field specification for the EMPLAST NAME field is set to "No Nulls."

❖ **Note** View implementation varies to some degree among most RDBMS software. Make sure you examine your RDBMS's documentation to determine how fully the RDBMS supports views and what types of constraints it imposes (if any) on modifying the data in a view.

Multitable Data View

As I mentioned at the beginning of this section, you can define a data view using two or more tables. The only requirement is that the tables you use to create the view must bear a relationship to each other; this helps ensure that the information the view presents is both valid and meaningful. For example, assume you're designing a database for a local community college and that the tables in Figure 12.3 are part of the database. You've just decided that you need to create a view called CLASS ROSTER that shows the name of each class and the names of the students who are currently registered to attend it. This will be an easy task for you to perform because you can use these three tables as the basis of the view; they contain the fields you need to define the view, and they bear a relationship to one another.

Now you define the CLASS ROSTER view by using the CLASS NAME field from the CLASSES table and the STUDFIRST NAME and STUDLAST NAME fields from the STUDENTS table. The appropriate student names will appear for each class because CLASSES and STUDENTS are related (and therefore connected) through the STUDENT CLASSES linking table. Figure 12.4 shows the diagram for the CLASS ROSTER view. Note that no changes have been made to any of the base tables.

Every time you access the CLASS ROSTER view, the RDBMS will rebuild and repopulate it using the most current data from the view's base tables. Figure 12.5 shows a *sample* of the view's data.

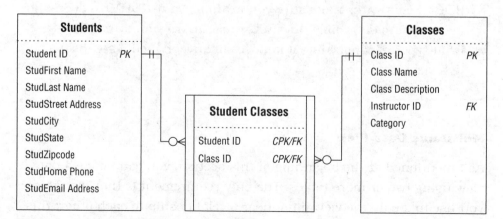

Figure 12.3. *Base tables for the CLASS ROSTER view.*

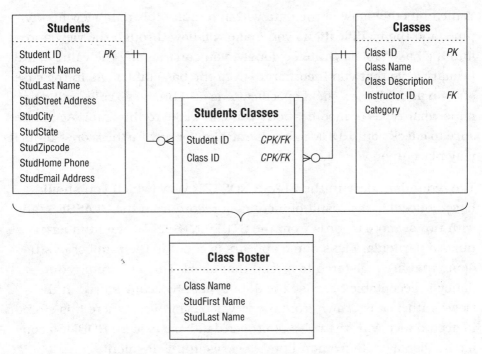

Figure 12.4. *The diagram for the CLASS ROSTER view.*

Class Roster

Class Name	StudFirst Name	StudLast Name
Advanced Calculus	Martin	Applebee
Advanced Calculus	Gina	Carter
Advanced Calculus	Joe	Rosales
Advanced Calculus	Sara	Ulrich
Advanced Music Theory	Mike	Hernandez
Advanced Music Theory	Susan	McLain
Advanced Music Theory	Lee	Turner
American History	Gina	Carter
American History	Susan	McLain
American History	George	Barlet
American History	Joe	Rosales

Figure 12.5. *A partial sample of data from the CLASS ROSTER view.*

You can modify *most* of the data within a multitable data view at any time, and the modifications you make will flow through the view and into the base tables. Quite obviously, you can't modify the value of any primary keys that you incorporate from the base tables. As in the case of a single-table view, field specifications and business rules will determine what types of modifications you can make to the data. (Again, be sure to check your RDBMS documentation for any further constraints it may place upon your views.)

The redundant data in the CLASS ROSTER view (which you should have noticed) is the result of merging a record from the CLASSES table with two or more records from the STUDENTS table; the number of times a particular class name appears is equal to the number of students that are registered to attend that class. This apparent redundancy is acceptable because the data *is not* physically stored in the view—rather, it is drawn from the view's base tables, where it is stored in accordance with the rules of proper database design. RDBMSs commonly display data from multitable views in this fashion.

Another point to note is that a data view does not contain its own primary key. It lacks a primary key because it is not a table; a true table stores data and requires a primary key to serve as a unique identifier for each of its records. You can incorporate a primary key from any (or all) of the base tables within the view, however, when you determine it will contribute to the information the view provides.

> ❖ **Note** In order to avoid any unnecessary ambiguity or confusion, make certain you do not have any primary key indicators within the view symbol when you diagram a *data* view.

Aggregate View

You use this type of view to display information produced by aggregating a particular set of data in a specific manner. As with a data view, you can define an aggregate view using one or more base tables. You can then include one or more calculated fields that incorporate the functions that aggregate the data and one or more data fields (drawn from the view's base tables) to group the aggregated data. Sum, Average (arithmetic mean), Minimum, Maximum, and Count are the most common aggregate functions that you can apply to a set of data, and every major RDBMS supports them.

Let's say that you wanted to know how many students are registered for each class, and you're using the tables from the school example shown in Figure 12.3. Your first impulse is to define a data view called CLASS REGISTRATION that will provide the information you need to answer your question. So, you use the CLASS NAME field from the CLASSES table and the STUDENT ID field from the STUDENT CLASSES table to build the view. Figure 12.6 shows a diagram for the new CLASS REGISTRATION view.

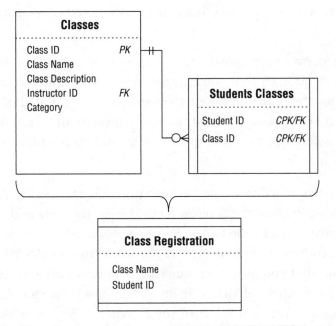

Figure 12.6. *View diagram for the new CLASS REGISTRATION view.*

Now you access the view so that you can answer your question. Figure 12.7 shows a *partial* sample of the data in the view.

Class Registration

Class Name	Student ID
Advanced Calculus	1003
Advanced Calculus	1025
Advanced Calculus	1073
Advanced Calculus	1110
Advanced Music Theory	1045
Advanced Music Theory	1066
Advanced Music Theory	1085
Business Administration	1025
Business Administration	1066
Business Administration	1017
Business Administration	1073

Figure 12.7. *A partial sample of data from the CLASS REGISTRATION view.*

In order to answer your question, you must now count each instance of a given class name so that you can determine how many students are registered for that class. Imagine the work you have ahead of you—this will not be an easy task! Rather than going though all this tedious work, you can answer your question quite easily (and more efficiently) using an aggregate view.

There's no need to define a new view because you can modify the one you have just now. Remove the STUDENT ID field from the view and replace it with a calculated field called TOTAL STUDENTS REGISTERED that counts the number of students per class. (When you work with a calculated field, make certain that you give it a name that is meaningful and that will distinguish it from other calculated fields in the view.) The calculated field will use a Count function to count the number of STUDENT IDs in the

STUDENT CLASSES table that are associated with each Class ID in the STUDENT CLASSES table. (Later, you'll learn how to document a view and record the expression the calculated field will use.) Figure 12.8 shows the revised diagram for the CLASS REGISTRATION view.

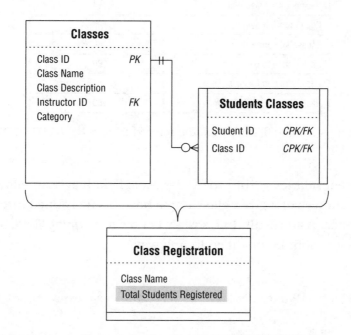

Figure 12.8. *Revised diagram for the CLASS REGISTRATION view.*

As was the case with the data view, the RDBMS will rebuild and repopulate the CLASS REGISTRATION view every time you access it, using the most current data from the view's base tables. Figure 12.9 shows a sample of the view's data.

There are three things to note about this view:

1. The Total Students Registered field displays a single number for each class name, which represents the total number of students registered for that class.

Class Registration

Class Name	Total Students Registered
Advanced Calculus	92
Advanced Music Theory	80
Business Administration	84
Computers in Business	98
English Literature	80
Introduction to Biology	60
Introduction to Database Design	84
Pan-American Studies	80

Figure 12.9. *A sample of data from the revised CLASS REGISTRATION view.*

2. The redundancy within the CLASS NAME field has been eliminated; all instances of a given class name have been grouped into a single instance. As a result, CLASS NAME is now a *grouping field,* and its values cannot be modified in any way.

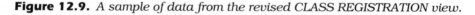
❖ Note All data fields in an aggregate view are grouping fields.

3. Because an aggregate view is composed entirely of grouping fields and calculated fields, you cannot modify any of its data.

An aggregate view is most useful as the basis of a report or as a means of providing various types of statistical information. You'll learn later that you can apply filtering criteria to this (or any) view in order to control and restrict the data that the view displays.

Validation View

A *validation view* is similar to a validation table in that it can help implement data integrity. When a business rule limits a particular field's range of values, you can enforce the constraint just as easily with a validation *view* as you can with a validation *table*. The difference between the two lies in their construction—a validation *table* stores its own data, whereas a validation *view* draws data from its base tables. Although you can define a validation view using one or more base tables, you'll commonly define a validation table using a single base table and incorporate only two or three of the base table's fields. (This structure is quite similar to that of a validation table.)

For example, let's say you're designing a database for a small contractor and you're working with the tables in Figure 12.10.

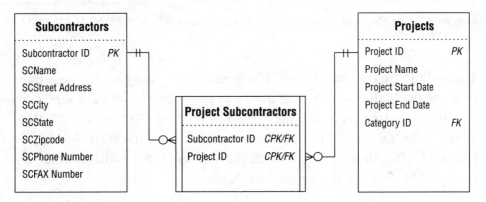

Figure 12.10. *Tables from a database for a small contractor.*

As you can see, the SUBCONTRACTOR ID field in the SUBCONTRACTORS table provides the range of values for the SUBCONTRACTOR ID field in the PROJECT SUBCONTRACTORS table. (Recall that a foreign key draws its values from the primary key to which it refers.) You've determined, however, that you want to restrict the access users currently have to certain fields in the SUBCONTRACTORS table; you've decided that the only fields users should be able to access are the SUBCONTRACTOR ID, SCNAME, SCPHONE NUMBER, and SCFAX NUMBER fields. So, you define a validation view called APPROVED SUBCONTRACTORS that will incorporate these fields and still provide the range of values for the Subcontractor ID field in the PROJECT SUBCONTRACTORS table. Figure 12.11 shows a revised diagram of the tables, including the new view.

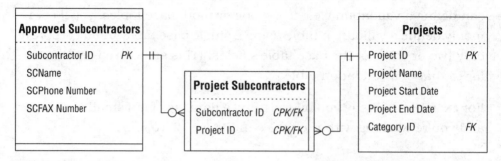

Figure 12.11. *Revised table diagram; note the new APPROVED SUBCONTRACTORS view.*

The APPROVED SUBCONTRACTORS view now gives users access only to those fields that you've indicated and provides the appropriate range of values for the Subcontractor ID field in the PROJECT SUBCONTRACTORS table. Additionally, the view will still enforce the relationship characteristics that exist for the SUBCONTRACTORS table because it (as you will recall) is the view's base table.

Determining and Defining Views

By now you've probably realized that views can be a substantial asset to the database. During this stage of the database-design process, you'll define a fundamental set of views for the database. Your definition of views won't stop here—you'll probably define more views when you implement the database within your RDBMS and as you create your end-user application programs. In these instances, you'll use views as a tool to support particular aspects of the implementation or application program. The views you define during the database-design process, however, will focus strictly on data-access and information-retrieval issues.

Working with Users and Management

You'll work once again with the organization's representative group of users and management to identify the types of views the organization requires. After you identify these views, you'll establish and document them, and then you and the group will review the views to make certain that they are properly defined.

Before you conduct your first meeting with the group, review the notes you've taken throughout the entire design process. Your objective is to get an idea of the types of views the organization might need. Almost every organization spends a large amount of time producing and reading reports, so you should focus on that aspect of your notes. You should also review the report samples you assembled during the analysis process.

When you and the group meet, consider the following points to help you identify view requirements:

- *Review your notes with the group.* In many instances, talking about a specific topic will spark an idea for a new or required view. For example, someone may realize a need for a view during a discussion of mission objectives.

- *Review the data-entry, report, and presentation samples you gathered during the early stages of the design process.* Examining these samples, especially summary-style reports, could easily illuminate the need for certain types of views.

- *Examine the tables and the subjects they represent.* Some individuals in the group may identify the need for a view based solely on a specific subject. If someone mentions a subject, such as Employees, it may cause someone else to say, "We definitely need a view that restricts certain employee data for confidentiality reasons."

- *Analyze the table relationships.* You'll most likely identify a number of multitable views that you should create for many of the relationships. Several of these views will coincide with views you identified for the report samples.

- *Study the business rules.* As you already know, you can use a validation view to enforce a rule that imposes a constraint on a particular field's range of values.

You and the group should be able to identify a number of views by going over the items on this list. After you've identified as many of the required views as possible, your next task is to define them.

Defining Views

You'll now define each view that you've identified using the appropriate tables and fields. Review the relationship diagrams to identify which tables and fields you need for the view's structure. When you've determined what you need, define the view and record it in a view diagram.

For example, say you've determined that you can use a view for the report shown in Figure 12.12; the name of the new view will be CUSTOMER CALL LIST.

The notes you've taken throughout the design process become useful once again. You reviewed this report during the analysis stage of the design process, and you've noted that this report represents information about customers and their orders; it is from the order data that you can determine when a given customer made his last purchase. Now, review the relationship diagram for the CUSTOMERS and ORDERS tables; you'll use fields from these tables to create the CUSTOMER CALL LIST view. Figure 12.13 shows the relationship diagram for these tables.

After examining the relationship diagram, you determine you need to use five fields to build this view: CustFirst Name, CustLast Name, CustPhone Number, and CustCity from the CUSTOMERS table, and Order Date from the ORDERS table. You now define the CUSTOMER CALL

Customer Call List			
City	**Customer Name**	**Phone Number**	**Last Purchase**
Bothell	Sara Anderson	542-0039	05/16/02
	Jim Booth	367-4495	02/11/02
	Larry Currey	445-3394	02/06/02
Bellevue	Jim Davis	545-9932	05/10/02
	Larry Lang	545-3384	01/22/02
	Sandra Wasser	367-2293	06/30/02
Edmonds	Julia Black	223-9943	04/12/02
Lynnwood	Mary McLain	562-1274	02/28/02
	Barbara Reeves	445-2094	03/07/02

Figure 12.12. *Report sample requiring a view.*

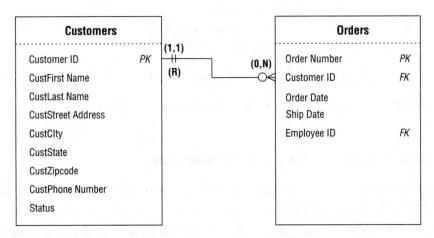

Figure 12.13. *Relationship diagram for the CUSTOMERS and ORDERS tables.*

LIST view by assigning the fields to the view and then recording them in a view diagram. When you're finished, your diagram should look like the one in Figure 12.14.

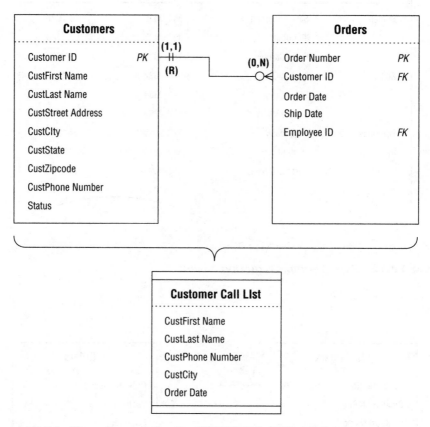

Figure 12.14. *View diagram for the CUSTOMER CALL LIST view.*

Using Calculated Fields Where Appropriate

Earlier in the database-design process, you learned that tables couldn't contain *calculated fields* for a number of good reasons. But one of the characteristics of a view that makes it so useful is that it *can* contain calculated fields. Recall that calculated fields will display the result of a concatenation, expression, or aggregate function; this makes them an extremely flexible structure to include in a view.

For example, consider the new CUSTOMER CALL LIST view. Although you have the fields you need for the view, you'll have to make one minor modification to the view so that it can display the appropriate data. One of the requirements for this view is that it must display the date of the last purchase made by each customer. In order to retrieve and display the proper date, you'll have to add a calculated field to the view. This field will use the Maximum function [commonly known as Max()] to retrieve the correct date from the ORDER DATE field. Name the new field LAST PURCHASE DATE and add it to the CUSTOMER CALL LIST view diagram. (You no longer need the ORDER DATE field in the view, so you can remove it from the view's structure.) This is the expression you'll use in the calculated field to retrieve the appropriate date:

   Max(Order Date)

Later in this section, you'll learn where and how to record this expression.

> ❖ **Note** Be sure to refer to your RDMBS's documentation to determine the correct syntax for this function and all of the other functions used in this chapter.

Another calculated field you might include in this view is one that displays the complete customer name by concatenating CUSTFIRST NAME and CUSTLAST NAME. Say, for example, that you want to display the customer name in this manner: "Hernandez, Michael." Create a calculated field called CUSTOMER NAME and use the following concatenation expression:

   CustLast Name & ", " & CustFirst Name

Add the new calculated field to the CUSTOMER CALL LIST view diagram and remove the CUSTFIRST NAME and CUSTLAST NAME fields from the view;

you don't need these fields anymore because you're now using the CUSTOMER NAME calculated field. (You'll soon properly record this expression as well.)

Figure 12.15 shows how your revised view diagram should look after you've completed these modifications.

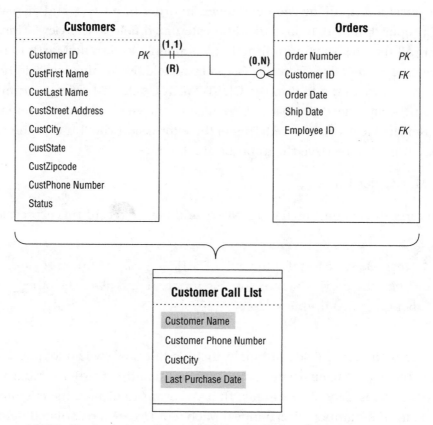

Figure 12.15. *Revised view diagram for the CUSTOMER CALL LIST.*

As you've just learned, calculated fields can be quite an asset because you can use them to enhance the information a view provides. You also learned earlier in this chapter that calculated fields are particularly crucial in aggregate views. A good rule of thumb to follow when you think you may need calculated fields is to use them if they will provide pertinent and meaningful information or if they will enhance the manner in which the view uses its data.

If you recall, you created a *calculated-field list* earlier in the design process (refer to Chapter 6). You can now use this list as a source of calculated fields that you might (or should) use in your views. Review the list as you define each new view and determine whether you can use one of the calculated fields on the list. When you find one that you can use, create it in the same manner as you did in the preceding examples. (If you create a new calculated field that does not appear on your list, however, be sure to add it to the list. This will help you keep your calculated-field list current and in order.)

Imposing Criteria to Filter the Data

Views have another characteristic that makes them extremely useful: You can impose criteria against one or more fields in the view to filter the records it displays. For example, say that the CUSTOMER CALL LIST view included the CustState field. Although the view would continue to display the set of records it did before, you would also see the state in which each customer lives. Assume, however, that you want the view to show a particular set of records, such as those for customers who live in the state of Washington. You can accomplish this by setting a specific criterion on the CustState field that will filter the data so that the view displays only those records of customers from Washington State.

> ❖ **Note** In database work, the word "criterion" refers to an expression that is tested against the value of a particular field. The view will include a given record if the value of the field meets the criterion.

This is the expression you will use to filter the records for the CUS-TOMER CALL LIST view:

CustState = "WA"

Now the view will display only customers from Washington. If you want to filter the records further to show only those customers who live in specific cities, you add a criterion such as this:

CustCity In ("Bellevue," "Olympia," "Redmond," "Seattle," "Spokane," "Tacoma")

The view will now display Washington State customers who live in the cities specified in the expression. You may wonder why both criteria are necessary—the criterion for the CustCity field should retrieve the appropriate records by itself. The trouble is that many cities are named for other cities, so that cities in two or three different states could have the same name. For example, there is a Portland, Oregon, and a Portland, Maine, both named after Portland, England. The point to remember is that you must use your best judgment when you establish criteria for a view—use the *minimum* number of criteria that will cause the view to display the records you require.

When you use a criterion in a view, you must make certain that the field you're testing in the criterion is included in the view's structure. If you do not include the field in the view, you have no way of imposing the criterion. This is an important point to remember because it is a requirement when you logically define a view *and* when you implement the view in your RDBMS.

The one problem with applying a filter to a view is that there is no way to indicate it on a view diagram; therefore, you must record it on a *View Specifications* sheet.

Using a View Specifications Sheet to Record the View

A View Specifications sheet *must* accompany each view diagram you create. It is on this sheet that you will record the characteristics of the view. The View Specifications sheet contains the following items:

- *Name.* This is where you indicate the name of the view. Before you record the name, however, test it against the *guidelines for creating table names* you learned in Chapter 7. These guidelines govern the naming of views as well, with *one* exception: The name of a view can implicitly or explicitly identify more than one subject. This is because you can define views from two or more base tables, so they do, indeed, represent more than one subject.

- *Type.* This is where you indicate whether you're defining a data, aggregate, or validation view.

- *Base tables.* This is where you specify the names of the view's base tables. Although the view diagram shows these tables, they appear here as a matter of convenience. The View Specifications sheet does not include field names, however, because you can record and display them more easily and efficiently on the view diagram.

- *Calculated-field expressions.* This is where you record the expressions for the calculated fields you included in the view. As you record the name of the calculated field, test it against the guidelines for creating field names you learned in Chapter 7. Calculated field names are governed by these guidelines with two exceptions: You can implicitly or explicitly identify more than one characteristic in a name, and you can use the plural form of the name. But it's still desirable to use the singular form of the name whenever possible.

- *Filters.* This is where you record the criteria that the view will use to filter the records it displays. You'll record both the field being tested and the expression used to test it.

> ❖ **Note** When you fill out the Calculated-Field Expressions and Filters sections of a View Specifications sheet, use the expressions with which you are most familiar. You'll modify them as necessary when you implement the database in an RDBMS.

Fill out a View Specifications sheet for each view you create and attach the sheet to the proper view diagram. Both of these items will serve to document the view fully. Figure 12.16 shows a completed View Specifications sheet for the CUSTOMER CALL LIST view. (Keep in mind that the view has been updated to include the CUSTSTATE field.)

Reviewing the Documentation for Each View

Once you've completed the task of defining and documenting each view, review all of your views once more—ensuring that the quality of the information each view provides is well worth the effort. As you review each view, keep the following points in mind:

- *Make certain that you've defined the view properly.* Think about the information the view should provide. Are you establishing the correct type of view for the required information? Did you use the appropriate base tables to define the view? Did you include all the necessary fields within the view's structure?

- *Make certain that the calculated fields you've created are suitable for the view.* Do they provide pertinent and meaningful information? Do they serve to enhance the manner in which the view displays its data?

- *Make certain that the filters will retrieve the required records.* First of all, do you need a filter for this view? If the answer is yes, do you know exactly which records you want the view to display? Do you believe that the filter will work correctly?

- *Above all, make certain that you have a view diagram and View Specifications sheet for each view.* This documentation will be very useful when you finally implement the database in an RDBMS.

VIEW SPECIFICATIONS

General Information

Name: Customer Call List   Type: [X] Data   [ ] Aggregate   [ ] Validation

Description: This view provides information that allows us to execute follow-up calls to our customers in Washington. Also indicated is the date of the customer's last purchase.

Base Tables

CUSTOMERS, ORDERS

Calculated Field Expressions

Field Name	Expression
CUSTOMER NAME	CUST LAST NAME & ", " & CUST FIRST NAME
LAST PURCHASE DATE	Max(ORDER DATE)

Filters

Field Name	Condition
CUST STATE	="WA"
CUST CITY	In ("Bellevue", "Olympia", "Redmond", "Seattle", "Spokane", "Tacoma")

Figure 12.16. *Completed View Specifications sheet for the CUSTOMER CALL LIST view.*

CASE STUDY

Your work on Mike's database is finally nearing an end. You meet with Mike and his staff to determine whether there is a need to establish views for the database. The agenda you've set up for the meeting involves the following steps:

1. Review the notes you've compiled during the design process.
2. Review each of the various samples you gathered during the early stages of the design process.
3. Examine the subjects represented by the tables in the database.
4. Analyze the table relationships.
5. Review and study the business rules.

As the meeting progresses, you identify several views that you need to define, including a PREFERRED CUSTOMERS view and a VENDOR PRODUCT COUNT view. The first view will provide the name and phone number of each customer who has a "Preferred" status, and the second view will provide information on the total number of different products each vendor supplies.

You base the PREFERRED CUSTOMERS view on the CUSTOMERS table and use the CustomerID, CustFirst Name, CustLast Name, CustHome Phone, and Status fields for the view's structure. Before you construct the view, however, Mike asks if there's any way to display the first name and last name together. You respond that it can be done, so you create a calculated field called Customer Name that concatenates both of the fields together; this field will now replace the CustFirst Name and Cust-Last Name fields. Figure 12.17 shows the view diagram for the PREFERRED CUSTOMERS view.

After you create the view diagram, you make note of the expression that you'll use to filter the view's data:

Status = "Preferred."

Then you complete a View Specifications sheet for the PREFERRED CUSTOMERS view. Figure 12.18 shows the results of your work.

Now you define the VENDOR PRODUCT COUNT view using the VENDORS and PRODUCTS tables as the view's base tables. You use the VENDOR NAME field from the VENDORS table to display the names of the vendors.

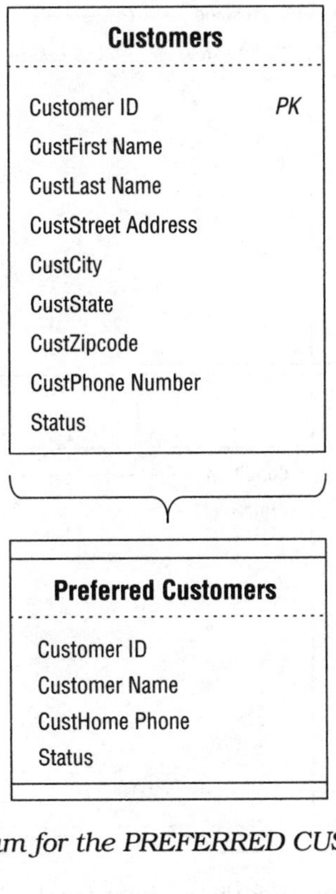

Customers

Customer ID	PK
CustFirst Name	
CustLast Name	
CustStreet Address	
CustCity	
CustState	
CustZipcode	
CustPhone Number	
Status	

Preferred Customers

Customer ID
Customer Name
CustHome Phone
Status

Figure 12.17. *View diagram for the PREFERRED CUSTOMERS view.*

VIEW SPECIFICATIONS		

General Information

Name:	Preferred Customers	Type:	[X] Data	[ ] Aggregate	[ ] Validation

Description: This View provides the names and phone numbers of our Preferred customers. We use this information in support of the services we provide to these customers.

Base Tables

CUSTOMERS

Calculated Field Expressions

Field Name	Expression
CUSTOMER NAME	CUSTFIRST NAME & " " & CUSTLAST NAME

Filters

Field Name	Condition
STATUS	="Preferred"

Figure 12.18. *The View Specifications sheet for the PREFERRED CUSTOMERS view.*

Next, you create a calculated field called PRODUCT COUNT to display the total number of products each vendor supplies. This is the expression the field uses to calculate the total:

Count(ProdName)

Now you create a diagram for the view, as shown in Figure 12.19.

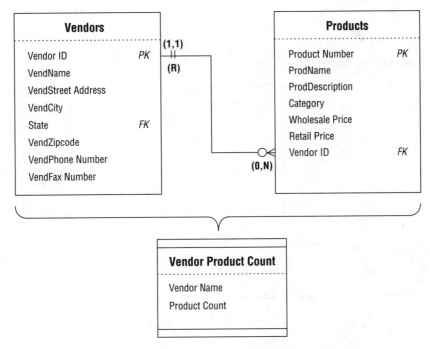

Figure 12.19. *View diagram for the VENDOR PRODUCT COUNT view.*

After determining that a filter is unnecessary for this view, you finish documenting the view by completing the View Specifications sheet shown in Figure 12.20.

You then repeat this process for every view you've identified for Mike's database.

VIEW SPECIFICATIONS					

General Information

Name:	Vendor Product Count		Type:	☐ Data	☒ Aggregate	☐ Validation

Description: This view tells us how many products are supplied by each vendor. This information will help us determine which vendors we might need to drop.

Base Tables

VENDORS, PRODUCTS

Calculated Field Expressions

Field Name	Expression
PRODUCT COUNT	Count(PRODNAME)

Filters

Field Name	Condition

Figure 12.20. *View Specifications sheet for the VENDOR PRODUCT COUNT view.*

Summary

We began this chapter with a definition of a view, and you learned that it is a virtual table that does not contain or store data. Views are useful for several reasons—they provide a means for you to work with data from multiple tables, they help enforce data integrity, and they help keep data secure or confidential.

We then discussed the three types of views: *data*, *aggregate*, and *validation*. You learned that each type of view can be based on one or more tables, other views, or a combination of both. Your RDBMS will rebuild and repopulate a view every time you access it, using the most current data from the view's base tables. As you now know, there must be relationships between tables in a multitable view (thus making the view's information valid and meaningful), and the characteristics of those relationships are carried forth through the view. Additionally, you can modify most views, and all the modifications you make to the data are passed through the view to the base tables. You also learned that *validation views* work in the same manner as validation tables and that they have distinct advantages over validation tables. For instance, validation views can incorporate data from multiple tables.

The chapter then continued with a discussion of determining and defining views for the database. Here you learned several specific points to keep in mind while you work with users and management to identify the organization's view requirements. Next, we discussed how to define a view, and you learned how to create a *view diagram* to document the view. Now you know how to select fields from the base tables and assign them to the view.

We then discussed how to use calculated fields in a view. You learned that you could use them to help provide pertinent information and to enhance how the view displays its data. You also learned that calculated fields are especially crucial in aggregate views and that each calculated field uses an expression to derive the value it displays. Next, you learned how to apply a filter to a view so that it will retrieve and display a specific set of records. The view will display a given record only if it meets the criteria you've imposed against one or more fields in the view. You frame each criterion as an expression and use it to test the value of a particular field.

The chapter closed with a discussion of the View Specifications sheet. Here you learned how to document the characteristics of the view, such as its name and type. You also learned about the items that compose the View Specifications sheet and how you use them to record the view's characteristics.

Review Questions

1.   Why can you refer to a view as a *virtual table*?

2.   State two reasons why views are valuable.

3.   Name the types of views you can define as you design the logical structure of the database.

4.   What does your RDMBS do each time you access a *data view* (or any type of view, for that matter)?

5.   What determines the type of modifications you can make to a view's data?

6.   What is the only requirement you must fulfill in order to define a *multitable data view*?

7.   Why doesn't a data view contain its own primary key?

8.   What is the purpose of an *aggregate view*?

9.   What are the most common *aggregate functions* that you can apply to a set of data?

10. What is a *grouping field*?

11. True or False: You can modify the data in an aggregate view.

12. What is the difference between a *validation table* and a *validation view*?

13. Name two points you would consider when identifying view requirements.

14. When should you use *calculated fields*?

15. How do you define a view that displays only science-fiction books?

16. Why must you complete a View Specifications sheet for every view in the database?

13

Reviewing Data Integrity

When you have eliminated the impossible, whatever
remains, however improbable, must be the truth.
—SHERLOCK HOLMES,
THE SIGN OF FOUR

Topics Covered in This Chapter

Why You Should Review Data Integrity

Reviewing and Refining Data Integrity

Assembling the Database Documentation

Done at Last!

Case Study—Wrap Up

Summary

You are now at the final stage of the database-design process. You've accomplished many things since you started the process. Thus far you have

- Perceived the advantages of the relational database model and how it compares to other database models

- Created a mission statement for a new database

- Defined mission objectives for the new database

- Performed a complete analysis of an old database

- Identified the organization's information requirements

- Defined all the appropriate table structures

- Assigned a primary key to each table

- Established field specifications for each field

- Established table relationships

- Defined and established business rules

- Defined all the appropriate views

- Established overall data integrity

For all intents and purposes, your new database is complete; nevertheless, it would be to your advantage to perform one final review of the overall data integrity of your database.

Why You Should Review Data Integrity

You're probably wondering why you should review the database structure one last time, given that you've paid attention to every detail and have focused on data integrity throughout the entire design process. The answer is simple: You want to make certain that the data integrity you've been so careful to establish is absolutely as sound as possible. As you well know, a crack in the integrity could result in inconsistent data or inaccurate information. However improbable, it is possible that you may have overlooked something. The peace of mind you gain from knowing that you have a solidly designed database is well worth the time and effort of this final review.

❖ **Note** Remember: Garbage in, garbage out!

Reviewing and Refining Data Integrity

Reviewing data integrity is a simple task if you take a modular approach, that is, if you sequentially review each component of overall data integrity: table-level, field-level, and relationship-level integrity and business rules. If you have carefully followed the design method presented in this book, you should encounter very few problems here. The following sections briefly outline the points you should keep in mind as you conduct the review, and they contain references to earlier chapters in case you encounter any problems.

At the Table Level

In order to ensure that you've properly established table-level integrity, review each table and make certain that the table conforms to all of the following points:

- There are no duplicate fields in the table.

- There are no calculated fields in the table.

- There are no multivalued fields in the table.

- There are no multipart fields in the table.

- There are no duplicate records in the table.

- Every record in the table is identified by a primary key value.

- Each primary key conforms to the Elements of a Primary Key.

If you believe you have problems with any of these items, resolve them using the techniques and concepts discussed in Chapters 6 through 8.

At the Field Level

You can ensure that you've properly established field-level integrity after you've done the following:

- Made sure each field conforms to the Elements of the Ideal Field

- Made certain you've defined a set of field specifications for each field

You can resolve field-level integrity problems with the techniques discussed in Chapter 9.

At the Relationship Level

Examine each table relationship to ensure that you've properly established relationship-level integrity. You've achieved this level of integrity when you've completed these tasks:

- Properly established the relationship

- Defined the appropriate deletion rules

- Correctly identified the type of participation for each table

- Established the proper degree of participation for each table

If you identify a problem with a relationship, use the techniques in Chapter 10 to resolve it.

At the Level of Business Rules

You can ensure that your business rules are sound by making certain these tasks are complete:

- You're sure that each rule imposes a *meaningful* constraint.

- You've determined the proper category for the rule.

- You've properly defined and established each rule.

- You've modified the appropriate field specification elements or table-relationship characteristics.

- You've established the appropriate validation tables.

- You've completed a Business Rule Specifications sheet for each rule.

If you encounter problems with any of your business rules, refer to Chapter 11 for the techniques necessary to solve them.

At the Level of Views

Although views are not directly connected to any component of data integrity, you should nevertheless review all of your view structures. As you examine each view, make certain you've addressed these items:

- Each view contains the base tables necessary to provide the required information.

- You've assigned the appropriate fields to each view.

- Each calculated field provides pertinent information or enhances the manner in which the view presents its data.

- Each filter returns the appropriate set of records.

- Each view has a view diagram.

- Each view diagram is accompanied by a View Specifications sheet.

If you encounter problems with any view, resolve them by using the techniques discussed in Chapter 12.

Once you've completed this entire review, you can be confident that the database structure is sound, the data within the database is consistent and valid, and the information you retrieve from the database will be accurate.

Assembling the Database Documentation

Throughout the database-design process, you've generated a number of lists, specification sheets, and diagrams used to record various aspects of the database-design. You should now assemble them into a central repository, preferably in a set of binders. (Incidentally, you could generate and store these documents using a computer program.) The design repository should consist of the following sets of documents:

Final table list	Relationship diagrams
Field Specifications sheets	Business Rule Specifications sheets
Calculated-field list	View diagrams
Table structure diagrams	View Specifications sheets

Two additional sets of items you may consider keeping with this documentation are the notes you compiled during the design process and the samples you gathered during the analysis stage of the design process. You can keep each of these items in a separate appendix at the end of the documentation.

All of these items constitute the complete set of documentation for the logical design of the database. This documentation is vital for three reasons:

1. *It provides a complete record of the database structure.* You can find every aspect of the logical structure of the database within the documentation. Additionally, you can answer almost any question concerning the database simply by referring to the documentation.

2. *It provides a complete set of specifications and instructions on how the database should be created during the implementation process.*

This documentation is similar to an architect's blueprints: It indicates how the database is to be constructed. It also identifies the integrity that needs to be established for the database. Because the database design is not directed to a particular RDBMS, the individuals implementing the database have full latitude concerning the manner in which they physically implement the database.

3. *Should it seem necessary to modify the database structure during the implementation process, the design documentation can be used to determine the effects and consequences of any modifications.* Any modifications you make to the database structure should be the result of an informed decision. You can make certain that a proposed modification will not have an adverse effect on the database structure by referencing the documentation first.

Done at Last!

Now that you've completed the integrity review and assembled all of the documentation for the database, the logical database-design process is complete. You can rest assured that you have a properly designed database and that its implementation will proceed smoothly. On to the next client and the next database design!

CASE STUDY—WRAP UP

This is your last meeting with Mike and his staff. Your objective is to review his database and its integrity one final time. Although you're confident that you will not find any problems, you want to give the database one final quality-control review.

During the meeting, you review each of the database structures to ensure that they are in accordance with the various elements that govern them. Then you review each component of overall data integrity to make certain that you've properly established table-level, field-level, and relationship-level integrity, as well as business rules. Finally you gather all of the documentation you've generated throughout the design process. After you've assembled all of the documentation into a set of binders, you give them to Mike and declare that his database is now complete. Mike expresses his thanks and gratitude for a job well done and promises your check will be in the mail by the 15th of the month. You express your thanks to Mike and his staff, say your good-byes and depart for new horizons. As you leave, Mike stares in your direction; one final thought occurs to him.

"Now, if I could just get you to *implement* my database for me . . ."

Summary

The chapter opened with a list of your accomplishments since you began the database-design process. It then continued with a discussion of why you should review overall data integrity one final time. This was followed by a brief discussion of the points to keep in mind as you review each component of overall data integrity. We close the chapter by discussing the importance of the documentation you've assembled during the entire design process.

Part III

Other Database-Design Issues

14

Bad Design—What Not to Do

Mistakes are always initial.
—Cesare Pavese

Topics Covered in This Chapter

Flat-File Design

Spreadsheet Design

Database Design Based on the Database Software

A Final Thought

Summary

You may have wondered why this chapter appears at the end of the book instead of at the beginning. The reason is simple: You can appreciate the dangers presented by a poorly designed database now that you've learned how to design a database properly. Additionally, you will be able to determine for yourself why a particular design is bad—you'll look at the design and be able to identify the problems with the structure immediately. You also possess the knowledge required to identify possible solutions to these problems.

In this chapter, you'll see the *three most common* design approaches that lead to poorly structured databases. The discussions are brief because they are only meant to illustrate types of design you should avoid. It should now be obvious that the way to resolve an improperly designed database is to take it through the complete design process you've just learned.

Flat-File Design

This type of design (sometimes known as the "throw-everything-into-one-big-table" design) has been in existence for many years and is common in databases that have been designed for implementation in nonrelational database-management systems. A flat-file design is fraught with problems, as you can see by examining the structure in Figure 14.1.

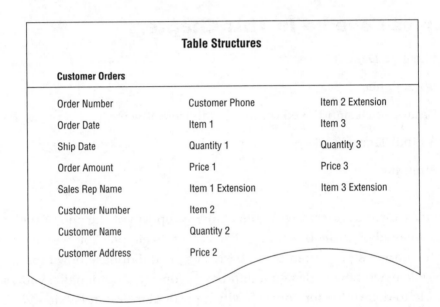

Figure 14.1. *An example of a flat-file structure.*

This diagram represents the structure of a *single* table. (Imagine how other tables within the database are structured!) You can readily see that this structure will inevitably cause problems with redundant data and inconsistent data and that it suffers from a lack of data integrity. As you've probably already noted, there are a few other problems with this structure:

- *Multipart fields.* Sales Rep Name includes the sales rep's first and last name, Customer Name includes the customer's first and last name, and Customer Address includes the customer's street address, city, state, and zip code.

- *Calculated fields.* The Order Amount field contains a value that is most likely manually calculated, especially if the customer is ordering more than three items. The Item # Extension fields are all likely to be manually calculated as well. The value for a given Item # Extension field is the result of multiplying the value of a related Quantity # field by the value of a related Price # field. (For example: Item 3 Extension = Quantity 3 × Price 3)

- *Unnecessary duplicate fields.* Each of the fields pertaining to a particular item is a duplicate. For example, the Item 1, Item 2, and Item 3 fields are unnecessary duplicate fields.

- *No true primary key.* There is no field or group of fields that can uniquely identify a single record in this table. The Order Number field is not a primary key in this table; if a customer orders more than three items, you'll have to enter another record into the table using the *same* order number.

- *The table represents more than one subject.* This table represents three subjects: customers, orders, and items. (Depending on your point of view, it also represents sales reps.)

Now that you know the elements of good database design, you're sure to avoid a design such as this.

Spreadsheet Design

A spreadsheet is certainly a good tool if you use it properly and for the purpose for which it was designed. For example, it is quite suitable for work that involves complex mathematical calculations and statistical analysis. Contrary to popular myth, however, a spreadsheet *does not* make a good relational database. If your organization has a need to collect, store, maintain, and manipulate various types of data, then use the proper tool for the job by designing and implementing a real database. For example, consider the spreadsheet in Figure 14.2.

	A	B	C
1	Store 100 (344-0029)		Store 103 (554-2993)
2	Manager: Mike Hernandez		Manager: Katie Christian
3	Asst. Mgr: Bob McNeal and		Asst. Mgr: Terri Sharpe
4	Suzi Thompson		
5	Store 101 (433-4872)		Store 104 (773-1837)
6	Manager: Abe Hernandez		Manager: Gary Holcomb
7	Asst. Mgr: Steve McMahn		Asst. Mgr: Barbara Cooper
8			and Tim Ennis
9	Store 102 (433-4872)		Store 105 (344-2883)
10	Manager: Susan McLain		Manager: Caroline Coie
11	Asst. Mgr: Diana Barlet		Asst. Mgr: LeRoy Bonnicksen

Figure 14.2. *An example of a typical spreadsheet "database."*

This spreadsheet is being used to keep track of store managers for a small chain of retail stores. As you can see, this approach has problems as well.

- *Duplicate fields.* Each field on this spreadsheet is a duplicate field. If you take the fields at face value, there are basically three fields in each instance: Store Number, Manager Name, and Assistant Manager Name.

- *Multipart fields.* Each field holds two values. The first field stores the store number and phone number, the second field stores the manager's first and last name, and the third field stores the assistant manager's first and last name.

- *Multivalued fields.* The ASSISTANT MANAGER field is a multivalued field because there can be more than one assistant manager assigned to a particular store.

- *This type of database is difficult to use.* Data-oriented tasks that can be performed with ease in an RDBMS program are tedious and time-consuming to carry out in a spreadsheet. For example, it would take you some time to create a list containing only the name of each store manager and his or her phone number.

After seeing the problems associated with a simple spreadsheet "database" such as this one, you can imagine the types of problems you would encounter with a more complex database. If you're currently using a spreadsheet as a database, you can improve the database's quality, speed, and versatility if you remove it from the spreadsheet, take it through the entire database-design process, and implement it in a suitable RDBMS.

Dealing with the Spreadsheet View Mind-set

When you begin to work with a true database and RDBMS, you must break away from a spreadsheet view mind-set. This means that you'll have to resign yourself to the fact that certain ways of viewing the data are now unavailable—you can no longer use typical spreadsheet layouts. For example, consider a typical spreadsheet report shown in Figure 14.3.

You cannot produce a report with this type of layout using a database. Whereas a spreadsheet stores the data exactly as you see it on the report, a database would store it in four separate fields within a table. Figure 14.4 shows an example of a database report you could generate for the same data. The database presentation is not the same as the spreadsheet presentation, but it is just as clear.

Branch Stores

Bellevue

Store 118	Store 201	Store 211
Manager: Katherine Ehrlich	Manager: Kevin Christian	Manager: George Chavez

Redmond

Store 27	Store 75	Store 322
Manager: Mark Rosales	Manager: Chris Weber	Manager: Steve Pundt

Seattle

Store 105	Store 187	Store 200
Manager: Caroline Cole	Manager: Julia Black	Manager: Sanjay Jacob

Figure 14.3. *An example of a typical spreadsheet report.*

Branch Stores

Bellevue		**Seattle**	
Store 118	Manager: Katherine Ehrlich	Store 105	Manager: Caroline Cole
Store 201	Manager: Kevin Christian	Store 187	Manager: Julia Black
Store 211	Manager: George Chavez	Store 200	Manager: Sanjay Jacob

Redmond	
Store 27	Manager: Mark Rosales
Store 75	Manager: Chris Weber
Store 322	Manager: Steve Pundt

Figure 14.4. *An example of a typical database report.*

The point to remember is that you'll have to adjust the manner in which you think about working with the data in your database. In the end, there are far more advantages to storing and using your data in an actual database than trying to use a spreadsheet in a similar manner. A database gives you much more control over data integrity and the consistency and validity of the data. It also provides an almost unlimited number of ways to retrieve the data, enabling you to obtain a wide variety of information.

Database Design Based on the Database Software

An RDBMS does not provide a basis or procedure or even a reason for designing a database in a particular fashion—it only provides the tools that you need to implement a design. In contrast, a formal database-design method provides both the principles and rationale necessary to define a database properly and effectively.

Many people unwittingly fall into the trap of designing a database based solely on the RDBMS software they will use for its implementation. In many cases, they do so because they are already somewhat familiar and skilled with a particular RDBMS. This is an unwise approach that you should avoid for several reasons:

- *You're likely to make design decisions based on your perceptions of what your RDBMS can or can't do.* For example, you may decide not to impose a degree of participation for a given relationship because you believe the RDBMS does not provide you with the means to do so.

- *You'll inadvertently let the RDBMS dictate the design of the database as opposed to driving the design strictly from the organization's information requirements.* This usually occurs when you discover that your RDBMS provides only limited support for certain aspects of the database, such as field specifications and relationship characteristics.

- *Your design will be constrained by your knowledge of the RDBMS.* For example, you may decide not to implement relationship characteristics simply because you don't know how to do so.

- *Your design will be constrained by how skilled you are with your RDBMS.* Your skill level affects how efficiently and effectively you can implement various aspects of the database, such as field specifications and business rules.

- *Using this approach to design a database commonly results in improper structural design, insufficient data integrity, and problems with inconsistent data and inaccurate information.* Defining a database within an RDBMS can be deceptively easy. You may create a database that works, but you're very likely to have a poor design without knowing it.

- *In the end, the RDBMS that you know and love so well may not be suitable for your organization's database requirements.*

You should always design the logical structure of your database without regard to any RDBMS. By doing so, you're more likely to design a sound structure because you'll be focused on the organization's information requirements. Once your design is complete, you can then clearly determine how you should implement the database (single-user application, client/server, Web-based, and so on) and which RDBMS you should use to facilitate the implementation.

A Final Thought

Through years of teaching database design and instructing people in how to use various RDBMS software programs, I've observed an interesting phenomenon: People who are familiar with the fundamental principles of proper database design have a better comprehension of their RDBMS and the tools it provides than those who know little at all about database design. I believe this is due to the fact that the people who know database design are able to understand *why* the RDBMS provides certain tools and *how* they can (and should) use them. For this reason—as well as the many others presented in this book—it is to your distinct advantage to learn and understand good database-design techniques. This book does not map the only road, but it is, I believe, the straightest, surest, and most easily traveled.

Summary

This chapter contrasted relational database design with weaker, less effective design formats. First, we looked at flat-file design. You learned that there are numerous fatal problems with this approach and that it should be completely avoided. We then examined spreadsheet design and you saw how constrained this approach can be. The chapter closed with a discussion of designing a database using RDBMS software. You learned that this type of design is perilously dependent on your familiarity and skill level with the software. Unlike a good database-design method, designing a database around an RDBMS does not provide you with principles and a rationale for designing a proper database structure. Superficially, in the short run, the software product looks as good—it just doesn't work as well in the long run as the design method discussed in this book.

15

Bending or Breaking the Rules

Nature never breaks her own laws.
—Leonardo da Vinci

Topics Covered in This Chapter

When May You Bend or Break the Rules?

Documenting Your Actions

Summary

I always advocate following proper database-design techniques. As you've already learned, there are numerous reasons for doing so. But first and foremost, you should use a good design method to ensure the integrity of the database. I cannot overstate how important this is. You now know the consequences of improperly establishing data integrity, so following the rules is of paramount importance.

When May You Bend or Break the Rules?

There are only two specific circumstances under which it is at all permissible to bend or break the rules of proper database design. Unless either of these is an inescapable imperative, you should use proper database-design techniques when designing your database.

Designing an Analytical Database

As you learned in Chapter 1, an *analytical database* stores and tracks historical and time-dependent data. This type of database often contains calculated fields within some of its table structures. The expressions used in many of these fields are meant to record the state of a particular set of data at a given moment in time; other fields store the results of aggregate functions.

You may have already surmised from the description that this type of database violates proper database design because its tables contain calculated fields (refer to Chapter 7). In this *particular* instance, the violation is acceptable because of the manner in which the data in the database is being used. I recommend that you *properly* design the database first and then break the rules only after judicious consideration—you should make a deliberate decision to break a rule and understand why doing so is necessary in the specific instance.

> ❖ **Note** Designing an analytical database requires a radically different design methodology than the one you learned in this book. If you determine that your organization requires an analytical database, I strongly recommend that you acquire a good book on the subject and learn how to design such a database properly.

Improving Processing Performance

This is by far the most common reason that people feel compelled to bend or break the rules. Whenever an RDBMS takes what seems to be an inordinate amount of time to process multitable queries or complex reports, many people believe that the solution to the problem is to alter the underlying table structures. For example, they would have you modify a table in such a way that it includes *every* field necessary for the query or report. While this modification does indeed increase the speed at which the RDBMS processes the query or report, it also introduces a number of new problems, such as unnecessary duplicate fields and redundant data. This is clearly not a desirable solution, because it violates proper database design.

Unfortunately, real life is not as ideal as we would like it to be, so you will sometimes find that you must decide between improving processing performance and holding to proper design principles.

Is It Worth It?

When you take a moment to really think about this dilemma, you'll soon realize that the question really isn't about performance; it's about data integrity. Anytime you break the rules for performance' sake (or any other reason, for that matter), you are surely going to introduce data-integrity problems. The question you must ask yourself, then, is this: Is the perceived increase in processing performance worth the price of reduced (and, therefore, weakened) data integrity? As you well know, the consequences of making imprudent modifications to your data structures will eventually spread, like ripples in a pond, throughout your database. Here are just a few of the problems you'll encounter:

- *Inconsistent data.* This is a result of introducing unnecessary duplicate fields into a table. It will be your responsibility (or that of your application program) to ensure that the data in these fields is synchronized; if you modify the value in a particular duplicate field, you'll have to make certain that the same modification is made to the remaining duplicate fields.

- *Redundant data.* Redundant data is also a result of introducing unnecessary duplicate fields into a table. When you edit a particular value in a field that contains redundant data, you must be sure to make the same modification for each instance of that value.

- *Impaired data integrity.* Bending or breaking the rules often violates one or more components of overall data integrity, such as table-level integrity and relationship-level integrity. It will be your responsibility (or that of your application program) to compensate for the lack of integrity—in whatever way it manifests itself—as best as you can.

- *Inaccurate information.* You cannot possibly expect the database to provide *accurate* information if it has any of the aforementioned problems.

Improving Performance by Other Means First

If you still think you want to pursue this course of action in order to improve processing performance, *do it only as a last resort.* Before you take these measures, however, try to improve performance by some other means first. Consider these alternatives:

- *Enhance or upgrade the computer hardware.* In spite of the cost involved, this is still the easiest way to increase processing performance. A faster CPU, more memory, and a printer that better meets your requirements will all help to greatly decrease the time it takes the RDBMS to process a complex query or report. Using a larger hard drive will also help increase the retrieval speed for disk-intensive queries. Larger hard drives incorporate technology that produces extremely fast disk-access times.

- *Fine-tune the operating system software.* Make certain that the computer's operating system is optimized for peak performance. This is especially important for networked computers. You can greatly enhance general processing performance by working with the settings of the network's configuration options. The types of modifications you make to the operating system in general will depend on the type of *software* you're using for the operating system, so you'll have to refer to the software's documentation to determine what types of modifications you can make.

- *Review the database structure.* Make absolutely certain that the database is properly designed. It makes quite a difference.

Poorly designed databases actually *contribute* to poor processing performance.

- *Review the database's implementation.* Examine how the database is currently implemented within the RDBMS. Make certain you've taken full advantage of the RDBMS's capabilities and defined the database as efficiently and completely as possible.

- *Review the application program used to work with the database.* Here's another area you should examine very closely. Is the application program well-written? Does it make the best use of the tools the RDBMS provides? Are the application's components well-defined? In some cases, a report may print more slowly because it is poorly designed—there may be more effective ways to design and generate the same report. Queries may run slowly because they are improperly defined. Make certain that each query is defined correctly and in the most efficient way possible.

If you believe you must depart from proper database-design techniques, carefully examine your situation. As I mentioned earlier, it's acceptable to suspend the rules *if* you are designing an analytical database. But I still strongly recommend that you design your database properly and thoroughly and relax the rules *only* for very specific reasons.

Documenting Your Actions

If you've exhausted all other options and still come to the conclusion that you need to bend or break the rules, then *you must document each rule you break and each action you take!* It is important that you document your changes because doing so will compel you to think about the consequences of what you are about to do and it provides a means of recording the changes you make to the database structure. Should you decide later that the modifications did not provide a significant increase in processing performance, you can use the documentation as a guide to reverse the modifications you initially made.

These are the items that you should record:

- *The reason you're breaking the rules.* Increasing processing performance and decreasing the time it takes to print complex reports are two of the most common reasons for breaking the rules. Whatever your reason, be sure to state it thoroughly and clearly.

- *The design principle you're violating.* Recording how you've altered the database design will give you the means to reverse these changes later should you determine that performance did not significantly improve. You might indicate that you're altering the structure of a table, for example.

- *The aspect of the database that you're modifying.* Indicate which particular field, table, relationship, or view you are going to alter. Once again, this information will be valuable should you decide to reverse the modifications.

- *The specific modifications you are making.* Once you determine which item you need to modify, record the *exact* modifications you make to that item. For example, if you need to modify a relationship, note the exact changes you make to its characteristics.

- *The anticipated effects on the database and the application program.* Any modifications you make to the database are going to affect all accompanying end-user application programs. For example, altering the structure of a particular table can affect data integrity, view structures, data-entry forms and reports built upon the table (either partially or totally), and macros or programming code that refer to the table. You must be sure to list every effect.

Add this document to the documentation you compiled for the database. Even if you reverse the changes later, this record could prevent you from yielding to a future impulse to attempt the same types of changes.

Summary

The chapter opened by examining the two circumstances under which you might feel compelled to depart from proper database-design techniques. You learned that breaking the rules is acceptable *if* you are designing an analytical database; otherwise, you should design the database properly first and then make deliberate decisions to break or bend specific rules. You then learned that the most common reason for departing from proper design techniques is to improve processing performance. Although this *is not* a satisfactory reason for breaking the rules, there are times when circumstances dictate that you must consider such changes.

We then continued with a discussion of the alternate measures you can take to improve processing performance, such as enhancing or upgrading the hardware and reviewing the implementation of the database. You learned that you should do all you can to improve performance first and depart from proper design techniques only as a last resort. The chapter then closed with a list of items you should record if you need to break the rules.

In Closing

*I'm not a teacher: only a fellow-traveller
of whom you asked the way. I pointed
ahead—ahead of myself as well as you.*
—GEORGE BERNARD SHAW

I've always believed that you shouldn't have to be a rocket scientist in order to design a database properly. It should be a relatively straightforward task that can be performed by anyone possessing a good amount of common sense. As long as you follow a good database-design method, you should be able to design a sound and reliable database structure.

You now possess the knowledge and skills necessary to design a relational database. You know how to define the necessary structures, establish table relationships, and implement various levels of data integrity. If you encounter improperly or poorly designed structures, you now know how to improve them.

Learning about database design is an ever-continuing process. You can learn enough to design the types of databases you require, you can turn it into a profession, or you can even make it a lifelong study. Whatever your approach, you'll encounter one inescapable fact: *The more you learn, the more you realize you don't know it all.* But don't be discouraged; this is true of any major subject you endeavor to learn, such as music, art, philosophy—or rocket science!

I sincerely hope you've enjoyed reading this book as much as I've enjoyed writing it. I know that most technical books of this nature can be a little dry, so I tried to inject a little humor every now and then, particularly in the interview and meeting dialogues. Those of you who thought the conversations were relatively realistic are quite perceptive—they were very loosely based on a number of interviews and conversations I've had with my clients over the years.

As a parting piece of advice, let me leave you with two words: *Always learn.* Never be afraid or intimidated or reluctant to learn something new. Learning opens the door to fresh ideas, different concepts, and new perceptions. It encourages participation and communication between individuals and broadens everyone's horizons.

Learning is a journey that begins with but one step. You've taken the first step by reading this book. Now you will continue your journey by learning about other facets of database management.

My book ends here, but your journey is just beginning. . . .

 **Part IV**
Appendixes

A

Answers to
Review Questions

Chapter 1

1. The two main types of databases in use today are *operational* and *analytical.*

2. An analytical database stores *static* data.

3. True. An operational database is used primarily in OLTP scenarios.

4. The *hierarchical* and *network* database models were commonly used in the days before the relational database model.

5. In a *parent/child* relationship, a parent table can be associated with one or more child tables, but a single child table can be associated with only one parent table.

6. A *set structure* is a transparent construction that establishes and represents a relationship in a network database.

7. The relational model is based on two branches of mathematics—*set theory* and *first-order predicate logic.*

8. A relational database stores data in *relations*, which the user perceives as tables.

9. The three types of relationships in a relational database are *one-to-one, one-to-many,* and *many-to-many.*

10. You retrieve data in a relational database by using SQL.

11. The advantages of a relational database include built-in multilevel integrity, logical and physical data independence from database applications, guaranteed data consistency and accuracy, and easy data retrieval.

12. A relational database management system, or RDBMS, is a software program you use to create, maintain, modify, and manipulate a relational database.

13. The object-relational model extends the relational database model by incorporating various object-oriented elements and characteristics, such as classes, encapsulation, and inheritance.

14. A data warehouse allows organizations to access data stored in any number of relational and nonrelational databases.

15. XML stands for *eXtensible Markup Language* and is quickly becoming a de facto data-transfer standard for sharing data across heterogeneous systems.

Chapter 2

1. The best time to use an RDBMS program's design tools is *after* you design the logical structure of the database.

2. True. Design is crucial to the consistency, integrity, and accuracy of data.

3. The most detrimental result of improper database design is inaccurate information.

4. The fact that the relational database model is based on *set theory* and *first-order predicate logic* makes the relational database structurally sound and able to guarantee accurate information.

5. These are the advantages to learning a design methodology:

   a. It gives you the skills you need to design a sound database structure.

   b. It provides you with an organized set of techniques that will guide you step-by-step through the design process.

   c. It helps you keep your missteps and design reiterations to a minimum.

   d. It makes the design process easier and reduces the amount of time you spend designing the database.

   e. It will help you understand and use your RDBMS software more fully and effectively.

6. True. Understanding database design will help you use your RDBMS program more effectively.

7. These are the objectives of good design:

   a. The database supports required and ad hoc information retrieval.

   b. The tables are constructed properly and efficiently.

   c. Data integrity is imposed at the field, table, and relationship levels.

   d. The database supports business rules relevant to the organization.

   e. The database lends itself to future growth.

8. Data integrity helps to guarantee that data structures and their values are valid and accurate at all times.

9. These are the benefits of applying good design techniques:

   a. The database structure is easy to modify and maintain.

   b. The data is easy to modify.

   c. Information is easy to retrieve.

   d. End-user applications are easy to develop and build.

10. False. You cannot take shortcuts through some of the design processes and still arrive at a good, sound design.

Chapter 3

1. Terminology is *important* for the following reasons:

   a. It is used to express and define the special ideas and concepts of the relational database model.

   b. It is used to express and define the database-design process itself.

   c. It is used anywhere a relational database or RDBMS is discussed.

2. The four categories of terms are *value-related, structure-related, relationship-related,* and *integrity-related.*

3. The values you store in the database are *data. Information* is data that you process in a manner that makes it meaningful and useful to you when you work with it or view it.

4. A *null* represents a missing or unknown value.

5. The major disadvantage of nulls is that they have an adverse affect on mathematical operations.

6. *Tables* are the chief structures in the database.

7. The three types of tables are *data* tables, *linking* tables, and *validation* tables.

8. A *view* is a virtual table composed of fields from one or more base tables in the database.

9. A key is a *logical structure* that you use to identify records within a table, and an index is a *physical structure* that you use to optimize data processing.

10. The three types of relationships that can exist between a pair of tables are *one-to-one*, *one-to-many*, and *many-to-many*.

11. You can characterize every relationship in three ways: by the type of relationship that exists between the tables, the manner in which each table participates, and the degree to which each table participates.

12. A *field specification* represents all the elements of a field.

13. A field specification incorporates three types of elements: *general*, *physical*, and *logical*.

14. *Data integrity* refers to the validity, consistency, and accuracy of the data in a database.

15. The four types of data integrity are *field-level*, *table-level*, *relationship-level*, and *business rules*.

Chapter 4

1. It is important to complete the design process thoroughly because it helps you assure a sound structure and data integrity.

2. True. The level of structural integrity is in direct proportion to how thoroughly you follow the design process.

3. The *mission statement* identifies the purpose of your database.

4. *Mission objectives* are statements that represent the general tasks your users can perform against the data in the database.

5. The list of fields and calculations that you compile during the second phase of the design process constitutes your organization's fundamental data requirements.

6. You determine the various subjects that the tables will represent from the mission objectives you wrote during the first phase of the design process and the data requirements you gathered during the second phase.

7. False. You establish field specifications for each field in the database during the *third* phase of the database-design process.

8. You establish a logical connection between the tables in a relationship either with a primary key or with a linking table.

9. The manner in which your organization views and uses its data will determine a set of limitations and requirements that you must build into the database.

10. You can define and implement *validation tables* as necessary to support certain business rules.

11. You identify the types of views you need to build in the database by interviewing users and management and determining how they work with their respective data.

12. You can implement the logical database structure in an RDBMS program after you've completed the entire database-design process.

Chapter 5

1. Interviews are important because they provide a valuable communication link between you (the developer) and the people for whom you're designing the database. They help ensure the success of your design efforts, and they provide critical information that can affect the design of the database structure.

2. The problem that arises when you conduct an interview with a large number of people is that the intimidation level of some of the participants will rise in direct proportion to the number of participants taking part in the interview as a whole.

3. The primary reason for conducting separate interviews with users and management is that each group has a different perspective on the organization as a whole and on how the organization uses its data on a daily basis.

4. False. You'll commonly use open-ended questions in your interviews.

5. You should try to elicit complete, descriptive responses from the interview participants.

6. The single most important guideline for every interview you conduct is to always maintain control of the interview.

7. A *mission statement* declares the specific purpose of the database in general terms.

8. A well-written mission statement is unambiguous, succinct and to the point, and free of phrases or sentences that explicitly describe specific tasks.

9. False. You must learn about the organization in order to compose a mission statement.

10. Your mission statement is complete when you have a sentence that describes the specific purpose of the database and that is understood and agreed upon by everyone concerned.

11. A *mission objective* is a statement that represents a single, general task supported by the data maintained in the database.

12. A well-written mission objective is a declarative sentence that clearly defines a general task and is free from unnecessary details. It is expressed in general terms, is succinct and to the point, and is unambiguous.

13. True. You should interview users and management to help you define mission objectives.

14. The staff's daily work relates to the mission objectives in that many of the tasks they perform will become mission objectives.

15. False. A mission objective cannot describe more than one task.

16. A mission objective can be derived from a response either explicitly or implicitly.

17. A mission objective is complete when it is both properly defined and well defined, and when it makes sense to you and to those for whom you are designing the database

Chapter 6

1. The goals of analyzing the current database are to determine the following:

   a. What types of data the organization uses

   b. How the organization uses its data

   c. How the organization manages and maintains its data

2. False. You *should not* adopt the current database structure as the basis for the new structure.

3. A legacy database is a database that has been in existence and in use for five years or more.

4. The analysis process incorporates these three steps:

   a. Reviewing the way data is collected

   b. Reviewing the manner in which information is presented

   c. Conducting interviews with users and management

5. The types of computer software programs you should review during the analysis include word processors, spreadsheets, databases, and Web pages.

6. You should conduct interviews after you gather data-collection and information-presentation samples for these reasons:

    a. They provide details about the samples you assembled during the previous reviews.

    b. They provide information on the way the organization uses its data.

    c. They are instrumental in defining preliminary field and table structures.

    d. They help to define future information requirements.

7. You use open-ended questions to focus on specific subjects and closed questions to focus on specific details of a certain subject.

8. The *subject-identification technique* allows you to identify subjects within a participant's response to a given question.

9. You identify specific attributes for a particular subject by using the *characteristic-identification technique.*

10. False. You should interview users and management separately.

11. The three basic types of information requirements you must identify are *current, additional,* and *future.*

12. The *preliminary field list* represents the organization's fundamental data requirements and constitutes the core set of fields that you must define in the database.

13. Each item on this list should have a unique name to ensure that the characteristic appears only once on the list.

14. A *value list* specifies the acceptable range of values for a particular characteristic and often enforces a given business rule.

15. A calculated field stores the result of a string concatenation or mathematical expression as its value. You should remove calculated fields from the preliminary field list and place them on a dedicated calculated-field list.

Chapter 7

1. You identify and establish tables for the new database using the *preliminary table list*.

2. You use the preliminary field list to help you define tables for the database because the fields on the list may imply subjects that the database needs to track.

3. When an item on the list of subjects and a differently named item on the preliminary table list both represent the same subject, you select the name that best represents the subject and use it as the sole identifier for that subject.

4. The *final table list* provides the name, type, and description of each table in the database.

5. These are the guidelines for creating table names:

   a. Create a unique, descriptive name that is meaningful to the entire organization.

   b. Create a name that accurately, clearly, and unambiguously identifies the subject of the table.

   c. Use the *minimum* number of words necessary to convey the subject of the table.

   d. Do not use words that convey physical characteristics.

    e. Do not use acronyms and abbreviations.

    f. Do not use proper names or other words that will unduly restrict the data that can be entered into the table.

    g. Do not use a name that implicitly or explicitly identifies more than one subject.

    h. Use the plural form of the name.

6.   These are the guidelines for composing table descriptions:

    a. Include a statement that accurately defines the table.

    b. Include a statement that explains why this table is important to the organization.

    c. Compose a description that is clear and succinct.

    d. Do not include implementation-specific information in your table description, such as how or where the table is used.

    e. Do not make the table description for one table dependent upon the table description for another table.

    f. Do not use examples in a table description.

7.   You assign fields to a table on the final table list by determining which fields best represent characteristics of the table's subject.

8.   These are the guidelines for creating field names:

    a. Create a unique, descriptive name that is meaningful to the entire organization.

    b. Create a name that accurately, clearly, and unambiguously identifies the characteristic a field represents.

    c. Use the *minimum* number of words necessary to convey the meaning of the characteristic the field represents.

    d. Do not use acronyms, and use abbreviations judiciously.

e. Do not use words that could confuse the meaning of the field name.

f. Do not use names that implicitly or explicitly identify more than one characteristic.

g. Use the singular form of the name.

9. Poorly designed fields can cause problems with duplicate data and redundant data.

10. You can resolve field anomalies by ensuring that the field complies with the Elements of the Ideal Field.

11. These are the *Elements of the Ideal Field:*

a. It represents a distinct characteristic of the subject of the table.

b. It contains only a single value.

c. It cannot be deconstructed into smaller components.

d. It does not contain a calculated or concatenated value.

e. It is unique within the entire database structure.

f. It retains a majority of its characteristics when it appears in more than one table.

12. Redundant data is acceptable when it is the result of resolving a multivalued field or an unnecessary duplicate field.

13. In general terms, these are the three steps you follow to resolve a multivalued field:

a. Remove the field from the table and use it as the basis for a new table.

b. Use a field (or set of fields) from the *original* table to relate the original table to the new table.

c. Assign an appropriate name, type, and description to the new table and add it to the final table list.

14. The only instance in which it is necessary to use a duplicate field is when the field serves to establish a relationship between two tables.

15. You can refine table structures by ensuring that each table complies with the Elements of the Ideal Table.

16. These are the *Elements of the Ideal Table:*

    a. It represents a single subject, which can be an object or event.

    b. It has a primary key.

    c. It does not contain multipart or multivalued fields.

    d. It does not contain calculated fields.

    e. It does not contain unnecessary duplicate fields.

    f. It contains only an absolute *minimum* amount of redundant data.

17. A *subset* table is a table that represents a subordinate subject of a particular data table.

Chapter 8

1. Keys are important for the following reasons:

    a. They ensure that each record in a table is properly identified.

    b. They help establish and enforce various types of integrity.

    c. They serve to establish table relationships.

2. The four main types of keys are *candidate, primary, foreign,* and *non.*

3. The purpose of a *candidate* key is to uniquely identify a single instance of the table's subject.

4.   These are the *Elements of a Candidate Key:*

   a. It cannot be a multipart field.

   b. It must contain unique values.

   c. It *cannot* contain null values.

   d. Its value is not optional in whole or in part.

   e. It comprises a minimum number of fields necessary to define uniqueness.

   f. Its values must uniquely and exclusively identify each record in the table.

   g. Its value must exclusively identify the value of each field within a given record.

   h. Its value can be modified only in rare or extreme cases.

5.   True. A candidate key can be composed of more than one field.

6.   Yes, a table can have more than one candidate key.

7.   A field you create for the sole purpose of serving as a candidate key is known as an *artificial candidate key.* You create this type of key when there are no "naturally occurring" candidate keys in a table.

8.   The *primary key* is the most important key you assign to a table.

9.   It is important for the following reasons:

   a. A primary key *field* exclusively identifies the table throughout the database structure and helps establish relationships with other tables.

   b. A primary key *value* uniquely identifies a given record within a table and exclusively represents that record throughout the entire database. It also helps to guard against duplicate records.

10. You establish a primary key by examining the table's pool of available candidate keys and then selecting one as the primary key.

11. These are the *Elements of a Primary Key:*

    a. It cannot be a multipart field.

    b. It must contain unique values.

    c. It *cannot* contain null values.

    d. Its value is not optional in whole or in part.

    e. It comprises a minimum number of fields necessary to define uniqueness.

    f. Its values must uniquely and exclusively identify each record in the table.

    g. Its value must exclusively identify the value of each field within a given record.

    h. Its value can be modified only in rare or extreme cases.

12. Before you finalize your selection of a primary key, you must make absolutely certain that it exclusively identifies the value of each field within a given record.

13. An *alternate key* is a candidate key that was not chosen to serve as the primary key of the table.

14. By establishing table-level integrity, you ensure the following:

    a. There are no duplicate records in a table.

    b. The primary key exclusively identifies each record in a table.

    c. Every primary key value is unique.

    d. Primary key values are not null.

15. You should review the initial table structures for the following reasons:

    a. To ensure that the appropriate subjects are represented in the database

    b. To make certain that the table names and table descriptions are suitable and meaningful to everyone

    c. To make certain that the field names are suitable and meaningful to everyone

    d. To verify that all the appropriate fields are assigned to each table

Chapter 9

1. *Field specifications* are important for these reasons:

    a. They help establish and enforce field-level integrity.

    b. They help enhance overall data integrity.

    c. They compel you to acquire a complete understanding of the nature and purpose of the data in the database.

    d. They constitute the "data dictionary" of the database.

2. *Field-level integrity* warrants the following:

    a. The identity and purpose of a field is clear, and all of the tables in which it appears are properly identified.

    b. Field definitions are consistent throughout the database.

    c. The values of a field are consistent and valid.

    d. The types of modifications, comparisons, and operations that can be applied to the values in the field are clearly identified.

3. The three categories of elements within a field specification are *general*, *physical*, and *logical*.

4. The three types of specifications are *Unique*, *Generic*, and *Replica*.

5. Composing a field description is extremely beneficial because it forces you (and everyone in the organization) to think carefully about the nature of the data that will be stored in the field.

6. The *Data Type* element indicates the nature of the data that the field stores.

7. The *Character Support* element indicates the type of characters that a user can enter into a given field value.

8. The *Display Format* element governs the appearance of a field's value when it is displayed on a screen or printed within a document.

9. The types of keys indicated on a field specification are *non*, *primary*, *alternate*, and *foreign*.

10. False. Null does not represent a blank—it represents a *missing* or *unknown* value.

11. The *Range of Values* element specifies every possible valid value for a field.

12. An *Edit Rule* designates at what point in time a user can enter a value into a field and whether he can modify that value.

13. The *Comparisons Allowed* element indicates the types of comparisons a user can apply to a given field value when he's retrieving information from the field.

14. A *value expression* is some form of operation involving field values, literal values, or a combination of both, and it returns a single value that you can then use for a comparison operation.

15. You use a *generic* specification for a field that serves as a template for other fields within the database.

Chapter 10

1. A *relationship* is important for the following reasons:

   a. It establishes a connection between a pair of tables that are logically related to each other.

   b. It helps to refine table structures and minimize redundant data further.

   c. It is the mechanism that enables you to draw data from multiple tables simultaneously.

2. The three types of relationships are *one-to-one*, *one-to-many*, and *many-to-many*.

3. The *many-to-many* relationship will pose the most problems.

4. You could possibly encounter problems such as these with a many-to-many relationship:

   a. It will be tedious and somewhat difficult for you to retrieve information from one of the tables.

   b. One of the tables will contain a large amount of redundant data.

   c. Duplicate data will exist within both tables.

   d. It will be difficult to insert, update, and delete data.

5. A *self-referencing relationship* is a relationship that exists between the records within a given table.

6. You begin the process of *identifying* the relationships among the tables in the database by creating a matrix of all the tables.

7. The *two types of questions* you can ask to help you identify existing relationships are associative and contextual.

8. You use a 1:N *shorthand symbol* to designate a one-to-many relationship in the table matrix.

9. You determine what type of relationship officially exists between each pair of tables in the matrix using formulas that correspond to the three relationship-type definitions.

10. You *establish* a one-to-many relationship by taking a copy of the primary key from the table on the "one" side of the relationship and incorporating it within the table structure on the "many" side, where it then becomes a foreign key.

11. True. Retrieving information from tables with a self-referencing relationship can be tedious and somewhat difficult.

12. You establish a self-referencing many-to-many relationship as you would a dual-table many-to-many relationship—with a linking table.

13. You *refine* the foreign keys in the database by ensuring that each one complies with the Elements of a Foreign Key.

14. The two element categories you must modify for a foreign key's field specification are the General Elements and Logical Elements categories.

15. A *deletion rule* determines what your RDBMS should do when you place a request to delete a given record in the parent table of the relationship.

16. The two *types of participation* you can designate for a table are Mandatory and Optional.

17. The *degree of participation* indicates the minimum number of records that a given table *must have* associated with a single record in the related table and the maximum number of records that the table *is allowed to have* associated with a single record in the related table.

18. A relationship attains *relationship-level integrity* after you've verified that it is properly established and its characteristics are suitably set.

Chapter 11

1. A *business rule* is a statement that imposes some form of constraint on a specific aspect of the database, such as the elements within a field specification for a particular field or the characteristics of a given relationship.

2. The two major types of business rules are *database oriented* and *application oriented.*

3. No. *Application oriented* business rules impose constraints that you *cannot* establish within the logical design of the database.

4. The two categories of database oriented business rules are *field specific* and *relationship specific.*

5. A *field specific business rule* is one that imposes constraints on the elements of a field specification for a particular field.

6. The constraint the business rule imposes is tested when you attempt to perform one of three actions: *inserting* a record into the table or an entry into a field, *deleting* a record from the table or a value within a field, or *updating* a field's value.

7. You document a business rule by filling out a Business Rule Specifications sheet for the rule.

8. The Business Rule Specifications sheet provides three advantages:

    a. It allows you to document every database oriented business rule.

    b. It allows you to document every application oriented business rule.

    c. It provides a standard method for recording all business rules.

9. The *Action Taken* section of a Business Rule Specifications sheet is the area where you indicate the modifications you've made to the elements of a field specification or to a relationship diagram.

10. A *validation table* (also known as a *lookup table*) stores data that you specifically use to implement data integrity.

11. Validation tables usually (but not always) comprise two fields: The first acts as the primary key and is what you'll use to help you enforce data integrity, and the second is simply a non-key field that stores a set of values required by some other field in the database.

12. You can use a validation table to enforce a constraint that a business rule imposes on a given field's range of values.

13. You should review each Business Rule Specifications sheet to ensure that you've properly established the rule it records and that you've clearly marked all of the appropriate areas on the sheet.

Chapter 12

1. You can refer to a view as a *virtual table* because it draws data from base tables rather than storing data on its own.

2. Views are valuable for the following reasons:

    a. You can use them to work with data from multiple tables simultaneously.

    b. They reflect the most current information.

    c. You can customize them to the specific needs of an individual or group of individuals.

    d. You can use them to help enforce data integrity.

    e. You can use them for security or confidentiality purposes.

3. The types of views you can define as you design the logical structure of the database are *data*, *aggregate*, and *validation*.

4. Each time you access a view, your RDBMS will rebuild and repopulate it using the most current data from the view's base tables.

5. Field specifications and business rules will determine what types of modifications you can make to a view's data.

6. The only requirement you must fulfill in order to define a *multi-table data view* is that the tables you use to create the view must bear a relationship to each other.

7. A *data view* does not contain its own primary key because it is not a table; a true table stores data and requires a primary key to serve as a unique identifier for each of its records.

8. The purpose of an *aggregate view* is to display information produced by aggregating a particular set of data in a specific manner.

9. *Sum, Average* (arithmetic mean), *Minimum, Maximum,* and *Count* are the most common aggregate functions that you can apply to a set of data.

10. A *grouping field* is a data field within an aggregate view that "groups" multiple instances of a given value into a single instance of the value.

11. False. You cannot modify the data in an aggregate view because it is composed entirely of grouping fields and calculated fields.

12. The difference between a *validation table* and a *validation view* lies in their construction—a validation *table* stores its own data, whereas a validation *view* draws data from its base tables.

13. You would keep the following points in mind as you identify view requirements:

    a. Review your notes with the group.

    b. Review the data-entry, report, and presentation samples you gathered during the early stages of the design process.

    c. Examine the tables and the subjects they represent.

    d. Analyze the table relationships.

    e. Study the business rules.

14. You should use *calculated fields* when they will provide pertinent and meaningful information or when they will enhance the manner in which the view uses its data.

15. You define a view that displays only science-fiction books by applying a filter to the appropriate field within the view.

16. You must complete a View Specifications sheet for every view in the database because it is on this sheet that you will record the characteristics of the view.

Diagram of the
Database-Design Process

The diagram on the following pages provides you with a map of the entire database-design process. It indicates each design phase, procedures within the phase, tasks within the procedure, and in some cases, subtasks within a task.

This legend shows the type of symbols you'll see in the diagram.

Legend

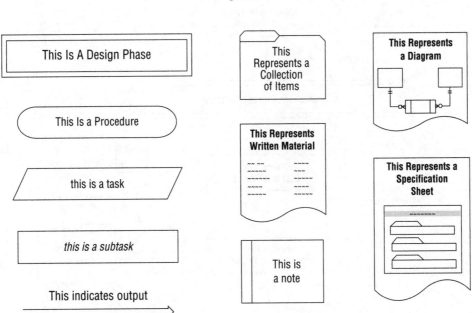

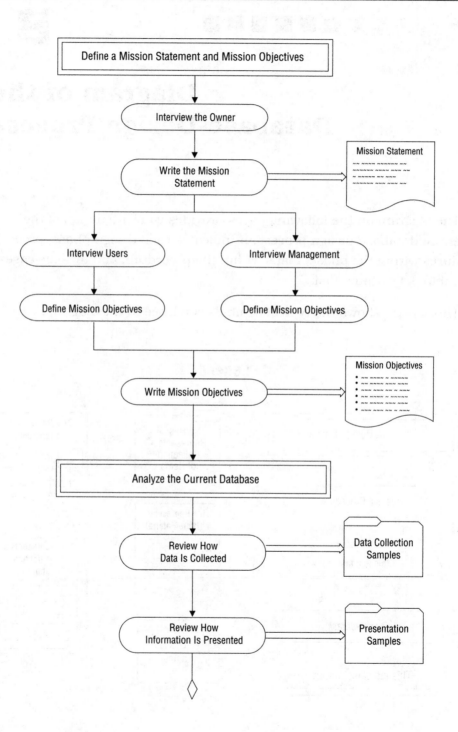

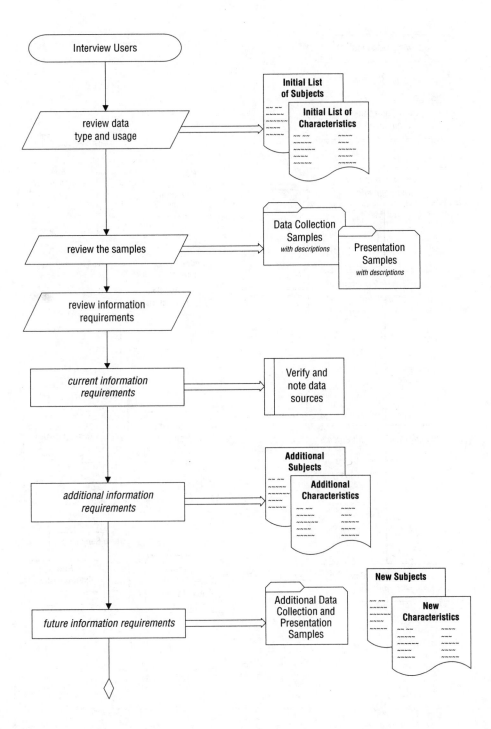

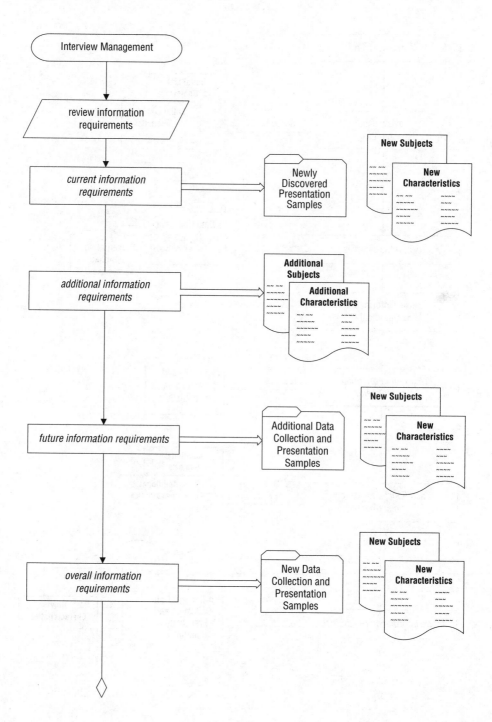

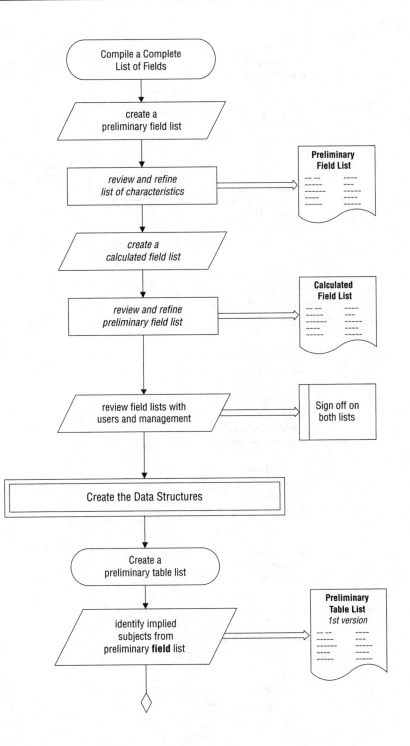

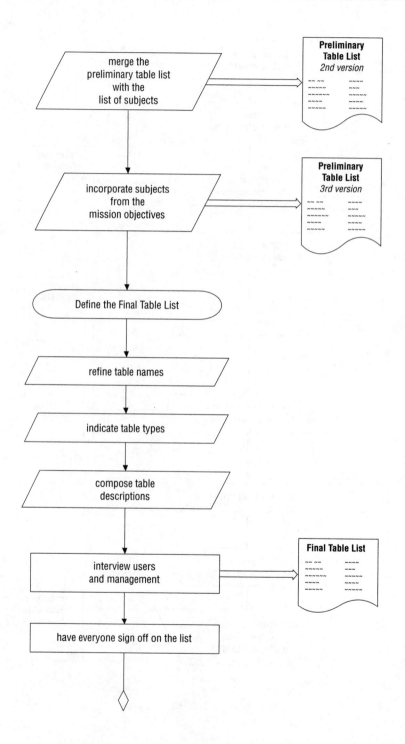

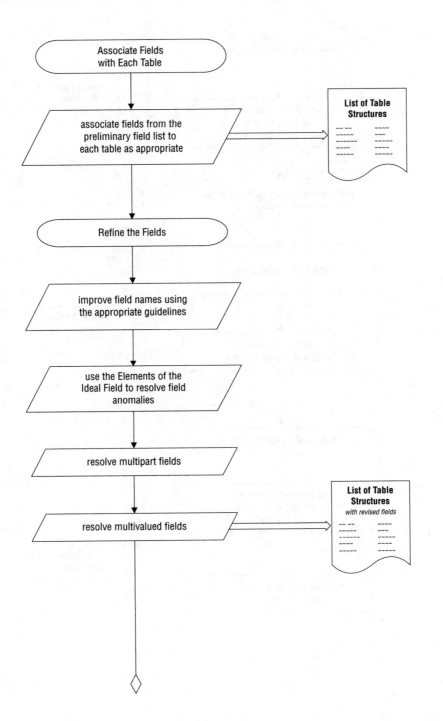

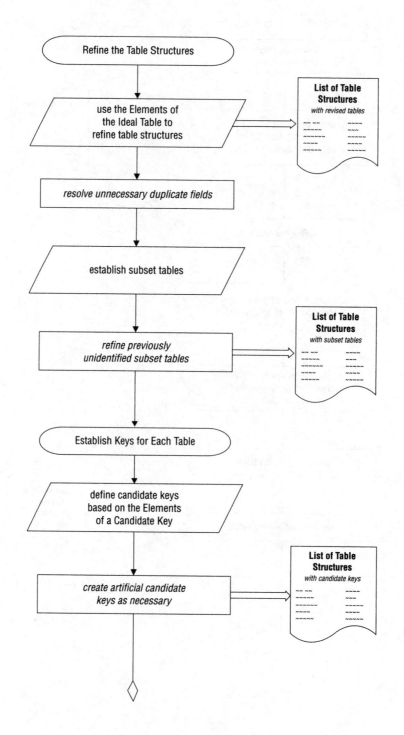

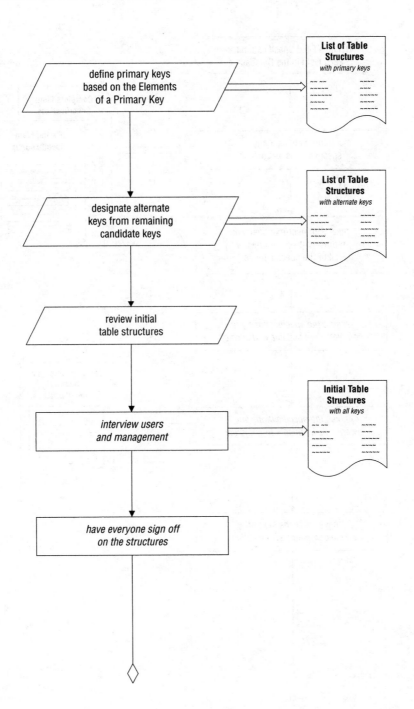

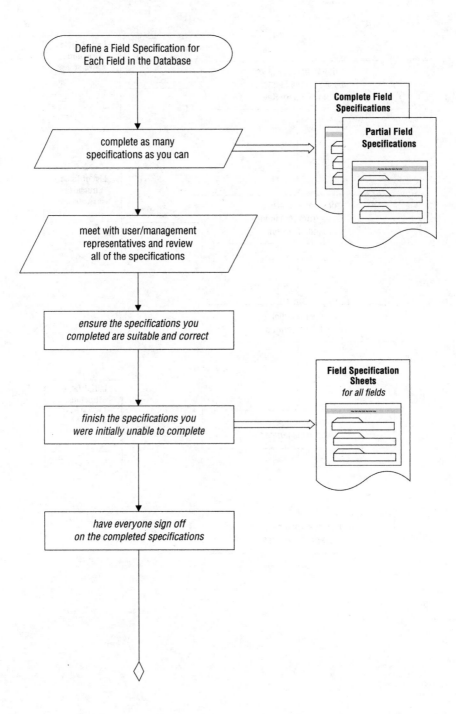

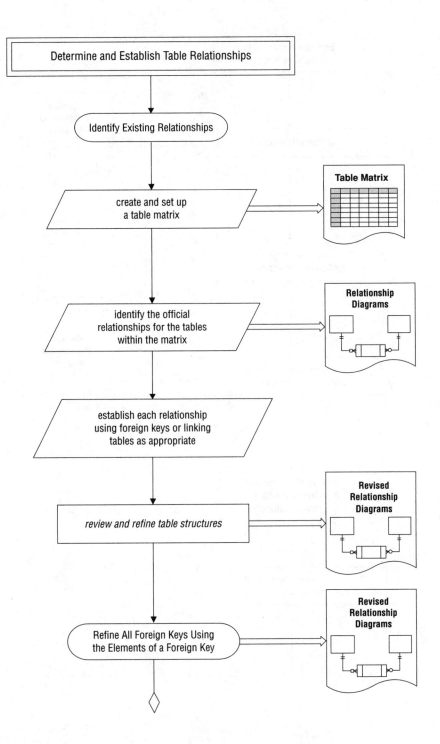

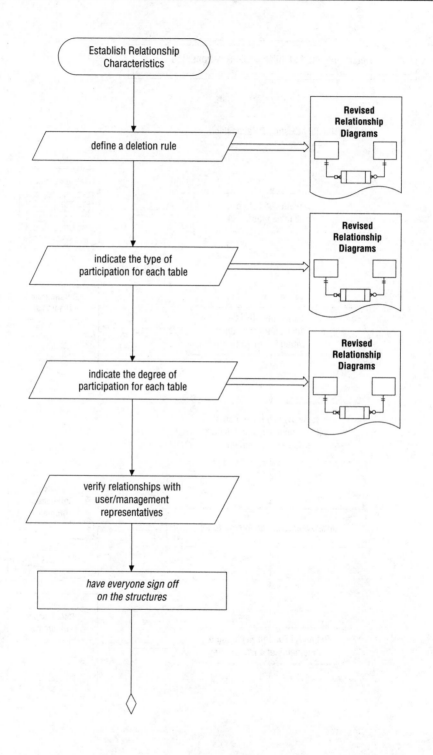

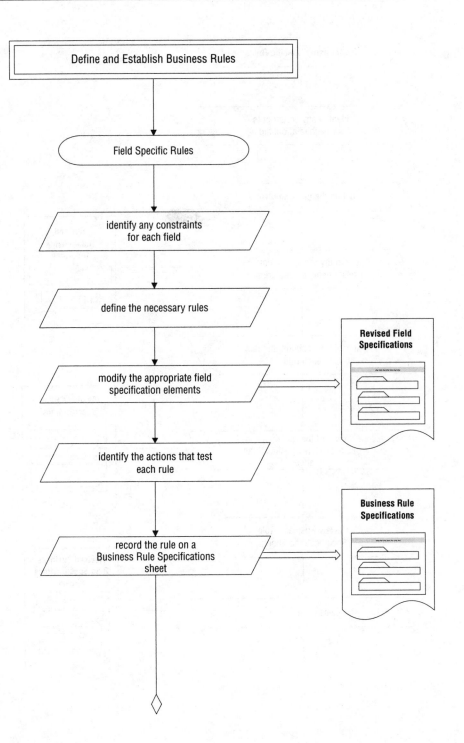

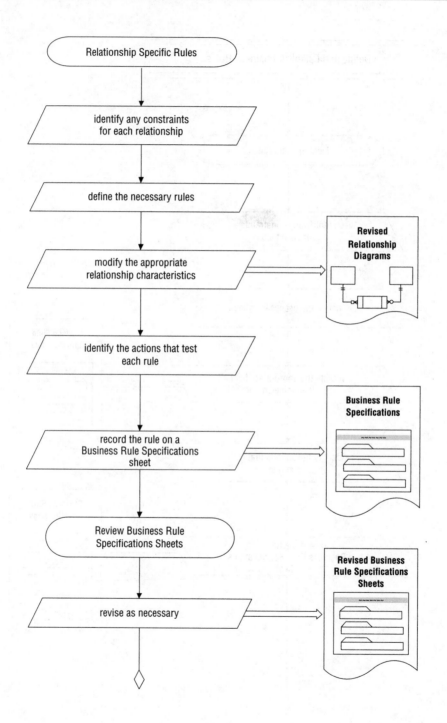

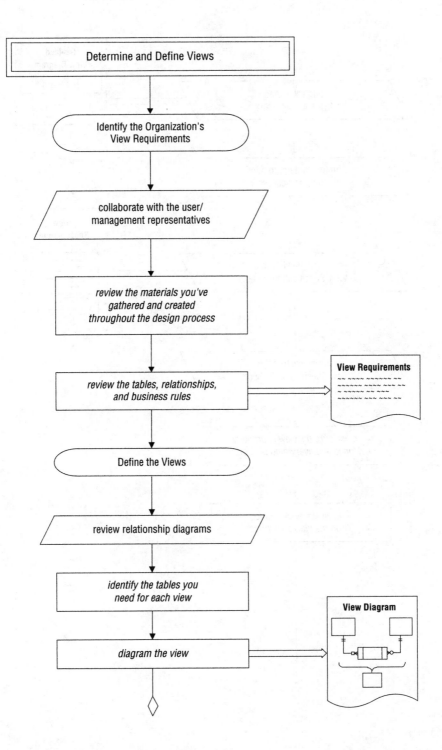

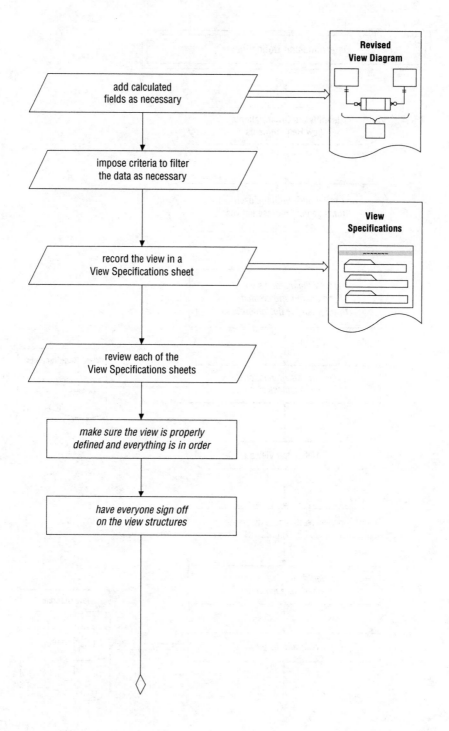

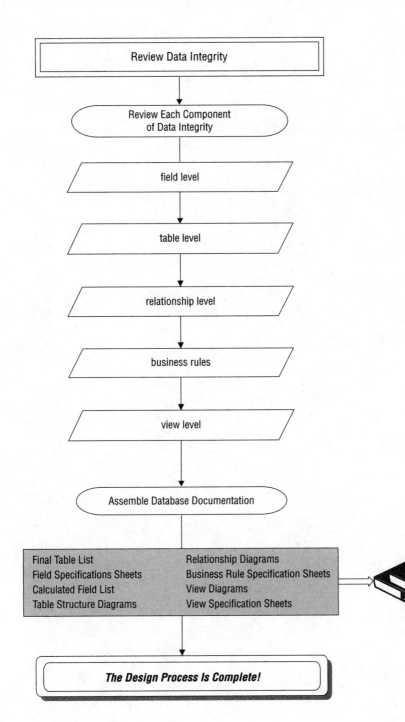

C

Design Guidelines

Here, in alphabetical order, are the various sets of design guidelines that appear throughout the book.

Defining and Establishing Field Specific Business Rules

1. Select a table.

2. Review each field and determine whether it requires any constraints.

3. Define the necessary business rules for the field.

4. Establish the rules by modifying the appropriate field specification elements.

5. Determine what actions test the rule.

6. Record the rule on a Business Rule Specifications sheet.

Defining and Establishing Relationship Specific Business Rules

1. Select a relationship.

2. Review the relationship and determine whether it requires any constraints.

3. Define the necessary business rules for the relationship.

4. Establish the rule by modifying the appropriate relationship characteristics.

5. Determine what actions will test the rule.

6. Record the rule on a Business Rule Specifications sheet.

Elements of a Candidate Key

- It cannot be a multipart field.

- It must contain unique values.

- It cannot contain null values.

- Its value cannot cause a breach of the organization's security or privacy rules.

- Its value is not optional in whole or in part.

- It comprises a minimum number of fields necessary to define uniqueness.

- Its values must uniquely and exclusively identify each record in the table.

- Its value must exclusively identify the value of each field within a given record.

- Its value can be modified only in rare or extreme cases.

Elements of a Foreign Key

- It has the same name as the primary key from which it was copied.

- It uses a replica of the field specifications for the primary key from which it was copied.

- It draws its values from the primary key to which it refers.

Elements of a Primary Key

- It cannot be a multipart field.

- It must contain unique values.

- It cannot contain null values.

- Its value cannot cause a breach of the organization's security or privacy rules.

- Its value is not optional in whole or in part.

- It comprises a minimum number of fields necessary to define uniqueness.

- Its values must uniquely and exclusively identify each record in the table.

- Its value must exclusively identify the value of each field within a given record.

- Its value can be modified only in rare or extreme cases.

Rules for Establishing a Primary Key

- Each table must have one—and only one—primary key.

- Each primary key within the database must be unique—no two tables should have the same primary key unless one of them is a subset table.

Elements of the Ideal Field

- It represents a distinct characteristic of the subject of the table.

- It contains only a single value.

- It cannot be deconstructed into smaller components.

- It does not contain a calculated or concatenated value.

- It is unique within the entire database structure.

- It retains the majority of its characteristics when it appears in more than one table.

Elements of the Ideal Table

- It represents a single subject, which can be an object or event.

- It has a primary key.

- It does not contain multipart or multivalued fields.

- It does not contain calculated fields.

- It does not contain unnecessary duplicate fields.

- It contains only an absolute minimum amount of redundant data.

Field-Level Integrity

This type of integrity ensures the following:

- The identity and purpose of a field is clear, and all of the tables in which it appears are properly identified.

- Field definitions are consistent throughout the database.

- The values of a field are consistent and valid.

- The types of modifications, comparisons, and operations that can be applied to the values in the field are clearly identified.

Guidelines for Composing a Field Description

- Use a statement that accurately identifies the field and clearly states its purpose.

- Write a clear and succinct statement.

- Refrain from restating or rephrasing the field name.

- Avoid using technical jargon, acronyms, or abbreviations.

- Do not include implementation-specific information.

- Do not make this description dependent upon the description of another field.

- Do not use examples.

Guidelines for Composing a Table Description

- Include a statement that accurately defines the table.

- Include a statement that explains why this table is important to the organization.

- Compose a description that is clear and succinct.

- Do not include implementation-specific information in your table description, such as how or where the table is used.

- Do not make the table description for one table dependent upon the table description for another table.

- Do not use examples in a table description.

Guidelines for Creating Field Names

- Create a unique, descriptive name that is meaningful to the entire organization.

- Create a name that accurately, clearly, and unambiguously identifies the characteristic a field represents.

- Use the *minimum* number of words necessary to convey the meaning of the characteristic the field represents.

- Do not use acronyms, and use abbreviations judiciously.

- Do not use words that could confuse the meaning of the field name.

- Do not use names that implicitly or explicitly identify more than one characteristic.

- Use the singular form of the name.

Guidelines for Creating Table Names

- Create a unique, descriptive name that is meaningful to the entire organization.

- Create a name that accurately, clearly, and unambiguously identifies the subject of the table.

- Use the *minimum* number of words necessary to convey the subject of the table.

- Do not use words that convey physical characteristics.

- Do not use acronyms and abbreviations.

- Do not use proper names or other words that will unduly restrict the data that can be entered into the table.

- Do not use a name that implicitly or explicitly identifies more than one subject.

- Use the plural form of the name.

Identifying Relationships

Use this procedure to identify the official relationship between a pair of tables within a table matrix:

1. Select a pair of tables and note the entry at the junction of the first table and the second table.

2. Locate the second table on the same side of the matrix you're working on and note the entry and the junction between it and the first table on the opposite side of the matrix.

3. Apply the appropriate formula (shown below) to the two entries and identify the official relationship between the tables.

   a. 1:1 + 1:1 = **1:1**

   b. 1:N + 1:1 = **1:N**

   c. 1:N + 1:N = **M:N**

4. Diagram the relationship in the appropriate manner.

5. Cross out both entries on the matrix.

Identifying View Requirements

Use this procedure to identify your organization's view requirements:

- Review your notes with the group of user/management representatives.

- Review the data-entry, report, and presentation samples you gathered during the early stages of the design process.

- Examine the tables and the subjects they represent.

- Analyze the table relationships.

- Study the business rules.

Interview Guidelines

Participant Guidelines

- Make the participants aware of your intentions.

- Let the participants know that you appreciate their taking part in the interview and that their responses to the interview questions are valuable to the overall design project.

- Make sure everyone understands that you are the official arbitrator if and when a dispute arises.

Interviewer Guidelines

- Conduct the interview in a well-lit room, separated from distracting noise, with a large table and comfortable chairs, and have coffee and munchies on hand.

- Set a limit of 10 people or fewer for each interview.

- Conduct separate interviews for users and management.

- When you have to interview several groups of people, designate a group leader for each group.

- Prepare your questions prior to the interview.

- If you're not very good at taking notes, either assign that task to a dependable transcriber for each interview or get the group's permission to use a tape recorder to record the interview.

- Give everyone your equal and undivided attention.

- Keep the pace of the interview moving.

- Always maintain control of the interview.

Mission Statements

A well-written mission statement has the following attributes:

- It expresses its point succinctly and immediately.

- It avoids unnecessary statements or details and is well-defined.

- It avoids phrases or sentences that explicitly describe *specific tasks.*

- It makes sense to you (the database developer) and to those for whom you are designing the database.

Mission Objectives

A well-written mission objective has the following attributes:

- It comprises a declarative sentence that clearly defines a general task and is free from unnecessary details.

- It expresses itself in general terms that are succinct, to the point, and unambiguous.

- It makes sense to you and to those for whom you are designing the database.

Relationship-Level Integrity

This type of integrity ensures the following:

- The connection between the two tables (or key fields) in a relationship is sound.

- You can insert new records into each table in a meaningful manner.

- You can delete an existing record without producing any adverse affects.

- There is a meaningful limit to the number of records that can be interrelated within the relationship.

Resolving a Multivalued Field

Use this generic procedure to resolve a multivalued field:

1. Remove the field from the table and use it as the basis for a new table. If necessary, rename the field in accordance with the field name guidelines that you learned earlier.

2. Take the primary key from the *original* table and incorporate it into the new table structure. This field will perform two specific functions in the new table: It will serve as part of the table's *composite primary key*, and it will serve as a foreign key that helps to establish the relationship between the new table and the original table.

3. Assign an appropriate name, type, and description to the new table and add it to the final table list.

Table-Level Integrity

This type of integrity ensures the following:

- There are no duplicate records in a table.

- The primary key exclusively identifies each record in a table.

- Every primary key value is unique.

- Primary key values are not null.

D

Documentation Forms

Blank copies of the Field Specifications sheet, Business Rule Specifications sheet, and View Specifications sheet are provided here for you to copy and use on your database projects.

FIELD SPECIFICATIONS

General Elements

Field Name:		Specification Type:	☐ Unique	☐ Generic	☐ Replica
Parent Table:		Source Specification:			
Label:					

Shared By:

Alias(es):

Description:

Physical Elements

Data Type:	Character Support:	
Length:	☐ Letters (A–Z)	☐ Keyboard (. , / $ # %)
Decimal Places:	☐ Numbers (0–9)	☐ Special (© ® ™ Σ π)

Input Mask:

Display Format:

Logical Elements

Key Type:	☐ Non	☐ Primary	Edit Rule:
	☐ Foreign	☐ Alternate	☐ Enter Now, Edits Allowed
Key Structure:	☐ Simple	☐ Composite	☐ Enter Now, Edits Not Allowed
Uniqueness:	☐ Non-unique	☐ Unique	☐ Enter Later, Edits Allowed
Null Support:	☐ Nulls Allowed	☐ No Nulls	☐ Enter Later, Edits Not Allowed
Values Entered By:	☐ User	☐ System	☐ Not Determined At This Time
Required Value:	☐ No	☐ Yes	

Default Value:

Range of Values:

Comparisons Allowed:

☐ Same Field	☐ All	☐ =	☐ >	☐ >=	☐ ≠	☐ <	☐ <=
☐ Other Fields	☐ All	☐ =	☐ >	☐ >=	☐ ≠	☐ <	☐ <=
☐ Value Expression	☐ All	☐ =	☐ >	☐ >=	☐ ≠	☐ <	☐ <=

Operations Allowed:

☐ Same Field	☐ All	☐ +	☐ –	☐ x	☐ ÷	☐ Concatenation
☐ Other Fields	☐ All	☐ +	☐ –	☐ x	☐ ÷	☐ Concatenation
☐ Value Expression	☐ All	☐ +	☐ –	☐ x	☐ ÷	☐ Concatenation

BUSINESS RULE SPECIFICATIONS

Rule Information

Statement:

Constraint:

Type:
- ☐ Database Oriented
- ☐ Application Oriented

Category:
- ☐ Field Specific
- ☐ Relationship Specific

Test On:
- ☐ Insert
- ☐ Delete
- ☐ Update

Structures Affected

Field Names:

Table Names:

Field Elements Affected

Physical Elements
- ☐ Data Type
- ☐ Length
- ☐ Decimal Places
- ☐ Character Support
- ☐ Input Mask
- ☐ Display Format

Logical Elements
- ☐ Key Type
- ☐ Key Structure
- ☐ Uniqueness
- ☐ Null Support
- ☐ Values Entered By
- ☐ Required Value
- ☐ Default Value
- ☐ Range of Values
- ☐ Comparisons Allowed
- ☐ Operations Allowed
- ☐ Edit Rule

Relationship Characteristics Affected

- ☐ Deletion Rule
- ☐ Type of Participation
- ☐ Degree of Participation

Action Taken

VIEW SPECIFICATIONS

General Information

Name: Type: ☐ Data   ☐ Aggregate   ☐ Validation

Description:

Base Tables

Calculated Field Expressions

Field Name	Expression

Filters

Field Name	Condition

E

Database-Design
Diagram Symbols

The symbols I've used throughout the book to diagram data structures, relationships, relationship characteristics, and key designations are presented here for quick and easy reference.

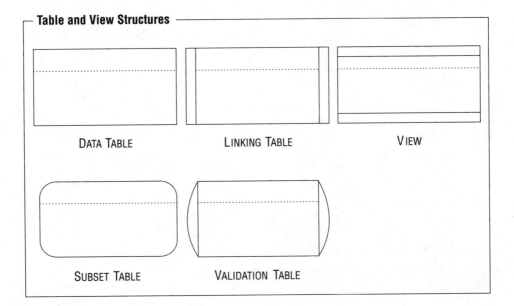

Table and View Structures

DATA TABLE   LINKING TABLE   VIEW

SUBSET TABLE   VALIDATION TABLE

Relationship Types

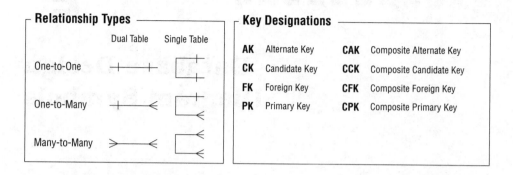

	Dual Table	Single Table
One-to-One		
One-to-Many		
Many-to-Many		

Key Designations

AK	Alternate Key	**CAK**	Composite Alternate Key
CK	Candidate Key	**CCK**	Composite Candidate Key
FK	Foreign Key	**CFK**	Composite Foreign Key
PK	Primary Key	**CPK**	Composite Primary Key

Deletion Rules

(C)	Cascade
(D)	Deny
(N)	Nullify
(R)	Restrict
(S)	Set Default

Type of Participation

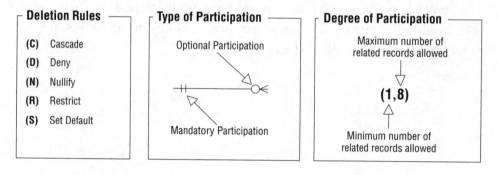

Optional Participation

Mandatory Participation

Degree of Participation

Maximum number of
related records allowed

(1,8)

Minimum number of
related records allowed

F

Sample Designs

I've provided these sample designs to serve as *ideas* for databases you may want or need to create. I emphasize the word "ideas" because five people can look at the same design and come up with five distinct variations based on their needs, backgrounds, and personal points of view. Remember that there is no right or wrong way to design a given database, but you do have to ensure that the tables, fields, relationships, and views all conform to the guidelines you've learned from this book.

I intentionally omitted all but the primary and foreign key fields from each table because I did not want to greatly influence you in any way as to how the tables should be populated. I also omitted a majority of the relationship characteristics for the same reason.

Should you see a design that you might be able to use, run it through the entire database-design process and treat it like an existing database. At the end of the process, you should have a database that suits your needs.

Entertainment Agency Database

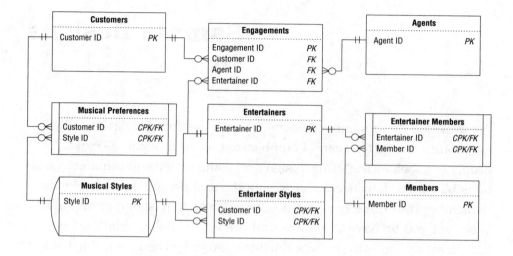

School Database

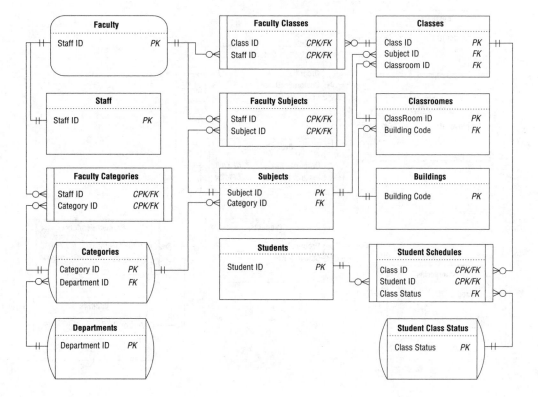

Sales Order Database

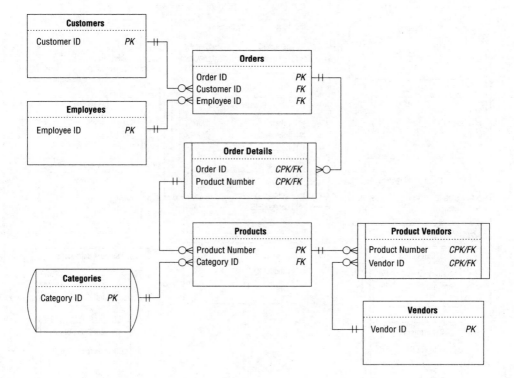

Office Inventory Database

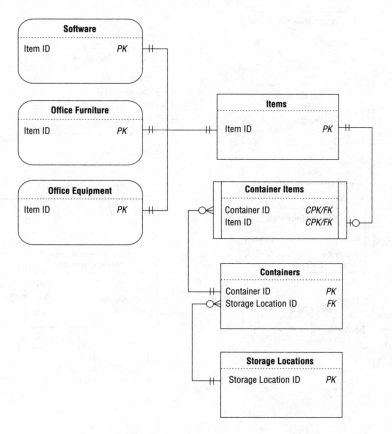

Bowling League Database

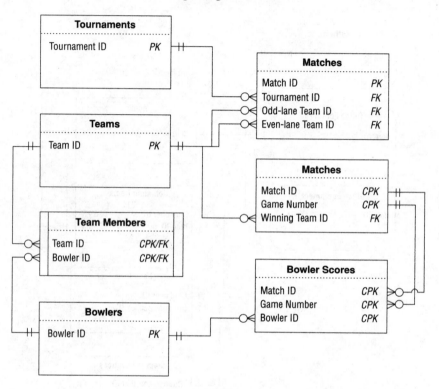

Car Rental Database

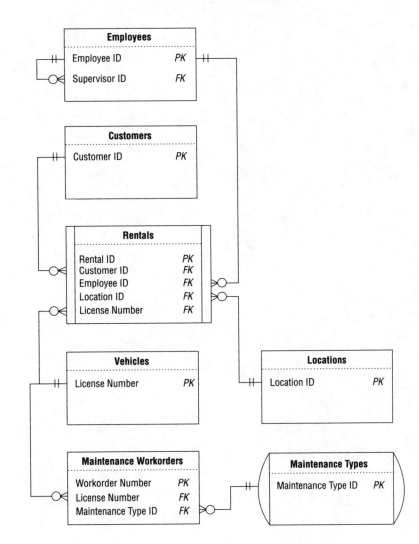

G

Recommended Reading

Should you be interested in pursuing an in-depth study of database technology, here are my recommendations for books on this subject. I've chosen these particular books because they have stood the test of time and have become standard reading within the database industry and academic institutions. (I'm pleased to state that my book has become part of this notable list.) Keep in mind that most of these books are going to be challenging to read; the authors presume that you have a fair amount of background in computers and programming or are pursuing a degree in computer science.

Codd, E. F. (1990). *The Relational Model for Database Management: Version 2.* Reading, MA: Addison-Wesley. (Note: This book is hard to find, but it's worth having in your library if you're going to become a serious database developer.)

Connolly, Thomas, and Carolyn Begg. (2002). *Database Systems—A Practical Approach to Design, Implementation, and Management, Third Edition.* Boston, MA: Addison-Wesley.

Date, C. J. (2000). *An Introduction to Database Systems, Seventh Edition.* Boston, MA: Addison-Wesley.

——. (2000). *The Database Relational Model—A Retrospective Review and Analysis.* Boston, MA: Addison-Wesley.

Date, C. J., and Hugh Darwen. (2000). *Foundation for Future Database Systems—The Third Manifesto, Second Edition.* Boston, MA: Addison-Wesley.

Fleming, Candace C., and Barbara von Halle. (1989). *Handbook of Relational Database Design.* Reading, MA: Addison-Wesley.

Hoffer, Jefferey A., Mary B. Prescott, and Fred R. McFadden. (2002). *Modern Database Management, Sixth Edition.* Upper Saddle River, NJ: Prentice Hall.

Kroenke, David M. (2000). *Database Processing—Fundamentals, Design, & Design, Seventh Edition.* Upper Saddle River, NJ: Prentice Hall.

I do recommend other books on a variety of subjects, such as database design and theory, data modeling, GUI design, SQL, Visual Basic, and .NET. You can review these recommendations by accessing my Web site at http://www.ForMereMortals.com.

Glossary

Aggregate Function A snippet of programming code that executes a particular type of mathematical aggregation on a set of data and returns a single value.

Aggregate View A view used to display information produced by aggregating a particular set of data in a specific manner.

Alternate Key A candidate key that has not been designated as a primary key.

Analytical Database A type of database that stores static data and is used when there is a need to track trends, view statistical data over a long period of time, or make tactical or strategic business projections; it is typically associated with OLAP.

Application A commercial or custom-built software program that is typically used to provide a user-friendly interface for a database.

Application Development The process of designing and creating an application that will serve as the user interface for a database.

Application Program Commercial or custom-built software that serves as the user-interface to a database.

Application Oriented Business Rule A rule that imposes constraints that you must establish within the physical design of the database or within the design of the database application.

Artificial Candidate Key A field created for the sole purpose of serving as a candidate key. It's existence is due to an absence of any "naturally occurring" candidate keys within the table.

Associative Table See *Linking Table*.

Attribute The relational model's equivalent of a field.

Base Tables Tables that form the basis of a view.

Business Rule Specification Represents all of the characteristics of a business rule, such as the rule statement, the constraint it imposes, the structures it affects, and so on.

Business Rules Restrictions or limitations on certain aspects of a database based on the ways an organization perceives and uses its data.

Calculated Field A field that contains a concatenated text value or the result of a mathematical expression.

Calculated-Field List A list of fields that can be defined only within an RDBMS. (Recall that you cannot define calculated fields within a table structure.)

Cardinality The type of relationship that exists between a pair of tables in a relational database. See *Relationship*.

Child Table Within a given relationship, a table containing records that are explicitly dependent upon the existence of records in the related table.

Client/Server RDBMS A type of RDBMS in which data resides on a computer acting as a database server and users interact with the data through applications residing on their own computer, known as the database client.

Closed Question A question that has a definitive, finite set of answers. This type of question leaves little opening for further follow-up questions.

Command Prompt A set of one or more symbols indicating the area within an operating system or command-driven software program in which a user can enter and execute commands. For example, C:\> is a command prompt within the MS-DOS operation system, and R> is the command prompt within R:BASE Technologies' R:BASE database software.

Composite Primary Key A primary key composed of two or more fields.

Data The values stored in the database.

Data Consistency Every occurrence of a given field value throughout the entire database is exactly the same.

Data-Entry Form A screen within an application program used to gather and collect data.

Data Integrity A set of rules or guidelines that governs the validity, consistency, and accuracy of the data in a database. There are four types of data integrity: table-level, field-level, relationship-level, and business rules.

Data Structure A particular construct used to store data, such as a field or table.

Data Table A table that stores data used to supply information; it is the most common type of table in a relational database.

Data View A view used to examine and manipulate data from one or more base tables.

Database Application Program See *Application Program*.

Database Developer A person who designs and implements a database.

Database-Design Process The set of actions required to design the logical structure of a database.

Database Oriented Business Rule A rule that imposes constraints that you can establish within the logical design of the database.

DBMS (Database-Management System) A software program that is used to create, maintain, modify, and manipulate a database.

Degree of Participation Considering a given relationship between a pair of tables within a relational database, this is the minimum and maximum number of records that one table can have associated with a single record in the related table.

Deletion Rule A rule that determines what the RDBMS should do when a user places a request to delete a given record in the parent table of a relationship.

Domain See *Field Specification*.

Domain Integrity See *Field-Level Integrity*.

Duplicate Data A nonprimary key value that appears in more than one table within the database.

Duplicate Field A field that appears in two or more tables for any of these reasons: It is used to relate a set of tables together; it indicates multiple occurrences of a particular type of value; or there is a perceived need for supplemental information.

Dynamic Data Data that changes constantly and always reflects up-to-the-minute information.

Elements of a Candidate Key This is a set of guidelines used to determine whether a given field is fit to serve as a candidate key.

Elements of a Foreign Key This is a set of guidelines used to determine whether a given field is fit to serve as a foreign key.

Elements of a Primary Key This is a set of guidelines used to determine whether a given candidate key field is fit to serve as a primary key.

Elements of the Ideal Field A set of guidelines used to create sound field structures and to help identify poorly designed fields.

Elements of the Ideal Table A set of guidelines used to create sound table structures and to help identify poorly designed tables.

End User A person who uses and works with a database or database application program.

End-User Application Commercial or custom-built software that serves as the user interface to a database.

Entity Integrity See *Table-Level Integrity.*

Event Something that occurs at a given point in time (such as a doctor's appointment or stock transaction) that can be represented by a table.

Explicit Information Information that is clearly stated within the response to a given question.

Extended Data Types Additional data types provided by many RDBMS programs that go beyond those specified by the SQL Standard.

Field The smallest structure in the database. It represents a characteristic of the subject of the table to which it belongs and is the only structure that actually stores data within the database.

Field Specification Represents all of the general, physical, and logical elements of a field. (This is traditionally known as a domain.)

Field-Level Integrity This type of data integrity warrants the following: the identity and purpose of a field is clear and all of the tables in which it appears are properly identified; field definitions are consistent throughout the database; the values of a field are consistent and valid; and the types of modifications, comparisons, and operations that can be applied to the values in the field are clearly identified.

Field Specific Business Rule A rule that imposes constraints on the elements of a field specification for a given field.

Filter A set of one or more constraints imposed on a view that causes it to return a specific set of information.

Final Table List This list contains key information (name, type, and description) on every table in the database.

First-Order Predicate Logic One of the two branches of mathematics upon which the relational model is based.

Hierarchical Database A database in which data is structured hierarchically and is typically diagrammed as an inverted tree.

Implementation Process The set of actions required to take a logical database design and incorporate it within a specific RDBMS.

Implicit Information Information that is not expressly stated within a response to a given question; you must derive it from your examination of the response.

Index A structure within an RDBMS program that can be used to improve data processing.

Information Data that is processed in a manner that makes it meaningful and useful to the person working with it or viewing it.

Information Requirements Information that must be supported by the data in the database in order for the organization to function properly, effectively, and efficiently.

Inherited Database See *Legacy Database*.

Keys Special fields that play very specific roles within a table; the type of key determines its purpose within the table. There are four significant types of key: candidate, primary, alternate, and foreign.

LAN See *Local Area Network*.

Legacy Database A database that has been in existence and in use for several years or more.

Linking Table A table that helps to establish a many-to-many relationship between a given pair of tables.

List of Characteristics A collection of nouns that imply various attributes of the items on the List of Subjects.

List of Subjects A collection of nouns that represent subjects that may be of interest to the organization.

Local Area Network (LAN) A group of computers and peripherals located within a relatively limited geographical area that share services and resources.

Logical Child Relationship A relationship that exists between a given table in one hierarchical database and another table in a second hierarchical database.

Logical Data Independence Changes made to the logical design of the database will not adversely affect the applications built upon the database.

Lookup Table See *Validation Table*.

Mainframe Computer A large, high-end, extremely powerful computer designed to handle literally millions of highly intensive computations simultaneously.

Many-to-Many Relationship A relationship between a pair of tables in a relational database in which a single record in the first table can be related to many records in the second table and a single record in the second table can be related to many records in the first table.

Member The subordinate node in a given relationship within a network database.

Missing Value A data value that has not been entered into a given field due to human error.

Mission Objective A statement that represents a general task that a user will perform against the data in the database.

Mission Statement A statement that establishes the purpose of the database and provides a distinct focus for your design work.

Multilevel Integrity This incorporates two or more of the following: field-level integrity, table-level integrity, relationship-level integrity, and business rules.

Multipart Field A field that contains more than one type of distinct value.

Multivalued Field A field that contains multiple instances of the same type of value.

Network Database A database in which data is structured hierarchically and is typically diagrammed as an inverted tree. Unlike the hierarchical database, however, it can contain several inverted trees that share branches.

Node A given collection of records within a network database.

Non-key A field that does not serve as a candidate, primary, alternate, or foreign key.

Normal Form A specific set of rules that can be used to test a table structure to ensure that it is sound and free of problems.

Normalization The process of decomposing large tables into smaller ones in order to eliminate redundant data and duplicate data.

Null This represents a missing or unknown value; it does not represent a zero or a text string of one or more blank spaces.

Object A tangible item (such as a person, place, or thing) that can be represented by a table.

OLAP (On-Line Analytical Processing) A method of presenting data from an analytical database in which the data is summarized and presented in the form of a table or cube.

OLTP (On-Line Transaction Processing) A system for processing transactions as soon as the computer receives them and updating master files immediately in a database-management system.

One-to-Many Relationship A relationship between a pair of tables in a relational database in which a single record in the first table can be related to many records in the second table, but a single record in the second table can be related to only one record in the first table.

One-to-One Relationship A relationship between a pair of tables in a relational database in which a single record in the first table is related to only one record in the second table, and a single record in the second table is related to only one record in the first table.

On-Line Analytical Processing See *OLAP*.

On-Line Transaction Processing See *OLTP*.

Open-Ended Question A question that can be answered in a variety of ways and can lead to further follow-up questions.

Operating System The complete set of software required to manage and provide services for the computer's hardware, peripheral equipment (such as printers and scanners), and all other software programs. The computer cannot function without the operating system.

Operational Database A type of database that stores dynamic data and is used in situations where there is a need to collect, modify, and maintain data on a daily basis; it is typically associated with OLTP.

Orphaned Record Given two related tables, this is a record in one table that is not associated with any record in the other table.

Owner The main node in a given relationship within a network database.

Owner/Member Relationship A type of relationship in a network database in which an owner table can be associated with one or more member tables, but a single member table must be associated with a specific owner table.

Paper-Based Database A loose collection of forms, index cards, manila folders, and so on, used to collect and maintain data.

Parent/Child Relationship A type of relationship in a hierarchical database in which a parent table can be associated with one or more child tables, but a single child table can be associated with only one parent table.

Parent Table Within a given relationship, a table containing records that are not dependent upon the existence of records in the related table.

Parse To decompose a given data value into smaller, distinct parts.

Physical Data Independence Changes the database software vendor makes to the physical implementation of the database will not adversely affect the applications built upon the database.

Pointer A mechanism that explicitly links a parent table to a child table in a hierarchical database.

Preliminary Field List A list of fields that represents the organization's fundamental data requirements and constitutes the core set of fields that must be defined in the database.

Preliminary Table List The core set of tables that must be defined in the database.

Primary Key A field or group of fields that uniquely identifies each record within a table.

Programming Environment The combination of a given computing platform (PC, client/server, mainframe, etc.), operating system, and programming language.

Programming Language A software program that can be used to define sets of instructions that will ultimately be processed and executed by the computer.

Query A request for information posed to the database via an SQL query statement.

Query Builder A tool within a database software program that allows a user to build a query via an easy-to-use graphical interface.

RDBMS (Relational Database Management System) A software program that is used to create, maintain, modify, and manipulate a relational database.

Record A structure that is composed of a complete set of singular values (regardless of whether any are null) for every field within a table and represents a unique instance of the table's subject.

Recursive Relationship See *Self-Referencing Relationship.*

Redundant Data A value that is repeated in a field as a result of the field's participation in relating two tables or as a result of some field or table anomaly.

Reference Field See *Duplicate Field.*

Referential Integrity See *Relationship-Level Integrity.*

Relation The relational model's equivalent of a table.

Relational Database A type of database that stores data in relations (perceived by the user as tables). Each relation is composed of tuples (records) and attributes (fields).

Relational Database Management System See *RDBMS.*

Relational Model A data model based on set theory and first-order predicate logic invented by Dr. Edgar F. Codd.

Relationship An interdependence that exists between two tables when records in the first table can in some way be associated with records in the second table. There are three types of relationships in a relational database: one-to-one, one-to-many, and many-to-many.

Relationship Diagram A graphic representation of the relationship between a given pair of tables or between a given set of records within a table.

Relationship-Level Integrity A type of data integrity that ensures that the relationship between a pair of tables is sound and that the records in the tables are synchronized whenever data is entered into, updated in, or deleted from either table.

Relationship Specific Business Rule A rule that imposes constraints that affect the characteristics of a relationship.

Report Any hand-written, typed, or computer-generated document used to arrange and present data in such a way that it is meaningful to the person or people viewing it.

Root Table The topmost table in a hierarchical database structure.

Screen Presentation A series of screens that discuss various topics in an organized manner.

Self-Referencing Many-to-Many Relationship A relationship that exists when a given record in a table can be related to one or more other records within the table and one or more records can themselves be related to the given record.

Self-Referencing One-to-Many Relationship A relationship that exists when a given record in a table can be related to one or more other records within the table.

Self-Referencing One-to-One Relationship A relationship that exists when a given record in a table can be related to only one other record within the table.

Self-Referencing Relationship A relationship that exists between the records within a table. Similar to its dual-table counterpart, a self-referencing relationship can be one-to-one, one-to-many, or many-to-many.

Set Structure A transparent construction that establishes and represents a relationship within a network database.

Set Theory One of the two branches of mathematics upon which the relational model is based.

SQL (Structured Query Language) A standardized language used to create, maintain, modify, and query relational databases.

Static Data Data that is never (or very rarely) modified.

Structural Integrity A set of rules or guidelines that governs the manner in which fields, tables, and views are defined.

Structured Query Language See *SQL*.

Subset Table A table that represents a subordinate subject of a particular data table.

Table The chief structure in a database. It is composed of fields and records and always represents a single, specific subject.

Table Description A statement that provides a clear definition of the subject represented by the table and states why the subject is important to the organization.

Table-Level Integrity This type of data integrity ensures that a table is free of duplicate records and that the values of the table's primary key are unique, never null, and exclusively identify the table records.

Tuple The relational model's equivalent of a record.

Type of Participation The manner in which a table participates within a given relationship in a relational database. The type of participation can be either mandatory or optional.

Type of Relationship The manner in which a given pair of tables can be related (one-to-one, one-to-many, many-to-many).

Unknown Value A value for a specific field that has yet to be determined or defined.

URL An acronym for Uniform Resource Locator. It represents an address for a given resource on the Internet, such as http://www.ForMereMortals.com.

Validation Table A table that stores data specifically used to implement data integrity. (This is also known as a lookup table.)

Validation View A view used specifically to implement data integrity.

View A virtual table composed of fields from one or more base tables in the database.

View Specification Represents all of the characteristics of a view, such as the name, type, base tables, and so on.

WAN See *Wide Area Network*

Web Page A document consisting of a Hypertext Markup Language (HTML) file and associated support files that can be accessed via the Internet.

Wide Area Network (WAN) A group of computers and peripherals located over a widespread geographic area that depends on various communications devices to share services and resources.

Zero-Length String Two consecutive single quotes with no space in between them.

References

Codd, E. F. (1990). "Relational Philosopher." *DBMS* December 1990, 34–40, 60.

———. (1990). *The Relational Model for Database Management Version 2.* Reading, MA: Addison-Wesley.

Connolly, Thomas, and Carolyn Begg. (2002). *Database System: A Practical Approach to Design, Implementation and Management, Third Edition.* Boston, MA: Addison-Wesley.

Date, C. J. (1994). "According to Date: Many Happy Returns!" *Database Programming and Design.* September 1994, 19–22.

———. (2000). *An Introduction to Database Systems, Seventh Edition.* Boston, MA: Addison-Wesley.

Fleming, Candace C., and Barbara von Halle. (1989). *Handbook of Relational Database Design* Reading, MA: Addison-Wesley.

Hoffer, Jeffrey A., Mary B. Prescott, and Fred R. McFadden. (2002). *Modern Database Management, Sixth Edition.* Upper Saddle River, NJ: Prentice Hall.

Kalman, David. (1994). "Moving Forward with Relational" *DBMS*, October 1994, 62–74, 109.

Kroenke, Dr. David M. (2000). *Database Processing Fundamentals, Design and Implementation, Seventh Edition.* Upper Saddle River, NJ: Prentice Hall.

McGoveran, David. (1994) "The Relational Model Turns 25." *DBMS* October 1994, 46–61.

Pascal, Fabian. (2000) *Practical Issues in Database Management: A Reference for the Thinking Practitioner.* Boston, MA: Addison-Wesley.

Stephens, Ryan K., and Ronald R. Plew. (2001) *Database Design.* Indianapolis, IN: Sams.

Teorey, Toby J. (1999) *Database Modeling & Design, Third Edition.* San Francisco, CA: Morgan Kaufmann.

Index

Also Available from Addison-Wesley

SQL Queries for Mere Mortals
A Hands-On Guide to Data Manipulation in SQL
Michael J. Hernandez, John L. Viescas

If you are accessing corporate information from the Internet or from an internal network, you are probably using SQL. *SQL Queries for Mere Mortals* will help new users learn the foundations of SQL queries, and will prove to be an essential reference guide for intermediate and advanced users. The accompanying CD contains five sample databases used for the example queries throughout the book, plus an evaluation copy of Microsoft SQL Server version 7.

0-201-43336-2 • Paperback with CD-ROM • 528 pages • © 2000

The Practical SQL Handbook, Fourth Edition
Using SQL Variants
Judith S. Bowman, Sandra L. Emerson, Marcy Darnovsky

This latest edition of the best-selling implementation guide to the Structured Query Language teaches SQL fundamentals while providing practical solutions for critical business applications. *The Practical SQL Handbook, Fourth Edition* now includes expanded platform SQL coverage and extensive real-world examples based on feedback from actual SQL users. This book begins with a step-by-step introduction to SQL basics and examines the issues involved in designing SQL-based database applications. It fully explores SQL's most popular implementations from industry leaders, Oracle, Microsoft, Sybase, and Informix. *The Practical SQL Handbook* is the most complete reference available for day-to-day SQL implementations.

0-201-70309-2 • Paperback with CD-ROM • 512 pages • © 2001

Practical SQL
The Sequel
Judith S. Bowman

Written by a co-author of the best-selling *Practical SQL Handbook*, *Practical SQL: The Sequel* picks up where the first book leaves off. It goes beyond basic SQL query structure to explore the complexities of using SQL for everyday business needs. It will help you make the transition from classroom to reality, where you must design, fix, and maintain imperfect SQL systems. For those who are working with SQL systems—or preparing to do so—this book offers information organized by use rather than by feature. Readers can turn to specific business problems and learn how to solve them with the appropriate SQL features. In particular, the sequel focuses on the real-world challenges of dealing with legacy systems, inherited problematic code, dirty data, and query tuning for better performance.

0-201-61638-6 • Paperback with CD-ROM • 352 pages • © 2001

CD-ROM Warranty

Addison-Wesley warrants the enclosed CD-ROM to be free of defects in materials and faulty workmanship under normal use for a period of ninety days after purchase. If a defect is discovered in the CD-ROM during this warranty period, a replacement CD-ROM can be obtained at no charge by sending the defective CD-ROM, postage prepaid, with proof of purchase to:

Editorial Department
Addison-Wesley Professional
Pearson Technology Group
75 Arlington Street, Suite 300
Boston, MA 02116
Email: AWPro@aw.com

Addison-Wesley makes no warranty or representation, either expressed or implied, with respect to this software, its quality, performance, merchantability, or fitness for a particular purpose. In no event will Addison-Wesley, its distributors, or dealers be liable for direct, indirect, special, incidental, or consequential damages arising out of the use or inability to use the software. The exclusion of implied warranties is not permitted in some states. Therefore, the above exclusion may not apply to you. This warranty provides you with specific legal rights. There may be other rights that you may have that vary from state to state. The contents of this CD-ROM are intended for personal use only.

More information and updates are available at:
http://www.awprofessional.com/